DESTINY BETRAYED

Jim Garrison, United States Army.

DESTINY BETRAYED:

JFK, Cuba, and the Garrison Case

By James DiEugenio

Introduction by Zachary Sklar

SHERIDAN SQUARE PRESS New York

LIBRARY OF CONGRESS CATALOGING-IN-PUBLICATION DATA

DiEugenio, James, 1952-
    Destiny betrayed : JFK, Cuba, and the Garrison Case / by James
DiEugenio : introduction by Zachary Sklar.
      p.   cm.
    Includes bibliographical references and index.
    ISBN 1-879823-00-4 : $19.95
    1. Kennedy, John F. (John Fitzgerald), 1917-1963—Assassination.
2. Garrison, Jim, 1921- .   I. title.
E842.9.D54 1992   92-15961
364.1'524—dc20   CIP

PHOTO CREDITS

All photographs courtesy of AP / Wide World Photos, except as follows: The Garrison family: ii, 124, 126, 268; Elsie Habighorst, 198; J. Gary Shaw, 26, 41, 61, 64, 70, 71, 78, 80, 101, 123, 130, 141, 263; Donn Young, 280; R.B. Cutler, 137; Edgar F. Tatro, 206; Corliss Lamont, 219; Orleans Parish District Attorney's office, 39; *CovertAction Information Bulletin*, 238; *Dallas Morning News*, 57; *New Orleans Times-Picayune*, 200; Warner Bros. Inc., Regency Enterprises V.O.F., and Le Studio Canal, 285, 286, 287.

Published in the United States by
Sheridan Square Press, Inc.
145 West 4th Street
New York, NY 10012

Distributed to the trade by
National Book Network

John F. Kennedy, United States Navy.

Dedication

To my mother, Flo: 1924-1991
With sorrow and regret that you weren't
here to see this book published.
Rest in peace, forever.

Acknowledgments

I owe much to my agent, Lee Matthias. On very short notice, he found a suitable publisher for this book and saw it through to completion.

That publisher, Sheridan Square Press, is operated by two of the most personable and helpful people a writer could hope for: Ellen Ray and William Schaap. They also put me in contact with editor Zachary Sklar, who made helpful suggestions, and with Bob Spiegelman, who did considerable additional research and fact checking for which I am extremely grateful. I also want to thank Sally Allen and Ellen Davidson for their assistance in the preparation of the manuscript.

I want to thank the staff at the Oviatt Library at California State University at Northridge, especially Kris Ecklund and Ramon Alvarado, who helped me find and secure books and documents I needed. I also wish to express my appreciation to Helen Dietrich, the stenographer at the Clay Shaw trial, who graciously let me use excerpts from the transcript.

But anyone who writes a book about the assassination of John Kennedy must mention the lonely, courageous group of men and women who spoke and wrote against the dogma and delusion of the Warren Report. This was not an easy or popular thing to do in those crucial years of 1964 to 1967. If it were not for that first wave of writers and researchers, most Americans might have believed the official story and the pursuit of the truth would have never begun. I mention some of the most influential writers in Chapter 8. Those I have found most valuable are Josiah Thompson, Sylvia Meagher,

Vincent Salandria, Richard Popkin, and Dr. Cyril Wecht, who has been a bulwark of bravery and honesty on the subject of the autopsy and related medical evidence.

Since 1967, literally scores of books have been issued on the assassination. It has become a cottage industry for publishers and a small sub-culture in America. Many of these works have been forgotten, for good reason. Some of them, in the hope of developing a "fresh angle" on the subject, have been nothing more than laborious stunts. But some writers have expanded on the work of that first generation in either research, analysis, and/or quality of writing and scholarship. People like Paris Flammonde, Howard Roffman, George Michael Evica, Anthony Summers, Michael Kurtz, Henry Hurt, Robert Groden, Seth Kantor, J. Gary Shaw, and Philip Melanson have distinguished themselves and justified their efforts. In 1989, Jim Marrs added a worthwhile desk compendium to the field.

Lastly, I should add some names of dedicated researchers, many of whom have not published in the mainstream press, or who have yet to complete their works, or who have been primarily researchers, and not writers. They include Gary Rowell, Mae Brussell, John Judge, Larry Harris, Gary Mack, Bud Fensterwald, Peter Dale Scott, Paul Hoch, Jerry Rose, Michael Levy, Joachim Joesten, R.B. Cutler, Jerry Policoff, Mary Ferrell, Gus Russo, Gary Schoener, and Hal Verb. These are the anonymous heroes of the JFK investigation.

Contents

Preface

Usually, books give birth to films. In this particular instance, the process was reversed. Let me explain.

Like most others who lived through the shock of John Kennedy's assassination, I accepted the Warren Report when it was first issued in 1964. I had no reason to question it at the time. The mass media wholeheartedly endorsed it; serious critiques were yet to come.

When New Orleans District Attorney Jim Garrison's investigation surfaced, I was confident he would not find anything. Suddenly, Garrison became front-page news. Even more suddenly, a campaign of calumny overwhelmed his investigation. Garrison was deluged, without any real opportunity to advance his discoveries and theory. At the time, I was not knowledgeable enough to form any sophisticated reaction to the extraordinary tidal wave of bad press. But I remember thinking two things almost subconsciously: No big city district attorney could be that awful. And why would any public official risk his career and reputation if he did not have at least some basis for his case? Nothing I read by the multitude of Garrison's critics answered or even seriously addressed these points, so I reserved judgment.

In the 1970s, three things happened that made me seriously delve into the field and arrive at a personal conclusion. Belatedly, I read Garrison's 1967 *Playboy* interview.[1] He made a respectable case for Lee Harvey Oswald's innocence. He provided a credible, if complex, alternative motive for the crime. In one of his many original achievements, he showed that the key to the assassination was in New Orleans in the summer of 1963, not Dallas in the fall. From here I went to the Warren Report. I found it quite unconvincing, even for someone with only a rudimentary knowledge of the case.

In 1975, I saw Robert Groden's optically enhanced print of the Zapruder film of the JFK assassination on national television.[2] Like millions, I thought it gave strong indication that a shot hit Kennedy from the front. In 1979, I saw the same film linked with a sound recording of the shots in Dealey Plaza (see Chapter 13). No one can see that version and not at least be open to the idea of multiple assassins.

At about this same time, I was writing a weekly column of film criticism back home in Pennsylvania; then I decided to move to Los Angeles to attend film school. One of my first ideas after graduation was to do a film treatment of the JFK assassination, which I thought a natural for the screen.

I totally immersed myself in the literature. I read as many works as I could, both supporting and attacking the Warren Report. The more I read the more I was convinced there must have been multiple assassins in Dealey Plaza. The problem was to find an alternative theory that fit all the facts. It was difficult. I found the Robert Sam Anson-Michael Eddowes school—Oswald is still in Russia, a double was sent over by the KGB—outlandish.[3] The Mafia theory was credible enough with Ruby, but strained with Oswald.[4] Some of the others were too weak to mention.

I then went back to the stigmatized Garrison case. I researched it in depth and at length, comparing the contemporary accounts to what had subsequently been confirmed as true. I matched Garrison's reconstruction of the event against the others. For me, the conclusion was inescapable. Garrison's explanation was the most logical, comprehensive, detailed, thorough, and demonstrable. No one else came close.

After a few years on other projects, I got as far as writing a treatment for a movie about the Garrison case. Then, in early 1991, I picked up a trade paper and read the news:

Oliver Stone, the three-time Oscar winning director, had purchased the rights to Jim Garrison's 1988 book, *On the Trail of the Assassins*, and had signed Kevin Costner to play Garrison. First, I went into a funk. But then I decided to turn my years of research into a book, this book.

By picking it up, you are delving further into one of the most enduring and fascinating puzzles of contemporary times, the resolution of which demands nothing less than a reinterpretation of the last thirty years of American history. No other single event can make that claim. I sincerely believe that the truth about that mystery illuminates and enlivens something in us all.

Introduction

I was 15 when John F. Kennedy was murdered. Like most Americans who lived through that bleak Friday, November 22, 1963, I remember exactly where I was when I heard the news. At 10:35 a.m., Los Angeles time, my tenth-grade biology teacher somberly told us that the President had been shot. Approximately an hour later, the announcement came over the p.a. system: JFK was dead.

I spent that weekend with my family, mesmerized in front of the TV set as the incredible events unfolded—the swearing in of the new President, the arrest and shocking murder of the suspect, the military funeral, the lighting of the eternal flame. I sat teary-eyed, stunned, deeply shaken. Something momentous had occurred, and though I did not know it then, things would never be the same.

It was not until I was a freshman in college, February 1967, that the assassination returned to the forefront of my consciousness. Much had changed by then. Rivers of blood flowed as U.S. Army tanks opened fire in the poor black neighborhoods of many of our cities. There was a military draft. More than 500,000 young American soldiers were fighting in a far-off land called Vietnam. Citizens were confused and bitterly divided about the war.

And then along came Jim Garrison, this eloquent, bigger-than-life district attorney from New Orleans, telling the world that President Kennedy had been assassinated not by Lee Harvey Oswald, whom the Warren Commission had fingered, but by a far-reaching conspiracy.

Many had doubted the lone-nut explanation from the moment they watched Jack Ruby execute Oswald on national television, while seventy cops stood by in the basement of Dallas police headquarters. Those doubts increased over the next three years as various researchers pointed out numerous problems with the Warren Report, among them that:

• The best marksmen in the world had been unable to duplicate the shooting feat attributed to Lee Harvey Oswald (a notoriously poor shooter);

• Oswald's nitrate test, which revealed no gun powder on his cheek, suggested that he had not shot a rifle on November 22;

• Most of the eyewitnesses in Dealey Plaza thought the shots came not from the Texas School Book Depository where Oswald worked but from the grassy knoll in front of and to the right of the President's motorcade;

• The best photographic record of the assassination, an 8 mm home movie taken by Abraham Zapruder, showed the fatal bullet snapping the President's head back and to his left, indicating that the shot came from in front and to his right.

But Jim Garrison went further—much further. He arrested local New Orleans businessman Clay Shaw on charges of conspiring to kill the President and, more breathtaking still, announced that our own intelligence community was behind both the assassination and the subsequent cover-up. Fanatical anticommunists in the defense industry, the Pentagon, and the intelligence community, Garrison explained, felt betrayed by the young President's attempts to end the Cold War. Rather than accept the nuclear test-ban treaty he had negotiated with the Soviet Union, his back-channel efforts to establish diplomatic relations with Cuba, and his plan to withdraw all U.S. advisers from Vietnam, these hardline Cold Warriors had simply eliminated Kennedy.

When my college friends and I read Garrison's bold interview in *Playboy* and a lengthy cover story on his investigation in *Ramparts* magazine, we were both excited and frightened. If Garrison was right, our so-called democracy was a sham, and our country was being run by an illegal, unaccountable, invisible government that would lie and kill to fulfill its secret agenda. When Martin Luther King, Jr., and Robert Kennedy, the two most charismatic opponents of the Vietnam War, were gunned down in rapid succession the next spring, everyone I knew was enraged—and terrified. I vividly remember sitting up late one night in a house in the woods and talking with friends about the assassinations, Garrison, and the Vietnam War. I remember how frightened we were even to mention the CIA or our growing conviction that it might have been behind the assassinations. From our experiences in the anti-war and civil-rights movements, we knew that phones were tapped, homes and offices were bugged, mail was opened. (All this was confirmed later in Freedom of Information documents about the FBI's COINTELPRO program.) Who knew how far the invisible government's reach extended? A squirrel scurried up a tree outside, and we jumped to the windows to see who might be spying on us.

Such paranoia may seem comical today, but that summer of 1968 the streets were filled with young people who felt it. Our government had been stolen, our leaders had been murdered, our friends and classmates were dying in a pointless war 9,000 miles away. We were being fed lie after lie by politicians and the media, and our protests were met with bayonets, beatings, and tear gas.

More than two decades later, of course, the lies and scandals of our government have jaded us into depressed resignation—Vietnam, Watergate, the CIA's covert actions around the world, the invasions of Grenada and Panama, the Iran-contra affair, the Persian Gulf War, the savings and loan debacle. After all that, who can even remember the assassination of John Kennedy, let alone muster any indignation about it?

Jim Garrison can. I met him for the first time in 1987, just after the Iran-contra affair blew open, and what impressed me most was how angry this man was. Not just about the machinations of Oliver North and William Casey, Bush and Reagan, but about the assassination of John Kennedy—still. For him, they were all connected. Some of the names may have changed, but it was the invisible government that was making deals in Iran, shipping guns to the contras, running drugs—the same invisible government that had killed the President and been controlling policy ever since. Jim Garrison could not figure out why everyone else was not as enraged as he was.

The occasion for our meeting was that I had been hired by Sheridan Square Press to edit Garrison's memoir about his investigation into the assassination—the book that eventually was published as *On the Trail of the Assassins* and became the inspiration for Oliver Stone's film *JFK*. I must confess that when I was first approached to work on a manuscript by Jim Garrison, I had reservations. Having edited a number of books on the CIA, I was more convinced than ever that employees of the Agency were capable of murdering their own President. But I also knew that Garrison had lost his case against Clay Shaw and had gone through two trials himself (both of which yielded verdicts of not guilty). The former DA had been discredited by the mainstream press as an opportunistic publicity-seeker at best, a kook and a crook at worst. Associating myself with him might destroy whatever credibility I had managed to earn as a journalist.

Garrison's manuscript persuaded me it was worth the risk. His firsthand experience and knowledge of the subject were unparalleled. His writing was eloquent, intelligent, witty, and convincing. Most of all, he managed to rekindle my own lost sense of outrage at the monumental injustice that the assassination and cover-up represented.

And so we met in the cozy Greenwich Village apartment of Sheridan Square publishers Ellen Ray and Bill Schaap to discuss the manuscript. Garrison was then 66 years old, an imposing six feet seven inches tall, dressed in elegant blue suit and tie, hair meticulously combed. He had a deep, reso-

nant voice as warm and rich as melted butter and slightly
bulging eyes that instantly made contact and set you at ease.
His manner was casual, but it could not mask the discomfort
that any author—even this one who had stood up to the might
of the federal government—feels when first confronting his
editor.

I asked him why he had chosen the third-person for his
narrative, leaving himself out entirely. He explained that he
wanted readers and critics to focus on the facts of the case,
the logic of the argument, rather than Jim Garrison as a
personality. He had done much the same thing at Clay Shaw's
trial. Realizing that the press would be eager to portray him
as a flamboyant publicity-hound rather than pay attention to
the prosecution's case, he decided to present only a short
opening statement and a low-key summation. Assistant DAs
handled the bulk of the case, and most of the time Garrison
was not even in the courtroom.

It took quite an effort to persuade Jim that he should
include himself in the book. My argument—that he was the
most important character in the investigation and had a
unique perspective—did not cut it with him. But when I said
that telling the story first-person would allow readers to go
through the same process that he went through as he tracked
down the evidence, that it would help them understand how
his thinking had changed, he finally agreed.

Over the next three years, as I worked on the book and the
screenplay of *JFK*, any doubts I had about the fairness of
putting Clay Shaw on trial were erased. Shaw was indicted
by a grand jury, and a three-judge panel ruled in a pre-trial
hearing that the prosecution had presented sufficient evidence to take him to trial. Moreover, during his trial, he
received help not only from supposedly impartial reporters
like *Newsweek*'s Hugh Aynesworth (who shared witness lists
and other information with defense lawyers) but also from
the CIA, according to Victor Marchetti, former assistant to
the Agency's director.

By contrast, Garrison's prosecution was sabotaged from day one. Every one of his attempts to extradite key witnesses from other states was rejected—something that had never happened in his previous six years as DA. His routine requests for important evidence such as x-rays and photos of the President's autopsy, and tax records and intelligence files on Lee Harvey Oswald and others, were denied. His office phones were tapped and, as Freedom of Information documents later revealed, he and his staff were followed everywhere by FBI agents. Key witnesses were bribed or died under mysterious circumstances. And the DA's files were stolen and turned over to Shaw's defense counsel before the trial began. (This was admitted by Tom Bethell, the man who did it, in his 1990 book *The Electric Windmill.*) If anyone did not receive a fair trial, it was Garrison and the people of Louisiana.

Not the least of these successful efforts at sabotage was the attempt to destroy Jim Garrison's personal credibility in the mainstream press. The portrait painted of him in the late 1960s and regurgitated in numerous books since—of a power-mad, egomaniacal DA who drugged and bribed witnesses, took payoffs from his friends in the Mob, and investigated the JFK assassination only as a vehicle for his grandiose political ambitions—was largely the result of smears orchestrated by the CIA and the FBI, both of which were endangered by what Garrison had to say.

Although we still do not know the full extent of the disinformation campaign against Garrison, some evidence of it surfaced in a CIA memo dated April 1, 1967, and released in 1977 under the Freedom of Information Act. It outlines a strategy to discredit critics of the Warren Commission by, among other things, planting stories with the Agency's "propaganda assets" in the press (see Appendix B). A letter discovered in 1982 in the LBJ Library, from Aynesworth to Lyndon Johnson's press secretary George Christian, reveals just how far some newspeople were willing to go. In this case,

Aynesworth admits he was regularly reporting on Garrison's investigation to the FBI as well as the White House (see Chapter 10).

In the three years I worked closely with Jim Garrison, I got to know him well. He does not in the least resemble the flamboyant, ambitious, corrupt politician portrayed in the press. When I first visited his home in a middle-class neighborhood of New Orleans, I expected the lavish furnishings and lifestyle of a successful politician, a judge earning a healthy salary. Instead I found a modest home in which there was only one precious item: the library. Jim's study is lined with hundreds of books from Shakespeare to John LeCarré, from Herodotus to former CIA case officer Philip Agee, from legal texts to all 26 Warren Commission volumes. A true intellectual, Jim is one of the few elected officials in America who would rather read a book at home than press the flesh at a cocktail party.

Personally, Jim is a reserved, almost shy man with an understated, sardonic sense of humor. He loves attractive women, the New Orleans Saints, his cat Max, a competitive game of chess, and intelligent conversation. Big-band swing music of the forties brings tears to his eyes, and he seemed genuinely offended at his book party in New York when several hundred people did not suddenly stop their chattering to listen in reverent silence to Gershwin's "The Man I Love" being played in the background by a flute-and-guitar duo. He enjoys fine New Orleans cooking and elegantly tailored clothes—a reaction, he explained to me one night, to a childhood during the Depression in which he was forced to line his shoes with cardboard to cover the holes and to sleep on concrete floors more often than he would like to remember.

But for a man who grew up under such conditions, he is remarkably indifferent to material things. He does not own a car or a CD player or a microwave. And his political campaigns have always been run on relatively small budgets because he does not enjoy raising money. One of his assistant

DAs, Andrew Sciambra, told me that he frequented a bar about two blocks from the DA's office. The owner was a great fan of Garrison's and told Sciambra that if Jim would just come in to the bar and shake his hand, he would give him a $5,000 campaign contribution. Sciambra eagerly conveyed the message to Garrison, but try as he might, he never got Jim to walk those two blocks to shake the man's hand.

Like everyone else, Jim has an ego and ambitions and character flaws. Sometimes he talks more than he should, he trusts too readily, and he can be too loyal to old friends. These personality traits did not serve him well during the Kennedy investigation. He had to operate in a fishbowl, with reporters constantly snooping around, and sometimes he talked to them in confidence about leads that had not yet been checked out. Too often these reporters betrayed his trust and misquoted him to the detriment of the investigation. His office was understaffed and overworked, and his instinct was to trust the numerous volunteers who had shown up to help out with the work. Though others on his staff voiced suspicions about some of these people, Jim stubbornly stood behind them. The result was disastrous, as one of them turned over crucial files to Clay Shaw's defense counsel.

Despite the not-guilty verdict in the Shaw trial, Jim never stopped investigating the Kennedy assassination. He and his family paid dearly for that commitment. They endured death threats and lived through two trials on trumped-up charges. Though Jim was found innocent in both cases, he was defeated in a bid for a fourth term as DA. He eventually stopped responding to the unceasing attacks on him in the press—"Why get into a pissing contest with a skunk?" he says—but he continued to pursue the truth. His passion for justice, his rage, his courage, have endured. And it is only now, more than two decades later, that his enormous contributions are receiving the recognition they deserve.

Jim DiEugenio's impressive book, *Destiny Betrayed*, performs a real service by taking readers back to Garrison's original case and setting the record straight. Hundreds of books have been written about the Kennedy assassination. Indeed, it is probably the greatest puzzle of the twentieth century. There are endless avenues to pursue, and it is easy to get lost in the minutiae of the whodunit—shots and angles, wounds and bullets, rifles and revolvers.

Jim DiEugenio cuts through all the clutter and focuses on the why of the assassination. In clear, simple prose, he explains and expands on the essential points that Garrison raised as early as 1967: 1. that the assassination could not have been the work of one person and was in fact the result of a conspiracy; 2. that members of the U.S. intelligence community were behind the conspiracy; 3. that the assassination was done in order to change government policy; 4. that the truth was covered up by an invisible government that still is operating in our country; and 5. that all this amounts to a coup d'état.

Though Garrison lost the Shaw case, DiEugenio points out that much of what we have learned since then through the Freedom of Information Act and other sources supports Garrison's original contentions. He has done excellent research and has admirably brought to life for a younger generation a case that is still having repercussions in all our lives. His book is an important contribution to the literature on the assassination of President Kennedy.

—**Zachary Sklar**

1

The Legacy

The events that exploded in Dallas on November 22, 1963, had their genesis in Washington on a February day in 1947. In a distant but very real sense, it was John Kennedy's resistance to the policy begun on that day that killed him.[1]

On February 17, 1947, H.M. Sichell, assistant to Lord Inverchapel, the British ambassador to Washington, sent a message to Dean Acheson.[2] The ambassador wanted to talk to Secretary of State George Marshall, but, since Marshall was out of town, the diplomats spoke instead to Acting Secretary of State Acheson. They told him the British were experiencing difficulty "administering" Turkey and Greece. For one thing, Britain was unable to quell Greek leftwing partisans in their civil war against rightwing monarchists. Indeed, the formidable strength of domestic leftists and economic havoc in both countries put the British in an unprecedented position. Still reeling from the economic effects of the war and already in need of a large loan from the United States, Britain was in no position to maintain its military involvement or extend aid to either country. The two diplomats impressed on Acheson their fears that a communist, neutralist, or even nationalist victory in the area would change the power structure in the Middle East, India, North Africa, and Italy. Their implication was obvious. England was stepping down as a "superpower," and America must fill the vacuum.

From this watershed meeting, three epochal events ensued: the United States assumed leadership of the West[3]; any hope of avoiding the Cold War was lost; and the initial steamrolling impact of the domino theory—the view that if one nation falls to communism, all those nearby will follow suit—commenced.[4]

A month later, on March 7, President Harry Truman stood before Congress to request $400 million in aid for Greece and Turkey. The request was overwhelmingly approved, for Truman couched it not in humanitarian terms, but in the terms he had received it: without it, the free world would end. With this, the Truman Doctrine was born and the Cold War became irreversible.

On June 5, after Truman's request was expedited, Secretary Marshall made a complementary speech at Harvard outlining the administration's intent to extend massive economic aid to the rest of Europe.[5] The expressed reason was to rebuild the shattered continent, to ensure its survival against a Moscow-led communist victory. The real reason was to reconstruct Europe's ability to buy American exports, to avoid either a depression or socialist advances.[6] The overall request was for $17 billion. A special session of Congress was called, and funding for the Marshall Plan was approved, despite considerable opposition.[7]

If the resulting economic isolation did not cause Stalin sufficient worry, the forthcoming Brussels Pact, signed by England, France, Belgium, the Netherlands, and Luxembourg, certainly did. It was a military pact formed in the name of thwarting communist aggression[8] and led to the formation of NATO, which added other nations, particularly the United States.

But the crucial year for us is 1947. In the context of the onrushing Cold War, one telling piece of legislation completed the construction of a national security state: the aptly named National Security Act. Signed on July 26, 1947, this law established the National Security Council to oversee all U.S. intelligence operations, created the Central Intelligence Agency, and gave the Director of Central Intelligence (DCI) the leadership of that agency.[9]

President Harry S
Truman, right,
with FBI Director
J. Edgar Hoover,
1950.

The odd thing was that the least discussed part of the act was potentially the most important: the intelligence functions of the CIA. It was not until the end of the congressional debate that they were even addressed. Congress had been preoccupied with the question of the jurisdiction of the CIA, specifically that it have no domestic purview. The head of the FBI, J. Edgar Hoover, emphatically concurred.[10]

Once these matters were decided and CIA responsibilities were ostensibly restricted to a foreign domain,[11] the Agency was delegated five functions: to correlate, evaluate, and distribute intelligence; to advise the President's National Security Council on national security matters; to recommend ways to coordinate various intelligence departments; to perform "additional services of common concern" for the government-wide intelligence community; and to perform "*such other functions* and duties related to intelligence affecting the national security as the National Security Council may from time to time direct"[12] (emphasis added).

The last clause was the key to Pandora's Box. Indeed, "other functions" became the linchpin for future covert and paramilitary operations, although the legislative history of the law shows that the phrase was not intended to justify those types of acts. It was meant to cover unforeseen circumstances. Congress never considered secret warfare or international coercion.[13]

As with every other aspect of the anticommunist national security state, this bill passed with alacrity. And six weeks after Truman signed it, the CIA was founded. The first DCI was Navy Rear Admiral Roscoe Hillenkoeter.

At first, the Agency had neither the skill nor the experience to extend its reach to overseas coercion.[14] But it learned quickly from its British cousins, first the SOE and then the SIS.[15] After setting up Radio Free Europe in 1950 and Radio Liberty in 1951, it went into partnership with the SIS in the Baltic republics of Lithuania and Estonia, but, due to Soviet counterintelligence and Agency incompetence, these first forays into covert operations failed. With the communist victory in China in 1949[16] and the outbreak of the Korean War in 1950, the power, range, and skill of the CIA were greatly expanded. Bases were opened everywhere, especially in the Far East.[17] Old intelligence officers from World War II were re-recruited. Expenditures were multiplied. Dummy fronts to conceal CIA operations were opened. Resupply operations were enhanced. By 1953 the Agency had over 10,000 employees.[18]

But there is more to the story of the birth of the CIA. Out of the ashes of World War II emerges an episode so dark in tone, so epic in scope, so powerful in its connotations that it was a state secret not exposed to any significant extent until the 1970s. And it sheds much light on the genesis and excesses of the Cold War and the national security state—excesses which John Kennedy was trying to control, but which ensnared and destroyed him.

As World War II drew to a close, many high-ranking Nazis, recognizing that defeat was coming, began to plan their own

Reinhard Gehlen in
1943, when he was a
Wehrmacht Colonel,
head of counter-
Intelligence on the
Russian Front.

escapes.[19] One was Reinhard Gehlen. He did not cut an imposing figure when he turned himself in to the victorious U.S. troops in May of 1945; and, over his protestations, he was immediately shunted off to a prison camp.[20]

Gehlen had been a commander in Hitler's Foreign Armies East, responsible for German military intelligence throughout Eastern Europe and the Soviet Union. In addition to intelligence work, he had created a network of fascist paramilitary groups to fight the vaunted communist threat in Eastern Europe. And by 1945 he was a potentially major player in any anti-Soviet agenda.

Gehlen had surrendered calculating that the best way to save himself was to offer his formidable intelligence organization to U.S. intelligence as a bargaining chip. He was sure that when the right people realized who he was, the fear in the Allied camp of the communist threat would induce the Office of Strategic Services (OSS), America's wartime precursor of the CIA, to consider his offer seriously.

Allen Dulles did not disappoint Reinhard Gehlen. Dulles was second in command at OSS, under General William Donovan. He had been dreaming of incorporating Gehlen's operation since 1944[21]; plans for a post-war, allied, anticommunist intelligence organization had been in the works since then. Donovan and Dulles had been against the official policy of prosecuting all Nazi war criminals, and had said so to Roosevelt.[22] Indeed, Dulles kept the details of his plans secret from Roosevelt and then Truman. Both Donovan and Dulles, it seemed, saw Gehlen's organization as a prime asset in their scenario for a postwar CIA.

By the end of 1945, Dulles had finished his negotiations with Gehlen. In August of 1945, Gehlen and six of his aides were flown to Washington by Eisenhower's chief of staff, General Walter Bedell Smith (another future DCI), for high-level meetings. The Gehlen Organization was transferred, and on Gehlen's terms.[23] It remained intact and under his control, "justified" under the rubric of mutual defense against the communist menace.

The United States agreed to finance and support the new network until such time as a new German state would take it over. Ultimately Gehlen would become the chief of intelligence of the Federal Republic of Germany. It was an incredible deal. Gehlen got everything he could have asked for. (In addition, this extraordinary agreement was what allowed men like Klaus Barbie and Josef Mengele, to escape to South America.[24]) From the ruins of defeat, the virtual head of Hitler's intelligence became the chief of one of the largest intelligence agencies in the postwar era. A man who should have been imprisoned and prosecuted for war crimes[25] became a wealthy and respected official of the new Germany.

By consummating the Gehlen deal, Allen Dulles accomplished two things. First, he signaled that the hallmark of the coming national security state would be anticommunism. Morality, honesty, common sense, these would all be sacrificed at the altar of this new god. Second, he guaranteed that the future successor to the OSS, the Central Intelligence Agency, would be compromised in a strange way: it would be viewing the new red threat not through American, but through German—indeed Nazi—eyes, an incredible distortion, since in essence Gehlen was selling Hitler's view of the Soviet Union and communism. Not coincidentally, this was a view that dovetailed with Dulles's. Morality fell by the wayside; in Dulles's words about Gehlen, "He's on our side and that's all that matters."[26] Finally, we see that Dulles had no compunctions about overriding orders from above when he felt that *his* vision of national security was at stake.

This was the line that Dulles sold Truman at the birth of the Agency,[27] the same line Dulles implemented as Eisenhower's Director of Central Intelligence. It was also a line to which Kennedy at first acquiesced, but which he later rejected. It is one of the more glaring ironies in recent history that this man, future CIA Director Allen Dulles, was appointed to the panel which investigated the circumstances of Kennedy's murder. If there were a plot which involved and exposed any part of the national security apparatus, Dulles would doubtless hide the trail in order to cover such a morally and legally indefensible deal.

Allen Dulles, Director of Central Intelligence, poses beside a poster stressing secrecy, 1961.

The clandestine incorporation of the Nazi spy apparatus into U..S. intelligence and the simultaneous recruitment of Nazi scientists into the heart of the defense establishment would not be things the Agency would wish to publicize. A president, like Kennedy, who eventually was at odds with the Agency could expose Dulles's secret to the considerable detriment of both the Nazis and the Americans involved in the transfers. Finally, he could reveal the great weight given to Gehlen in measuring the Soviet threat.[28]

In 1953 General Dwight D. Eisenhower took over the White House. Although his public image was that of an avuncular, charming old man—a university president and citizen-soldier—he was in reality a hard-nosed warrior, adept on the international stage of power plays and intimidation. Ike had developed a healthy respect for espionage and secret operations through his experience in World War II with the SIS, the French Resistance, and the OSS. He firmly advocated and implemented the full use of this type of agency in a wide variety of roles. In 1952, the Democratic Party's response to the communist threat, commonly named "containment," was inadequate, according to Ike's Republican Party. In the presidential campaign, the GOP ridiculed the idea of keeping the

President Dwight D. Eisenhower awarding J. Edgar Hoover the National Security Medal, 1955.

Soviet empire confined, of merely parrying future expansion and waiting for the communist world to collapse. Its spokesmen advocated something more radical and dangerous. Sometimes it was termed "liberation." Sometimes it was called "rollback." Either way, it meant that the U.S. should go beyond resisting future Soviet advances. It should actively begin to free those people it considered already enslaved by communist doctrine and power.

While Eisenhower never clearly embraced this policy, he came close.[29] He had no problem with its endorsement by Secretary of State John Foster Dulles or Vice President Richard M. Nixon. But secretly, Eisenhower agreed with containment. After all, he had been in conference with Truman and Marshall right at its creation in 1947 during the Greek-Turkish crisis. And during the Hungarian crisis of 1956, when Ike was urged by advisers like Nixon and Dulles to intervene directly against Soviet tanks and liberate Hungary, he chose not to. ·

Although he stopped short of rolling back the communists, Ike was a dedicated practitioner of an active containment policy, at any price, in any place, or at the slightest provocation. His tool was the CIA. Indeed, during his administration, the CIA perfected the art of the covert, paramilitary operation. In 1953, Eisenhower authorized Operation AJAX to undermine the moderate Mossadegh government in Iran, facilitating the return from exile of the Shah. In 1954, Operation SUCCESS caused the overthrow of the progressive Arbenz government in Guatemala. In 1957, the operation against Sukarno in Indonesia nearly destroyed his neutralist state. In Vietnam, the Agency maintained the Diem government in the south, backing its refusal in 1955 to agree to elections mandated by the Geneva Accords, the pact that ended the first Indochina War in 1954.[30] In 1960, Dulles warned against an imminent communist takeover of the Congo and authorized a $100,000 fund to replace the country's first prime minister, Patrice Lumumba, with a "pro-western" group. This triggered a chain of events ending in Lumumba's assassination.[31]

And finally, there was Cuba. When Fidel Castro overthrew the Batista government in 1959, his political programs took Eisenhower by surprise. Since the Guatemala operation in 1954, the general had focused his attention on the Middle East, Europe, and the Soviet Union. Consequently, Eisenhower refused to commit himself against the Castro government. He wanted to see if he could find a "third force" between Castro and the remnants of the former regime. In this way the U.S. began slipping down the slope that would lead to the CIA's watershed—the Bay of Pigs disaster of April 1961.

For the CIA, the "third force" consisted of the Cuban refugees and exiles who had fled the revolution. In the face of Castro's confiscation of their property, thousands of middle and upper-class Cubans had left with whatever wealth

Fidel Castro in the Sierra Maestra mountains, 1957, with Raul Castro, left, and Camillo Clenfuegos, right, described in the AP caption as "two armed followers."

they could smuggle out. Most settled in the American Southeast: Florida, Georgia, Louisiana. Many had only one goal in mind after their resettlement: working for the immediate overthrow of this communist government.

By late 1959, the President agreed with the Cuban exiles: he called Allen Dulles in and recommended a stepped-up secret war against Castro.[32] The U.S. would first isolate Cuba diplomatically and economically by breaking off relations, embargoing the island, and urging other countries to do the same. It would also launch a propaganda drive against Castro, culminating in the clandestine recruitment of Cuban exiles. These policies were to be kept secret because they would offend Latin-American sensitivities by the raw display of American might, and because one of the alternatives was Castro's assassination.

As it turned out, the actual assassination attempts made public by the Church Committee investigation of 1975[33] were of the Keystone Kops variety. They included attempts to get the Mafia to gun down Castro, poison cigars and ice cream sodas, and even the use of a poisoned seashell at his favorite skin diving beach. It is not clear whether or to what extent Eisenhower approved these or any other specific parts of the plan. He was skilled enough to do so orally and preserve deniability in the event these bizarre schemes were exposed.

In March of 1960, DCI Allen Dulles—brother of the late Secretary of State—and his special assistant on Cuba, Richard Bissell, met with the President to discuss a Guatemala-type incursion against Cuba.[34] There were four main parts to the plan: creating a credible government-in-exile; lauching a full propaganda offensive aimed at both Cubans in exile and those on the island; creating on the island a guerrilla unit sympathetic to the government-in-exile; and creating a paramilitary force outside Cuba to precipitate action.

Eisenhower approved the plan but insisted that all four parts be in place, especially the first, before he would initiate hostilities. Dulles thought this would take about six to eight

John F. Kennedy pins the National Security Medal on Richard M. Bissell, Jr., April 1962.

months. Eisenhower wished to get rid of Castro before he left office. But if he did not, he felt that Richard Nixon, who both enthusiastically supported the plan and, as White House Cuba Project action officer, knew its details, would succeed him as President and carry it out well.[35]

Unfortunately for Eisenhower, Nixon, and Dulles, Jack Kennedy's election in 1960 was a big surprise.

2

Kennedy, the Agency, and Cuba

It is difficult to imagine two major politicians as seemingly different as Dwight David Eisenhower and John Fitzgerald Kennedy. Their superficial differences are easy to list. Ike was a conservative Republican. Kennedy was a liberal Democrat. At the time, Eisenhower was the oldest President to hold office, while Kennedy was the youngest ever elected. That age difference was visually dramatic: the former general was partly bald, white-haired, wrinkled, and stooped; Kennedy was youthful, with a full head of wavy, brown hair; he was effervescent, vibrant, with fashion-model good looks.

In the 1960 election, the Kennedy braintrust was well aware of these differences and worked tirelessly to take advantage of them. Indeed, the idea of the "New Frontier" theme was created at the nominating convention in Los Angeles, when, with more than 50,000 in attendance, then Senator Kennedy accepted the nomination with these words:[1]

We stand today on the edge of a New Frontier—the frontier of the '60s—a frontier of unknown opportunities and perils—a frontier of unfilled hopes and threats.

Kennedy was challenging an image of eight Republican years of apparent security and quietude; or, as one commentator has termed it, "years of excitement cushioned in complacency."[2] For Kennedy seemed a new kind of liberal—well-informed, dynamic, moderate, fiscally prudent, yet one who could reach across lines of class and politics to create a consensus. Unlike Adlai Stevenson or Hubert Humphrey, Kennedy could not easily be pigeonholed by the Republicans.

But if there was one area where Kennedy and Eisenhower seemed to intersect, it was in their response to the communist threat. For all his freshness and energy, Kennedy was a prudent politician. He knew that to be branded soft on communism would be to invite political oblivion. Throughout his career, he had assiduously cultivated anticommunist credentials, even on domestic issues. For instance, when he first began investigating labor issues in the House of Representatives, he targeted communist membership in American unions.[3] During the Senate voting to censure McCarthy for witch-hunting against the army, JFK carefully dodged the roll call, failing to phone in his vote from his hospital bed. It was Kennedy's fence-sitting on the McCarthy issue that cost him the support of the liberal paragon, Eleanor Roosevelt, in his drive for the vice-presidential nomination in 1956.[4]

In the 1960 campaign, Kennedy was strong on national defense, claiming a huge missile gap existed between the U.S. and U.S.S.R. (In fact, the "gap" was decidedly in our favor; the U.S. had a ten-to-one advantage in missiles[5] and the Soviet Union had cut its military budget by one-half between 1955 and 1960.[6]) He was strong on defending the tiny islands of Quemoy and Matsu off the coast of China against the Chinese Communists—a crisis that had been all but extinguished by that time.[7] Most of all, he was tough on Cuba. In the famous election debate against Nixon, Kennedy used the Cuban issue like a billy club.[8] When Nixon attacked the Democrats for "losing China," Kennedy shot back that Nixon was in no position to accuse anyone of not standing up to the communists, since his administration had allowed a communist takeover ninety miles off the Florida coast.[9]

**Kennedy and Eisenhower
strolling together
after the 1960 election.**

Kennedy was even more specific in his prescriptions for dealing with Castro: "We must attempt to strengthen the non-Batista democratic anti-Castro forces.... Thus far these freedom fighters have had virtually no support from our government."[10] It is hotly debated how much Kennedy knew about the Bay of Pigs during the campaign. Dulles briefed JFK on the operation twice, once in July and again in September. Dulles has stated that at the first meeting only generalities were discussed and the only clandestine operations he revealed were radio broadcasts. Dulles did not reveal the substance of the second meeting, but after it, Kennedy went on record in two speeches in support of the freedom-fighting forces in exile.

Then, on November 18, president-elect Kennedy received a fuller briefing from Dulles on the proposed invasion. Again, it seems that specific details were not discussed. But Kennedy seems to have developed other channels both inside and outside the government to gather information on the planned operation.[11] In any event, Kennedy then showed some affinity with Nixon and Eisenhower about the need for alternatives to Castro. In 1960, whether because of or in spite of these similarities to the Nixon-Eisenhower positions, JFK won the closest election victory in American history. Out of nearly 70 million votes cast, Kennedy won by a bit over 100,000. The electoral vote was a more solid 303-219.

But below the level of campaign rhetoric, John Kennedy was not simply a more youthful version of Eisenhower. This was especially marked in his attitude toward the communist threat and with respect to what was becoming known as the "third world," those developing former European colonies just achieving their independence.

In the late 1950s, there was massive conformity in American politics about counteracting alleged communist infiltration or expansion into so-called free or neutral areas: it must be prevented, no matter what the price or circumstances. Since 1946, this attitude was increasingly vehement, explaining in large part the intensity of reaction to Castro's leftward turn in Cuba.[12] Despite its internal differences the communist world was portrayed as a hulking monolith, poised to enslave a precarious free world. Soviet actions right after World War II, the Alger Hiss case, the Rosenbergs' alleged theft of atom bomb secrets, the activities of the House Committee on Un-American Activities—of which Nixon was a member— the wild accusations of Senator Joe McCarthy, all these and more seemed to paralyze rational analysis and, ironically, give the lie to the self-proclaimed serenity of the golf-playing Eisenhower and the era taking his name. But what ensured a rigid, overwrought, knee-jerk reaction was the juggernaut of the domino theory.[13]

Like most political boilerplate, the theory had some relation to fact. After World War II, every Eastern European government had gone communist. All but Yugoslavia were closely allied with Stalin. Extrapolating from this, jingoists postulated that this chain reaction would be repeated if another country in any other area were to fall to communism.

The peculiar relationship of the Soviet Union to Eastern Europe, Stalin's legitimate fear of Germany,[14] the fact that China went communist under totally different circumstances and by itself in 1949,[15] the indigenous nature of most Third World liberation struggles—all this was ignored or distorted in this oversimplified, self-serving theory. Once the dominoes started falling, there was no telling where they would stop: the Philippines, Australia, Hawaii, maybe even San Diego.

Eisenhower was an avid believer in the domino theory. During his administration, one domino after another seemed to be constantly falling. After the French defeat at Dien Bien Phu in Vietnam, a treaty organization had to be formed or "the whole anti-Communistic defense of that area [would] crumble and disappear."[16] The democratically elected Arbenz government of Guatemala had to be subverted, or it would endanger Central America all the way up to the Rio Grande: "My God," Ike told his Cabinet, "just imagine what it would mean to us if Mexico went communist!"[17] The U.S. could not even "lose" tiny islands like Quemoy and Matsu "unless all of us are to get completely out of that corner of the globe."[18] He even postulated that the threat must be met in Vietnam or the dominoes would fall across the Pacific to Australia.[19]

This was a frightening scenario for politicians to ponder. Who would want to be responsible for the loss of whole areas of the globe?[20] And who better to broadcast the alarm than the aged eagle who had saved us from the barbarous Nazis?

As we have seen in the intervening years, the Communist Bloc was not a monolith, nor did the domino theory describe the real world; although the fear of it and of "losing Vietnam" led Lyndon Johnson into both national and personal tragedy in Southeast Asia. At the time there were some scholars and politicians (and many ordinary people) who were bold and imaginative enough to think of the world as more than just bipolar, free versus enslaved, and who wished to penetrate the surface of this new constellation of ideas and how they worked—especially in the third world.[21] One such person was Jack Kennedy.

Kennedy had always held a strong interest in and curiosity about foreign affairs. His first published book, *Why England Slept*,[22] was an analysis of the reasons for that country's reluctance to face up to Nazi aggression prior to 1939. In 1950, Congressman Kennedy toured the Far East. According to his biographer, Herbert Parmet, it changed him a great deal:[23]

> He returned highly critical of ... British and French colonialism.... It enabled him to understand the potency of nationalism as a force more significant than communism and as something utilized by them to gain their own ends.

Thus, in truth, Kennedy was not a hard-line Truman clone. He was more sophisticated and penetrating on the issues, more subtle and sensitive, closer to FDR.[24] In fact, he made his most courageous and insightful speeches on the Senate floor when he addressed the two French colonial dilemmas of Algeria and Vietnam.[25] Kennedy pushed for granting complete independence to both states.[26] He felt that once independence was granted, the nationalist movements would mushroom into an anticommunist force that would place the U.S. on the right side of history. His approach was through politics and economics, rather than the knee-jerk militarism of many Cold Warriors. He was consistent on the issue, because he also linked it with granting aid to Iron Curtain countries like Poland[27] that showed the desire for self-rule.

So even initially JFK was not a doctrinaire Cold Warrior, but a much subtler politician open to new possibilities. Indeed, by 1963, he would tell Walter Cronkite that the Vietnam War was not primarily an American struggle; ultimately it was South Vietnam's war to win or lose.[28] Eisenhower, however, supported the war well into 1966[29] and Nixon throughout his presidency.

By the time Kennedy entered office the planned action against Cuba had gotten out of executive control. In its operational phase, it included ships, planes, landing craft, diversionary tactics, preliminary bombing, and, most importantly, the recruitment of thousands of anti-Castro Cubans. Most of them were enlisted around Miami and shipped to Guatemala for training. The operation had become so large that Eisenhower had reluctantly postponed it, handing it over to Kennedy. The new President downsized it slightly[30] but continued to maintain it as a "go" project. By now, it had gained its own inner momentum. In CIA Director Allen Dulles and Richard Bissell, two holdovers from Eisenhower, it had two stalwart defenders.

But it was *too* big.[31] Castro was tipped off early and cracked down on rebels inside Cuba, choking off aid to incoming groups. Stories on the guerrillas' training in Guatemala began to appear in the American press: *The Nation* ran an editorial in its November 19, 1960, issue; pictures appeared in the *Miami Herald* the same month; in January 1961, a detailed account finally made the front page of the *New York Times*.[32]

The number of CIA employees and Cuban refugees involved in the April 17 invasion exceeded 3,000. Dulles and Bissell assured Kennedy of its success. But from the beginning, the assault degenerated into a debacle.[33]

The fact that the planes used in the preliminary bombing expeditions on April 15 were owned by the United States was exposed. Due to heavy waves, the diversionary landing near Guantanamo Bay could not take place.[34] The main invasion force at the Bay of Pigs landed successfully, but one of its supply ships sank on hidden reefs, with communications gear and aviation fuel, crippling radio contact among the exiles.

But the two biggest mistakes were in the Agency's predic-

Left, three members of the
Invasion force In a Cuban Jall;
above, one of the Invaders'
planes, with Cuban Air Force
Insignia, shot down at
Playa Giron, the Bay of Pigs.

tions of Cuban responses. Dulles and Bissell had told Kennedy it would take days for Castro to get troops, artillery, and tanks to the front. They also had stated that large numbers of Cubans would join the brigade once it landed. Both assertions were dead wrong. The Cuban people rallied to the island's defense, and large forces were deployed against the invaders within 24 hours. Not one sympathizer reached the shore to aid the exile army.

By April 19, the invasion force was reeling. The CIA appealed frantically to Kennedy to send in air power. He came close to doing so, but decided against direct U.S. intervention.[35] When the invasion was defeated, U.S. ships ferried survivors back to Florida. Castro captured more than 1,200 soldiers.

Evidently, some people in the CIA never believed there would be a spontaneous uprising against Castro sparked by the invasion. In fact, weeks after the fiasco, Dulles went on *Meet the Press* and stated, "A popular uprising? ...That's a popular misconception. But no I wouldn't say we expected a popular uprising. We were expecting something else to happen in Cuba ... something that didn't materialize." The implication is that this "something else" was likely the "diversionary landing" that had gone awry.[36]

According to Warren Hinckle and William Turner, the landing was an Agency pretext to force Kennedy to commit U.S. forces to the invasion through a secret expansion of the planned activities. It consisted of ploys by Cuban exiles, masquerading as Castro's troops, either to attack the American base at Guantanamo or to attack Cuban forces *from* Guantanamo. The "something else" also included at least two Castro assassination plots timed with the invasion and meant to facilitate it.[37] One of these plots was coordinated with the Mob, and the man who enlisted the actual assassin was E. Howard Hunt, a major recruiter in the exile community and a strong advocate of Castro's assassination.[38] As with the incorporation of the Gehlen organization, the Agency and Dulles kept their ostensible bosses in the dark about the "something else."[39]

From this point on, Kennedy grew less enamored of Dulles, Bissell, and the Agency. Feeling angry, misled, even betrayed, he swore to, "splinter the Agency into a thousand pieces and scatter it to the wind!"[40] Indeed, if Dulles was telling the truth on *Meet the Press*, it demonstrates the depth of the deception he had practiced on the president and helps explain Kennedy's rage upon learning of it.

Dulles was fired shortly after, replaced by John McCone.[41]

Bissell was also asked to resign. When he resisted, he was transferred to the Institute for Defense Analysis, a military think tank.[42] Dozens of older officers were asked to relinquish their posts, including Deputy DCI General Charles Cabell (the brother of Dallas Mayor Earle Cabell, who rode in the fateful motorcade).

But Kennedy kept the CIA Miami station, JM-WAVE, alive. A new bureau chief was installed and given an annual budget of $500 million.[43] In the eighteen months between the

Lt. Gen. Charles Cabell, DDCI, 1957, left; his brother Earle, running for Congress in 1964, above.

Bay of Pigs and the Cuban Missile Crisis, there were more attempts to infiltrate Cuba, mostly failures. Distrusting the CIA, Kennedy assigned his brother to supervise this new operation, codenamed MONGOOSE.[44] Again, assassination was part of the campaign, but Robert Kennedy apparently shielded his brother from the fact.[45]

Then came the Cuban Missile Crisis of 1962.[46] In October, the high-altitude spy plane, the U-2, had photographed the installation by the Soviets of missile bases on the island. Kennedy summoned a circle of senior advisers known as his Executive Committee, or ExComm. Three alternatives were recommended: air strikes to take out the missile sites; an invasion to secure their dismantlement; or a blockade to stop their completion.

There was a fierce internal debate in which Kennedy took a relatively moderate stand amongst military hawks wanting immediate invasion, diplomatic doves wanting a negotiated settlement, and a range of tactical suggestions in between.

Future Warren Commission member John McCloy, then a director of Chase Manhattan Bank and long-standing national security strategist, initially counseled that if need be, an air strike should be launched and the island invaded by American troops. Dean Acheson, Truman's former Secretary of State, was for an immediate surgical air strike against the missiles and opposed any course leading to a protracted showdown. Defense Secretary Robert S. McNamara urged a blockade or "quarantine" of ships headed for Cuba, followed by a gradual increase of pressure as warranted. This, in the end, was Kennedy's final strategy. After days of global fear of imminent nuclear war, the crisis ended with the Soviets pulling out their missiles and JFK promising not to invade Cuba, as well as withdrawing some of America's (obsolete) missiles from Turkey (on the Soviet border). JFK also called on the Soviets now to focus on "the great effort for a nuclear test ban," a limited version of which both signed in 1963.[47]

It is crucial to note that in both Cuban crises, Kennedy was very subtly beginning to show a softer line towards Cuba and communism. While many liberals and leftists score Kennedy's willingness to risk a nuclear war, he did not escalate the crises, something Acheson, Eisenhower, and Nixon said they would have immediately done. Kennedy decided on solutions that would not spark further conflagrations or even more anti-Americanism. In this second crisis, his lack of macho posturing, his cool flexibility, allowed the Soviets a way out without risking their complete humiliation.

This outcome was hailed in the media as Kennedy's finest hour. In Cold Warrior terms, the new President had proven his mettle and done much to redeem himself from the Bay of Pigs disaster. But there was much more to the picture: in the resultant euphoria, three aftereffects of the crisis went unnoticed. First, the U.S. did not demand on-site inspection of the missile removal. It was to be monitored by the same planes that had spotted them. Second, two days after the resolution of the crisis, Kennedy finally pulled the plug on Operation MONGOOSE and began moving toward a possible accommodation with Castro. And third, notwithstanding the media's Cold War triumphalism, JFK began to move toward a lowering of the nuclear threat and Cold War tensions with the Soviets.

Few people foresaw the disappointment, bitterness, resentment, and rage the first two actions by the President would produce among the Cuban exiles and the operational CIA employees close to the scene. By apparently stopping the efforts to unseat Castro, Kennedy was telling thousands of people whom the U.S. had recruited and given hope that all the promised support—without which success was impossible—was gone.[48] In essence, Cuba was now Castro's forever. Not having on-site inspection forced the CIA in theory to trust the Soviets and Cubans with nuclear stakes, a hitherto unthinkable proposition. These were bitter pills to swallow, and some refused to do so. Thus, the conspiracy to kill the President had its roots in the remnants and resentments of the Cuban operations.

To understand its Dallas denouement, we must understand its New Orleans genesis.

3

New Orleans

In retrospect, the key was always New Orleans. It seems strange that no one picked up a pattern at the time. But hindsight is always 20/20.

Very late on November 19, 1963, a small 1957 two-tone Ford pulled off Route 190 on its way out of Baton Rouge, northwest of New Orleans.[1] Two men were in the front seat, and a young woman was in the back. Her name was Rose Cheramie, and she worked for Jack Ruby at his Dallas saloon. She was a narcotics addict, and she was in terrible need of a fix. She was writhing and moaning as she lurched around in the back seat. The two men, underworld friends of Ruby's, were arguing over how to handle her. She seemed too big a risk to their activities. One of them had talked to her too much. When the other found out about it, he realized that Rose had to be eliminated. After pulling over in front of a lounge and trying to slap her into shape, they got back in the car and took off. They opened a door and dumped her out, thinking she could not survive and that her death would be considered a hit-and-run accident.

Badly bruised, but still alive, Rose Cheramie was found by Officer Francis Fruge and taken for treatment to East Louisiana Hospital, in Jackson. After being treated for her injuries and her drug problem, she was asked by a nurse what had happened. She said she had been deliberately ejected from a car by business associates of Jack Ruby, her Dallas employer. She added that they were returning to Texas after making a drug pickup in Miami. When asked why she was thrown from the car, she replied that "transporting drugs was one thing, but murder is something else." She went on to say that President Kennedy would be killed in Dallas within a few days. She said the same thing to other nurses and to Officer Fruge, but this was dismissed as the ranting of a junkie.

After the assassination, Fruge returned to the hospital and took Cheramie into custody. On the trip to Texas, after Ruby had shot Oswald, she picked up a paper in which her employer was quoted as saying that he never knew his victim. She turned to Fruge and laughed as she told him that Ruby and Oswald were good friends; Oswald had visited him in the bar.

On September 4, 1965, the body of Rose Cheramie was found on the side of a highway running east between Texas and Louisiana. This time she was dead. A motorist told authorities that as he was driving, he came upon her body and, swerving to avoid her, ran over her head. The investigating policeman, Officer Andrews, could find no relationship between the woman and the driver. He had strong reservations about the story, but since no family members pursued the investigation, it was closed. Fruge heard about the accident much later. He asked Andrews for the driver's address

Rose Cheramie.

and when he tried to track him down in Tyler, Texas, he found the location to be nonexistent.

In the late afternoon of November 22, 1963, two men sat in the Katzenjammer Bar in New Orleans.[2] The taller, huskier one was Guy Banister, former Bureau Chief of the FBI's key Chicago office,[3] now running a private detective firm out of a nearby office. The smaller, skinnier man was his investigator, Jack Martin. Guy Banister had an aggressive, overbearing personality to begin with, and the day's events seemed to have made him even edgier. Before dusk, after much alcohol, the two men headed back to their office. Once there, Banister accused Martin of having stolen a file. Martin denied it, taking offense. The recriminations escalated into a hot argument, and finally Martin informed his boss that he was aware of the strange people and events going on around his place during the previous months. He knew, he hinted, what they added up to. He had barely finished his statement when Banister pulled out his .357 Magnum and started to beat his face in with it.

Martin was so badly hurt that he was driven to Charity Hospital, where a police report of the incident was filed. Embarrassed and outraged by Banister's violent outburst, Martin later confided to a friend that his boss and an associate, David Ferrie, had been involved in the plot to assassinate President Kennedy, with Ferrie as the getaway man. It was this knowledge that had driven Banister to assault and battery.

As early as the night of the assassination, there was a hint that the machinations in and around New Orleans were connected to Washington. On that evening of November 22, 1963, Gary Underhill was a deeply troubled man. What he had learned, and the fact that *they knew* he had learned it, were too much for him. He had to escape. Once he was out of Washington, he could regain his equilibrium. Then he would decide what to do. He had friends in New York he could talk to without fear of the word getting back to Washington.

He arrived on Long Island the next morning.[4] His friend Robert Fitzsimmons was asleep. He and his wife Charlene— Bob called her Charlie—were about to leave on a long trip to Spain that day. When Underhill learned of the trip, he said, "You're going to Spain? That's the best thing to do. I've got to get out of the country, too. This country is too dangerous for me now." He paused and added, "I've got to get on a boat, too. I'm really afraid for my life."[5]

Charlene Fitzsimmons realized something was wrong with the usually rational and objective Underhill. But Underhill insisted he had not been drinking. It was the Kennedy assassination, he explained. It was not what it seemed to be. "Oswald is a patsy. They set him up. It's too much. The bastards have done something outrageous. They've killed the President! I've been listening and hearing things. I couldn't believe they'd get away with it, but they did!"

Charlie did not know what he was talking about. Who were "they"?

"We, I mean the United States. We just don't do that sort of thing! They've gone mad! They're a bunch of drug runners and gun runners—a real violence group. God, the CIA is under enough pressure already without that bunch in Southeast Asia. Kennedy gave them some time after the Bay of Pigs. He said he'd give them a chance to save face."

He could tell Charlie did not believe him. "They're so stupid," he continued. "They can't even get the right man. They tried it in Cuba and they couldn't get away with it. Right after the Bay of Pigs. But Kennedy wouldn't let them do it. And now he'd gotten wind of this and he was really going to blow the whistle on them. And they killed him!

"But I know who they are. That's the problem. They know I know. That's why I'm here. I can't stay in New York. Can you put me up?"

Charlie reminded him they were leaving for Europe in a

few hours and would be gone for months.

"Well, maybe I can go with you."

Charlie was frightened now. Recovering, she said he could stay there for a few hours. When Bob came down he might let him have the key to the place for a few days.

Underhill mulled it over for a few seconds. "No, that's all right. Maybe I shouldn't leave the country." He turned toward the door. "I'll come back in a couple of hours. Bob will be up by then." He walked out without saying where he was going. It was the last time the Fitzsimmonses would see their troubled friend.

John Garrett Underhill knew whereof he spoke. He had attended Harvard and served in the OSS.[6] His family had been active in military-political affairs for a long time. Underhill himself was an expert on limited warfare and small arms. After the war he had shuttled back and forth between special assignments for the CIA and consulting for Henry Luce at *Life* and *Fortune*. He had had a strong influence on Luce's views of both World War II and Korea.[7]

John Garrett Underhill, June 16, 1955, when he was Deputy Civilian Defense Director for Wardens in Washington.

Underhill was close to top military brass and higher-ups in the CIA,[8] and had voiced his fears about these people to another friend, Asher Brynes,[9] a writer for *The New Republic* who also knew Underhill's estranged wife, Patricia.[10] Underhill did not leave the country after his visit to the Fitzsimmonses. He returned to Washington and began quietly to investigate the assassination. He spoke about it to Brynes.

On May 8, 1964, Brynes visited Underhill's apartment. When no one answered, he walked in, to discover Underhill in bed sleeping. As he approached his friend, he noticed that his face seemed discolored. It had a yellow-green hue.[11] Brynes drew closer and saw a bullet hole in his friend's head. Underhill was dead and had been for days. Yet no one in the apartment house had heard a gun go off. Odder still, Underhill had been shot behind the left ear and the gun was under his left side, yet Underhill was right-handed.[12] Despite these strange circumstances, the coroner ruled the death a suicide. Brynes was disgusted with the conclusion, but did not pursue the matter. Patricia Underhill would not talk to anyone about her husband's death and refused to turn over any papers he may have written concerning the assassination.[13]

Dean Andrews was a short, roly-poly New Orleans attorney who walked with a jaunt and spoke in an offbeat manner, using words like "Daddy-o" and "cool cat" and "my man."[14] It was hard to see exactly what he looked like because he wore a set of oversized sunglasses through which he could see the world but no one could see him. He wore them constantly, indoors and out, no matter what the weather.

Andrews was not an upper-echelon, corporate lawyer. He had a small office in a seedier part of the city and was not above letting clients and friends buy him lunch. Heavyset, he suffered from a heart condition which he did little to counter. Much of his practice dealt with morals charges like prostitution—including homosexual prostitution—and he also did immigration work. He did not deal with deep-south high

Dean Andrews leaving the Orleans Parish Grand Jury, March 1967. A few days later, he was indicted for perjury.

society, which might help explain his demeanor. It certainly explains his clientele, which included many Hispanics and poor whites. In the summer and fall of 1963, both groups called on him for services which would lead him into unwanted prominence and later into perjury.

Sometime in late May, a group of young Hispanics, or as Andrews called them, "gay Mexicanos," were brought into his office by a slender white man of medium height. Andrews knew the man, and he agreed to represent the youngsters on charges of lewd behavior. After they left, the man stuck around and chatted with the attorney about some of his own legal problems: his military discharge, his own citizenship, and the citizenship of his Russian wife. Andrews told him that they were not serious problems. They would be easy to solve. Some he could handle himself. He advised him where to get the proper forms and how much it would cost.

A few months later, Andrews received a call from a friend named Clay Bertrand. Bertrand called him occasionally to defend his friends who, like the young Latins, got involved in minor scrapes or morals charges. Unlike most of his other clients, Bertrand was not lower class, poor, or indigent. He was wealthy, educated, respected. He occupied a different social stratum, so much so that Andrews rarely saw him. He was calling Andrews now because he knew someone in Dallas who needed his services. It was the man with the previous citizenship problem. His name was Lee Oswald, and he was accused of murdering John F. Kennedy.

Perhaps no one noticed a pattern in these seemingly unconnected events because the individuals involved seemed themselves so unconnected. But if the authorities had dug a bit deeper and traced their travel and their associations in the New Orleans-Dallas-Miami corridor that summer, they would have found a connection: a time and a place that linked three of the main characters and witnesses who could have testified to their association.

Clinton is a small agricultural village in the extreme south of Louisiana, southwest of New Orleans.[15] That summer of 1963, the civil rights movement was picking up steam everywhere in the South, and in Clinton a major drive to register voters, sponsored by the Congress of Racial Equality, was taking place. Most of the town's adult population was out on that September day. They congregated around the registrar's office. Blacks wanted to prevent any intimidation by whites to stop black registration; whites were checking on any possible outsiders rolling into town to organize and encourage the drive.

They were concerned, therefore, when a large black limousine drove into town that day. Alarmed, the town marshal approached the automobile. He thought they might be from Washington, looking for any irregularities in the registration process. He was relieved when the man said he was from the International Trade Mart in New Orleans, and started to produce an ID to that effect. The ITM was cofounded in 1947 and directed ever since by Clay Shaw, whose striking appearance fit the description given by the townsmen of the driver of the limousine.[16]

One of Shaw's companions, the one who stayed in the car with Shaw most of the time, was even more unmistakable.

Dave Ferrie suffered from a rare disease called alopecia. Untreated, this disease causes complete hair loss. Ferrie had been receiving treatment, but it was only partly successful. To alleviate his bizarre appearance, he wore a red, homemade mohair wig that he glued on himself. He did the same for eyebrows, or, at times, simply brushed them in with grease-paint. The weird makeup gave him an unforgettable Halloween clown appearance.

The third man, who was out of the car and talking most of the time, was Lee Harvey Oswald. Edwin McGehee, the town barber, was the first to talk to Oswald. He had just turned off the air-conditioning and opened the door to his shop when the young stranger walked in and requested a haircut. This took about 15 minutes; during the time, Oswald showed him his Marine discharge card and mentioned that he was trying to get a job at a nearby hospital. Oswald seemed taken aback when the barber informed him it was a mental hospital, but he did ask whom to see about a position. The barber suggested Reeves Morgan, the State Representative for the district.

It was a cool day and Morgan sat in front of a fireplace with Oswald as he discussed the job with him. He suggested that Oswald register in the district if he really wanted to pursue it. Oswald seemed a bit less eager about the prospect as he left.

How to explain this strange, almost dreamlike trip? What was Oswald doing looking for a job in Clinton, away from New Orleans, when he did not drive? What was Ferrie, a maniacal anticommunist, doing with Oswald? Strangest of all, why was Shaw there? What was the handsome, dignified, upstanding representative of upper-crust New Orleans doing in this sleepy hamlet with these two characters from the opposite end of the social spectrum?

The thread running through the relationships was the left-over flotsam of the Bay of Pigs. As noted, the CIA had done much to recruit anti-Castro Cubans in the Southeast to participate in the enterprise. Even after its spectacular 1961 failure and the ensuing changes within the Agency, the operations against Castro persisted. This was in large part because the internal CIA investigation that followed the Bay of Pigs was led by Allen Dulles. In a grave error, Kennedy had asked the DCI to uncover the operation's faults. JFK felt he had protected himself by putting his brother Robert on the committee, but two things happened which swung the proceedings to Dulles's advantage. First, Dulles managed to control the proceedings, presenting only the evidence that put the Agency's errors in the softest light. Second, Bobby was as innocent about the Agency as his brother. Dulles noted this and carefully manipulated this naiveté into enthusiasm for covert action in the Caribbean.[17] Thus, Operation MONGOOSE was hatched.[18]

The supposedly secret training camps for the operation included sites in Louisiana. One was at Lacombe, across from Lake Pontchartrain, directly northwest of New Orleans.[19] The camp was on land owned by Bill McLaney, an old business friend of Jack Ruby's. Ferrie had been an instructor at the camp.[20] His interests and talents fit right in there. He had once tried to secure an Air Force commission by writing Truman's Secretary of Defense Louis A. Johnson. In the letter, Ferrie accented both his flying and instructional skills with young pilots:[21]

> ...and by God they will get into action to kill those Russians—they should have been wiped out years ago. When am I going to get the commission: When the Russians are bombing Cleveland?

When the commission was not forthcoming, Ferrie tried writing the Air Force directly, in similar terms:[22]

> There is nothing I would enjoy better than blowing the hell out of every damn Russian Communist, Red, or what

have you.... I want to train killers, however bad that sounds. It is what we need.

He confided to a friend that he was training small units in guerrilla warfare and was personally dropping off and returning his trainees from raids inside Cuba.

Ferrie's activities in this area went back even further. One of the ships used in the Bay of Pigs invasion, the *Santa Ana*, had been stacked with arms supplied by Ferrie. In early April of 1961, he and an admitted CIA agent named Gordon Novel had raided an explosives bunker in Houma, a town south of New Orleans. They had taken land mines and hand grenades and stored them in their apartments.[23]

After the failure of the Bay of Pigs operation, Ferrie, a fervid anticommunist, developed an intense antipathy for John Kennedy. He made little effort to restrain his hatred. At one meeting with some of the Cuban refugees, he spoke at such length and with such bitterness toward the President that even the anticommunist Cubans walked out on him. As a friend commented, Ferrie "became obsessed with the idea of Kennedy and what he was doing to Cuba...."[24]

Then, after the missile crisis, Kennedy began to dismantle MONGOOSE. Operatives at all levels were enraged. Many refused to accept the decision. Secretly, the Agency still funded some of its southeastern cadre and their efforts. Some of them turned to private funding and became rogue operatives, linking themselves with the Mob and rightwing paramilitary groups like the Minutemen, who did the actual supplying of money and weapons.[25] When Kennedy discovered this, he decided to play hardball with the Agency.

On July 31, 1963, the FBI raided a pink cottage near the Lake Pontchartrain site.[26] There they confiscated a broad array of munitions: dynamite, bomb casings, fuses, and fuel explosives. McLaney, the camp's owner, planned to bomb oil refineries in Cuba. The FBI had been tipped off to this violation of the Neutrality Act and proceeded on the President's orders. They also captured some key players in the movement but, oddly, released them without filing charges.[27]

Ferrie, and others, now grew even more resentful of Kennedy. For the first time, Ferrie mentioned to a young protégé a design to do away with JFK.[28] But he never included himself in the plans. He talked about it in the second or third person.

In this light, perhaps, the Clinton trip of that motley trio is more clear. It helps explain Oswald's surprise on learning that the hospital was a mental institution. It was not his idea. He had not checked it out. He was not a permanent resident of the area, as were his two calculating companions. Who would have thought that one day soon, one of the trio would be asking Dean Andrews to represent another of the group. For Dean Andrews knew that Clay Bertrand was only an alias. The caller's real name was Clay Shaw.

4

Witches' Brew

In the immediate aftermath of the assassination, Oswald seemed less a person than a projection of our own personal demons and our disdain for the image of Dallas: nouveau riche, coarse, rightwing, and redneck—the only big city that pelted and spat on then U.N. Ambassador Adlai Stevenson. And so with Oswald.

Due to the shock of the assassination and the biased and shallow reporting, the picture we received of him, the one the general public retains, is foreshortened, superficial, distorted.[1] Unfortunately, Oswald had no opportunity to correct it. The Dallas police took no notes or audio tapes of his twelve hours of questioning.[2] He requested legal counsel, but none came to his aid.[3] Then his life was snuffed out while he was literally in the arms of the police. Oswald never admitted shooting anyone, which would seem odd in the wake of a politically motivated crime. What most people remember is the image that was heard and seen and read over those two days of incarceration and accusation: a poor, white non-conformist who was a warehouse worker at the book depository in front of which the Presidential motorcade passed. Whatever was known about his past beyond the commonly reported events of his time in the Soviet Union and his military service, seemed reduced to a single photo-image: film clips of him in dark clothes passing out "Hands Off Cuba" flyers in downtown New Orleans.[4] The picture seemed to sum up the case: a lonely figure in black, passing out communist literature as people walk by. Oswald's sponsoring organization was the Fair Play for Cuba Committee. The Committee did exist, based in New York City,[5] but Oswald was the only member of the New Orleans chapter. The address stamped on the literature was 544 Camp Street.

In one of its many glaring omissions, the Warren Report never got to the bottom of the intriguing mystery of 544 Camp Street. If Oswald was the only member of the organization, why did he use that address, the Newman Building?[6] It was not his home address. If he was making about a hundred dollars a month and spending about sixty on rent, how could he afford an office?[7] For that is what the Camp Street address was, an office building. If he did not rent space there—as the owner of the building, Samuel Newman, said— did someone rent a room for him or lend him an office to use?[8]

This mystery could have been solved by looking through one of the FBI reports submitted to the Warren Commission. The report is a nine-line summary of an interview with former G-man Guy Banister, the detective who beat up his assistant, Jack Martin, on the day of the assassination. The address given in the report for Banister's office is 531 Lafayette Street.[9] Newman's office building is located at the corner of Lafayette and Camp. If one enters on the Lafayette side, the address is 531; if one enters on the Camp side, it is 544.[10]

Banister, who died of a heart attack in 1964, was a compelling character.[11] Apparently he spent his life in law enforcement. During World War II, he worked in Naval intelligence. After the war, he became head of the Chicago FBI office. In 1955, he moved to New Orleans and joined the police force. He was relieved of duty over a strange and dubious affair[12] in which he was supposed to have drawn his gun on a waiter in a restaurant. After this, he set up Guy Banister Associates, his private detective office at 531 Lafayette Street.

Banister seemed to do little detective work himself. Apparently, men like Jack Martin and David Lewis were hired to do the gumshoe work, leaving Banister free to pursue his

**Guy Banister, former SAC
of the Chicago FBI office.**

other interests. One of these was publishing a periodical called the *Louisiana Intelligence Digest*. This publication stated that the civil rights movement was a communist front and ridiculed Kennedy for being soft on communism because he supported the movement. Banister also funded a network of informants at nearby colleges like Tulane and LSU to gather details about leftist activities on campus so he could monitor and perhaps infiltrate them.

Banister was also a member of the Anti-Communist League of the Caribbean, a pet project of the Somoza dictatorships of Nicaragua.[13] By 1962, he had become Louisiana coordinator of the militant reactionary group, the Minutemen. Banister boasted of having the best rightwing intelligence agency in the state. His files proved it. Some of the titles include: "CIA," "Civil Rights Program of JFK," "Anti-Soviet Underground," "Missile Bases Dismantled—Turkey and Italy." The files were deemed so sensitive that within days of his death his potentially explosive papers were seized by government agents and carted away never to be seen again.[14]

So what was Banister really up to in New Orleans? Apparently he was running a clearinghouse for anti-Castro Cu-

bans.[15] After Miami, New Orleans had the highest number of
Cuban refugees in the U.S. Banister monitored them, aided
them in many ways, and even got them offices at 544 Camp
Street, as he did for Sergio Arcacha Smith of the Cuban
Revolutionary Council.[16] So what would Banister, so far to
the right as to be a proto-fascist, be doing with an alleged
Marxist like Oswald? Others, like Banister's secretary, Delphine Roberts, wondered about this inconsistency. When she
spotted Oswald handing out his literature on the street, she
asked her boss about it. He reassured her, "He's with us. He's
with the office." Roberts understood the answer. She was
aware of concepts like agents and double agents and their
significance.[17]

How did Banister know and meet Oswald? Why did this
tough, fanatical, hard-nosed man have someone like Oswald
come to his office, fill out a form, and then go into a closed-
door meeting with him when he first showed up?[18] The
connection between the two is the same as the one between
Shaw and Oswald: David W. Ferrie.

Total hair loss was hardly the only singular trait about David
Ferrie.[19] Beyond his appearance, his was a personality that
no one could forget. He was an exceptionally intelligent man
who, without much advanced education, had mastered a wide
range of subjects. For example, he experimented with mice
and prepared a paper on the viral origins of cancer. And from
his days of study as a priest, before being defrocked, he had
acquired strong foundations in Latin, Greek, and mathemat-
ics. He spoke French and Spanish. He adored Socrates. In a
tough situation, he would burst out, "What would Socrates
do?"[20] Along with his medical dabblings he had a background
in hypnosis about which he liked to brag. He once boasted,
perhaps prophetically, to a young friend, "I could kill myself
and no one would find the cause."[21]

Then there was his flying. He did not merely pilot the Lake
Pontchartrain trainees on overnight raids into Cuba. He had

been involved in the air war over Cuba as far back as 1959. There are reliable reports that he was paid by ex-Batista officials $1,500 per bombing raid.[22] His reputed ability to fly out of tight situations was legendary in the underground, making him a skilled operative in spite of his eccentricities.

Ferrie acquired his skills as a pilot in the early fifties as a member of the Civil Air Patrol (CAP). It was at this time and as a member of the CAP that he met Oswald.[23] Oswald had moved to New Orleans with his mother in 1954, and joined the CAP while Ferrie was its leader. Many members of the outfit at the time remember a friendly relationship between the two.

As we have seen, by this period—1954-1956—Ferrie had already developed a strong antipathy for communism. Yet his sidekick Oswald seems to have been politically neutral. His brother Robert has written:[24]

If Lee was deeply interested in Marxism in the summer of 1955, he said nothing about it to me. During my brief visit with him in New Orleans, I never saw any

Ferrie, right, in the Civil Air Patrol.

books on the subject in the apartment.... Never, in my presence, did he read anything that I recognized as Communist literature.

Yet a year later, Oswald was writing to a communist group for samples of their literature.[25] While Oswald's political life may have begun in New Orleans in late 1955, what those leanings really were remains a subject of debate.

But there is no debate about Ferrie's relationship with both Oswald and Banister. Ferrie's ties to Banister were clear as early as the Bay of Pigs, as many of the Cuban exiles confided to Haynes Johnson, a journalist writing a book on the operation from the exiles' point of view.[26] In fact, Banister had so much respect for Ferrie that he flew to Miami to testify for him at a dismissal hearing by his employer, Eastern Airlines.[27] Eastern wanted to remove him for the same reason he was defrocked from the priesthood, and relieved of his CAP command. Dave Ferrie was openly homosexual at a time when it was not socially tolerated, much less acceptable, to be gay.

Ferrie's homosexuality was known; it had been reported in the *New Orleans States-Item* in 1961.[28] The reasons it made the press were twofold. First, Ferrie had a proclivity for young boys, sometimes as young as fifteen. Second, when the charges were made, Ferrie tried to intimidate witnesses by threatening harm through a third party, a Cuban friend.

It was after the unsuccessful Eastern hearing, when Ferrie lost his job, that he and Banister joined forces, although Ferrie moonlighted as a private investigator for G. Wray Gill, an attorney.[29]

So there was no reason for ex-G-man Guy Banister to harbor any doubts about Lee Oswald in the summer of 1963. His partner Ferrie had known Oswald for a long time and had vouched for him. In fact, he apparently used Oswald, without his knowledge, back in 1961, in preparation for the Bay of Pigs. On January 20 of that year, two young men, a Hispanic

**Oscar Deslatte,
New Orleans
truck salesman.**

and a Caucasian, visited a Ford dealership in New Orleans. They wanted to buy ten pickup trucks. They told the salesman, Oscar Deslatte, that they should be able to purchase the vehicles at cost because they were part of a patriotic cause, the Friends of Democratic Cuba. The Hispanic told Deslatte his name was Joseph Moore. His sidekick, the one with the money, was named "Oswald." Of course, he could not have been the real Lee Oswald. He was still in the Soviet Union at the time. So how could these two anti-Castro Cubans know his name, and why would they use it? Perhaps because one of the founders of Friends of Democratic Cuba was Guy Banister.[30]

5

A Question of Motive

If Lee Oswald was being manipulated by Shaw, Ferrie, and Banister, then was he really a Marxist? Or, to look at it the other way: if Oswald were a true believer in the communist cause, why would he be associating with rightwing extremists?

Of course, it would not be necessary for Oswald to be a rightwinger in order to be useful to these men. In fact, who would expect them to be associated with a crazed Marxist? But at this point in his life, was Oswald a true Marxist and did his psychology fit into the profile of an assassin?

Oswald never had the opportunity to argue his case in court. The media and the Warren Report seized on some of the facts of his life and some statements to prove the case against him. Some of these included conversations with friends in the service and later, his journey to Russia, his mailings for communist literature, his aforementioned distribution of pro-Cuba flyers, and the ensuing radio debate in New Orleans in which he defended Marxism. But does this collection of exhibits add up to a convincing indictment? Does it encompass all pertinent details and exclude other alternatives?

A brief outline of Oswald's life until his return to Dallas in 1963 seems in order.[1] He was born in New Orleans in 1939. He had two brothers, one from his mother's previous marriage. His father died before he was born and, until moving to Texas in 1945, Marguerite raised her children herself. She suspected her new husband, correctly, of infidelity and divorced him in 1948.[2] When Lee's two older brothers joined the military, Marguerite and Lee lived together by themselves

Lee Harvey
Oswald,
center, aged 5;
Brother Robert,
left, aged 10;
and brother
John, aged 12.

Below, Oswald aged 19, In the
Marines; right, Marguerite
Oswald photographs wax
museum Image of her son.

for a while. In 1952, the pair moved to New York City, where Lee's half-brother was stationed in the Coast Guard. Later, the two moved to their own apartment in the Bronx. Lee was unhappy in the New York City schools because he was teased about his dress and his southern accent. He began skipping school and was caught and placed in detention for examination. The results were not unusual. They showed him to be inquisitive, above average in intelligence, but somewhat withdrawn.

From New York, mother and son moved back to New Orleans. Here Lee went to high school, joined the Civil Air Patrol, and tried to join the service by lying about his age. Before finishing school, when he turned 17, he enlisted in the Marines. He went through training in California and Florida, was stationed in Japan and the Philippines, got a hardship discharge, and returned to Texas in 1959.

From there he defected to the Soviet Union, where, at the U.S. Embassy, he renounced his U.S. citizenship, announcing that he intended to help the Soviet Union. Few details of his stay there are known, but he reportedly grew disenchanted rather soon.[3] He was given a job with an electronics firm in Minsk, where he met Marina Prusakova, the niece of a KGB colonel, whom he married after a whirlwind romance. While still in Russia, their first child, June, was born, on February 15, 1962. Oswald left the U.S.S.R. in June of 1962 with Marina and their daughter and arrived in Fort Worth two weeks later.[4] They moved to Dallas, where he worked at Jaggars-Chiles-Stovall, which helped produce classified government maps, and stayed until early April of 1963. Then, for no apparent reason, he and his family moved in stages to New Orleans.[5] They stayed for about five months. There, from May to July, Oswald worked in some capacity at the Wm. Reily Coffee Company, just around the corner from 544 Camp Street. Again, for no apparent reason, they returned to Texas.

At the time of the assassination, many commentators, official and otherwise, examined the facts of his life as if it were an algebraic equation leading to the death of JFK. The Warren Report devoted more than 160 pages to a detailed summary of his life and his psychology; television devoted hours of documentary and news time to a rerun of the saga; books were published to show how his aimless, ragged days led him to kill two people in an hour, one of them the President of the United States.

The discussion was, of course, one-sided. Jack Ruby, another supposedly motiveless murderer, had robbed Oswald of his day in court. The Warren Commission gave him no attorney, just like the Dallas police.[6] Yet after all this, no real motive was adduced. The first attempt at a posthumous conviction was the Marxist angle. When that showed strain, the psychopath angle was tried. Finally, a mixture of both was settled upon. No one seemed to consider Oswald the perfect pawn. However, so many contradictions abound that the possibility, even the probability, cannot be ignored. Consider the most obvious:

Do sophomores in high school develop serious political consciousness? If Oswald did, would a young Marxist then join the U.S. Marine Corps? Would a young Marxist then leave Russia? Why would a loving father and faithful husband never make an attempt to settle down? Why would a communist start a one-member Fair Play for Cuba Committee in New Orleans, a hotbed of anti-Castro activity? What sort of communist would proudly pose for a photo holding both the Trotskyist *Militant* and the Communist Party *Daily Worker*, the organs of two profoundly antagonistic factions? Why would an unemployed communist *pay* people to pass out leaflets? If, on the other hand, Oswald was in New Orleans to infiltrate anti-Castro groups, for whom was he doing this? If the assassination were a political crime by Oswald, why did he never own up to it, as other political assassins have done?

In 1963 and 1964, none of these serious questions was ever dealt with, in the Warren Report or elsewhere. All were generally ignored. The implication was simply that Oswald was a fringe character who was gradually going over the edge. Yet the only psychiatric examination ever given him, when in detention in school in New York, was not a diagnosis of psychosis.[7] So all the psychological attributes foisted on him later are just that, painted on by speculators. No one brought before the commission ever delivered any such judgment.

Yet the desire to portray Oswald as a sick man was so overwhelmingly necessary to make the official case that some of the most embarrassing parts of the Warren Report are precisely in this area. Oswald is painted as living in a fantasy world, one that "was a product of his imagination."[8] We are to believe he was a political megalomaniac who was never appreciated for his great political acumen and potential. He therefore struck back at an unappreciative world through one symbolic act. But even here, the commission hedged its bets. Its psychological profile ends with this conclusion:[9]

Many factors were undoubtedly involved in Oswald's motivation for the assassination and the commission does not believe that it can ascribe to him any one group of motives.... Out of these and many other factors ... there emerged a man capable of assassinating President Kennedy.

This performance was so weak that even one of the commission counsels had to write in reflection, "Why did Oswald kill Kennedy? It is a question not satisfactorily answered by the Warren Commission."[10] Or, one might add, by anyone.

But a plausible explanation of Oswald's trips to New Orleans and Texas can be constructed from the details of his life, most of them not difficult to locate.

As friends and relatives have attested, Oswald was in the New Orleans Civil Air Patrol.[11] Here, he met David Ferrie, a strong political personality, the first he had been exposed to. Then he joined the Marines and at El Toro base in California, he took a Russian exam at age 17. Oswald, who got only to the tenth grade and liked to skip class, had learned one of the most difficult languages of all. To explain this extraordinary fact, the commission squelched a report that he had attended the Monterey School, now called the Defense Language Institute, the government version of Berlitz.[12] They substituted the explanation that he listened to records and read books, even though none of the witnesses from the service remembered him listening to Russian records at the time.[13] Oswald was then stationed at Atsugi Air Base in Japan, home of the First Marine Air Wing. Atsugi was also the home of the "Joint Technical Advisory Group," jargon for its being the main operational base in the Far East for the CIA. It was opened in the early 1950s for operations into China and Korea.[14]

At Atsugi, Oswald had the highest security clearance in his unit—quite odd for a self-proclaimed Marxist. One of his buddies referred to it as a "crypto" security clearance.[15] Later, a former CIA finance officer, James Wilcott, testified that "cryptos" were the code names given to undercover CIA agents and operatives. And Atsugi was a base for the high-speed, high-altitude U-2 spy plane developed during the Eisenhower years and then used by the CIA to gather intelligence by flying over Russia and later Cuba.[16] After finding a way to get out of the service, one that the Marine Corps did

Oswald in May 1958 at Atsugi, Japan, home of the First Marine Air Wing and of the CIA's "Joint Technical Advisory Group."

not contest (he got his hardship discharge, but it was under other than honorable conditions, an undesirable discharge, which disqualified him from most veterans' benefits), he returned to America and defected almost immediately.[17] The Marines did only a cursory check on this, the first of their ranks ever to defect. Oswald, the Marxist, then became disaffected with the Soviet Union and easily got out.[18]

When he returned home to Dallas, this alleged Marxist was befriended by the White Russian community—those Russians who had supported the Czar in the Russian Civil War following World War I. But not only were Oswald's friends odd, so also was a job he had at a company called Jaggars-Chiles-Stovall. JCS handled, among others, contracts for the U.S. Army Map Service.[19] It is strange they would employ a Marxist defector. While there, Oswald developed a friendship with a co-worker named Dennis Ofstein, who knew a bit of Russian.[20] Oswald showed Ofstein photos of military headquarters he had taken while in the Soviet Union. Oswald commented on them, making detailed remarks about ammunition, orders given the guards, and the deployment of armor, infantry, and aircraft in divisions. Even more revealing are the following notations in Oswald's address book alongside the address and phone number of JCS: "TYPOGRAPHY" and "micro dots."[21] As Philip Melanson has noted, typography was a sophisticated technique of photographic reduction used by JCS in its advertising work. A micro dot is a method employed in espionage to reduce large amounts of printed information photographically down to the size of a period. The dot is then passed on in the text of a letter or document.[22]

When Oswald left Dallas in the spring of 1963 and met his old mentor and new friends at 544 Camp Street, he also had an odd job. It was at the Reily Coffee Company, within a few blocks of Banister's office, and owned by a wealthy New Orleans reactionary, William Reily. Reily, like Banister, was a supporter of Cuban exiles, in particular the CIA-backed Cuban Revolutionary Council.[23] There are two very peculiar

Dante
Marachini
leaving
Garrison's
office after
responding to
his subpoena,
March 3, 1967.

things about Oswald's stay at this job. First, he would take long breaks quite often. Sometimes he would go next door to the local FBI-Secret Service garage, run by Adrian Alba.[24] Also, toward the end of his stay at Reily Coffee, he told Alba he expected soon to be joining the aerospace industry at the nearby NASA installation.[25] He did not, of course. But why did he think so? Because everyone working with him or above him would be transferred there soon. And they were (and three of them—Dante Marachini, James Lewallen, and Melvin Coffee—knew Shaw or Ferrie).[26]

In October, Oswald moved back to Dallas, separated from his wife, courtesy of Ruth Paine. With Mrs. Paine's help, he secured his job at the Texas School Book Depository. The next month, from that building he allegedly performed a fantastic feat of marksmanship and killed the President. Soon afterwards, a rabid Oswald got the drop on an armed policeman, Officer J.D. Tippit. Two days later, in yet another seemingly motiveless "lone-nut" murder, he was killed himself.

A coherent explanation for this odd sequence of events, one that does not strain credulity or suffer from enormous internal contradictions, was not that difficult. The key was lying on the floor of the Dallas Police property room. The police had collected Oswald's personal effects and deposited them there. One item was a Minox camera, a miniature camera smaller than a pack of cigarettes, with an odd, tubular shape.[27] It is the camera with which he took the pictures he showed Ofstein. When the FBI took over the investigation, they tried, unsuccessfully, to convince the police to remove the camera from their manifest.[28] They claimed it was not a camera at all, but a light meter.[29] When this failed, they tried to convince the local authorities that the camera really belonged to Michael Paine, Oswald's then companion in Dallas. But the serial numbers were not domestically available at the time.[30]

Why was the federal government so intent on separating Oswald from the high-speed camera that was used almost exclusively for espionage in 1963?[31] Because Oswald's possession of it would have explained some of the seeming incongruities in his life. It might explain why a Marine Private was learning Russian and why the Marines would tolerate a "Marxist." It might explain why a defector would have no trouble getting into and out of the country, why an allegedly dedicated Marxist would not know the difference between Trotskyist and Stalinist newspapers. It might explain why he was so interested in typography and microdots and took pictures of military installations.

Finally, it could explain why an intelligent young man who was dedicated to his family never seemed to settle into a steady career. He already had one. Oswald was an American agent *posing* as a Marxist. Lee Harvey Oswald was a spy.

6

The Regicide Succeeds

The plot that would snuff out the lives of both Jack Kennedy and Lee Oswald began to unfold almost immediately after Oswald left New Orleans near the end of September 1963.[1]

On September 25, a young man who called himself Harvey Oswald appeared at the Selective Service Office in Austin, Texas.[2] He was looking for help in upgrading his Marine discharge. He talked for more than half an hour to Mrs. Lee Donnelly, the Assistant Chief of the Administrative Division. He told her he was registered in Florida,[3] was living in Fort Worth, and was having difficulties finding employment because of the undesirable discharge he had received from the Marines. Mrs. Donnelly listened to him but told him that employment problems were not in the Selective Service's jurisdiction. He should go to the Veterans Administration.

On September 26, a young woman named Sylvia Odio answered the door of her apartment in Dallas.[4] Three men were outside, none of whom she knew. Mrs. Odio was the American-educated daughter of a couple who had been prominent in pre-Castro Cuba. Her parents were political prisoners on the Isle of Pines off the south coast of Cuba. Two of the men were Cubans and said they were members of JURE, an anti-Castro group led by Manolo Ray. Ray had been a friend of Sylvia's father, who had let Ray hide out in his home on more than one occasion. They introduced themselves as Leopoldo and Angelo and won her confidence by reciting details about her parents' activities, details that only a good friend or confidant would know.

Mrs. Odio realized that Leopoldo and Angelo were probably aliases or "war" names, a device used to hide their identities from possible Castro spies. They added that they had just left New Orleans with their friend, the third person there, whom they called Leon Oswald. They said they were leaving on a trip and were interested in enlisting her in their group. They would like to see her on the way back.

The next day, Leopoldo called her back. He asked, "What did you think of the American?" She replied she did not think anything of him. "You know our idea is to introduce him to the Cuban underground because he is great, kind of nuts." He went on to add that Oswald thought the Cubans were gutless. Kennedy should have been shot after the Bay of Pigs. It would be easy to do and the Cubans should have done it. He also said that Oswald had been in the Marines and was an excellent marksman.

On November 9, a man named Lee Oswald walked into a Lincoln-Mercury car dealership up the street from the Texas School Book Depository near the triple underpass.[5] In the showroom, he approached salesman Al Bogard and said he wanted to test drive a new car. They both got in a car, and the driver took the red Mercury Comet out on the Stemmons Freeway. Once there, the customer, named Oswald, revved up to more than seventy miles an hour and began weaving through traffic in race-car-driver style. Bogard, shaken by the trip, told one of his colleagues that Oswald drove like a madman.

On returning to the showroom, there was some haggling over the method of payment and the amount of the down payment required. Another salesman overheard Oswald say, "Maybe I'm going to have to go back to Russia to buy a car." He told Bogard that he would be coming into enough money in a couple of weeks to pay for the car in cash. Bogard took his name down on a card. He then told Oran Brown, another salesman on the floor, to take note of him if he should come in one night and Bogard was not there.

In early November, a man with some spectacular, if ostentatious, skills made a few appearances at the Sports Dome Rifle Range in Dallas.[6] In a city that prides itself on gun ownership and sharpshooting, the impression left by this particular marksman was indelible. Thirteen-year-old Sterling Wood was shooting with his father when the two noticed an unusual flame spouting from the rifle of the man next to them. The father told the boy it was okay; the rifle was only an Italian carbine, and the man was an excellent shot. When Dr. Wood looked over at his neighbor's target, he saw that most of the hits were in the bull's-eye. The few that missed were outside it by an inch or two. After watching this for a while, Sterling walked over to the man and asked if it was a 6.5 Italian carbine with a four-power scope. The man replied that it was.

Garland Slack had talked briefly to this mysterious marksman on November 10 at the same range. Exactly one week later the man burned himself into Slack's memory. While on the next firing slot, he began shooting at Slack's target. And hitting it.

All three witnesses later identified the rifleman as Lee Oswald. Sterling was also right about the rifle.

Around the second week of November, a man was driving through Irving, Texas, near Dallas, looking for a gun repair shop.[7] He pulled up with his wife in front of a gunsmith's in a two-tone blue-and-white Ford. The store had a sign that said "GUNS" on it, but the two women inside told him that the gunsmith had moved. The place was now a furniture shop. The man called in his young wife to look at some furniture. During the conversation, the man mentioned that the object wrapped in paper in his hand was the plunger (firing pin) to his rifle and needed repairing. He also added that his wife had just given birth to a girl. One of the women, Mrs. Whitworth, directed him to the Irving Sports Shop where he could get the weapon fixed. Later this man did go to the sports shop. He left a ticket with the name Oswald on it.[8]

These "Oswald" sightings—and more—all have several things in common. First, they all occurred after the mid-September announcement of the Kennedy trip to Dallas and after Oswald's move back to Dallas had been decided.[9] They continued up to the day of the assassination; for example, there was a reported sighting on November 21 at the same rifle range. There is in them a pattern of growing instability mushrooming into homicidal intent. The first incident in Austin shows us a man who is disgruntled because the bad discharge the military gave him is causing employment and financial problems. The second depicts a Marxist associating with anti-Castro Cubans to leave the impression of a hatred of Kennedy leading to the contemplation of murder. The third introduces monetary reward for the prospective act, perhaps from Soviet agents. The last two see him honing his skills and preparing his weapon for the fatal act.

The problem is that none was the real Oswald.[10] Some of the time, as in the Selective Service and Odio instances, Oswald was not in Austin or Dallas. It could not have been Oswald knocking down bull's-eyes at the rifle range because, as we shall see, not only was he a poor shot, but at the times in question he was home or at work. Neither was it Oswald at the furniture store, nor speeding with Bogard on the freeway, because Lee Harvey Oswald did not drive.

The first overt step of the Dallas conspiracy was to incriminate Oswald by having one or more persons who resembled him involve themselves in what would later appear as compromising situations. In retrospect, it seems so simple-minded and the situations so contrived that the events appear plotted by a hack TV writer. However, this ploy succeeded with the Warren Commission. In each case, the man who doubled for Oswald was undoubtedly a dead ringer, but the resemblance was only facial. He was a daring driver and a crack shot, two qualities that Oswald lacked. Physically, he differed in two respects: he was a bit huskier, and he had a slightly receding hairline.[11]

The second step in the plot was to place President Kennedy in position for an ambush between a crossfire. This was done by placing his motorcade route on a path that no security chief would permit.

If one looks at the issues of the *Dallas Morning News* in the days leading up to Kennedy's arrival, there seems to be confusion about the route of the motorcade.[12] On November 16, reporter Carl Freund wrote on page one, "The President and Mrs. Kennedy are expected to drive west on Main Street at noon next Friday." But on November 19, the route published on page one included the two turns that would actually be taken on November 22, the right-angle turn on Houston and the 120-degree turn left onto Elm. But just one day later the

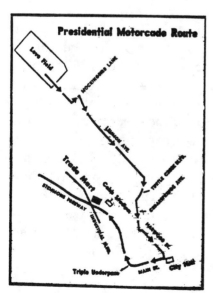

The map of the parade route as it appeared on the front page of the *Dallas Morning News* the morning of November 22, 1963. Note that the path went straight along Main Street through the triple underpass, with no turns on Houston or on Elm.

route was again reported to be only on Main Street, no turns. Finally, on the day of Kennedy's arrival, the map on the front page of the newspaper depicted a straight path down Main.

The reason for the confusion has never been cleared up. But the effect of the route actually taken is obvious when one visits Dealey Plaza where those sharp turns were negotiated. First, the cars had to slow down drastically, down to 11 miles per hour, far below the recommended speed. Second, because of the misinformation in the newspapers, the crowds in Dealey Plaza were much thinner than on Main Street. One can see this clearly in films taken on that day. Third, the layout of Dealey Plaza was absolutely perfect for an ambush by rifle-fire. As the car made the last turn onto Elm, there were high buildings behind it on either side. To the front there was a patch of grass with a fence behind it. Behind the fence was a parking lot and two railroad tracks. You could hardly ask for more if you were planning an assassination: perfect positions for snipers, a target open from all directions, easy access and exit, witnesses in front of you with obstacles hiding their vision if they turn around after the shooting.

The third step in the plot was to set up Oswald to be in the right place at the right time in order to be framed for the assassination. This process began in October of 1962, shortly after Oswald's return from Russia. He was befriended by a mysterious, complex man named George DeMohrenschildt. As Edward Epstein has noted, one of the inscrutable DeMohrenschildt's aims seems to have been separating Oswald from his wife.[13] He accomplished this by April of 1963 and then left the scene, never to see Oswald again. The woman whom Marina Oswald moved in with at this time was Ruth Paine. Mrs. Paine had been introduced to Marina by DeMohrenschildt in February of 1963.[14] Ruth was separated from her husband at the time (but would reconcile with him after the assassination).[15] The reason Ruth Paine gave for wanting to have Marina and her child move in with her was that she wanted to learn Russian, even though she already knew the language well enough to teach it.[16] Mrs. Paine, who had just separated from her husband when she met Marina, took the initiative in their relationship. After obtaining Marina's address, she wrote her asking to visit, and Marina invited her over.[17] They became friends, and when Lee was preparing to move to New Orleans, Marina moved in with Ruth before joining Lee later.

Once Ruth Paine had Marina at her house she was persistent in keeping her there and diligent in her vigilance over her. After making a cross-country trip—about which the records are still classified[18]—she picked up Marina in New Orleans in September of 1963 and drove her back to Dallas. Again, Marina lived with Ruth Paine and was separated from her husband until his death on November 24. As for Ruth Paine's vigil over Marina, the Warren Report openly says that "Ruth Paine has stated that she always accompanied Marina Oswald whenever Marina left the house with her children."[19] It was Ruth Paine who convinced Marina not to have her husband at the Paine home the weekend of November 16-17, right before the assassination.[20]

Ruth Paine's influence extends beyond separating Marina from Lee, a fact that would tend to make him seem even more isolated and offbeat at the time of the assassination. It was Ruth Paine who placed Oswald at the Texas School Book Depository just one month before Kennedy's motorcade passed in front of it. Upon hearing of a job opening at the depository, Ruth Paine personally called the superintendent and heartily recommended Oswald for the position.[21] Oswald was hired within 24 hours. Within that same time period, two calls came in about another position, an airline cargo loader, which paid more than the depository job. The calls came to the Paine household. Oswald never got word of them.[22]

Some of the connections between the New Orleans conspirators and the Dallas assassination were provided by the man

**Jack Ruby, about to go
on trial for the murder
of Lee Harvey Oswald,
February 1964.**

whose act eliminated the plot's discovery: Jack Ruby. Ruby
knew Bill McLaney, the owner of the Lake Pontchartrain
training camp. Ruby was also involved in the anti-Castro
effort himself. One of Ruby's many activities was gunrunning to the Cuban exiles.[23] Once, when he was in prison in
1964, he became hysterical and started weeping to a guard
that he had been running guns to Cuba.[24] Ruby, forever
duplicitous, later composed himself and said it was only four
handguns to a friend.

Ruby told his first lawyer, Tom Howard, that something he
feared coming out at his trial was his association with a man
named Tom Davis. There is a CIA file on a Thomas Eli Davis
who died in 1973.[25] Davis was an Agency contract employee
who first smuggled arms to Castro when he was fighting
Batista.[26] When Davis realized Castro was a socialist, Davis,
like many others in this saga, began working against him.

Davis's movements in November 1963 are interesting, to say the least. Just before the assassination, he was running guns in Algeria. Right after November 22, he was jailed in Tangiers, apparently possessing a mysterious note about Oswald and Lyndon Johnson. He was quickly freed on orders of William Harvey, director of the CIA's Executive Action Department, in charge of international assassinations.[27]

Ruby was working with Davis in 1959, although it is not clear that Ruby did this for explicit political reasons. Unlike Ferrie, Shaw, and Banister, Ruby was not a fanatical patriot. He apparently used the opportunity to make money, as he always seemed in debt.[28]

Another witness who verified Ruby's association with these activities was Nancy Perrin Rich.[29] She worked for Ruby in Dallas as a hostess at his bar. She was a remarkably candid and convincing witness before the Warren Commission, testifying, among other things, to Ruby's plying of police officers with free drinks. Her most startling testimony, however, was the story of an offer she and her husband received from a group of Cuban exiles and an Army colonel— $10,000 to bring a boatload of Cuban refugees to Miami. The

**Nancy Perrin Rich
with Robert Perrin.**

couple replied that they would consider the job for more money, including a large advance. A few nights later, they met with the same group and were told the money was on its way. They waited, and in her words:[30]

> I had the shock of my life. Apparently they were having some hitch in money arriving. No one actually said that's what it was. A knock comes to the door and who walks in but my little friend Jack Ruby. You could have knocked me over with a feather ... and everybody looks like this, you know, a big smile—like here comes the saviour, or something.

The more Ruby's case is investigated, the more about his Cuban and New Orleans relationships is revealed. Ruby is said to have made four trips to the island, though many credible commentators believe the number to be higher.[31] The frequency increased as time went on, and the Warren Commission had evidence that Ruby had visited Havana as late as June of 1963![32] Curiously, Ruby was also in New Orleans around that time, supposedly checking out a stripper for his nightclub. But on this trip, no one saw or heard from Ruby for a three-day period from June 5 to June 8, something quite unusual for the peripatetic and voluble bar-owner.[33]

To clinch the New Orleans-Dallas connection, there is Emilio Santana, a friend and former employee of Clay Shaw's.[34] Santana revealed to Jim Garrison in 1967 that Shaw and Ruby had traveled to Havana together in the early days of the Castro regime. Santana, once an Agency employee in the huge anti-Castro effort, stated that this is how Shaw and Ruby met.

Finally, let us return to another former Ruby employee, the unfortunate Rose Cheramie. In *Betrayal*, Robert D. Morrow states that it was she who impersonated Marina Oswald as part of the masquerade at the Irving furniture store.[35] The car from which Rose Cheramie was dumped near Baton Rouge, and the car parked in front of the furniture store, were both two-tone Fords. It seems likely that the men who disposed of her were involved with the plot, and Morrow believes that one of them was an Oswald double.

One of the most puzzling aspects of the conspiracy, and a riddle that will probably never be solved, is the extent of Oswald's knowledge of a plot. The evidence is certainly strong that Oswald never fired a rifle on November 22.[36] Whatever his involvement, there can be little doubt that he was tagged to take the rap. The announcement of the Presidential trip was in September, and this was when the pattern of the "second Oswald" began. The actual motorcade was announced the next month, and, as we have seen, the charade activities gained in frequency, obviousness, and gunplay as the date of the President's visit drew near.[37] At the gun range in Dallas the Oswald impersonator was observed picking up his bullet shells as they ejected.[38] And the FBI report on the shells found at the depository reveal that they had double markings, as if they had been loaded twice.[39] The plot may have been unsubtle, but it was extensive and elaborate.

And there were also forewarnings. Other attempts in the fall to kill JFK were arguably slated for Chicago and Miami.[40] And, on November 9, a Miami police informant met with wealthy, rightwing extremist Joseph Milteer.[41] The informant, who was taping their conversation, steered the dialogue to Kennedy's upcoming trip to Miami:[42]

Milteer: You can bet your bottom dollar he [Kennedy] is going to have a lot to say about the Cubans, there are so many of them here.... The more bodyguards he has, the easier it is to get him from an office building with a high-powered rifle.... He knows he's a marked man.
Informant: They are really going to kill him?
Milteer: Oh yeah, it's in the works.... An investigation wouldn't leave any stone unturned, no way. They will

Joseph Milteer.

pick up somebody within hours ... just to throw off the
public.

As a result of this taping, Kennedy's planned motorcade
through Miami was dropped. He instead flew to his scheduled
speech by helicopter. Milteer told the same informant after
the assassination not to worry about the capture of Oswald,
"because he doesn't know anything. The right wing is in the
clear, the patriots have outsmarted the communists...."[43]

Sadly, President Kennedy himself seemed to be aware of
the strong possibilities Dallas held for an assassination attempt. On the morning of November 22, he was in a Fort
Worth hotel room with his wife, Jackie. As he was waiting
for his flight to Dallas, someone showed him the venomous
ad, accusing him of being a communist sellout, that was in a
Dallas newspaper that morning. Kennedy turned to his wife
and said, "We're really in nut country now."[44] He read the ad
and began pacing the room. "Last night would have been a
helluva night to assassinate a President. I mean it. There was
the rain, the dark, and we were all getting jostled. Suppose a
man had a pistol in a briefcase." He then raised his hand,

pointing it like a pistol, and fired off some shots, his thumb imitating the gun's hammer. "Then he could have dropped the gun into the case, dropped the case, and melted into the crowd."[45]

John Kennedy had foreseen his own death that morning, but Milteer had the circumstances down more accurately. It was definitely an overkill operation, no fooling around with pistols and briefcases. These men used scopes and rifles and crossfires. Its speed, precision, efficiency, and cohesiveness eliminate Oswald as a gunman. In fact, as Kennedy was predicting his own demise, Lee Oswald was being dropped off by Wesley Frazier and his sister at his workplace, the Texas School Book Depository. He ambled into the building with a brown paper bag that he said contained curtain rods for his apartment, which, as a photo revealed later, was curtainless.[46]

That morning, between 9:30 and 10:00, Oswald encountered co-worker James Jarman on the first floor.[47] At the time, Oswald was standing at and staring out a window. He noticed a gathering crowd around the corner. As Jarman approached, Oswald asked him what the crowd was doing there. Jarman informed him that President Kennedy was going to pass by in a motorcade. Oswald asked which way he was coming, and Jarman told him he would probably be coming down Main, turning on Houston, and going back down on Elm. Oswald replied, "Oh, I see," and walked away. Unless Oswald was a consummate actor, this is probably the best piece of direct evidence showing that Oswald was a complete patsy.

At about this time, Kennedy was addressing a Chamber of Commerce breakfast.[48] When his wife arrived later, it gave him an opportunity to flash his sharp wit: "It takes Mrs. Kennedy a bit longer to organize herself, but then she looks so much better than we do." He added to this: "In France two years ago, I became known as the man who accompanied Mrs. Kennedy to Paris. I'm getting that same sensation here. Nobody wonders what Lyndon and I wear." Indeed, his Vice

President had proposed the trip,[49] both as a way of approaching the 1964 campaign and as a method of mending fences
between the two feuding wings of the Texas Democratic
Party, one under conservative Governor John Connally, and
the liberal wing under Senator Ralph Yarborough.

After breakfast, the party left for the airport and the jump
flight to Dallas, where Kennedy was to address a luncheon.
Ironically, here in the heart of the military-industrial complex, Kennedy was to speak out against the forces of reaction,
like those who had placed the ad in the newspapers that day.
One of the lines from his speech attacked those "voices
preaching ... that vituperation is as good as victory and that
peace is a sign of weakness."[50]

Air Force One arrived at Love Field in Dallas at 11:37 a.m.
Even though it had rained early that morning, a crowd of
several thousand cheered the arrival with big placards saying
"Welcome to Dallas," and "Hooray for JFK!" Jackie received
a bouquet of roses, and the President stopped to shake a few
hands. The organizers steered the Kennedys toward the open
limousine with the Connallys on the jump seat in front of
them. The black Lincoln had been flown from Washington

President and
Mrs. Kennedy
greeting
wellwishers
upon their
arrival at Love
Field, Dallas,
shortly before
noon, November
22, 1963.

President and Mrs. Kennedy with Texas Governor John Connally leaving Love Field for the motorcade.

for this occasion. Because of the weather, a warm 75 degrees, the bubble top was removed and the bullet-proof side windows rolled down. The circuitous 11-mile route would lead through downtown Dallas to the Trade Mart, where Kennedy would make the speech. Before arriving there, the cars would go down Main Street to Dealey Plaza, turn right on Houston Street and make a sharp left on Elm Street, in front of the Texas School Book Depository, before approaching a triple underpass near the Stemmons Freeway.

The procession rolled out of Love Field at 11:50 a.m. Five minutes later, according to the Warren Report, the last witness saw Lee Harvey Oswald on the sixth floor of the depository.[51] That morning, a crew had been putting down flooring on the sixth floor. At about 11:45 a.m., they decided to break for lunch. Going to the northeast corner, they began to race downstairs. They noticed Oswald on the fifth floor, where he was waiting for an elevator. One of these workers, Charles Givens, testified that at 11:55 a.m., he returned to the sixth floor for his cigarettes. There he saw Oswald, clipboard in hand. He asked him if he was going down. Oswald replied, claimed Givens, that he was not.[52]

Givens's is not the last report on Oswald's movements before the motorcade passed the depository. Co-worker Eddie Piper reported to the Dallas police that he saw and spoke to Oswald on the first floor at 12:00 noon while he was preparing for lunch. Carolyn Arnold, a secretary, said she saw Oswald on the first floor at 12:15. She had left her office on the second floor to go downstairs to stand in front of the building to view the motorcade. There she saw Oswald in the hallway between the front door and the double doors leading into the warehouse.[53]

This was crucial testimony. First, because it clashed with the first sighting—at 12:15!—of a gunman on the sixth floor by Arnold Rowland, who timed his view of the gunman by the large clock on the Hertz sign atop the depository.[54] Second, because it tied in cleanly with the first encounter with Oswald after the shooting, with Marrion Baker, described below. Thirdly, it dovetails with the testimony of co-worker Bonnie Ray Williams. Williams testified that he was eating *alone* on the sixth floor of the depository while waiting for the motorcade. He said that he left at about 12:20.[55]

Meanwhile, the motorcade was progressing slowly through thick crowds. The limousine stopped twice, once for Kennedy to shake hands and once for him to speak to a Catholic nun with a group of small children. The cars proceeded west through downtown Dallas toward Houston Street, at the beginning of Dealey Plaza. As the procession turned right from Main onto Houston, it passed the Criminal Courts Building and then the County Records Building. If Oswald were the assassin and if he had been on the sixth floor at 12:30 p.m., this is when he should have fired.

Looking south on Houston Street, there was no foliage between the window and the target. The car was moving toward the depository, getting closer and larger. But, in reality, the assassins let the limousine come up Houston and make a sharp left turn onto Elm Street. Now heading away from the depository, it progressed down Elm at eleven miles per hour,[56] through the thinner crowd on that street. As the procession moved toward the grassy knoll in front of the underpass at the right of Elm, Mrs. Connally turned to President Kennedy and said, smiling, "You can't say that Dallas doesn't love you."[57] Before Kennedy could reply, the fusillade began.

Miraculously, Abraham Zapruder, a Dallas dress manufacturer, was in Dealey Plaza with his 8 mm movie camera that day. His secretary had urged him to retrieve the camera from home when the weather cleared. He then took his place on the grassy knoll with the cars rolling right at him and a stockade fence and parking lot behind him. As the presidential limousine began to approach on Elm Street, Zapruder pressed the shutter release and recorded perhaps the most dramatic, macabre, and shocking 22 seconds in American history.

The first shot ripped through the air at 12:31 p.m. The President raised his clenched hands upward in front of his face, clearly hit.[58] At the precise instant of impact, no one in the car seemed aware of his plight. Mrs. Connally turned around at the noise and saw his clenched fists in the air and his body seem to slump. Governor Connally, perhaps recognizing a rifle shot, turned to his right, but could not see Kennedy from that angle. Mrs. Kennedy turned to her right and saw a pained expression on her husband's face. Secret Service Agent Roy Kellerman, at the right front of the limousine, heard Kennedy say, "My God, I am hit!"[59]

As Connally began to turn back toward his left, he was hit through the back and began to pitch sideways towards his wife. As he did so, he cried out, "Oh, no, no. My God, they are going to kill us all."[60] Kellerman told the driver, "Let's get out of here; we are hit. Get us to a hospital immediately!"

Then, as Kennedy was sliding into his wife's arms and pitching forward, the tremendous last blast hit. As Jackie Kennedy was trying to pull her husband into her arms, the last shot drove the President upward, backward, and to his left. His head exploded with a halo of blood and scalp and

Zapruder film, frame 228: Kennedy reacts to the neck shot.

Zapruder film, frame 274: Kennedy slumps toward his wife.

Zapruder film, frame 313: The fatal shot impacts the President.

brain tissue that splattered over the rear of the car and onto the two motorcyclists riding behind the limousine. Agent Clint Hill jumped out of the trailing car and onto the rear of the Presidential limousine. Mrs. Kennedy seemed to be trying to help Hill up, but she later said she was attempting to retrieve part of her husband's skull.[61] As the car began to pull away, Jackie got back in her seat and cried, "They've murdered my husband. I've got his brains in my hand."[62]

At this point, after rifle fire that lasted about six seconds, the motorcade sped off to Parkland Hospital. John Kennedy would be pronounced dead at 1:00 p.m.[63] But the drama playing out at Dealey Plaza was not yet finished.

The consensus of the eye- and earwitness testimony at the site suggests a triangulation of fire.[64] The majority of witnesses thought they heard shots from the grassy knoll. Some even threw themselves to the ground because they thought the shots were coming from over the stockade fence and they were right in the line of fire. A slightly smaller number thought the shots came from the depository. A much smaller number felt they came from a building adjacent to the deposi-

Witnesses running towards the grassy knoll.

tory, either the Dal-Tex Building or the records building. All three areas were searched immediately after the shooting. Footprints, cigarette butts, and mud on a car fender were all found behind the stockade fence—a curious place from which to be viewing the motorcade with so much space available on the grassy knoll. Six witnesses testified that they saw either a puff of smoke or a flash of light originating there; some of them rushed to the scene along with at least two policemen. S.M. Holland, who had been on the overpass, was one of the first witnesses there, and he was puzzled by both the proliferation of footprints and the pattern of their grouping:[65]

That was the mystery to me, that they didn't extend further than from one end of the bumper to the other. That's as far as they would go, it looked like a lion pacing a cage.

Holland was looking for shells on the ground when two policemen approached, Patrolman Joe Marshall and deputy sheriff Seymour Weitzman.[66] Marshall smelled gunpowder

S.M. Holland, signal supervisor for the Dallas Union Terminal Railroad, who saw a shot fired from the fence at the grassy knoll.

after being alerted by a witness to the origin of the shots. When they searched the area, they came across a still-unidentified man. They had drawn pistols but put them down when the man produced credentials from the Secret Service. This would not be odd except for the fact that when the individual reports of all Secret Service agents were filed, it was established that not one remained at Dealey Plaza after the limousine sped away. They were all at Parkland Hospital with the motorcade.[67]

Something even more interesting was happening at the depository. The building was not sealed after the assassination.[68] Any rifleman had ample opportunity to escape. Dallas Patrolman Marrion Baker, who had been on a motorcycle in the procession, thought he heard shots from the depository. He parked his cycle and ran through the main entrance of the building. There he met Roy Truly, the building manager. The pair ran up the stairs to the second-floor landing. Baker stopped here because he saw a man through the glass window in the vestibule door. The man was walking toward the lunchroom. Baker approached the man with his gun drawn.[69] Truly followed him and told him the man was all right, he was his employee, Lee Harvey Oswald. The two then continued upstairs.[70]

By this time, several other officers were in the building. At around 1:00 p.m., Deputy Sheriff Luke Mooney noticed a pile of cartons in front of the southeast corner of the sixth floor window.[71] The double-marked shells were found lying neatly three in a row nearby. The well-hidden rifle was found later after a longer, more arduous search. One bullet was found in the breech.

About the same time that Mooney was making his discovery, two witnesses saw a man escaping from the rear of the depository. Marvin Robinson testified to the FBI that he saw a light-colored Nash Rambler station wagon pull up alongside the building.[72] As it stopped, a white male came down the grass-covered incline between the building and the street and entered the station wagon. The car then drove away toward the Oak Cliff section of Dallas.[73]

Even more startling is the testimony of policeman Roger Craig.[74] Craig saw a white male running down the hill from the direction of the depository toward a light-colored Rambler station wagon driven by a dark-complectioned, probably Hispanic, male. Craig tried to cross Elm to stop the car, but the heavy traffic prevented him from doing so. Craig ended his testimony with this:[75]

> Later that afternoon, I heard that the City had a suspect in custody and I called and reported the information about the suspect running down the hill and getting into a car to Captain Fritz and was requested to come at once to City Hall. I went to the City Hall and identified the subject they had in custody [Oswald] as being the same person I saw running down the hill and into the station wagon and leave the scene.

This testimony came from a very credible source and dovetailed with Robinson's and the theory of an Oswald impersonator. It had to be vehemently attacked by both the Dallas police and the Warren Commission. The police even denied that Craig saw Oswald in the interrogation room that day. Later, Craig's testimony was vindicated by a photo that showed him in the room.[76]

Did Craig really see Oswald running from the depository? Did Robinson? The evidence indicates that the man Craig saw was Oswald's double, the man who had earlier impersonated him in public. He was the sharpshooter at the rifle range seen by the Woods and Gordon Slack, and he did at least some of the shooting that day.

The real Oswald made his way to his rented room at 1026 North Beckley in the Oak Cliff section of Dallas.[77] The time was around 1:00 p.m. The housekeeper, Earlene Roberts, stated that he was in and out of the place in less than

Oswald's
rooming house
at 1026 North
Beckley.

five minutes. While he was there, he donned a jacket and picked up his .38 Smith and Wesson revolver.[78] Another curious thing happened at the same time. A police car stopped in front of the house and honked a few times. Then it drove off. Ms. Roberts watched Oswald leave the house and stand on the curb at a bus stop nearby.

Then the next mysterious murder took place. For some reason, Policeman J.D. Tippit was out of his assigned region, driving in the wrong area of Oak Cliff.[79] He was not heading toward the assassination scene, as all cars in the area had been notified to do. A highly suspect police radio transcript (submitted later by the Dallas Police Department) told Tippit to stay in Oak Cliff and "be at large for any emergency that comes in."[80] This, when the President of the United States had just been murdered five miles away! At 1:00 p.m., the police dispatcher was seeking someone to pick up blood at a blood bank near the 2000 block of Commerce Street, nowhere near where Tippit was at that time. Tippit did not respond to this dispatch. Why? Could he have been at 1026 North Beckley honking his horn? The times almost match. Tippit then signaled the dispatcher twice at around 1:08 p.m., but the dispatcher did not respond.

Sometime between 1:08 and 1:16 p.m., J.D. Tippit was shot four times and killed almost instantly.[81] The official story has him killed by Oswald, but as we shall see in the next chapter, that is unlikely. Why Tippit was in this area, why he supposedly called out to the suspect on the basis of a vague description of a man carrying a rifle (Oswald was not),[82] why he tracked a murder suspect while he was still in his car with his gun holstered—all these questions have never been answered.

But it is interesting that the Warren Report leaves out valuable information that illuminates some of this relentless randomness. Again, Jack Ruby, may provide the key. First, as Rose Cheramie later revealed, Ruby knew Oswald. There are several other witnesses who have also testified to this effect, including Dallas policemen. Second, when Oswald returned to Dallas in October, his family had preceded him. Yet he checked into a downtown Dallas YMCA on October 3 and stayed there for two nights. That same YMCA was frequented by Jack Ruby.[83] It was at this time that Kennedy's trip to Dallas had recently been announced.

Tippit was mysteriously out of his sector, and not headed toward Dealey Plaza. He also approached his suspect in an unusually casual manner. At this time, Oswald was headed in the general direction of Jack Ruby's apartment in Oak Cliff.[84] Tippit had been behaving strangely that day, not just in his route, but also to people who had seen him on his beat. Five witnesses saw him sitting in his patrol car parked at a service station in Oak Cliff.[85]

He waited there for ten minutes and then drove off, gunning the engine. Tippit then went into a record shop where he frequently used the phone. This shop was seven blocks from the site where he was to be killed and one block from the Texas Theatre, where Oswald would be apprehended in less than ninety minutes. On this day, Tippit entered the shop in a huff. He cleared people from the phone so he could use it. Then he dialed and let the phone ring for a minute or two.

He said nothing, hung up, and rushed out.[86] A few minutes
later, he was dead.

Jack Ruby knew at least two hundred policemen.[87] At one
time, Ruby's sister owned a nightclub close to where Tippit
was living. Ruby himself later operated that club.[88] He and
Tippit were close to another Dallas policeman named Harry
Olsen. Olsen, in turn, was near Tippit at 1:00 p.m., a few
minutes before his shooting, allegedly guarding an estate in
Oak Cliff for its absent owners.[89] Olsen had access to the
house phone, since this is how he learned of the assassination. That evening, Ruby spent an hour talking to Olsen about
the assassination.[90]

From all these circumstances, a clear question arises: Did
Tippit know whom he was tracking in advance? The Warren
Report denies the possibility. Yet, in its own volumes of
testimony, there is jarring evidence that this may have been
the case. A waitress at Dobbs House, a Dallas restaurant,
testified that two days before the assassination she saw:[91]

> ...the person now recognized as Oswald ... in the res-
> taurant at about 10:00 a.m., Wednesday, November 20th,
> at which time he was "nasty" and used curse words in
> connection with his order. She went on to relate that
> Officer J.D. Tippit was in the restaurant, as was his habit
> at about that time each morning, and "shot a glance at
> Oswald."

Another waitress at Dobbs House recalled seeing Oswald
there on that occasion and numerous others.[92] Is it too much
to suggest that these associations and sightings mean something? Why would a ten-year veteran policeman pull over a
suspected armed killer without getting out of his car, drawing
his gun, or even calling for a backup car *unless* he knew the
"suspect" in advance?

If Tippit was expecting an easy arrest, he must have been
shocked. If Ruby had expected Tippit to take care of Oswald,

he was also surprised. If the Oswald double was expecting no policeman to accost him, he must have been totally disconcerted. But whatever really happened, this turnabout led to two events: First, the real Oswald was captured, ostensibly for the Tippit murder, and this led to his being charged with the assassination. Second, with Oswald poised to stand trial, it was now necessary for Ruby to eliminate him.

Allegedly, Oswald then went from the scene of the Tippit murder to the Texas Theatre, a movie house about eight blocks away. He was seen by a clerk at a nearby shoe store, Johnny Brewer, sneaking into the theater. Brewer alerted the cashier, Julia Postal, who called the police. After a brief altercation, Oswald was arrested, at about 1:50 p.m., allegedly for the Tippit murder.

It was a busy week for Jack Ruby, but his life up until then had prepared him for it. Jacob Rubenstein had ties to the mob as far back as 1939 in Chicago. When organized crime moved

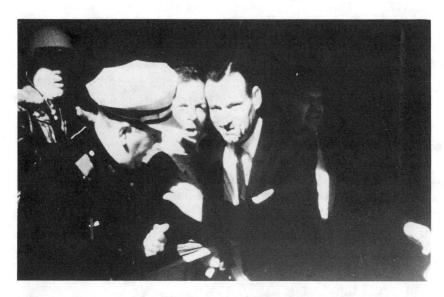

Oswald being arrested at the Texas Theatre, one hour and 20 minutes after the assassination. This and other photos of the scene were taken by passerby S.L. Reed.

into Dallas in the late forties, Ruby moved in with it.[93] As noted earlier, through his gunrunning activities Ruby also had ties with the anti-Castro exiles and with contract CIA agents like Thomas Davis. As Ruby authority Seth Kantor has shown, he consciously and assiduously plied the Dallas police force with liquor and women.[94] He was also very in debt to organized crime figures and in no position to face the consequences of disobeying any orders from above. For all these reasons, he was indispensable to the New Orleans plotters.

Ruby used most of his connections in the days leading up to his murder of Oswald. As was discovered later, the night before the assassination Ruby had a very late dinner at the Cabana Motel.[95] Close to midnight he met two people at the Bon Vivant Room there. One was Lawrence V. Meyers, supposedly a Chicago businessman. Meyers was accompanied by a woman named Jean Aase, also of Chicago. Ms. Aase was also known as Jean West (in the Warren Commission volumes, she has a third name, Miss A. Asie). On September 24, 1963, David Ferrie called Jean West's phone number. This was the day before Lee Oswald left New Orleans for Dallas, allegedly via Mexico.[96] And it should be noted that in the days preceding the assassination, Ruby placed several calls to both Chicago and New Orleans.[97]

Ruby's stay at the Cabana is even more intriguing because he did not leave at midnight when the Jean West rendezvous ended. Also at the Cabana, was Eugene Brading, also known as James Braden.[98] Brading was a con man with mob connections in Dallas who had been run out of town in 1952. Two years later he was jailed for embezzlement in California. After he got out of jail, he developed his mob connections and also made some oil investments. In September Brading made a trip to Houston using his pseudonym. On November 21, he made a second Texas trip—this time to Dallas—with Morgan Brown. Brown was supposedly another successful oil man; however he later went to jail for selling phony oil stocks. Both men stayed at the Cabana and had reservations until the 24th.

On November 22, Brading was at Dealey Plaza.[99] He was arrested in the Dal-Tex Building, across the street from the depository and gave his name as Jim Braden, which was also on his driver's license. He told the police he had been walking down Elm Street unaware of the motorcade or the assassination. In the midst of the confusion that followed, he ran into the Dal-Tex Building to use the phone. But, he said, he did not. The elevator operator turned him over to the police because he was a stranger. Unaware of his alias, the police believed his story, which contained the lie that he was unfamiliar with and new to Dallas. When the FBI interviewed him later in California, they also thought his name was Jim Bra-

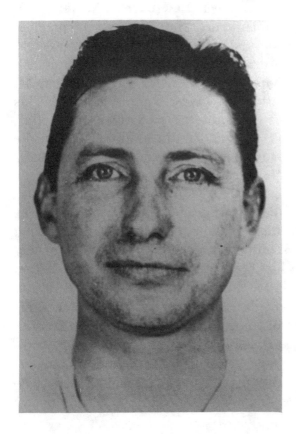

Eugene Brading, alias Jim Braden.

den, and apparently failed to uncover his shady past or real name.

Morgan Brown, Braden's companion, checked out of the Cabana Motel at 2:00 p.m., less than thirty minutes after Kennedy was pronounced dead. There is no explanation of why he left or where he went. But we do know that Brown and Brading were at the Cabana the previous night. And we know that Ruby told an employee that he was there at 2:30 a.m. on the 22nd.

At the time of the assassination, Ruby was reportedly at the offices of the *Dallas Morning News*.[100] The man who claimed he shot Oswald out of sympathy for Jack Kennedy's family was not attending his triumphal procession through Dallas. Yet once the news of the shooting was broadcast, Ruby rushed to Parkland Hospital, where he was seen by two witnesses. Why would a man who did not care for JFK in life—who actually made derisive comments about him—rush to the scene of his death?[101]

That question may never be answered definitely, though it is logical to conclude that he was making sure that the victim of the plot was dead. And there can be no doubt that Ruby began to stalk Oswald that Friday evening. He was at the police station that night to deliver sandwiches. While there he told someone his function was transcriber for a Jewish newspaper. Fantastically, he corrected Dallas Police Chief Henry Wade about the name of Oswald's Cuban organization in New Orleans.[102]

The busy Jack Ruby did not get to bed until 6:00 a.m. the next morning.[103] He was back at police headquarters on Saturday when he found out about Oswald's tentative transfer that afternoon. When this was postponed until Sunday, Ruby left.[104] On Sunday morning, he was across the street from the police station, waiting for the transfer. There is strong evidence he was tipped off to its time by two police friends.[105] Somehow, Ruby got into the basement, waited for the escort of the prisoner, and pumped one fatal bullet into

Oswald.[106] A detective who observed Ruby immediately after
the shooting said he appeared sweaty, hyper, nervous. He
asked for a cigarette after being stripped down. The detective, Don Ray Archer, later told a British TV reporter that,
after he told Ruby Oswald was dead,[107]

> ... he became calm, he quit sweating, his heart slowed
> down. I asked him if he wanted a cigarette and he
> advised me he didn't smoke. I was astonished at the
> complete difference of behavior....

Dave Ferrie also had a hectic November 22. That evening,
during a fierce thunderstorm, Ferrie and two friends drove
all night—more than 400 miles—to Houston from New Orleans.[108] Ferrie later said that he and his friends had wanted
to relax and go ice skating. But at the rink, he did not go
skating. He took up a post next to a pay phone and waited
there for two hours. When it rang, he answered. After talking,
he left. The trio then went to Galveston, a city to which Jack
Ruby placed a call that day. Ferrie's later excuse to Jim
Garrison for being in Texas was to go goose hunting. Evidently, knowing that downtown Houston was not a good
hunting spot, they did not bring guns. On their way back to
New Orleans, the group stopped at a gas station to watch the
news of Oswald's murder by Ruby.[109]

There was another reason for Ferrie's obsession with Dallas on the 22nd. He seemed intensely worried that Oswald
had borrowed his library card and that his possession of it
would reveal their association and unravel the conspiracy.
Right after the assassination, Ferrie first visited one of Oswald's former neighbors, and then his landlady, to inquire
about the card. Ferrie's lawyer also seemed to worry about
this. And, strangely, when the Secret Service interviewed
Ferrie after the assassination, an agent asked him if he had
lent his card to Oswald.[110] Ferrie even went to former CAP
members' homes to see if any remembered that he and Os-

wald had been in the same unit and to collect any photos of the pair in uniform.[111]

The most eerie aspect of Ferrie's involvement with the assassins in Dallas was one of his myriad odd hobbies: Ferrie seems to have developed an interest in ballistics. A book on firearms was found in his apartment. In the section dealing with the distance and direction a shell travels after ejection, Ferrie had scribbled the figures "50° and eleven feet."[112] This may explain why no bullet shells were found in Dealey Plaza except, of course, those so conspicuously on display in the TSBD in a neat row beneath the sixth-floor window.

The last damage control measure from New Orleans may have been Clay Shaw's Sunday call to Dean Andrews. By calling a friend who also knew Oswald, Shaw appeared to throw a lifeline to the self-proclaimed patsy. But in actuality Shaw was possibly ensuring, if it came down to that, that an undistinguished attorney would represent the hated assassin and the competency of the representation would be undermined from inside by the attorney's secret acquaintance with at least one of the undisclosed conspirators, or an accessory. It was a wise measure in case Ruby failed.[113]

All in all, it was an impressive operation, featuring intricate planning, precision, lethal means, and camouflage of those at the operational level, and preserving plausible deniability at higher levels. In its simple effectiveness, it was reminiscent of the CIA successes of the Eisenhower era. With the aid of the Warren Commission, its triumph and secrecy would be complete. At least for a while.

7

The Official Story

The origins of the Warren Commission were political, not investigatory.[1] After Kennedy was dead and buried, one panel was set up and another was on its way. The State of Texas, the site of the crime, was going to start a lawful court of inquiry, headed by Attorney General Waggoner Carr. Carr announced this on Monday, November 25, after a phone conversation with President Johnson's aide, Walter Jenkins.[2] Jenkins put him in touch with Abe Fortas, Johnson's private counsel. Johnson had designated Fortas to coordinate the efforts of the FBI and the Justice Department, and the Texas inquiry headed by Carr. He added that he would have the Assistant Attorney General, Herbert Miller, call that night to begin the formal process of coordination.[3]

J. Edgar Hoover was also on the phone to Dallas that weekend. Dallas District Attorney Henry Wade agreed to turn over state's evidence to the FBI at Hoover's request. Wade said, "they agreed to let us have it back any time we wanted it."[4] Neither Carr nor Wade seemed to realize the momentous significance of giving up local jurisdiction over a murder case. With Oswald's death, the forces pulling the investigation toward Washington became irresistible.

But by the next day, there was a strong movement under way in Congress to launch its *own* formal investigation. Johnson faced problems from the Republican opposition. Specifically, Senate Minority Leader Everett Dirksen (Rep.-Ill.) pushed for a Judiciary Committee probe, while Congressman Charles Goodell (Rep.-N.Y.) proposed a joint

House-Senate committee. As his party's likely presidential candidate the next year, Johnson foresaw a long, drawn-out political sideshow lasting well into 1964. This could jeopardize his chances: after all, if the inquiry was not complete by November of 1964, the legitimacy of his presidency could be called into question by rumors and political rivals. In the worst case scenario, if the uncovering of a conspiracy were to reveal that Kennedy had been eliminated because the conspirators favored Johnson, it would create explosive October-November headlines and make Johnson the issue.

Consequently, Johnson decided to preempt both investigations with the appointment of his own special committee. To deflect the objection that he was taking the matter out of congressional hands, he cleverly appointed two members from each chamber to his new commission.

The investigatory panel was created on November 29, 1963, and it was called the Warren Commission. It took its

The Warren Commission's formal portrait, left to right: Rep. Gerald Ford (Rep.-Mich.), Rep. Hale Boggs (Dem.-La.), Sen. Richard Russell (Dem.-Ga.), Chief Justice Earl Warren, Sen. John Sherman Cooper (Rep.-Ky.), John J. McCloy, Allen Dulles, and chief counsel J. Lee Rankin.

name from Earl Warren, Chief Justice of the United States, who became its chairman.[5]

Warren seemed very reluctant to take the position, but Johnson convinced him by using his fabled powers of persuasion mixed with some standard Cold War demagoguery about national security. He began with, "Wild rumors have been circulating" that an emergency situation confronted the country. He then raised the possibility of 40 million people dying in a nuclear holocaust.[6] Warren tried to resist, but Johnson persisted, and the Chief Justice eventually succumbed. Johnson had his man, a seal of integrity for the inquiry. Reportedly, Warren left the meeting in tears.

Warren could hardly have performed better for LBJ. At the first formal meeting of the Warren Commission staff, he told the newly hired lawyers that their investigation might include national security problems and they should not discuss their work outside the Commission.[7] A month later, when asked by a reporter if the Commission's inquiry would be made public, he replied:[8]

> Yes, there will come a time. But it might not be in your lifetime. I am not referring to anything especially, but there may be some things that would involve security.

The other choices were less distinguished. Senator Richard B. Russell, a Georgia Democrat and a powerful figure in the upper house, chaired the Senate Armed Services Committee and its subcommittee on intelligence. John Sherman Cooper was the senior senator from Kentucky and a Republican; his image was that of an elder statesman. His previous assignments had been as ambassador to India and as U.S. adviser to the United Nations and NATO, the Cold War military command. Representative Hale Boggs of Louisiana was the Democratic Whip.

Representative Gerald R. Ford was a congressman from Michigan and chairman of the House Republican Conference. Why Johnson picked him remains something of a mystery, since he does not seem to have had much respect for Ford's intelligence. "Ford is kind of dense. He must have played too much football without a helmet," he once said. He added that Ford had difficulty walking and chewing gum at the same time.[9] But Johnson must have known that Ford had a reputation as the CIA's best friend in Congress, since that fact was common knowledge in Washington.[10] Ford's voting record also reveals he was a staunch ally of the Pentagon.[11]

Once he was on the Commission, Ford performed as his record would predict. He seems to have been an FBI informant. In a December 12, 1963, internal memo from Hoover aide Cartha De Loach to the Director, De Loach noted: "Ford indicated he would keep me thoroughly advised as to the activities of the Commission. He stated this would have to be done on a confidential basis, however, he thought it had to be done."[12]

Ford went to great lengths in his role as an informant to Hoover. He pointed out to the Director which members of the Commission needed convincing on certain points of the Report. He also revealed the names of prospective assistant counsel so they could be vetted in advance.[13] Ford then placed John Stiles on his own personal staff. Why he needed him seemed puzzling at the time, since the Commission had many assistant counsel. Later the matter was cleared up when Stiles became the ghost writer for Ford's book about the Warren Commission, *Portrait of the Assassin.*[14]

The final two members came ostensibly from the private sector. They were both corporate lawyers and bankers with strong government experience. They were to be the two most questionable, most important, most insidiously powerful appointees. Allen W. Dulles had been head of the CIA for nine years under both Eisenhower and Kennedy. Dulles had overseen the incorporation of Gehlen's Nazi spy network into the OSS. He had also been the DCI who had deceived JFK about certain aspects of the Bay of Pigs operation before Kennedy removed him. To say the least, Johnson's choice of Dulles was dubious. The choice of John J. McCloy parallels that of Dulles at the same time that it completed a then-invisible alliance.[15]

It is generally said of McCloy that he was a high-powered lawyer who served as Assistant Secretary of War and as U.S. High Commissioner in Germany at the end of World War II. This is accurate as far as it goes, but it does not go far enough. McCloy's career lies in the heart of the Wall Street-Washington power and money connection. He served as chairman of Chase Manhattan Bank. He was a director of such companies as Westinghouse, AT&T, Allied Chemical, and United Fruit. In the 1960s he served as chief counsel to some of the largest oil companies in America including Standard Oil, Mobil, Texaco, and Gulf.

Most of these corporate achievements came toward the end of his career. Prior to this, McCloy had concentrated on government service. As a young lawyer, he had litigated the Black Tom Island case, involving an alleged act of German sabotage against the United States in New York Harbor during World War I. McCloy conducted the latter part of the dragged-out settlement agreement and ended up talking to Rudolph Hess and other Nazi officials in 1936 (he actually watched the 1936 Berlin Olympics from Hitler's box seat).

McCloy was involved in creating an intelligence office to break Japanese codes. He persuaded Roosevelt to accept an alliance with Jean Darlan of Vichy France, a notorious Nazi collaborator. He helped defeat Churchill's plan to summarily execute Nazi leaders after they were captured. The infamous Japanese-American internment program, in which more than 100,000 citizens were rounded up and placed in prison camps, was supervised by McCloy (and supported by then California Attorney General Earl Warren). McCloy objected to making raids against the Nazi death camps proposed in 1944. He also opposed bombing the railroad tracks used to transport victims into the camps. He felt it "might provoke even more vindictive acts by the Germans." As many have replied, what could be worse than the Holocaust?

It was as High Commissioner in occupied Germany that McCloy made some of his most controversial decisions. There he had almost free rein to make his own rulings, for, as he himself stated, "Washington left me alone, and I was like a Roman proconsul." At the time, many were advocating a complete de-Nazification of Germany. At first, McCloy seemed to concur with this view. But when he realized what a bulwark Germany would be in the struggle against the Soviets, he abandoned this line. He allowed former Nazis who "recanted" to work in the new government. He then allowed the verdicts at the Nuremburg trials to be reviewed. As a result, 74 jail terms were reduced and 24 death sentences were commuted. (He once told documentary filmmaker Marcel Ophuls, "Let's not philosophize about Nuremberg.")

The act that brought the most protest about McCloy's tenure was the freeing of Alfred Krupp, heir to the fortune of the celebrated German arms-manufacturing family. Krupp was imprisoned because he knowingly employed slave labor—Jews and other camp inmates—in his factories during the war. McCloy not only released Krupp, but also forced restitution of the German's confiscated estate, saying the confiscation set a dangerous and illegal precedent. But when Krupp was asked why he thought McCloy had released him and returned his property, he replied, "Now that they have Korea on their hands, the Americans are more friendly."

Like Dulles, McCloy's ethos was forged in the crucible of the defeat of Nazism and the rebirth of the Red Menace. In fact, McCloy often spoke of a world that thirsted for American guidance, a world that looked to America "as the stabilizing influence which can give them the hope of a return to decent living." American prestige was "terrifyingly high ... terrifying when you see how much the rest of the world depends on us for leadership."

This attitude was both condescending and chauvinistic, and it jibed with McCloy's views of the Warren Commission, the purpose of which, he said, was to "show the world that the U.S. was not a banana republic where a government could be changed by conspiracy." McCloy once said that he entered the investigation thinking "there must have been a conspiracy." He later had a quick change of heart. "I never saw a case that I thought was more completely proven."[16] At times, McCloy's militant anticommunism seemed reminiscent of David Ferrie. When Truman decided to go forward with the hydrogen bomb, therefore escalating the Cold War one more notch, McCloy said, "If there were an oxygen bomb bigger than the H-bomb, I would build it."

It is hard not to conclude that the Commission was ideologically unbalanced. Dulles and McCloy were ideological soulmates. Both were obsessed with American dominance in the world after World War II. Both had little compunction about going easy on Nazi war criminals. Both were preoccupied with the defeat of Soviet Communism by American capitalism. The pair would provide a focus strongly resistant to the idea of an internal conspiracy and predisposed to paint Oswald as a leftist lunatic at the mercy of twisted Marxist motivations. Joined by the intimidated Warren and their sympathetic and carefully chosen protégé Ford, Dulles and McCloy had almost free rein over the inner workings of the Commission. In fact, at the very first meeting, Dulles pushed copies of a book that (falsely) portrayed American political assassinations as the work of crazed lone gunmen.[17] When the possibility of Cuban exile involvement in the assassination surfaced, Dulles never revealed the CIA-Mafia plots that had originated under his watch at the Agency.[18]

In following the inner workings of the Warren Commission, one can see the influence of the Dulles-McCloy axis. Very early, Dulles argued against the need for independent investigators.[19] When key questions about the motorcade route arose, McCloy twice asked to go off the record momentarily.[20] When Officer Seymour Weitzman was questioned about the rifle he found at the depository, which he reported as a Mauser, McCloy said he had filed no such report and again the discussion went off the record.[21] When Commission counsel Wesley J. Liebeler began to write the section of the Report concerning Oswald's motivation for the shooting, McCloy pressed the "killer-instinct" angle on him in spite of Oswald's reported meek and mild nature.[22] Through their pointman Arlen Specter, it was Dulles and McCloy who foisted the "single-bullet" hypothesis on a reluctant Commission.[23] It was Dulles and McCloy, the latter in particular, who demanded that a Report get out quickly to quell "ugly rumors" in Europe, which would "spread like wildfire" if there were a delay.[24]

With these two Commissioners leading the way, it was fitting that the final draft was produced by a man on Temporary Duty Transfer from the Army Historical Division, insuring that the Report would be strongly national-security oriented. The Army Historical Division was one of the drop points for the Gehlen network after World War II and the historian, Otto Winnaker, was one of Hitler's 26 official historians.[25]

Since the Commissioners had other pressing duties, much of the actual day-to-day work of the committee was handled by counsel and staff members.[26] Chief counsel was J. Lee Rankin, a friend of Warren's for more than ten years. But Rankin had not been Warren's first choice as chief counsel. He had wanted to choose a man he had known three times longer than Rankin and whose record as a criminal investigator he much admired. That was Warren Olney, who had been his deputy when he was DA of Alameda County, California. When Olney's name was advanced by the Chief Justice, some Commissioners said he lacked nationwide name recognition, whereas Rankin had been U.S. Solicitor General.[27] But the real reason goes deeper, in a way that illustrates both the innate bias of the commissioners and Dulles's protective influence. Olney, as an assistant U.S. Attorney General, had once been asked by the CIA to hold back on prosecuting a New York company that was an Agency front. The company had been caught smuggling arms into pre-revolutionary Cuba. Olney, not part of the good ol' boy network, refused the overture and pursued the charges. The Agency passed the word on to Dulles, and he objected quite strongly to having Olney as chief counsel. Dulles was supported by Boggs and Ford. Boggs, who would later acknowledge grave doubts on the Report, went as far as threatening to resign if Warren insisted on Olney. Warren backed down and Olney was dropped.[28]

Rankin then went on to select assistant counsel and staff members, twenty-six people in all. Most of the choices were bright, young lawyers who would go on to better, even significant things. Some examples are William T. Coleman, Jr., the sole black, who would become Gerald Ford's Secretary of Transportation and board member of several major firms; Charles N. Shaffer, Jr., who would defend Nixon's White House counsel, John Dean, in the Watergate hearings; Albert E. Jenner, Jr., who later served as minority counsel in the Nixon impeachment proceedings; and Arlen Specter, who became counsel to Nixon and then Senator from Pennsylvania.[29]

Rankin and four others had inordinate influence over the path of the investigation and the final Report: David W. Belin, Wesley J. Liebeler, Norman Redlich, and Arlen Specter. Belin, a natural infighter and blind believer in Oswald's guilt, oversaw the Oswald, Tippit, and Ruby areas of the Report.[30] Liebeler came as close to anyone to being the conscience of the Commission. He was responsible for most of the biographical section on Oswald. Toward the end, he wrote a twenty-six-page devil's-advocate critique of the Commission Report, which is the most intelligent and honest document the Commission turned out. Redlich, because of

Wesley J. Liebeler at a January 1992 press conference he called to denounce Oliver Stone.

his endless energy and command of most substantive issues, had much input into the overall design and shape of the report. Specter[31] had special access to the reclusive Rankin and was the inventor of the Commission's most controversial theory, the "single-bullet hypothesis."

From the beginning, the Commission and its staff did not work well together. Politics and the CIA had forced Warren to jettison Olney. Then, some ultra-conservative members of Congress tried to get Rankin to sack Redlich because they felt that communists were trying to blame anticommunists and the right wing for the assassination and Redlich would lend them a sympathetic ear. The charge was ludicrous, but that did not prevent Ford from airing it at a closed-door session. Redlich actually offered to resign, but finally Rankin decided this would compromise the Commission's appearance of independence and asked him to stay. Afterwards, Redlich was a less frisky investigator.[32]

Ford also figured in a dispute with J. Edgar Hoover. Rankin was disturbed by leaks to the media and asked Hoover if his agents had been talking to the press. Hoover replied that the leaks came from the Commission, specifically Congressman Ford.[33] Ford had given a story to *Life* magazine about the discovery of Oswald's "secret diary." Later he would write an article for *Life* the week after the report was released. From this, we can deduce that, for at least one member, leaks to the press, incriminating a dead man before the verdict was in, were part of Washington politics.

Which is not really surprising. The Dallas police, though now off-stage, had no qualms about broadcasting their opinions about the guilt of the prisoner who had been murdered in their custody. In fact, on November 24, the day of Oswald's death, Captain Will Fritz, of Dallas Homicide, told the *New York Times*, "We're convinced beyond any doubt that he [Oswald] killed the President ... the case is clinched."[34]

The police made this claim before any of the medical evidence was submitted for analysis, before the weapon was tested for fingerprints (none was found), before the ballistics evidence about the Tippit murder was in, and while Oswald was denying his guilt and virtually begging for an attorney to "step forward" (he never got one). The media swallowed the barrage. The next day's stories about Oswald's death referred to him not as "the accused assassin," but simply as "the assassin." The *New York Times* was the most flagrant; its November 25 headline read, "President's Assassin Shot to Death in Jail Corridor by a Dallas Citizen."[35] This took some of the heat off the superficiality of the Dallas investigation and the shoddy security for Oswald.

With Oswald's death, and because of the forcible and illegal removal of the President's body from Texas,[36] the FBI took over the investigation.[37] The day of Oswald's murder, though, Hoover's organization announced that the case was still open and that their investigation was pressing onward. This pressing investigation lasted just two-and-a-half more weeks. In the interim, Hoover leaked stories to the *Washington Post* and *Time* magazine informing them that the case against Oswald was solid and that the upcoming report "will indicate that Oswald, acting in his own lunatic loneliness, was indeed the President's assassin."[38]

To no one's surprise, the secret FBI report—made public in 1965—concluded that Oswald was the sole killer of Kennedy.[39] How it could do this with the medical evidence it had is puzzling. The FBI report on the autopsy revealed a back wound "less than a finger length"[40] in penetration. The rifle tests later performed showed that this would be impossible with Oswald's Mannlicher-Carcano at his presumed distance. The bullet had to penetrate much deeper. Also, the FBI created a problem that the Commission would never be able to solve. Their report stated that Governor Connally was hit by a bullet other than the one that hit Kennedy. As we shall see, if the Commission had accepted the FBI's statement, it would have had to admit that there were at least two assassins. But the Warren Commission was already committed to convicting Oswald as the sole killer.

The FBI report of December 9, 1963, and its supplement of January 13, 1964, had a strong influence on the Warren Report. First, both reports—as did the Dallas police—placed the guilt for both Kennedy's and Tippit's deaths on Oswald. In other words, what the police concluded in two days, what the FBI concluded in two weeks, the Warren Commission formally agreed to after ten months. The Warren Report does more of the same in another respect. The first FBI report spent twenty pages on the actual evidence of the crime and fifty-five pages on background information and extraneous matters such as Oswald's elementary school days. In fact the supplemental report is even more unbalanced: it has nine pages of analysis of the shootings and fifty-nine pages of background material.[41]

Unfortunately, the Commission seems to have taken the FBI reports seriously, because its basic conclusions were the same and the methodology was similar. It focused on the background and circumstances of Oswald's life rather than on evidentiary analysis, and it highlighted the background witnesses who would place him in the worst possible light. The reliance on the FBI report is a symptom of the worst shortcoming of the Commission's investigation: its dependence for evidence and analysis on government investigative bodies, bodies like the FBI, CIA, and Secret Service.

The Commission did not hire its own investigators. This was a grievous error, for once the FBI had submitted the very first reports, there was no way the stubborn, vain, unchallengeable Hoover would back down from their initial conclusion. Also, the Bureau and the Secret Service[42] were under fire for their security failures during the Dallas trip—Hoover eventually disciplined seventeen officers for negligence; and the Warren Report, shutting the barn door after the horses were stolen, dedicated a section to recommendations for Secret Service reforms.[43] Thus, it was in the interest of both agencies to minimize damage, get the inquiry over quickly, and blame an unbalanced fringe character whose actions would understandably be too difficult to anticipate or predict. The alternative, to have been victimized by a well-planned and coordinated conspiracy, would make both bodies look bad, especially if the conspirators carried forged Secret Service credentials. As for the CIA, if the assassination had begun as an outgrowth of the Agency-sponsored, anti-Castro effort and was organized by higher-ups and/or contract employees, the Agency might be forever dismantled beyond recognition. So the pattern of half-hearted, incomplete investigation and response began.

Very early, the Commission indicated that it would not be an open-minded, curious, aggressive panel of inquiry. At a minimum, the Commissioners ought not have made up their minds or begun drafting their report until all, or at least a majority, of the important witnesses had testified. But on January 11, 1964, just after the Commission had assembled a staff and before it had heard a single witness, Chief Counsel Rankin had assembled a loaded outline organized by these tell-tale headings: "Lee Harvey Oswald as the Assassin of President Kennedy," and "Lee Harvey Oswald: Background and Possible Motives." Subheads further reveal the deeply ingrained bias against Oswald. For instance, after touching on Oswald's movements following the assassination, these topics are included: "Murder of Tippit" and "Evidence Demonstrating Oswald's guilt."[44] In this regard, the Commission even surpassed the FBI, since the Bureau neither drew a solid conclusion on Tippit's murder nor assembled a wealth of evidence about it.

This early outline of the report also shows how "seriously" the Commission dealt with the possibility of a conspiracy. The outline heading lettered "H" is "Evidence Implicating Others in the Assassination or Suggesting Accomplices." The first subhead beneath this reads "Evidence of shots other than from the Depository?"[45] That question mark is revealing, as we shall soon see. As stated earlier, more witnesses—a total of 52—testified that shots came from the knoll than from the book depository. Second, the Zapruder film depicts clearly and compellingly that the last, fatal shot came from in front of the car.[46]

But the last subhead may well explain the question mark. It reads: "Refutation of Allegations."[47] The notion of a conspiracy was not just being minimized early, it was being *refuted* early. One can fairly say that it was dropped before it was considered.

One of the Commission's most egregious errors was its handling of the autopsy. To be more accurate, the Commission could not botch what was already a mess, but what it did with those results is still reprehensible. After the last shot, Kennedy and Connally were whisked away to Parkland Hospital. There, a tracheotomy was performed over the President's throat wound (this is a common, simple surgical procedure to assist the breathing process). The twelve doctors who worked on Kennedy at Parkland did not flip the body over to discover the back wound. When the President died, the body was soon forcibly removed, perhaps at gunpoint. The White House staff and Mrs. Kennedy left Parkland and returned to Washington before the local coroner's autopsy could be performed, a clear violation of Texas law. Given the choice of Bethesda Naval Hospital or Walter Reed Army Hospital in Washington, Mrs. Kennedy then opted for Bethesda for the autopsy.[48]

That evening, between 8:00 and 11:00 p.m., one of the most important autopsies in American history was performed under complete military control and deplorable circumstances. More than two dozen people were in the room, including FBI and Secret Service agents, top military brass, and White House advisers, with Jackie and Robert Kennedy outside.[49] Perhaps the reason the three autopsy doctors "tolerated" this much congestion at a sensitive autopsy was because none of them had any extensive experience in gunshot autopsies. A better reason was that they had no say: the autopsy was held under control of their military superiors (see Appendix A). Of the trio, Navy Commanders James Humes and J. Thornton Boswell seem to have had no experience at all in the field, being more involved in administration. Army Colonel Pierre Finck did have experience, but he was called in late, perhaps for that reason. Only Finck belonged to the American Academy of Forensic Sciences. And, on top of all this, while civilian Parkland had wide experience in these kinds of cases and was equipped for them, the reverse was true of the Bethesda military facilities.

Supposedly, 45 photographs and 20 x-rays were taken of the body.[50] The number is conditional, because each time some photos were released (they were originally sealed by the Kennedy family), the total given changes. Important photos and x-rays have apparently disappeared. In fact, these seemingly critical exhibits were not even subpoenaed by the Warren Commission, which accepted artist's drawings in their place. Moreover, the drawings were not rendered from the original pictures, but from the doctors' memories of the wounds!

To add to the mystery, sometime since the autopsy, the President's brain—perhaps the key exhibit in the crime of the century—has been lost or stolen, and thus cannot be re-examined. This is crucial because the brain was never sectioned so the bullet paths through it could be definitively tracked for their direction. The bullet path through the back also was never tracked.

A further dispute between the two hospitals over the nature of the throat wound also persists. At Parkland, the doctors reported it as an entrance wound, which would mean it was fired from the front, necessitating two assassins. The doctors at Bethesda, not knowing about the tracheotomy, thought the wound at the front of the neck was an exit wound, since these are always wider than entrance wounds, indicating a shot from behind. Also, since no bullet was found in the body,[51] they concluded that the neck wound was a logical place for its exit.

The autopsy defies logic and common sense. The only running commentary on the autopsy, the Sibert-O'Neill FBI report, says that when the doctors probed the back wound, not only was no bullet found, but the path extended only a few inches inward and its end could be felt. Where was the bullet? Second, how could a rifle shot from the sixth floor of the depository enter the President's upper back and then exit out the base of his throat? How could it be an exit wound? The trajectory would be wrong. The only way this would make sense is if the bullet had hit some thick bone and been seriously deflected upward. But, as the report says, this is not the case.

JFK's head wound is equally confusing. At Parkland, it was reported that an exit wound in the rear of the head revealed much of the rear of the skull to be blasted away. This too would indicate a shot from the front. Again, this was reversed at Bethesda. Thus, the wound became a rear shot that exited the front of the head. How an entrance wound from the rear could shatter the back of the skull is unexplained.

But this only begins the mysteries of the medical-ballistics evidence. Commander Humes found no bullet in the body, even though he found a hole in the back, only two to four inches deep. Since he had heard that heart massage was done, he assumed that the bullet in the back had worked itself loose during this process, but he remained puzzled until he heard that a bullet—the eventual magic bullet—was found on one of the stretchers in Dallas.

The Commission had another piece of evidence that precluded Humes's simplistic conclusion: the Zapruder film. By synchronizing the film speed with the capability of Oswald's Mannlicher-Carcano rifle, it was concluded that the time span for Oswald's alleged series of three shots could be no more than 5.6 seconds. This was the reasoning: First, it took at least 2.3 seconds to operate the bolt on the Carcano. Since a bullet was already in the chamber for the first shot, the Commission allowed a split second for the assassin to line up Kennedy in the cross hairs of his scope and pull the trigger. Secondly, the 5.6 seconds approximate the time from when Kennedy was first hit to the time the last shot hurls him backwards. Because James Tague, a bystander under the triple underpass, was struck by a flying concrete chip, the Commission decided that one of the shots missed altogether. This was probably, but not certainly, the second one.[52] If this were true and one shot alone, the last one, smashed the President's skull, then another shot, the first one, must have hit him in the upper back and exited his throat.

But if this was what happened, then which of these bullets hit Connally in the back, exited his chest, smashed his wrist, and then lodged in his thigh? Here the Commission faced a huge dilemma. Only three shells were found on the sixth floor of the depository. There was only enough time, according to the tests, to fire the Carcano once every 2.3 seconds. Connally, however, appears in the Zapruder film to be hit about

1.2 to 1.5 seconds after Kennedy. Thus the logical inference would be that Connally was hit by a separate shot. But as Commission investigator Norman Redlich put it, to say that he was hit separately is to say there were two assassins, because no one could fire that rifle that quickly.[53]

Here is what Governor Connally said on the subject:[54]

They talk about the "one-bullet" or "two-bullet" theory, but as far as I'm concerned, there is no theory. There is my absolute knowledge, and Nellie's too, that one bullet caused the President's first wound, and an entirely separate shot struck me. No one will ever convince me otherwise. It's a certainty. I'll never change my mind.

He should know. Like many Texans, he is an experienced rifleman. He was one of the few people in Dealey Plaza who recognized the first crack as a rifle shot. Connally went on

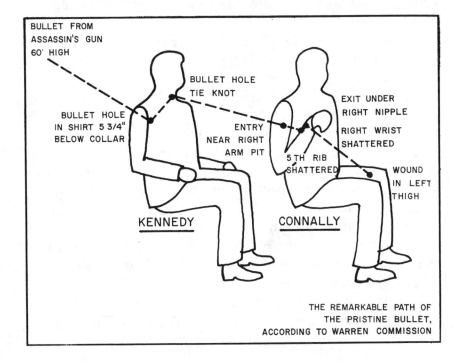

BULLET FROM
ASSASSIN'S GUN
60' HIGH

BULLET HOLE
TIE KNOT

BULLET HOLE
IN SHIRT 5 3/4"
BELOW COLLAR

ENTRY
NEAR RIGHT
ARM PIT

EXIT UNDER
RIGHT NIPPLE

RIGHT WRIST
SHATTERED

5TH RIB
SHATTERED

WOUND
IN LEFT
THIGH

KENNEDY

CONNALLY

THE REMARKABLE PATH OF
THE PRISTINE BULLET,
ACCORDING TO WARREN COMMISSION

to add that except for this point, he agreed with the rest of the Warren Report. But he did not realize what the Commission was all too aware of: if Connally was right on this matter, the entire 888-page document was wrong. So the commissioners had a choice: Either believe Connally, admit a second gunman—thus a conspiracy—and start over. Or disbelieve Connally and eventually lose credibility by being forced to adopt a highly suspect invention, Arlen Specter's "single-bullet" theory.[55]

Consider: A bullet is fired at a downward angle; it hits Kennedy's body; without striking a bone it reverses course upward and exits the throat. Then it changes trajectory in mid-air, while hanging suspended for a second, then goes downward to enter Connally's back, smashes a rib, exits, deflects right 90 degrees, smashes a wrist, deflects left 120 degrees, and lodges in his thigh. Thus, what researchers now call "the magic bullet" enters the lexicon. Consequently, the Commission was left defending an unheard-of bullet trajectory.

The story is not over. With the "discovery" of a bullet on a stretcher at Parkland Hospital, we now actually have the bullet that allegedly performed these acrobatic feats. This projectile, known as Commission Exhibit 399 (CE 399), has been one of the most controversial pieces of evidence ever produced in a case that contains almost nothing but controversy. This bullet was allegedly found on Connally's stretcher at the hospital after the assassination. The Commission—specifically the magic bullet mastermind, staff lawyer Arlen Specter—shamelessly badgered hospital engineer Darrell Tomlinson into saying he found it on Connally's stretcher. This was because, if the bullet had been found on Kennedy's stretcher, Connally's wounds would have had to come from other bullets and another gunman.[56]

So this was the "magic bullet." What did it look like after smashing two bones while penetrating two bodies, four limbs, and several layers of muscle and tissue? Like it had

A young Arlen Specter, District Attorney of Philadelphia, In 1967, when he was chosen to run for Mayor. According to the AP caption, Specter "Is credited with writing major part of the Warren Commission's final report."

just been purchased from a gun shop. Yes, except for a slight flattening at the base, there is no observable deformation of the bullet.

The Commission had a devil of a time proving that a bullet could do this much damage and remain unscathed. Every test conducted proved otherwise. The Commission fired bullets from an identical rifle through human corpses, animal corpses, gelatin blocks, and cotton piles. Even these tests could not have proved that what CE 399 allegedly did was possible, because the obstacles were not lined up consecutively, like Kennedy and Connally, and the path of the single bullet could not be replicated. This alone should have destroyed the single-bullet theory. Yet the Commission persisted, with the results one would have expected. In fact, no bullet fired through any obstacle—not even through cotton and gelatin— could emerge as intact as the pristine CE 399. This so embarrassed the Commission that it did not reproduce the worst exhibits in the photos included with the Report.[57]

Why did the Commission accept such a wild conclusion about CE 399? Because to reason logically that the bullet was fired from the Carcano,[58] but did not hit anything, would lead to the inescapable fact that someone had planted the bullet, thus suggesting a plot. And the Warren Commission was painfully aware that two witnesses placed Jack Ruby at the hospital within minutes of the President's arrival.[59]

The Warren Commission never analyzed the rest of the cartridge case evidence found near the sniper's lair on the sixth floor of the depository. It would have produced some interesting results.[60] One of the shells contained a dent so deep it could not house a bullet. Two of the shells had not been marked by the bolt of Oswald's rifle, which would indicate they had not been ejected from the Mannlicher-Carcano. Two of the shells were marked by the rifle's magazine follower. Yet the follower marks only the last cartridge in the clip, and there was a live bullet found in the rifle's chamber.

Also, the cartridge case with the dent had markings on its base from the firing pin strikes that could only be present if the cartridge were empty. The FBI tried to duplicate these markings. They could only do so when they fired an empty shell from Oswald's Mannlicher-Carcano. Thus there was strong evidence that both CE 399 and the other cartridges were previously fired and/or tampered with and then planted to incriminate Oswald. This was all ignored.

Once the Commission had decided on the rifle, a sequence of three shots, a trajectory from the TSBD, and a lone bullet, it had to prove that ex-Marine Oswald could have achieved the amazing feat of marksmanship displayed at Dealey Plaza. No fingerprints were found on the rifle, and no one found gloves on or near Oswald while he was alive.[61] If Oswald could not have done the shooting, this would further suggest that a real sharpshooter did it and then wiped the rifle clean. So the Commission reconstructed the motorcade in front of the depository and got three master marksmen to duplicate Oswald's feat.[62]

But the Commission must have known something, because these reenactments, like the testing of CE 399, were not accurate.[63] First, they were conducted from only thirty feet up, though Oswald was on the sixth floor. Second, the targets were stationary while Oswald's was moving. Third, the Commission's National Rifle Association (NRA) masters fired at full-bodied models, whereas Oswald could only aim at the head and shoulders of Kennedy. Finally, and crucially, the NRA riflemen took as long as they needed to aim the first shot. But Oswald had to get his first shot off immediately, because Kennedy'a car was just emerging from behind the branches of an oak tree and was moving away from him steadily. The first shot was the most difficult for Oswald, because the target had just popped into view, and he had a split-second to aim and fire to fit the time frame of 5.6 seconds. It was the easiest shot for the marksmen.

Given all these advantages, what were the results? Not one of them could do what Oswald allegedly did.[64] They either could not fire the weapon fast enough, or they could not get two out of three hits, or they could not hit the head or shoulders of the target.

Was Oswald really this good a shot? Did he really belong in a rodeo show shooting cigarettes out of an assistant's mouth? Not according to the record.[65] When he left the Marines, Oswald was classified at the lowest level attainable as a rifleman. According to the testimony of his Marine colleagues, Oswald's shooting was something of a joke. He often missed the entire target.

It is common knowledge among marksmen and hunters that the key to maintaining skill is, above all, practice. From the time he left the Marines until the assassination, a period of more than four years, the Commission produced, at most, twelve instances of "practice."[66] This includes rabbit hunting with shotguns and "dry runs," *i.e.*, just picking up a rifle and aiming it. It also appears that none of the practice sessions found by the Commission occurred in the two months before November 22, 1963, when one would expect someone contemplating shooting the President of the United States would try to brush up on his skill.

Yet in the face of this formidable pile of evidence, the Warren Commission concluded:[67]

Oswald's Marine training in marksmanship, his other rifle experience and his established familiarity with this particular weapon show that he possessed ample capability to commit the assassination.

The adjective "ample" is interesting. Does it mean Oswald could have hit the President at 400 feet with the car going 25 miles per hour? One of the Commission's investigators, Wesley Liebeler, noted in an internal memo:[68]

The fact is that most of the experts were much more proficient with a rifle than Oswald could ever be expected to be, and the record indicates that fact.... To put it bluntly, that sort of selection from the record could seriously affect the integrity and credibility of the entire Report.... [These] conclusions will never be accepted by critical persons anyway.

Can there be any doubt that the commissioners knew they were risking all but decided to gamble with history anyway?

The case made by the Commission regarding Officer Tippit was as flimsy as the one about Kennedy. First, some witnesses to the shooting or its aftermath, like Acquilla Clemons, were not called to testify.[69] They all thought the killer was not Oswald. But even some of the witnesses the Commission did call would not identify Oswald. In fact, the closest eyewitness, Domingo Benavides, could not identify the shooter and was not taken to the lineup.[70]

The other eyewitness to the shooting was Helen Markham, who has become legendary in the literature on this subject. First, while the authorities decreed that Tippit had died instantly, Ms. Markham insisted that she had talked to him for

25 minutes after the shooting.[71] Testifying to the Commission, this is how she described a lineup on the day of the shooting to Assistant Counsel Joseph Ball:[72]

Mr. Ball: Did you recognize anyone in the lineup?
Mrs. Markham: No, sir.
Mr. Ball: You did not? Did you see anybody—I have asked that question before—did you recognize anybody from their face?
Mrs. Markham: From their face, no.
Mr. Ball: Did you identify anybody in these four people?
Mrs. Markham: I didn't know nobody.
Mr. Ball: I know you didn't know anybody, but did anybody in the lineup look like anybody you had seen before?
Mrs. Markham: No. I had never seen none of them, none of these men.

Finally, Mr. Ball did what the Commission usually did when they could not elicit the testimony they needed. He asked Markham about the number two man in the lineup, who, of course, was Oswald. This was a leading question that

Helen Markham on her way to work in Dallas, September 29, 1964, two days after she appeared on a CBS-TV news program stating she had seen Lee Harvey Oswald shoot officer J.D. Tippit.

would have any defense attorney jumping out of his or her chair if it were to happen in a court of law.[73]

There is another telling indicator of Mrs. Markham's credibility. Three weeks before she testified, she told Mark Lane, an attorney contacted by Oswald's mother, that Tippit's killer was short and stocky with bushy, black hair. Clearly this does not describe Oswald, who was of medium height, quite slender, with thin, brown hair. When Lane confronted the Commission and Mrs. Markham with this testimony, Earl Warren and others doubted his word. Fortunately, Lane had taped the phone call. When confronted with the tape, Mrs. Markham simply admitted she had given a different description to Lane.[74] Still, her testimony is given probative value in the Warren Report.

The other Tippit witness the Commission used was William Scoggins. Scoggins was a cab driver eating lunch near the scene. Scoggins, who did not actually see the shooting, and who denied that Mrs. Markham was even there, identified a fleeing man, "and he never did look at me." Before he was taken to the lineup, he saw Oswald's picture on television and was shown photos of him and told who he was by policemen at the station.[75] He identified Oswald out of the same lineup that William Whaley, another cab driver, described as follows:[76]

> [Y]ou could have picked [Oswald] out without identifying him just by listening to him because he was bawling out the policemen, telling them it was not right to put him in line with these teenagers.... [T]hey were trying to railroad him and he wanted his lawyer.... Anybody who wasn't sure could have picked him out just for that.

Needless to say, Scoggins's identification would not have been allowed in court.

The ballistics evidence in the Tippit case was also dubious. First of all, shells were found at the scene, yet Oswald's gun was a revolver; the killer would have had to unload the cylinder and sprinkle the shells on the ground at the scene of the crime. Also, the FBI expert who testified before the Commission could not determine if the bullets found in Tippit's body could be matched to Oswald's revolver. Finally, of the four shells retrieved from the street, two were Winchesters and two were Remingtons. Of the four bullets found in Tippit's corpse, three were Winchesters and one was a Remington.[77] Does not this evidence suggest either that the shells were planted—as at the depository—or that someone else shot Tippit?

This, then, is the sum of medical, ballistics, rifle, and revolver evidence against Oswald for two shootings. Some would call it the "best evidence," because this kind of evidence does not rely on the vagaries of memory or of sight lines. But one can only imagine what a skilled attorney familiar with the case could have done with it. Not to mention the use he or she could have made of witnesses who would have provided an alibi for Oswald, such as Truly, Officer Baker, and Ms. Arnold. When the weight of the Zapruder film is thrown in—the best evidence in light of the hapless autopsy—how could a jury not have found a reasonable doubt that Oswald killed Kennedy or Tippit?

The faults of the Warren Report do not end here. Consider:

•The Warren Report states that both sets of doctors at Parkland and Bethesda *agreed* on the autopsy. As we have seen, this is misleading at best.[78]

•The "second Oswald" sightings around Dallas prior to the assassination are dismissed because the person, or persons, could not be Lee Harvey Oswald. This misses the point smashingly.

•The Commission was not above manhandling witnesses who would not perform. Yet it babied ones it liked or needed. The handling of Marina Oswald—who legally could not have testified against her husband in court—is a shining example of this.[79] And, as Sylvia Meagher has pointed out, a case could be made that the Commission suborned perjury at least once.[80]

• The character profiles and histories of the principals like Oswald, Ruby, and Tippit are shockingly shallow. Ruby is described as a man without mob influence and as an acquaintance of 25 policemen. Oswald's connections to intelligence, his ties in New Orleans, his easy access to passports after his defection, all these and much else go unexplored. Tippit is only a cipher.

• The lack of professional, let alone vigorous, questioning is disheartening. When, for example, Liebeler discovered that Oswald knew Ferrie through the New Orleans Civil Air Patrol, he stopped questioning the witness, and therefore dropped the whole New Orleans connection.[81] As Jim Garrison would later show, the key to the assassination was lost.

Finally what sinks the Warren Report is its lack of respect for itself and the reader. We are asked to believe a string of happenstance, improbabilities, incongruities, and flat-out impossibilities.

It would have us believe that a man (Oswald) could be downstairs on the first floor fifteen minutes before the shooting, run upstairs, set up a sniper's lair, commit the act, and fly downstairs 75 seconds after it was completed. That on his way down, two women descending from the fourth floor would not see him.[82] That a lousy shot like Oswald could hit a moving target two out of three times in 5.6 seconds. That a victim's head and body would recoil backwards *toward* the shooter with such force as almost to topple out of the back of the car. That a bullet fired downwards could reverse direction and go upwards without being deflected. That the same bullet could create seven wounds in two people, smash two bones, and remain undamaged. That the man who had just committed the crime of the century would catch a bus going the wrong way in making his escape and later give up a cab to an elderly person after getting off the bus.[83] That in shooting a policeman, he would load his gun with cartridges that did not match the bullets and then eject shells from a revolver to leave at the scene.

It is all too much. Superficiality is not reality. Things like will, planning, and volition—dismissed as "conspiracy theory"—make up at least as much of life as randomness, luck, and coincidence. Even more so in a planned political crime like an assassination. But to convict the dead Oswald, the Commission could mold the alleged facts to fit its portrait of the accused.

Later, not even the Commissioners or counsel could swallow the official story. Liebeler, Russell, Boggs, and even Belin all expressed doubts about their performance and their case.[84] Towards the end of his life, the man who created the Commission, Lyndon B. Johnson, told others he doubted its conclusions.[85]

Yet it served its immediate purpose. It incriminated a lone assassin and shoved the issue under the table for the 1964 election. But such a story could only last a while. The monument to investigatory excellence that was supposed to close the door on the execution of President Kennedy lasted less than three years. It deserved its quick death.

8

Like a House of Cards

The Warren Report was issued in late September of 1964. Its release was designed to maximize and manipulate its acceptance by the media. The Report was issued without the volumes of testimony and exhibits, so there was no way to compare conclusions with witness reports. The first chapter of the Report, "Summary and Conclusions," served as a perfect press release for afternoon newspapers and nightly news shows. But the Commission's manipulations went even further.

By leaking certain elements of its findings, the Commission had given away what its general conclusions would be. But even as early as the summer of 1964, some writers had become aware of unexplainable contradictions on the surface of the story. These doubts first arose in Europe, in a series of articles written for *L'Express* by American expatriate Thomas Buchanan. The articles were collected into a book, *Who Killed Kennedy?* published abroad in 1964, before being released in America. Another book, by the German-American Joachim Joesten, *Oswald: Assassin or Fall Guy?* was also published abroad in 1964, before its American debut. The Warren Commission requested copies of both books, and, innocently enough, both authors complied, thinking perhaps that the points they developed—about the number of shots, for example—would be seriously considered. Cynically, the Commission used the rather sensible arguments of these men to manufacture a section of the Report called "Speculations and Rumors." The criticisms of these two men were baldly denied, at times with faulty logic and evidence, *e.g.*, about the announced route of the motorcade, the throat wound found at Parkland, and the reports about a Mauser being found at the depository before the Carcano was located.[1]

Buchanan's book is looser and more rambling, but it has an interesting opening section on the history of American political assassinations, in which he attacks the myth that they have generally been the work of lone gunmen.[2] He also asks some pointed questions about Oswald's curious actions and associations in New Orleans.[3] Joesten's book is more systematic and analytical. It is instructive to follow the course of the Commission's relations with Joesten. When they heard about his book, a letter was sent to him in Germany. Through chief counsel Rankin, the Commission requested a copy of the book, and an emissary was sent to retrieve it personally. Joesten met him in Hamburg and gave him the book and some research materials.[4] Joesten said he believed the assassination had been the work of a conspiracy that Oswald might have known about, but which had made him the fall guy. He thought Oswald was perfect for the role, since he suspected Oswald had ties to both the CIA and the FBI. Both agencies would now try to conceal those ties and paint him as a lone, crazed killer.[5]

When Joesten returned to his home in America, his wife told him that the FBI had been there. When he asked why, she replied that the Warren Commission had sent them. Joesten was puzzled, since he had already given his materials to the representative of the State Department in Hamburg. Joesten did not realize at the time that the Commission had launched an investigation of him, since they considered his book subversive, as it cast aspersions on the FBI, the CIA, and the Dallas police. Joesten had been in Germany at the time of Hitler's rise to power, fled to Denmark in 1933, and warned of a coming Nazi invasion of that country. When it came, he fled to the United States. The Gestapo had a file on Joesten that labeled him a Marxist. The Commission secured this file from British intelligence through the CIA. The Agency then used the file material in its internal directive against critics of the Report.[6]

Despite the attacks on the critics, the Commission could not dodge two realities: its report had to be issued soon, and it contained gaping holes.

When the Report and (two months later) the accompanying volumes were issued, it took little time for a reaction to set in. Vincent Salandria, a Philadelphia attorney, wrote a series of magazine articles in early 1965 in which he carefully measured the medical and ballistic evidence against the Zapruder film to reveal the inherent improbabilities in the bullet trajectories as projected by the Report. These underlined the breathtaking assumptions of the single-bullet theory.[7] In 1966 and 1967, some of the photographic evidence depicted in *Esquire* and the *Saturday Evening Post* also deflated the hypothesis that all the shots came from behind.[8]

But the real knockout blows to the Report came in 1966 and 1967, with a series of well-researched, annotated, passionate, and provocative books that were irresistible in force and logic.

Buchanan and Joesten had written books that were essentially collections of essays and reports. Neither work had a bibliography or footnotes. The Buchanan book did not even have a table of contents. So the Commission could easily dodge their arguments, labeling them "speculations" even if they were real or true. But with the release of the 26 volumes, it was now the Commission's turn to be exposed as a paper tiger. The Commission failed to provide a subject index to the 18,000 pages and persistently misspelled the names of participants and witnesses. Still, new writers soon discovered the main weakness in the Report, namely, that the conclusions did not follow from the evidence but were made in spite of it. Once this became evident, it was open season on the Commission.

In rapid succession, six books appeared that could not be ignored as "speculations and rumors": Edward Epstein's *Inquest*, Mark Lane's *Rush to Judgment*, Harold Weisberg's *Whitewash*, Richard Popkin's *The Second Oswald*, Josiah Thompson's *Six Seconds in Dallas*, and Sylvia Meagher's *Accessories After the Fact.*

They were generally more balanced and thoughtful than the Report. And they wasted little time on amateur psychology. They went right to the heart of the case. In courage, insight, and logic, these works were reminiscent of Wesley Liebeler's critical internal memorandum, the path *not* chosen by the Report. In fact, one of these books, Epstein's *Inquest*, had Liebeler's assistance. Originally written as a master's thesis, it was meant to illustrate the political problems of government-sponsored inquiries. Liebeler was Epstein's primary conduit to the inner workings of the Commission, and he revealed how personalities and factions undermined the Commission's purported aim to seek out only the truth.[9]

Epstein's book was the first close-up, inside look at the personalities and workings of the much-heralded Commission. Epstein had conducted extensive interviews with both Commission members and staff. Wesley Liebeler had talked to him at length and given him his files. Some of the rather unflattering facts revealed by the book are:

•The investigation did not last ten months. Because of problems in organization at the start and a lengthy writing process at the end, the actual investigation went on for only five months.[10]

•The Commission did little besides interview witnesses in closed session. The bulk of the investigation—legwork, weighing reports, collating documents—was done by the staff.[11]

•By July of 1964—two and a half months before the Report was released—all the senior staff had returned to private practice. Only three junior members remained full-time.[12]

•The Commission did not have a direct line to either the FBI or the CIA. There was a Justice Department liaison. When a report surfaced that Oswald had been an FBI informant—complete with employee number and monthly salary—the Commission had no alternative but to ask Hoover if it were true. He denied it, and that was that.[13]

In short, Epstein's portrait is one of a centralized, confused, weak, helpless bureaucracy working under intense political pressure and an unrealistic deadline. At the beginning of his book, the author strongly implies that the purpose of the Commission was to centralize the fact-finding mission and to delay or close down the more independent inquiry being launched by Texas Attorney General Waggoner Carr.[14] (Carr had given the Commission the information about Oswald's FBI status.)

Epstein's book was serious, well-documented, and included exclusive reports—like abridgments of the first two FBI reports, and photos and descriptions of Kennedy's clothes after the autopsy. The portrait was accurate. When Warren saw Liebeler in Washington after the book's publication, he commented, "It looks like you wrote about half of Epstein's book."[15]

Epstein's book cast no aspersions on anyone directly. He analyzed very little of the evidence or the conclusions drawn from it. In the last chapter, he stated that the Commission did what it did because it was under tremendous pressure—not specified—to come up with a palliative political truth rather than an honest, thorough criminal investigation.[16]

The job of attacking the actual findings of the Report was left to two works that came out almost simultaneously: Mark Lane's *Rush to Judgment* and Harold Weisberg's *Whitewash*. These two books showed no respect for the Report; in that respect their authors showed considerable courage. In essence, they said the government was lying—Oswald did not shoot either Kennedy or Tippit.

Lane was a New York lawyer whose early argument for Oswald's innocence—published in the *National Guardian*, a leftwing alternative weekly—attracted the attention of Marguerite Oswald, Lee's mother.[17] He went to Dallas, the first of seven visits, and began to collect an impressive array of evidence to counter the Warren Report. He all but gave up his law practice to devote himself to finding the truth about the assassination. His *Rush to Judgment* reads like a dazzling defense brief for Oswald. One of its achievements is that its citations are drawn almost exclusively from the Report or the accompanying 26 volumes. Consequently, Lane established that the Commission convicted Oswald *first* and then sifted through the evidence to prove its case, leaving a welter of exculpatory evidence unpresented. He is particularly strong on the Tippit murder and on the witnesses from the grassy knoll. In the former, he successfully attacked witnesses like Helen Markham and William Scoggins and found new witnesses like Acquilla Clemons and Frank and May Wright, who failed to identify Oswald.[18] In the latter, Lane destroyed the Commission's contention that, "No credible evidence suggests that the shots were fired from ... any place other than the Texas School Book Depository Building."[19] He did what the Commission did not; he placed nearly all the witnesses in Dealey Plaza and showed that most of them heard shots not from the depository but from the knoll, and that several of them saw smoke rising from that area.[20]

Harold Weisberg's *Whitewash* was self-published in 1965. He had submitted it to 63 publishers in the United States.[21] No one picked it up. Weisberg, at great personal expense, published the book himself. It sold well, and Dell picked it up in 1966. The book is a passionate—perhaps too passionate—defense of Oswald. In his introduction Weisberg makes it clear that he saw the assassination as a political crime. He was the first to sound that note. He had nothing but scorn for both the Commission and the FBI, and he often refers to them in sarcastic, derogatory terms. The book seems strident, but Weisberg still scores some bull's-eyes. He skewered the myth of Oswald the marksman and was one of the first to note that shells left at the scene were suspiciously marked.[22] He is especially good at demonstrating the hollowness of the Commission's reconstructions of Oswald's movements after the shooting. For example, he showed how it would be difficult, if not impossible, for Oswald to have encountered Truly and Baker at the soda machine less than a minute and a half after the shooting.[23] As improbable as it would have been for Oswald to have walked from his rooming house to the scene of the Tippit murder in time to kill the officer.[24] And Weisberg should be singled out for devoting an entire chapter to the abuse of Oswald's legal rights after he was arrested.[25]

Also appearing in 1966 was a uniquely incisive book, *The Second Oswald*. It had its genesis as a series of articles in the *New York Review of Books* by philosophy professor Richard Popkin. He collected these, expanded them, and added other materials to produce a brief but provocative book focusing on the possibility of a conspiracy. In the first part of the book, he detailed what he saw as some of the strongest evidence pointing away from a single assassin—the Zapruder film, the FBI report suggesting a separate bullet hit Connally, and the location of the back wound, which is lower than the throat wound.[26] Then he noted what he saw as traces of a conspiracy: the planting of CE 399 at Parkland Hospital, perhaps by Ruby,[27] and the numerous sightings of a "second" or "false" Oswald after the Mexico trip in late September,[28] which he described in detail. Popkin may have been the first to postulate that this "false" Oswald was one of the actual assassins.[29] Acutely, he separated the red herrings from reality and showed how the Commission fell for a set-up, hook, line, and sinker.

In 1967, two heavyweights appeared to deliver the coup de grâce to the Report. Josiah Thompson was another professor of philosophy who had become fascinated by the assassination. He convinced *Life* magazine to let him use the Zapruder film to advance a theory about the assassination.[30] Thompson felt that the single-bullet theory was untenable in light of the timing between Kennedy's and Connally's reactions to their respective hits. He methodically built a case for four shots from at least two directions. He supplemented his observations of the Zapruder film with a catalog of eye- and ear-witness testimony at the scene, the FBI report on the autopsy, Connally's testimony and subsequent interviews, witnesses who saw smoke and light behind the stockade fence on the knoll, and the ballistics evidence showing that the Carcano could not do what the Commission said it could.

Thompson's professorial tone is even, unruffled, cool, and logical. The evidence he mounts and the way he presents and arranges it, are convincingly scientific. His recreation of the

Josiah Thompson in 1988, after the publication of his book, *Gumshoe*; "operative" Jacqueline Tully stands next to him.

Sylvia Meagher in her
Greenwich Village apartment,
June 1977, with a copy of
Accessories After the Fact.

sequence of shots was more credible than anyone else's at the time, and he paved the way for the idea of a "hit team" in Dealey Plaza, with *at least* four shots being fired.

Thompson made two enduring observations. He was the first to postulate that two shots hit Kennedy in the head, almost simultaneously, one from the back and one from the front, at Zapruder frames 310-315.[31] Also, by closely examining a film made facing the depository, Thompson was the first to discern the outlines of *two* individuals in the sixth-floor window from which Oswald was supposed to have fired.[32] Apparently, *Life* thought the demonstration too effective, because just as Thompson's book was to be published, it withdrew the rights to the film it had purchased from Abraham Zapruder. Thompson went ahead and published *Six Seconds in Dallas* with artist's drawings that approximated the frames from the film.

Later in 1967, another book appeared, written by a woman who had viewed the Zapruder film at *Life* with Thompson,

Sylvia Meagher. She knew the Warren Report and the 26 volumes of testimony and exhibits better than the Commissioners or their staff. Outraged that the government could issue such a bloated compendium without a subject index, she produced one herself.[33] Because it affords researchers a roadmap through the intentional morass of the Report, it remains the standard guide. Fellow writers and researchers were so appreciative of her efforts they urged her to write her own critique. She did, and when *Accessories After the Fact* appeared, it was immediately recognized as one of the best—if not the best—polemic against the Report.

It has often been said that the Commission produced not a single piece of uncontestable evidence incriminating Oswald. One of Meagher's strengths is that her work is encyclopedic, taking on almost every piece of evidence the Commission could mount, and discrediting almost all of them. Her tone is also judicious; one does not feel one is hearing a one-sided argument. Meagher believed in Oswald's innocence, but she considered each of the Commission's arguments before exploding them.

Some of these books were popular with the public. All of them were serious and scholarly and had some arguments that were cogent and irresistible. Together, as they seeped into public awareness, they created a growing wave of public criticism against the vaunted Warren Report. Indeed, by 1967, more than forty percent of the American public had serious qualms about the lone assassin thesis.[34] Four major magazines—*Life, Esquire, Ramparts*, and the *Saturday Evening Post*—called for a new investigation based on the points made by the critics.[35] Their efforts were bearing fruit. The public was paying attention and the Report was in grave jeopardy. The stage was now set for a new investigation. Enter Jim Garrison.

9

New Orleans Redux

Jim Garrison, the District Attorney of Orleans Parish, Louisiana, had actually begun investigating the assassination on November 25, 1963, four days before the Warren Commission had been announced. Even then, he was closer to the truth than the Commission. Unfortunately, Garrison did not pursue the matter as he could have. If he had, the assassination might have been solved in a matter of weeks.

Shortly after the ex-FBI man and private detective, Guy Banister, had pistol-whipped his employee Jack Martin into a hospital bed, one of Garrison's Assistant DAs came to him with some provocative information. Martin's tongue had been loosened by Banister's beating, and he had told a mutual acquaintance about a strange ice-skating and goose-hunting trip on the day of the assassination by a David Ferrie. Hurt and resentful, Martin had cast the excursion in a particularly dark light. Something about Ferrie being a "getaway pilot" in an elaborate assassination plot.[1]

Garrison had a slight acquaintance with all three characters named. He had known Banister when Banister was a policeman, and they had traded stories about their previous work in the FBI. Through Banister, he knew Martin. He had met Ferrie only once. After his election as District Attorney, the odd-visaged pilot had congratulated him on the street. At this point, Garrison was harboring no suspicions about any of these men. His next encounter with Ferrie, however, would change that attitude quickly.

Jack Martin.

On the weight of Martin's accusations and a previous police complaint record, Garrison sent assistants from his office to Ferrie's apartment. When they arrived, they found two young boys inside, waiting for Ferrie. They said he had left for a trip to Texas on the 22nd and had not yet returned.[2] This was also Garrison's first knowledge of Ferrie's odd living conditions. The apartment had a collection of rabbits for Ferrie's cancer research, a batch of Army rifles and other military equipment, and a wall map of Cuba.

When Ferrie returned from Texas, Garrison brought him in for questioning. Ferrie's answers were a mixture of truth, lies, and subterfuge. He admitted going to Houston on the 22nd. He denied ever knowing or meeting Oswald. When Garrison pressed him on his reasons for driving to Texas through a fierce rainstorm, he gave the ice skating-goose hunting story described earlier (he once changed this to an interest in building a rink himself).[3] To Garrison, this was like driving four hundred miles for a hamburger. The DA was also suspicious of Ferrie's nervous and evasive demeanor. On November 25, he decided to arrest Ferrie and turn him over to the FBI for questioning; but they released him quickly when they determined his plane could not fly that weekend. Evidently they were not concerned that Ferrie would not need his plane in Houston and had already arranged for another plane to be waiting there.[4] Garrison automatically accepted the decision of the FBI, his former employer. As we shall see, it was the biggest mistake of his career.

For the next three years, Garrison continued in his role as vigorous, colorful, humorous prosecutor and dedicated husband and father. Then, on an airplane trip in November 1966 with Senator Russell Long and New Orleans oilman Joseph Rualt, the conversation turned to the Kennedy assassination,

One of Jim Garrison's favorite photos. When he had occasion to have an official White House photo taken with President Johnson, just as the photographer was about to snap the picture, Johnson jumped several feet in front of him towards the photographer. Johnson was extremely vain and did not like to appear shorter than anyone else in a picture. When faced with a giant like Garrison, he solved the problem by moving closer to the camera.

and Long made a comment that set off a time bomb in Garrison: "Those fellows on the Warren Commission were dead wrong. There's no way one man could have shot up Jack Kennedy that way."[5] This stunned Garrison both because of its source—a man whose intelligence he respected—and because he himself had conducted a brief and aborted investigation of Ferrie three years before.

He was so disturbed by this brief conversation that he began reading every book and article he could find on the assassination: Salandria, Weisberg, Lane, Epstein, *et al.* He then ordered the Warren Report and its 26 volumes of testimony and exhibits. That was the clincher. Garrison's reaction was disbelief, or as he termed it, "the end of innocence":[6]

It is impossible for anyone possessed of reasonable objectivity and a fair degree of intelligence to read those twenty-six volumes and not reach the conclusion that the Warren Commission was wrong in every one of its major conclusions concerning the assassination.

It was at this point, around October 1966, that the DA decided to reopen his investigation. Oswald had been in New Orleans for six months before going on to Dallas less than two months before the assassination. Garrison's initial assumptions about the assassination, about the probity of the Warren Report, the FBI inquiry, about his own brief investigation, all these were now crumbling. Was it too late to discover the truth? Garrison felt it was not.

It was time to uncover the mystery of 544 Camp Street.

Here, it is useful to describe the man who was about to step onto the world stage to become perhaps the most famous DA in American history.[7] To comprehend the truth or falsity of the charges later to be leveled at him once his investigation was made public, we must know something about who he was before the media lit him up like a Christmas tree. Garrison did not do this in 1967, so he was painted in by a hostile media before he could define himself. It would seem only fair to do that now before proceeding.

Garrison's family hails from Iowa. His two grandfathers represent two strains of American history that are evident in the man's psyche and have affected his life. His grandfather on his father's side, Thomas Jefferson Garrison, an attorney for Northwestern Railway, once worked with the legendary lawyer Clarence Darrow. (Jim Garrison idolized Darrow so much that he named one of his sons after him.) His grandfather on his mother's side, William Oliver Robinson, was a typical early 20th-century American-Irish businessman. From him, Garrison inherited his strong individualism, patriotism, love of the good life, and his height—he is 6 feet 7 inches tall.

Born on November 21, 1921, he was named Earling Carothers Garrison (he understandably changed it to Jim in 1946). His parents divorced when he was three. His father eventually moved to Arizona and Garrison had little further

**Jim Garrison, fresh
in the U.S. Army.**

contact with him. His mother moved with Jim to Chicago and then south to New Orleans.

Garrison joined the army at age nineteen, well before Pearl Harbor, and during World War II became an artillery spotter pilot over Germany and France, quite a dangerous position. He was one of those who discovered the terror and madness of Nazism firsthand. His unit was involved in the liberation of Dachau concentration camp. Its horrors were a sight that never left him, and the fear of fascism and authoritarian rule frequently appears in his writings and interviews.

Garrison enjoyed his military service so much that he joined the National Guard when he left active duty and stayed in it for eighteen years. He belonged to the Guard when he began his investigation in 1963.

Following in his grandfather's tradition, Garrison went to Tulane and received a law degree. He then worked for a short time with the FBI in the Pacific Northwest. He rejoined the service for the Korean War, and, afterwards, returned to New Orleans. Once there, he served as an assistant DA before going into private practice. In 1960 he ran for a Criminal District Court judgeship and lost. Then, in 1961, he ran for District Attorney and, in a huge upset, defeated the incumbent.

Garrison had promised reform, and he delivered. He came down hard on prostitutes, both female and male. He also went after honky-tonk bars and strip joints. But his outspokenness raised controversy. He assailed the police for being lazy and soft on crime. He criticized New Orleans' eight criminal court judges for not authorizing funds for investigations of organized crime and said this "raised interesting questions about racketeer influences." The judges sued him for defamation of character and the case ended up in the U.S. Supreme Court, where on November 23, 1964, Garrison won a landmark case protecting citizens' rights to criticize public officials as "the essence of self-government."[8]

There seem to be two constants in Garrison's record as DA. One is diligence in his function as crime-fighter in New

"Battling District Attorney," the May 1963 AP headline reads, as Garrison poses on Bourbon Street during his "war against French Quarter vice."

Orleans. On more than one occasion he said he relished his job and felt fortunate to have it. The other is a strange one for a DA outside a liberal big city: a preoccupation with the civil liberties of the defendant. For example, Garrison intervened in the police arrest of a bookseller who sold James Baldwin's *Another Country*. Standing up for a black author in the Deep South was a brave move that cost Garrison popularity among racist voters and won him the enmity of the local White Citizens' Council[9] (but he has always been popular with the black voters of Orleans Parish). He also reinvestigated cases that his office had won and had convictions overturned on the basis of new evidence. And he wrote an eloquent law review article in 1965 that indicated his deepest feelings about the triangle of the law, the state, and the individual:[10]

It may well turn out, in the course of time, that our expanding concept of the fair trial, of the rights of the defendant against the state, may come to be seen as the greatest contribution our country has made to this world....

Garrison depoliticized the DA's office by choosing his assistants on merit from the upper echelon of local law schools like Tulane and LSU without regard to party affiliation. This would aid him immeasurably in his reopened inquiry. It is testimony to the energy and acumen of his young staff that they accomplished so much in such a short time with so few resources.[11] Comparing Garrison's office to the bloated, big-budgeted Warren Commission, we see how the values of intelligence, drive, and the sheer will to discover the truth can outweigh things like money and experience. If there ever was a case of a group of young lawyers having to rise to an occasion, this was it.

This was Garrison's background when he began to crack the most sensational murder of our time. He had little with which to start besides Martin's lead. The Warren Commission had spent very little time on the New Orleans portion of Oswald's life. Commission lawyer Wesley Liebeler had interviewed some witnesses in Louisiana, and Ferrie's name had come up, but it had been disposed of quickly. (The testimony appears in Volume VIII with interviews of Edward Voebel and Frederick O'Sullivan, who testified they recognized both Oswald and Ferrie as CAP members.) Liebeler had also interviewed local New Orleans lawyer Dean Andrews, whose testimony was rather relevant, to say the least.

Andrews had related the story of the enigmatic Clay Bertrand, the man who asked him to defend Oswald.[12] Liebeler seems to have been put off by Andrews's argot and attitude, neither of which suited Liebeler's Ivy League pedigree. But whatever the reason, the Report discounted his testimony. This seems unwarranted, if predictable, because Andrews's original story was buttressed by the testimony of three people: his assistant, Preston Davis; Eva Springer, his secretary to whom he told the story; and his colleague, Monk Zelden, whom he called and asked to help him in the case.[13]

But besides these and a few other bits and pieces, the only lead the Warren Commission left to Oswald's trail in New Orleans was an interview with Sam Newman. Newman was the owner of the building at 544 Camp Street, the address stamped on Oswald's pro-Castro pamphlets. The FBI dropped its investigation of this address when Mr. Newman said he rented no office there to the Fair Play for Cuba Committee and did not recognize Oswald's photo.[14]

This was where the Commission ended its inquiry into Oswald's stay in New Orleans. It is where Garrison began.

While inspecting the building, Garrison realized that its other address was 531 Lafayette and recognized Guy Banister's office there. This, of course, led Garrison to solving the Camp Street mystery and to establishing Oswald's association with Ferrie and Banister. Unfortunately—and this is what makes Garrison's failure to follow up his 1963 inquiry so crushing—Banister and his associate Hugh Ward had both died in 1964. (Bannister's death was reportedly due to a heart attack, but Ward died in a mysterious plane crash along with DeLesseps Morrison, a former New Orleans mayor and JFK's representative to the Organization of American States.) Nevertheless, Garrison managed to get the title cards to Banis-

Guy Banister.

ter's files and uncovered his façade as a private detective. One of the files was entitled "Shaw," but its papers had disappeared within days after Banister's death.[15]

David Lewis, a former investigator for Banister, talked to Garrison very early in 1967 and confirmed Jack Martin's story suggesting the New Orleans origin of the conspiracy. He said that at least five men—Oswald, Banister, Ferrie, Carlos Quiroga, and Sergio Arcacha Smith—were involved in the planning stages of the assassination while frequenting 544 Camp Street. He said it was a quick, overkill-type of operation. Lewis later got cold feet and disappeared, presumably when he saw what happened to Dave Ferrie and linked it with Oswald's fate.[16]

When Garrison realized that Banister's office was a front for rightwing intelligence activity, he began to rethink the conventional perception of Oswald the communist. Given Oswald's likely presence at 544 Camp Street, Garrison decided Oswald's leftist persona had to be as much a cover as Banister's detective office. When one of Garrison's busy assistant DAs discovered the Shaw-Oswald-Ferrie Clinton

David F. Lewis, who had been an investigator for Banister, holding the Warren Report, February 21, 1967, after announcing to the press that he believed his life was in danger.

trip, Garrison began to realize that Oswald was being used as some sort of informant—to win the sympathy of, and then infiltrate, suspect organizations to collect information and, perhaps, when necessary, steer the organization a particular way.[17]

If we follow this model, some of the otherwise inexplicable parts of Oswald's life became coherent. For example, Oswald's mastery of Russian, his defection from and then easy reentry to the U.S., his one-man chapter of the FPCC, his attempts to infiltrate anti-Castro Cuban organizations in New Orleans, and, above all, his Mexico trip on which he was likely accompanied by three CIA contacts, all become less aimless.[18]

But Garrison's scenario went deeper. He had never believed in Oswald's ability to fire the fatal shots. For him, the timing of the shot sequence, the paraffin test, and the impossibility of the single-bullet theory eliminated Oswald as the assassin. With this in mind, he began to see that, toward the end of his New Orleans stay, Oswald the manipulator was being manipulated; that Shaw, Ferrie, and Banister had hatched a plot in which the agent provocateur who masqueraded as a pro-Soviet, pro-Cuban Red would be set up as the perfect patsy for the assassination.

With this perception, Garrison also shed light on another enigma. He linked George DeMohrenschildt with Banister. DeMohrenschildt was one of the most baffling characters to appear before the Commission. In retrospect, he played the Commissioners like Solti conducting the London Symphony. He was a White Russian of strong anticommunist leanings who had ostensibly made money in the Texas oil and geology business. He and his wife, Jean, lived in a refined, cultivated, and comfortable social world, very different from the Oswalds'. Yet when Marina and Lee arrived back in Texas from Russia, it was the charming, affable DeMohrenschildt who convinced the Oswalds to move from Fort Worth to Dallas and stay with friends of his.[19] It was this aristocratic couple

George DeMohrenschildt
and his wife Jean, holding
a photo of President and
Mrs. Kennedy at Love Field.

who got the anticommunist White Russian community to befriend this communist who had defected to the Soviet Union.[20] Here was a man who was Oswald's political antithesis, social opposite, and economic superior; yet he was lending his valuable time and influence to a so-called misfit and loner. As Garrison said in 1967, "What did they talk about— last year's season at Biarritz, or how to beat the bank at Monte Carlo?"[21]

When he appeared before the Warren Commission, DeMohrenschildt played the political novice, implying he had no political interests and hardly bothered to vote.[22] The Commission let this pass, ignoring the fact that he had a strange itinerary in his geological work: Haiti, Yugoslavia, Costa Rica, Guatemala, and Ghana. Not exactly an OPEC lineup when it comes to potential oil reserves, but plenty interesting when CIA interests are considered.[23]

DeMohrenschildt pulled another reversal before the Commission. Although he and his wife were supposed to be best friends of Lee Oswald, he said he broke with Oswald just before he left for New Orleans and never saw or heard from him again. This was another contradiction the Commission, guided by its foregone conclusion, failed to pursue. Then, during their testimony, both George and Jean went out of their way to paint Oswald as the stereotypical assassin type: alienated, abusive, unstable. Jean described an afternoon scene in which she saw Oswald and his daughter in the park, with Lee carrying his rifle. Occasionally, he would pull it out and fire at some birds in the area. Even the Commission took that one with a grain of salt.[24]

Subsequently it was learned that DeMohrenschildt was a CIA contact as far back as 1957, who had tried to join the OSS during the war.[25] It appeared, as Garrison began to suspect, that he was "baby-sitting" Oswald in Dallas [26] and may have debriefed him on his return from Russia,[27] and that he then passed him on to Banister in New Orleans as he stepped offstage in this penultimate act in the drama.

Later, as his story began to come unhinged, so did DeMohrenschildt's mental state. In 1977, when Edward Epstein was interviewing him on the Oswald-DeMohrenschildt friendship for his book *Legend*, he was served with a subpoena from the House Select Committee on Assassinations. Three hours later, he was dead, allegedly by his own hand.[28]

Garrison had now seemingly penetrated the covers of Banister, DeMohrenschildt, and Oswald. He also had some ideas about the meaning of the Clinton trip. What he needed next was to piece together the actual mechanics of the assassination and the explicit CIA connection. With Banister dead and DeMohrenschildt's apparent Agency deep cover still in place, Garrison had to find some links, particularly a clear connection between Ferrie, Shaw, Banister, and the Agency. To this end, the pursuit of Gordon Novel was about to begin.

Novel was perhaps the primary CIA contact for the New Orleans part of the anti-Castro efforts.[29] A communications and electronics expert, he had funds channeled to his Evergreen Advertising Agency, a CIA front, to fuel the effort. With this, he helped pay for radio commercials that contained cryptic messages to alert agents to the Bay of Pigs invasion date. Novel and his first attorney, Jerry Weiner, originally denied his Agency connections. But after Garrison uncovered Novel's participation with Ferrie in the Houma arms raid and the *New Orleans States-Item* broke a story about his CIA connection, Novel and his second attorney, Steve Plotkin, dropped the denials and changed their response to a "no comment." Later, this ploy was also dropped; in a letter discovered in his abandoned New Orleans apartment, Novel revealed his CIA employment.[30]

Novel is connected through the Houma weapons raid on the Schlumberger warehouse not only to Ferrie but also to Banister. It was at Banister's office that many of the stolen munitions were stored for later use at the Bay of Pigs.

Novel denied that the Houma operation was a heist at all. He claimed it was nothing but a "patriotic" pickup of stored war material. Privately, he said that on the day of the pickup, he was phoned by his CIA contact and told to lead a group to the Schlumberger bunker, and then transport the weapons by laundry truck to their eventual debarkation point, Miami.[31] He said the people he worked with—Ferrie, Sergio Arcacha Smith, and Layton Martens, Ferrie's then roommate—were all supposed to be working with the CIA.

Novel's statements were critical to the Garrison probe because he not only provided a CIA link to Ferrie and Banister, he also stated that he knew both Clay Shaw and Dean Andrews.[32] Novel's specialty was electronics. He also owned a restaurant which he almost never frequented. Shaw was in the international trade business and wrote plays. We have seen that Andrews was an undistinguished attorney. How did Shaw know Novel? How did Andrews know Novel? And who was Novel's "CIA contact" who called him the day of the Houma "raid"?[33]

These questions became even more compelling in view of what Novel did next. He had appeared before the Grand Jury on March 16, 1967, and discussed some general matters. But on March 22, the day he was scheduled to return for more detailed questioning, he disappeared. He had sold his interest in the restaurant and cleared out his apartment. He then began a national and international junket denouncing Garrison from Columbus, Ohio, McLean, Virginia, and Montreal, Canada, sidestepping the DA's efforts to extradite him.[34]

But Novel had slipped up when he left New Orleans in such a hurry. Two young girls who rented his apartment found a letter written by him. One of their friends gave it to Hoke May, a reporter, who, in turn, gave it to Garrison. A handwriting analyst verified it as Novel's. It was dated in January 1967, before Garrison's probe was made public. Made out to a "Mr. Weiss," it began:[35]

I took the liberty of writing you directly and apprising you of current situation expecting you to forward this through appropriate channels. Our connection and activity of that period involved individuals presently about to be indicted as conspirators in Mr. Garrison's investigation.

The letter went on to warn that Garrison was close to discovering Novel's association with Double-Chek Corporation in Miami, another CIA front that coordinated the anti-Castro Bay of Pigs efforts in Florida. He added that, when questioned by the FBI, "My reply on five queries was negative. Bureau unaware of Double-Chek association in this matter."

Novel was getting frantic and said he could not use the Fifth Amendment, immunity, or legal dodges and had to be out of New Orleans by March. He then threatened that if the Agency left him out in the cold or harmed him, he would release sealed Agency files on the matter to expose it. Novel closed by urging the Agency to aid him:

Some researchers
believe Gordon
Novel was on the
grassy knoll at
the time of the
assassination. This
series of blowups,
compared to a
mug shot of Novel,
suggests that the
man at the far right
in the top shot may
well be Novel.

Gordon Novel In a
taxi outside the
courthouse after
testifying before
the Grand Jury,
March 16, 1967.

...appropriate counteraction relative to Garrison's inquisition concerning us ... may be handled through military channels vis-à-vis DIA [Defense Intelligence Agen-
cy] man. Garrison is presently colonel in Louisiana Army National Guard....

The Agency took Novel's threat seriously, and came to his
rescue. It supplied Plotkin as his attorney, and his journey
across America smearing Garrison began. But now neither
Plotkin nor Novel could credibly deny their Agency ties.
Garrison could therefore show the connection between the
CIA and Ferrie, Banister, and perhaps even Clay Shaw.

The DA also probed for the actual dynamics of the plot. Once
Garrison's investigation was made public in 1967, people
whom the Warren Commission ignored and those who discovered information after 1964 came to him with their stories. For instance, Francis Fruge, the policeman who had
discovered Rose Cheramie and brought her to Texas, told
Garrison about this powerful encounter, highlighting the role
of Jack Ruby.[36] Garrison realized its importance and linked
it to what he knew about Ruby's relationship with Bill Mc-
Claney, owner of the Lake Pontchartrain training camp. He
also connected it to the testimony of Nancy Perrin Rich about

Jack Ruby,
center, at a
bail hearing,
December 24,
1963, with
his attorneys,
Joe Tonahill,
left, and
Melvin Belli.

Ruby's payoffs in Cuban exile gunrunning schemes. From all
this, the DA deduced that Ruby's tale of killing Oswald out
of sympathy for Jackie Kennedy was just a ruse (it was later
revealed that this was a defense ploy dreamed up by Tom
Howard, Ruby's first attorney).[37] Garrison now saw Ruby as
part of the plot, his shooting of Oswald as a desperate, but
rational and deliberate act. Ruby was the low-level operative
in Dallas. He had strong, plentiful ties to the police and
therefore access to the station that day. He had seen the Tippit
rendezvous go awry. He was aware that Oswald was denying
his guilt and was, in fact, insisting he was the fall guy. If
Ruby did not silence him, Oswald was the one man at that
time whose trial could expose the conspiracy.

Garrison eventually discovered more about the inner workings of the plot and its increasingly probable relation to the
Agency. This was revealed to him by a former intelligence agent who also felt his life was endangered by the
plotters.

This former agent, Richard Case Nagell, appears in the Warren Commission exhibits only briefly, in a one-sentence FBI
report that has been obviously censored:[38]

For the record, he would like to say that his association with Oswald [meaning Lee Harvey Oswald] was

purely social and that he had met him in Mexico City
and in Texas.

There was no background to this report. Not even a hint
why the man was being questioned, or where. As it happened,
he was in jail at the time.[39]
   In late September 1963, Nagell had entered a federally
chartered bank in El Paso, Texas. He pulled a gun and began
firing. But he was not trying to rob the bank. His shots were
aimed at the ceiling. After firing a few rounds, he waited
outside on the curb to be arrested.
   Despite this obvious lack of intent to rob the bank, he was
not indicted for a misdemeanor, but for the serious felony of
armed robbery. He was convicted in Federal court and sen-
tenced to ten years (the sentence was later reduced and he
was out in three).
   Nagell told Garrison that in mid-1963, his intelligence
agency (never named but apparently the CIA) had strong
suspicions that a large plot by a group of contract employees
in New Orleans to kill President Kennedy was under way. The
weapons for use in the assassination were ordered by Shaw
through the Agency. (Ferrie ordered the weapons he used to
train Cuban exiles through Permindex,[40] a shadowy, rightwing international trade organization, on whose board Shaw
served.) When the DA pressed the reluctant Nagell to reveal
the men involved in the plot, he admitted that the three he
knew of were Clay Shaw, Guy Banister, and David Ferrie.
When asked if Oswald was a witting or unwitting participant
in the conspiracy, Nagell replied that he was not sure, but
thought Oswald was unwitting.
   Nagell had been told by his contact that he was to penetrate
this circle to see if the suspicions were justified. He went to
Louisiana to ingratiate himself with this group. The more he
learned, the more he was convinced that his contact was
correct, a conspiracy was afloat. It would be executed the last
week of September, and its target was JFK.

Richard Case Nagell.

Two events caused Nagell to fire the shots in the El Paso bank. First, his contact was reassigned, and he could not reach him. Second, when this happened, he wrote a registered letter to Hoover to tip off the FBI. When the letter went unacknowledged, he acted to save himself. He thought the conspiracy was bigger than he dreamed. Even worse, he feared that somehow he would be sucked into it and be accused of being a plotter through his association with Oswald and the trio. That is when he decided to be arrested for a misdemeanor and be in custody during the assassination. That would be preferable to being accused of a conspiracy to murder the President. He did not foresee that the plot would be postponed or that he would be convicted of a felony.

Gordon Novel and Richard Nagell provided further evidence of some CIA relation to a plot. But the plot was not necessarily hatched in Langley, Virginia, headquarters of the Agency. It may have developed in a compartmentalized manner out of Miami (perhaps at Ted Shackley's JM/WAVE or Ed Lansdale's Operation MONGOOSE) and forged links in New

Orleans and Dallas. Very likely, it related to Kennedy's decision to dismantle Operation MONGOOSE after he made his
pledge not to invade the island. CIA operations are compartmentalized, organized on what is often called a "need-to-
know" basis. Some operatives are not aware of others in the
same area.[41]

In the cases of Novel and Nagell, their employment by the
Agency seemed more evident; they were closer to being
full-time field officers than local contract agents—people
with looser ties,[42] as was the case with Ferrie, Banister, and
Shaw. If his amazing story is true, it would appear that Nagell
was assigned to penetrate the plot because some part of the
compartmentalized Agency feared the devastating effect of
an exposé of the plotters' ties to the CIA. For the same reason,
the Company could never cooperate in any investigation or
even admit they had smelled a whiff of the plot beforehand.[43]
This fear was justified because, in the 1970s, when the Castro
assassination schemes were publicized by Senator Frank
Church's committee, the effects on the CIA were quite serious and the Agency did not recover for years. The Agency
doubtless realized that if the plot were uncovered, it would
not matter if linked plotters comprised a rogue, outlaw band
operating independently of the center. The headlines would
not explain this fine distinction, politicians would blur it, and
the public would not understand it. Moreover, the exposure
of any involvement in one domestic operation by the Agency
might lead to the exposure of other fully authorized but
illegal domestic activities, like disruption of lawful domestic
organizations, mail openings, and considerable other domestic covert operations.[44]

The gravity of the plot was made clear to Garrison in his
meeting with his old law school chum, Dean Andrews. Garrison was intensely curious about who Clay Bertrand really
was. From 1963, when Andrews had first told the FBI of his
phone call from Bertrand to defend Oswald, the lawyer had

backpedaled from his original story. Bertrand had shrunk from 6 feet 2 inches to 5 feet 8 inches, and Andrews almost begged not to be interviewed anymore.[45] To Garrison, this meant that Andrews's original corroborated testimony was true. But due to his reception by the Commission and his realization of what had happened to others like Ferrie who were extensively questioned, he had decided to tapdance away from it.

Garrison invited Andrews to lunch early in 1967 and asked him Clay Bertrand's true identity. When Andrews would not respond truthfully—he insisted he did not know what the mysterious Bertrand looked like—the conversation turned dramatic. Garrison grabbed his arm and warned him that he would take him before the grand jury and, if he dodged the question on the stand, he would go to jail for perjury. Andrews's response was equally intense. He told the DA that if he revealed the identity of Clay Bertrand, "it's goodbye Dean Andrews ... I mean like a bullet in my head." Garrison was adamant. He would still call him to testify. Garrison realized now that those involved in the plot would go to any length to stymie his inquiry. What he did not know was that his own life would soon be threatened and that Andrews would be aware of it.

Garrison was now filling in much of the conspiracy: its origins, its geographical base, and the identity of some plotters. What he needed was a witness to its planning. That was supplied in the person of a young college student and insurance salesman named Perry Russo. In February of 1967, Russo had written to Garrison when he became aware of his investigation, but the letter was never delivered. Russo then gave interviews to both a local TV station and a reporter from the *Baton Rouge State-Times*.[46] When the interviews appeared, stating that Russo had been at a meeting at Ferrie's where killing the President had been discussed, Garrison immediately sent Andrew ("Moo Moo") Sciambra, a young assistant DA, to take a deposition from Russo in Baton Rouge. Russo said he was a friend of Ferrie's and had attended a party at Ferrie's apartment in mid-September of 1963.[47] He revealed that, late in the evening, after most had left, he, Ferrie, two of Ferrie's friends, and several Cuban exiles remained. Russo had brought two friends to Ferrie's that night, Sandra Moffett and Niles Peterson. Both left early, but Peterson later vaguely remembered a man named Leon Oswald.[48] By the time the discussion took place, both Russo's friends were gone. Almost everyone else had left except Ferrie, Leon Oswald, and a tall, distinguished, white-haired man named Clem Bertrand.[49]

The group, reported Russo, discussed Cuban-American politics and everyone expressed their distaste for both Castro and Kennedy. Then, the assassination of Fidel Castro was raised, but Bertrand noted that there would be a real problem getting at him inside Cuba.

**Perry Russo at Clay
Shaw's preliminary
hearing, March 15, 1967.**

Around this time the Cubans left, and only Ferrie, Oswald, Bertrand, and Russo remained. Ferrie continued the conversation saying that if they could not get at Castro, they certainly had access to Kennedy. Russo said this was characteristic of Ferrie. Since he had known him, Ferrie had become more and more embittered at the President. Russo had no liking for Kennedy either. He was a Republican and a Goldwater supporter. Joined by their stated hatred of JFK, the men now turned to the details of a plot to do away with him.

Ferrie became intense. Pacing the floor, he expostulated on the way to do it: in a "triangulation of crossfire"—shooting at Kennedy from three directions. Ferrie insisted this would ensure that one of the shots would be fatal. As Ferrie became more excited and voluble, Bertrand remained calm, smoking, and added, coolly, that if it happened, they had to be away from the scene. Ferrie said he would be at Southeastern Louisiana campus in Hammond. Bertrand said he would be on a business trip to the West Coast.

Russo realized that the discussion had now transcended the hypothetical. They were talking about where they would be *when it occurred*. Indeed, on his way back from Texas the weekend of the assassination, Ferrie did go see a friend at the university in Hammond. And on November 22, Shaw did have a speaking engagement in San Francisco.

Ferrie kept on talking about a triangulated crossfire. But Russo was now tired and his memory weak. Ferrie drove him home that night.

When Sciambra showed Russo a photo of Clay Shaw, he immediately identified him as Clem Bertrand. When shown photos of Oswald, Russo could not positively identify him. But when artists drew in renditions with whiskers, Russo made a positive ID.[50]

Garrison now had a sufficient case to go forward. Russo was his eyewitness to the planning stage of the assassination. But not satisfied with Russo's memory, he decided to subject him to the tests of hypnosis and the so-called truth serum, Sodium Pentothal®, tests that are not allowed in court but which prosecutors often use to check and corroborate testimony. Dr. Nicholas Chetta, the Orleans Parish Coroner, administered the Sodium Pentothal®. Dr. Esmond Fatter, an expert in hypnosis and memory, coordinated the questioning.

The story held up to Garrison's satisfaction, and the case seemed solid. Here, for the first time, was a plausible alternative to the sham assembled by the Warren Commission. A case that included the classic elements of assassination, elements abundantly lacking in Oswald's instance: motive, means, and opportunity. A group at the operational level—the Cuban exiles—with real reasons to want Kennedy dead. A group at the organizational level—the CIA—with resources and experience to plan and execute such an operation. Both had access to the kind of marksmen necessary to pull off the lethal, military-style ambush in Dealey Plaza. In this scheme, the conflicting earwitness testimony in Dealey Plaza made sense, as did the Zapruder film. From this perspective, Oswald's odd associations with people like DeMohrenschildt and Ferrie fit in. So did the call from "Bertrand," and Ruby's final, culminating murder.

Garrison felt he had a case. He had enough to go to a preliminary hearing, to get an indictment. Three years of questions would now be silenced. The critics, like himself, would now be vindicated.

But Jim Garrison did not know that this was as good as it was going to get. This was the peak of his inquiry. From this point on, his investigation would be a long toboggan slide toward ruination. The seeds of destruction had already been sown.

10

Inferno

The date Garrison's investigation began to collapse can easily be fixed: February 17, 1967. On that day, the *New Orleans States-Item* published a story headlined, "DA Here Launches Full JFK Death Plot Probe," by a young reporter, Rosemary James.[1] The story described how Garrison had funded his secret investigation through judicially approved vouchers from his fines and fees account. The vouchers included trips to Florida, Washington, and Texas. James described this as "pouring out-of-the-ordinary sums of money into a probe of a possible assassination plot." Since the probe had been secret, a fact that James treated as scandalous, there was no indication of what the DA and his small staff had achieved with the minuscule $8,000 expenditure.

Rosemary James maintained that she had shown the story to the DA before publication and he had read part of it before responding with a "No comment." When Garrison was told of this, he said, "Anyone who says I saw that story in advance is a liar."[2] And his response to the newspaper and its reporter—locking them out of a press conference—would surely indicate his anger at the disclosure. James never revealed what had provoked her to begin looking through the vouchers. She later remarked in a book that there were rumors around town that Garrison was working on something big. She never got more specific than that. For good reason. There is strong evidence that the leak came from inside Garrison's office and that David Ferrie knew it was coming.[3]

Ferrie had been placed under surveillance by Garrison in

late 1966, and cameras had been fixed outside his apartment
to record his comings and goings. A change had come over
Ferrie. Two changes, to be exact. The first had come right
after the assassination. In late November 1963, Ferrie dropped
out of sight for a while and seemed directionless. He quit his
job with Banister and the two parted ways. This may have
been because he was the only one of the group to be questioned by the FBI or mentioned in the Warren Commission
documents. A friend, Raymond Broshears, said in a Los
Angeles TV interview with Stan Bohrman that Ferrie actually
confessed the plot to him in one of the erratic moods that then
began to consume him, and which he tried to combat with
pills and alcohol.[4] He stated that his function was to fly the
assassins from Houston to South America. From there, they
would fly to South Africa, which had no extradition treaty
with the U.S. (Interestingly, Johannesburg is where the CIA
front, Permindex, co-directed by Shaw, had been recently
relocated, following its expulsion from Italy.)

And Ferrie's behavior became even more extreme after
Garrison reopened his inquiry in late 1966. He had become
an emotional wreck, existing on coffee, cigarettes, and tran-
quilizers. His behavior toward Garrison was mercurial.
Sometimes he would call and ask how the investigation was
proceeding. Other times, he would tell him that he was now
a marked man. But after Ferrie read that he would be the first
conspirator indicted, he decided to fight back through the
media. He leaked the story about his involvement in the probe
to several reporters, and, the day the story broke, Ferrie
began to denounce Garrison to any reporter who would listen.
He called the inquiry a "big joke," and said that he had been
tagged "as the getaway pilot in a wild plot" to kill the
President.[5] Ferrie seemed to be doing a good job in promoting his cause and deflating Garrison. *Washington Post* national security reporter George Lardner, Jr., who to this
day—especially in the controversy over Stone's *JFK*—rabidly berates Garrison, referred to Ferrie as "an intelligent,

well-versed guy on a broad range of subjects."[6] Lardner did not seem to realize that he was saying just what Ferrie needed him to say.[7]

Unfortunately, Garrison played right into Ferrie's hands. The day the story broke, Garrison stayed silent. The next day, when New Orleans became a seething cauldron of publicity and reporters, he evaded reporters by using a back entrance to his office. There he read Ferrie's comments and an editorial criticizing him for spending the $8,000 and implying he was using it for vacation trips for his staff and to get national publicity.[8] Garrison was highly offended by these remarks because he sincerely believed in his case and devoted so much of his own time to pursuing it. So, smarting from the editorial, Garrison began to make statements that were, at best, ill-advised and, at worst, inflammatory:[9]

My staff and I solved the case weeks ago. I wouldn't say this if I didn't have *evidence beyond a shadow of a doubt.* We know the key individuals, the cities involved and how it was done....

We are building a case and I might add, it's a case *we will not lose,* and anyone who wants to bet against us is invited to. But they will be disappointed.

There will be arrests, charges will be filed, and on the basis of these charges, *convictions will be obtained.*

We solved the assassination.... We're working out details of evidence which will probably take months. We *know* that we are going to be able to *arrest* every person involved—at least every person who is still living. [Emphases added.]

From his own perspective, these quotes were justified. Garrison had figured out the general design of the plot, and some of the people and places that were involved. But it was a major mistake to issue these sweeping statements. First, his investigation had been exposed before it was finished, as some of the quotes indicate. Also, the collecting of evidence was by no means complete. Nor had Ferrie yet been indicted, or even called before a grand jury to testify. And equally, if not most importantly, this was the first time Garrison had been exposed to worldwide media attention. He had no experience in this arena and no advisers to help him. His candor, his way with words, his predilection for hyperbole, which may have worked locally, all played into the worst aspects of global pack journalism: sensationalism and caricature. He was setting himself up for a fall. A conscious campaign by selected journalists to derail and discredit his case was gearing up.[10]

Ferrie's attempt to derail the probe went beyond throwing the press in Garrison's path. Before alerting the media, Ferrie had made a call to a long-time criminal named Ed Whalen, asking him for a meeting in New Orleans.[11] There, Ferrie promised him a big payoff for a job and safe passage out of New Orleans after performing it. The next night, they met at a bar, and Ferrie brought a friend named Clem Bertrand. As with Perry Russo, Whalen's later description of Bertrand matched that of Clay Shaw. The trio went to Ferrie's apartment, where Ferrie advanced a proposition: he and Bertrand wanted Whalen to perform a murder for $25,000, ten up front and fifteen afterwards. Afterwards, Bertrand would secure him a passport, and Ferrie would fly him to Mexico. They did not give him the name of the man they wanted rubbed out. They only said he was a witness in an upcoming case, someone who could put them behind bars. Over the course of two further meetings, however, Ferrie revealed that the man they wanted eliminated was Jim Garrison. Whalen did not recognize the name, but when Ferrie told him he was the local District Attorney, Whalen grew cool to the offer.

At Shaw's home, the pair again tried to convince Whalen

to take the contract; Whalen still refused. Shortly thereafter, Dean Andrews arrived and spoke privately with Shaw. Andrews left, and Ferrie and Shaw made one last appeal, promising money and aid to Whalen's polio-stricken daughter. When they told him that Garrison's charge would be plotting to kill the President, Whalen thought they were making a desperate grab at him. He insisted he would not kill a DA and left.[12]

It was September 1967, when Whalen went to Garrison and told his tale. By then, it was clear that Ferrie's attempt to recruit Whalen had been a last, desperate act by a crumbling man. On February 22, 1967, the same day Garrison had decided to call him before the grand jury, David Ferrie was found dead.[13]

Ferrie's death was as strange as his life. His body was found naked on his living room sofa; a sheet was pulled over his head. Two *typed* suicide notes were found. The table next to his body was strewn with medicine bottles, several of them empty. Coroner Nicholas Chetta had had the body moved out quickly, before Garrison and his staff arrived. Garrison took

Coroner's Office removing the body of David Ferrie from his home, February 22, 1967.

Orleans Parish Coroner,
Dr. Nicholas Chetta,
shows newsmen a photo
of David Ferrie's brain, at
a February 28, 1967, press
conference to announce
that Ferrie died of
natural causes.

some of the medicine bottles in order to check them out. On February 28, Chetta ruled that Ferrie had died of natural causes, specifically, an aneurism or broken blood vessel in the brain.

Garrison had his doubts, especially in light of the two typed suicide notes. He had Proloid®, one of the drugs found in the apartment, analyzed and discovered that with Ferrie's hypertension, this drug could cause death by brain aneurism without a trace.[14]

There are other mysteries beyond the two suicide notes and the deadly drugs. *Washington Post* reporter George Lardner, Jr., claims he was with Ferrie until 4 a.m., a time the coroner insisted was "absolutely the latest possible time of death." If Lardner was not involved—and there is no reason to believe he was—this means that Ferrie must have died by whatever means within minutes of Lardner's departure.[15] This would suggest that, if Ferrie was murdered, the killers were waiting for Lardner to leave. The youth who found Ferrie claimed he "didn't know Ferrie" and "just happened to wander in."[16] This is strange, considering that Ferrie's apartment was on the second floor.

Even more compelling are photographs from Ferrie's autopsy, recently disclosed by Dr. Chetta's successor, Dr. Frank Minyard.[17] The photos reveal contusions on the inside of Ferrie's mouth and gums, which suggest that his mouth was forced shut, perhaps to make him swallow something against his will. Ferrie's death remains a mystery.[18]

Garrison felt pity for Ferrie, whom he considered a genuinely brilliant man whose personality was warped by his appearance and twisted emotions. But whatever his feelings about Ferrie's death, it was a staggering body blow to the inquiry. Commenting to the press, the DA again characterized his feelings in the overstated, colorful language that would come to plague him:[19]

> [David Ferrie] was a man who, in my judgment, was one of history's most important individuals. Mr. Ferrie was one of those individuals I had in mind when I said there would be arrests shortly. We had reached a decision to arrest him next week. Apparently we waited too long.

With Ferrie gone, Garrison faced a grim decision: should he move against Clay Shaw now or wait to build a stronger case? Ferrie had been the link to Shaw. Without him, the case would be much more difficult to prove. On the other hand, suspects in this case had a strange way of dying unexpectedly. Garrison decided he could not wait. On March 1, 1967, at 5:30 p.m., Garrison issued an arrest warrant for Clay Shaw and a search warrant for his home in the French Quarter. When Garrison's investigators came back from Shaw's house, they had with them some strange artifacts: two large hooks that had been screwed to the ceiling of Shaw's bedroom, five whips, several lengths of chain, a black hood, a webbed hat, and a cape. Shaw passed this off as Mardi Gras attire.[20]

Explanations aside, it was clear that the 54-year-old bachelor was into the nether regions of sado-masochist activity. In fact, Shaw's position as director of the International Trade Mart had caused him to come under the all-seeing eyes of J. Edgar Hoover. Hoover had in his Bureau files a report by an informant who stated that his homosexual relations with Shaw included sadism and masochism.[21] It all explained Shaw's use of Andrews to defend the "gay Mexicanos." It accounted for his use of an alias. Shaw's homosexuality may also have provided a bond between the cool, wealthy, well-mannered Shaw and the excitable, rootless, eccentric Ferrie, a bond beyond their politics, and (as later revealed) their Agency ties.

The search of Shaw's home turned up another interesting tidbit. In his address book, there appeared the following entry:

Lee Odom
P.O. Box 19106
Dallas, Texas

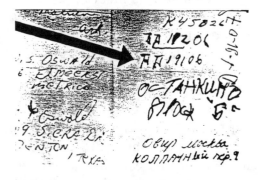

The pages of Shaw's diary, top, and Oswald's notebook, bottom, both with the number 19106.

Garrison was aware that this same post office box number also appeared in Lee Oswald's address book.[22] Shaw's lawyers later produced a man named Lee Odom who said he was from Dallas. The box number, he said, was that of a company he once worked for, and that he had tried to contact Shaw about "promoting a bullfight" in New Orleans. To Garrison, this was all reminiscent of Ferrie's story about setting off for Texas to ice skate and hunt geese in a lightning storm.

But there was another entry in Shaw's book that was even more interesting. Although the entire book listed addresses and phone numbers, on one otherwise blank page were scrawled the two abbreviations "Oct." and "Nov." and next to these, the word "Dallas."[23]

On March 14, 1967, Garrison initiated a preliminary hearing against Shaw. This is a process usually requested by the

Clay Shaw entering his home at 1313 Dauphine Street, March 15, 1967, before attending the second day of his preliminary hearing.

defense, because it requires the DA to present a *prima facie* case to a judge or panel of judges. Prosecutors do not normally request it because, at such a hearing, the defense can cross-examine witnesses, which they cannot do in a grand jury proceeding.

At the hearing, Garrison presented Perry Russo and Vernon Bundy, a drug addict who testified to seeing Shaw meet with Oswald on the shores of Lake Pontchartrain and pass him money. Russo and Bundy held up well under defense cross-examination, and the three-judge panel held that there was enough evidence to charge Shaw with conspiracy to murder John F. Kennedy. Then, Garrison took his case to a grand jury, and it issued the indictment.

Garrison made a tactical error in requesting the preliminary hearing. This was a public proceeding, and now the media were able to see Shaw and his lawyers in court. Shaw presented a stark contrast to his two accusers. His appearance was almost regal; his suave, genteel, mild-mannered personality reinforced this image. After the shock of the preliminary hearing wore off, Shaw's attorneys—F. Irvin Dymond, Edward Wegmann, Bill Wegmann, and Sal Panzeca—began to use this image blatantly, to cultivate the press and curry favor in the news stories. After the preliminary hearing, for example, they held a brunch at which Shaw and his attorneys fielded questions.[24] Shaw was careful not to attack Garrison personally. He just expressed puzzlement at his actions, comparing himself to a Kafka character, an innocent man hounded, for unknown reasons, by the State. Shaw's baffled, victimized posture advanced his lawyers' strategy of placing Shaw above the battle. How could anyone believe that such a pillar of the community could be involved in *any* crime, let alone such a dastardly one? Whom would *you* believe, an insurance salesman and a drug addict, or an international businessman and playwright? Shaw was cast perfectly for the part.

In this effort, Shaw was aided by many prominent friends and acquaintances in the upper echelons of New Orleans society. The motive was obvious. They did not wish to see their city tarred with the conviction of one of its leading lights for conspiracy to murder President Kennedy. Many luminaries in the local media came over to Shaw's camp, including local journalists David and Patricia Chandler and eventually Rosemary James.

The national and international media were met, wined, and dined by the wealthy New Orleans philanthropists, Edith and Edgar Stern. Edith Stern was the daughter of Julius Rosenwald, one of the founders of Sears, Roebuck and Company. She and her husband owned WDSU, the local NBC affiliate, and Shaw attended social functions at their estate. (In the late 1960s, the Stern Family Fund was a major backer of the fight against the proposed Vieux Carré Riverfront Expressway. Shaw was also active in that battle, as one of the promoters of the restoration of the French Quarter.) The Sterns extended their hospitality to sympathetic reporters, who attended their tony parties and dinners.

Both tactics, Shaw's gentle but superior attitude and the courting of print and electronic journalists both local and national, succeeded resoundingly. Taking in the media was almost too easy. Very soon there was an astonishing role reversal: Garrison became the accused.

First, some of the major daily newspapers, including the *New York Times*, the *New York Post*, and the *Los Angeles Times*, began to express doubts about the validity of Garrison's case.[25] Then, in May, there was a double-barreled media attack.

First, in the May 6, 1967, issue of the *Saturday Evening Post*, James Phelan wrote an article entitled "Rush to Judgment in New Orleans." From the title (borrowed from Mark Lane's book on the Warren Commission) on to the last sentence, the article was a one-sided attack on almost every aspect of Garrison's probe—written in a belittling, amused style that revealed the author's supercilious attitude toward the subject. Garrison, about whom Phelan had written a favorable piece in 1963, was pictured as an egocentric megalomaniac whom Phelan called a "one-man Warren Commission."[26]

The bias of Phelan's phrase was enough to expose the distorting lens of the author's analysis. Unlike the Commission's, Garrison's investigation had to be carried out within the strict rules of our legal system. He had to investigate and depose suspects, and find and secure evidence admissible in court. He had to secure indictments from a grand jury, and test his case in an adversarial procedure, all to be decided by a jury selected by both sides. None of these strictures had applied to the Warren Commission. They had investigated no one but Oswald. A great deal of their evidence was created, manipulated, or, when exculpatory of Oswald, ignored. There was no grand jury proceeding. Much of their testimony—like that of Marina Oswald—was not acceptable in court. Oswald was allowed no defense. And, of course, the Commission was its own jury.

Phelan's five-page article was filled with snide characterizations, half-truths, and innuendo. But he saved his harshest blast for the end. He wrote that when assistant DA Sciambra first interviewed Perry Russo, his notes made no mention of the party at Ferrie's. Phelan then suggested that all of Russo's testimony at the preliminary hearing had been pumped into him under drugs and hypnosis by Dr. Chetta and Dr. Fatter. It did not matter to Phelan that both Russo and Sciambra denied this to his face before he went to press. Nor that Russo had talked about the fateful party at Ferrie's to the Baton Rouge press and television *before* Sciambra had ever met with him.[27] Or that neither Dr. Fatter nor Dr. Chetta would sacrifice his reputation or career for Garrison (as Chetta had clearly shown during his coroner's report calling Ferrie's death "natural"). And, of course, Garrison's fair record, his writings on the rights of defendants, and his choice of a preliminary hearing were completely ignored.

Phelan had developed an animus toward the DA of which this would be only the first manifestation. He and his friend Hugh Aynesworth would cooperate in trying to torpedo Garrison and his case throughout the two-year interlude between the preliminary hearing and the Shaw trial. Aynesworth had been a reporter for the *Dallas Morning News* at the time of the assassination. Like so many other journalists, Aynesworth had bought into the Warren Report and had previously attacked Mark Lane for criticizing it.[28]

Aynesworth's article appeared nine days after Phelan's. On May 15, 1967, *Newsweek* published his "J.F.K. Conspiracy," the most violent attack on Garrison's investigation thus far. The first two sentences set the tone for what followed: "Jim Garrison is right. There has been a conspiracy in New Orleans—but it is a plot of Garrison's own making."[29] The piece made numerous bizarre accusations against Garrison: that the investigation had financially ruined several men; that the DA's office had offered a witness $3,000 and a job to give false testimony; that Garrison's staff had threatened to murder a witness; that Garrison himself had threatened a man who tried to talk him out of his probe; that Russo had testified at the preliminary hearing under post-hypnotic suggestion; that Garrison was holding the citizenry of New Orleans in terror in order to manufacture more headlines; and that Garrison's theory of the assassination had gone through so many changes that his conspirator was now a composite of "Oswald, homosexual, rightwing extremist, FBI agent, Cosa Nostra hood, CIA operative and Russian double-agent."[30]

That a magazine like *Newsweek* would print such a lurid piece shows how far in just two months the media had tilted toward protecting the government against the DA. It also foretells the extreme divisions the case would engender. This all-out campaign would match any modern national political media campaign in intensity.

The charges in the article were beneath comment, in fact, as we shall see, sheer conscious disinformation,[31] the kind which the witty Garrison would later answer with, "Well, I've stopped beating my wife."[32] In fact, the charges were not meant to be answered; they were designed to destroy Garrison. Both authors had already passed judgment on the case a full two years before the trial. What is surprising is that a mainstream newsmagazine like *Newsweek* printed such a blatantly biased attack.[33]

But this was just the first of many lows to which both *Newsweek* and *Time* would sink over the next year. Consider some of the titles that followed:

"Bourbon Street Rococo"—*Time*, March 3, 1967
"Carnival in New Orleans"—*Newsweek*, March 6, 1967
"Something of a Shambles"—*Time*, June 30, 1967
"Law Unto Himself"—*Newsweek*, January 8, 1968
"Jolly Green Giant in Wonderland"—*Time*, August 2, 1968

Media attacks got so out of control that Garrison's staff collected the most purple ones and pinned them to the bulletin board for laughs.[34]

But the worst was yet to come. In the spring of 1967, NBC television decided to do a documentary on the case.[35] The producer was Walter Sheridan, an ex-FBI man[36] who had been a prosecutor under Bobby Kennedy in his pursuit of James Hoffa. Sheridan and his crew never bothered to interview Garrison or any of his assistants for on-camera quotes or even for background material. They talked to Perry Russo, but the subject was not Dave Ferrie. They talked to Gordon Novel's ex-wife, but the subject was not Mr. Novel. They talked to Bill Gurvich, a former aide to Garrison, but they did not ask him what evidence he had developed earlier for the DA. The target of all these interviews was not the Kennedy assassination but Jim Garrison.

The program aired on June 19, 1967. The "White Paper" began with commentator Frank McGee saying, "We have no right to prejudge Jim Garrison's case.... But let us legitimately examine his record of the Kennedy probe up to now." Very quickly, it became clear that this TV special would not only prejudge the case, but would rehash the Phelan-Aynesworth charges against it. In fact, both had cooperated in its making.[37]

Some of the people interviewed included Dean Andrews; John Cancler, a convicted burglar; Miguel Torres, another convicted burglar; Fred Leemans, a Turkish bath owner; and Phelan himself.

This motley crew repeated the same laundry list of allegations against Garrison and his office: bribing witnesses, falsifying and forcing testimony, suborning perjury, and harassing innocent men. The program was shot and edited to convey the illusion that the people interviewed were on a witness stand, testifying in court against the accused, in this case, Garrison. But funny things happened when Garrison called these same men to testify in a real proceeding, under oath, and to tell the grand jury about this new and critical information. Andrews was convicted of perjury; Cancler and Torres took the Fifth Amendment against self-incrimination, were cited for contempt, and had time added to their sentences; Phelan failed to appear, even though Sciambra offered to pay his expenses; and Walter Sheridan, the show's producer, skipped town. When Leemans was contacted by the *New York Times*, he refused to expand on his appearance, saying that he had already sold an exclusive story to the Associated Press.[38]

It later transpired that Phelan and Sheridan had visited Perry Russo four times to ask for his cooperation in demolishing Garrison's case.[39] In return, they promised to set him up in California, protect his job, get him an attorney, and guarantee that Garrison could never have him extradited back to Louisiana. Because Russo refused to cooperate, the docu-

Walter
Sheridan, left,
leaving a
hearing, July
27, 1967, at
which the
presiding judge
ruled he must
appear before
the Grand Jury
and denied his
request that
Garrison not be
permitted to
advise the
Grand Jury.

mentary did the next best thing: it stated that both he and
Bundy flunked their polygraph tests. Like nearly every other
statement on this program, this claim was hotly denied by
Garrison. He even offered to resign if it were proved true.[40]
   It never was.

Was there a deeper reason for the ferocity of these attacks?
One that went further than just disagreement with Garrison
or empathy for Shaw? In Aynesworth's case the hidden motives seem clear. At the time of the assassination he was a
conservative reporter at the *Dallas Morning News*.[41] He reported to the Warren Commission and received bits of information in return. Not long after the assassination he was
involved in the sale of Oswald's diary to the *News* for
$50,000 and he became a close associate of Marina Oswald
for about a month. He once told an interviewer that he was
the first to hear of the Tippit murder and was in one of the
first cars to arrive at the scene. He said he heard of it at 1:00
p.m. and arrived at 1:05.[42] But, as we have seen, Tippit was
not killed until 1:07 at the earliest. As Joachim Joesten tells
it, Aynesworth arrived in a police car at both the scene of the

Tippit murder and the theater where Oswald was arrested, revealing his close police ties. But he betrayed those ties by copying purloined documents from the police archives for Mark Lane. Then he attacked Lane's work. Before writing the May 15 *Newsweek* column, Aynesworth had been in public relations. His byline had never before appeared in that magazine. He did not belong to its regular staff.

An opportunist? Probably. But it goes further than that. He once told a reporter for Dallas PBS affiliate KERA:[43]

I'm not saying there wasn't a conspiracy.... I know most people in this country believe there was a conspiracy. I just refuse to accept it and that's my life's work.

And he acted on those objective journalistic impulses. But not just for newsmagazines. Aynesworth was an informant for both J. Edgar Hoover and Lyndon Johnson. In a document obtained through the Freedom of Information Act by researcher Gary Mack from the Lyndon B. Johnson Library, Aynesworth reveals his intent with regard to Garrison in the following telegram to Johnson's Press Secretary, George Christian, at the White House. Attached to a draft of his upcoming article, it reads in full:[44]

Here is the rough draft of the story we discussed this morning. It will be changed in a minor way, but for the most part will be just this.

The story will break late Sunday via the wire services. Naturally, the strength and seriousness of it will evoke considerable reaction. I thought the President might be interested in this advance version.

I am not offering this for comment of any kind, nor a check of the validity of any part. Simply, it's FYI....

Naturally, I would expect this to go no further.

My interest in informing government officials of each step along the way is because of my intimate knowledge of what Jim Garrison is planning. The subpoena of two FBI agents Saturday (today) is another step in his plan to make it seem that the FBI and CIA are involved in the JFK "plot." He is hell-bent on involving several high officials, is considering embarrassing others. In his devious scheme he can—and probably will—do untold damage to this nation's image throughout the world.

I am well aware that Garrison wants the government to defy him in some manner or to step in to pressure a halt to his "probe," but, of course, this should not happen … for that is exactly what Garrison wants.

I intend to make a complete report of my knowledge available to the FBI, as I have done in the past.

Regards,

Hugh Aynesworth

James Phelan managed to hide his deep-seated prejudices until 1982. In his book *Scandals, Scamps and Scoundrels* he devoted a chapter to the Shaw trial. Writing thirteen years after the verdict, years after both the Church Committee revelations about the CIA and the House Select Committee on Assassinations conclusion that there was a 95 percent probability of a conspiracy to kill JFK, Phelan had not changed: Garrison's case is specious; Shaw is as "near to a true hero as any man I have encountered";[45] Garrison is implicated as the cause of Shaw's death;[46] as the Warren Report states, Oswald was a communist.[47] Phelan believes the FBI investigations of both Ferrie and Shaw were complete;[48] and even after the exposure of Shaw's double life, he still questions whether or not Shaw used an alias.[49] For Phelan, nothing had happened, no new information had come to light, in the fifteen years between the publication of his piece in the *Saturday Evening Post* and the publication of his book. So much for the canons of impartial, objective "investigative" journalism.[50]

Something Phelan does not reveal in his book is that when Garrison gave him the Sciambra memorandum in Las Vegas, he took it to Robert Maheu's office to photocopy. Maheu, of course, was the liaison between the CIA and the Mob in the earlier Castro murder plots, the exposure of which Garrison's investigation threatened. Phelan, who closely followed Howard Hughes's career, had a long and enduring friendship with Maheu, Hughes's top assistant. Maheu also knew Martin Ackerman, president of Curtis Publishing, which owned the *Saturday Evening Post*, the magazine that published Phelan's story.[51]

And what of Walter Sheridan? The conventional wisdom places him as a former FBI man who went to Bobby Kennedy's Justice Department, where the Attorney General gave him more or less carte blanche over the "Get Hoffa" unit.[52] That summary is superficially accurate, but the picture it paints is both narrow and incomplete.

Sheridan's ties to the intelligence community, *beyond the FBI*, were wide, deep, and complex. He himself said that, like Guy Banister, he had been with the Office of Naval Intelligence.[53] Then, *after* he left the Bureau, Sheridan moved over to the National Security Agency.[54] This was a super-secret body created by Truman in 1952 both to protect domestic codes and communications and to gather intelligence through cracking foreign codes. It was so clandestine that, for a time, the government attempted to deny its existence.

It was after his service at the NSA that Sheridan joined forces with RFK. The intelligence connections he garnered there served Sheridan well in his new position. Both he and the AG were on shaky ground with Hoover—Sheridan for quitting the Bureau and RFK for encroaching on the Director's turf.[55] As a result, Hoover extended minimal help to the Hoffa effort. Also, Hoffa was so elusive that the tactics the pair used in his pursuit were legally questionable. They needed tough, experienced, wily veterans to get a solid indictment of the Teamsters' chief. Therefore, Sheridan and

Kennedy availed themselves of another intelligence unit at their disposal.

In 1961, they began farming out the brunt of their investigatory work to a private proprietary, seemingly created for their own purposes. The company was International Investigators Incorporated[56] (nicknamed "Three Eyes"). According to a Senate investigator, it was "owned lock, stock, and barrel by the CIA."[57] Two of the original principals, George Miller and George Ryan, were, like Banister, former G-men who later went to work for CIA cover outfits.[58] According to another source, not only was Sheridan the liaison to Three Eyes, he "disposed over the personnel and currency of whole units of the Central Intelligence Agency out of the White House."[59] By 1965, when the investigatory phase of the Hoffa case was complete, Three Eyes was taken over by two former CIA officers.[60] One of them, Beurt Ser Vaas, later purchased the *Saturday Evening Post.*[61]

This relates to another of Sheridan's skills, one that he honed to a needle-point in his campaign against Garrison— the use of media assets. Hoffa always maintained that, because they could not beat him in court, Kennedy and Sheridan would try to win their case in the press.[62] As Jim Hougan pointed out, the pair assiduously cultivated a series of media contacts with whom they planted material for lurid exposés of Hoffa and his union. Two of the more cooperative contacts were Time-Life and NBC.[63] As we have noted, the former printed many pejorative articles about Garrison's inquiry. The latter sponsored Sheridan's special. Given his experience, connections, and influence, Sheridan, it is safe to assume, was the in-house ringleader and overall coordinator of the national media campaign that crested in the summer and fall of 1967, leaving Garrison's credibility and reputation permanently scarred.

The sustained media attack was not just jackal journalism. For Garrison—and the public's right to know—it went deeper than that. As in political campaigns, the person who attacks first has the advantage. The other is forced on the defensive and has to waste precious time denying absurd accusations. In Garrison's case, the story he had to relate was complex, long, and detailed and did not lend itself to TV soundbites as does political sniping. It is no coincidence that Garrison's most compelling appearance was in the long *Playboy* interview in October of 1967. Allowed the freedom of dialogue, the DA gave a tour-de-force performance—penetrating, comprehensive, masterful in detail, sardonically humorous about himself and his critics. But what chance did he have against the multinational forces of the networks, the newsweeklies, and the giant newspapers?

Garrison was also somewhat restricted because Edward Haggerty, the trial judge, limited his pre-trial comments in public in order not to prejudice the case, a stricture Garrison referred to often in the *Playboy* interview.[64] Sheridan, however, was not limited by any such order, and, since he was working with Shaw's lawyers, he could comment at will on the evidence in the upcoming trial.

As we can see in retrospect, Rosemary James's disclosure of the probe was an unmitigated debacle for Garrison. As long as he was working in secret, as long as his discoveries and the gravity of their implications could only be spread by word of mouth, Garrison had a fair chance of succeeding, because the obstacles thrown in his path would be limited. For instance, Gordon Novel had actually tried to infiltrate Garrison's probe very early on, even before the James disclosures.[65] And then he was hired as a consultant to the NBC show on February 1.[66] The Agency was working in tandem with the media to torpedo the inquiry.

There were more insidious relationships. Phelan tried to convince Russo and other witnesses that Shaw-Bertrand was really the dead Banister.[67] Shaw's legal team supplied information for the NBC special.[68] Then, when Garrison requested equal time to reply to the unfair NBC attack, Shaw's attor-

neys tried to stop Garrison's petition.[69] Since Garrison's tale
was as complex as it was shocking, it was conducive to two
types of unfavorable coverage: on the one hand, from reporters with biases toward the intelligence community, and on
the other, from simply lazy and incompetent journalists, as
represented by the *Time* and *Newsweek* articles listed above.
Whatever the reason, Rosemary James's exposé provided an
opening for those who wished to trash Garrison and hide the
truth about the crime from the American public. After February 17, 1967, a pall was cast over the investigation that the
DA could never dispel.

There were some liberal-left publications that came to
Garrison's defense, *e.g.*, *Ramparts*, the *New York Review of
Books*, and *The New Republic*.[70] Of course, the combined
circulation of those three magazines was about one-thirtieth
that of just *Newsweek*. Garrison tried to press the case himself on July 15, 1967, by appearing on a 30-minute "equal-
time spot" untimately granted him by the FCC to answer the
hour-long NBC show. After this he appeared on TV's "Issues
and Answers" and, on January 31, 1968, for forty-five minutes on Johnny Carson's "The Tonight Show." It was all too
little, too late. Garrison had been mortally wounded. As we
shall see, the public bloodletting would spill over into the
courtroom.

11

The DA Stumbles

Under the impact of the May-June media blitz, Garrison had fallen from a position of strength in early February of 1967, to a position of weakness by summer. The press disclosure of his secret investigation and the death of his prime suspect, David Ferrie, had been twin disasters. But some of his problems had been of his own making. Not arresting Ferrie earlier, was a key error. In fact, Garrison's staff had been friendly with the pilot up to the day of his death. When Ferrie's behavior became erratic and manic, Garrison's assistants arranged for a room for him at the Fountainbleau Motel.[1] Had they taken him into custody, the entire case might have turned out differently.

Garrison's overstated remarks to the international press corps also served as ammunition to be shot back at him later. His precautions in verifying witnesses' testimony with the use of polygraphs, Sodium Pentothal®, and hypnosis were successfully distorted as "mind control" by his attackers, and were much too exotic for the public to understand.

It has become a commonplace of political discourse today that perception is reality. In 1967, the media image of Jim Garrison was a case study in this phenomenon. By the fall of that year, the media attacks increased to the point where *Life* magazine, which had earlier advocated a new investigation and sought to cooperate with the DA, was accusing him of ties with the Mafia.[2]

But, the press coverage notwithstanding, Garrison had done fairly well in spite of his missteps. He had convicted

Dean Andrews of perjury for reversing his Warren Commission testimony and for denying that a Clay Bertrand existed
or that he knew who he was.[3] He had won the preliminary
hearing in the Clay Shaw case and had obtained an indictment. He had discredited Aynesworth's May 15 *Newsweek*
story by obtaining a retraction from Alvin Beaubeouf, who
Aynesworth said had been bribed and intimidated by Garrison's staff. In fact, a subsequent police investigation demonstrated that a tape recording supposedly proving the bribery
attempts had been doctored.[4] He had secured contempt citations against two of the witnesses who appeared on the NBC
show, and faced down Sheridan and Phelan by challenging
them in court, the former for attempted bribery of witnesses.

Internationally, Garrison's probe received considerable
support. But at home, Garrison's victories were never trum-
peted as conspicuously as were the charges against him or his
reversals. (His gains might get local coverage, but negative
attacks were broadcast nationally.) Sometimes his victories
were not even published. When one of the DA's attackers was
forced to recant an accusation, Garrison wryly commented:
"You might have seen that on page 46 of the *New York Times*,
right next to ship departures."[5] In the arena of public opinion,
Garrison himself became the issue, instead of his investigation. The assassination became incidental, if mentioned at
all.[6] The defenders of the Warren Report, like Aynesworth
and former commissioners and staff, all joined in the sound
and fury to make Garrison a pariah in official circles. And
the establishment position, though on tottering legs, still had
potent defenders whose job was to see that the Warren Report
died an honorable death after a decent interval, and not at the
hands of a half-baked New Orleans DA.

One point man for the Johnson Administration in damaging
Garrison's case was Ramsey Clark.[7] In March of 1967, right
after his confirmation as Attorney General by the Senate
Judiciary Committee, Clark made an extraordinary intervention into the case: he told a group of reporters Garrison's case

was baseless. The FBI, he said, had already investigated Shaw in 1963 and found no connection between him and the events in Dallas. When pressed on this, Clark insisted that Shaw had been checked out and cleared.[8]

But in his haste to discredit Garrison, Clark had slipped. The obvious question, though not pursued by the Washington press corps, was *why* back in 1963 the upstanding citizen Shaw had been investigated concerning the assassination *at all*. Shaw and his lawyers realized the implication of Clark's gaffe even if the Attorney General did not. When one of Shaw's attorneys, Edward F. Wegmann, requested a clarification of Clark's statement, a Clark subordinate tried to control the damage by asserting that the original statement was without foundation: "The Attorney General has since determined that this was erroneous. Nothing arose indicating a need to investigate Mr. Shaw."[9]

Things got even worse for Clark. The same day he made his original announcement, a *New York Times* reporter, Robert Semple, wrote that the Justice Department was convinced that "Mr. Bertrand and Mr. Shaw were the same man."[10] Semple had gone to the National Archives seeking Warren Commission references to Clay Shaw. Finding zero, he was told that the Justice Department believed that Ber-

Attorney General Ramsey Clark, center, with J. Edgar Hoover, left, and President Johnson, at the White House, May 1968.

trand and Shaw were actually the same man, and that this belief was the basis for the Attorney General's assertion.

Clark had come to praise Shaw but instead had implicated him. However, Clark was not through trying to aid Shaw and sandbag Garrison. The AG would have a surprise for the DA at the upcoming trial.

Buried in those same National Archives files was an equally interesting episode recorded by the Secret Service. On November 24, 1963, Marina Oswald, who was not yet an American citizen, was spirited away by the authorities.[11] It was the beginning of a three-month seclusion after which she became the prime witness against her late husband. A report of the interview conducted that day was unearthed by Commission critic Harold Weisberg. One of the questions asked Marina was, "Do you know a Mr. David Farry?"[12] She replied in the negative.

There is no "David Farry" in the name indices of the Commission exhibits and testimony. But there is a David

Marina Oswald Porter being
interviewed for a French
television show, 1979.

Ferrie. Given the relentless misspellings of key names throughout all 26 volumes, there seems little doubt that he is the same one referred to in the question. Indeed, in this same memorandum, the name Paine is spelled "Payne." (The Paines housed Marina Oswald on her return to Dallas in September of 1963.[13])

The time frame is critical. The question was posed on November 24. Yet Garrison did not question Ferrie until the next day and only thereafter was he turned over to the FBI.

Were the FBI and the Secret Service already investigating Shaw-Bertrand *and* Ferrie by November 24? If so, why? If not, how did their names get into the record or at least circulated by Justice? Neither Clark nor anyone else ever attempted to answer these disturbing questions that go to the core of the Garrison inquiry. Again Garrison was made the issue, while disturbing questions about the suspicious circumstances surrounding the death of a President became unimportant. Federal officials and the major media were single-minded: they wanted to discredit totally the New Orleans trial before it got started.

Garrison's case was already weakened through the unfortunate deaths of so many people who were either major elements of his conspiracy case, or who had important testimony to contribute about the assassination. Both Guy Banister and Hugh Ward had died in 1964, the former of a heart attack, the latter in a plane crash. Oswald was murdered on national television, and his slayer, Jack Ruby, had died in prison of cancer in January 1967, just after being granted a new trial. Ferrie died the next month.

The same day that Ferrie died, Eladio del Valle, a man who had paid Ferrie for his flights over Cuba, was brutally murdered in Miami. The killers did not leave his survival to chance: del Valle received a bullet through the heart and an axe through the head.[14] Witnesses at Dealey Plaza who could have testified also had a high mortality rate, *e.g.*, S.M. Holland and Lee Bowers, who disagreed with the Warren Report about the direction of the shots. Even famous columnist and TV celebrity Dorothy Kilgallen, the last journalist allowed to interview Ruby, who then professed to a friend to have information that would "blow the lid" off the Kennedy case, died immediately afterwards under mysterious circumstances.[15] Author Penn Jones made a good compilation of the high number of strange deaths in a series of books called *Forgive My Grief.*

As a result of this crescendo of unusual deaths, some witnesses either fled or changed their stories. One, David Lewis, the former Banister employee, left New Orleans rather than testify about the strange goings-on at 544 Camp Street during the summer of 1963.[16] Warren Reynolds, a witness to the Tippit murder who had denied that Oswald was the killer, reversed his story at the Warren Commission—six months after someone shot him through the head and he miraculously survived.[17]

But there was another reason many important witnesses were not available to testify. The media and the federal government had branded Garrison such an eccentric renegade that many governors refused to honor his requests to extradite witnesses back to Louisiana.

For instance, on March 27, 1967, Garrison's office issued a subpoena for Sandra Moffett, the girl Perry Russo said had gone with him to Ferrie's party the night of the assassination discussion. The legal papers were signed by Judge Edward Haggerty, who would preside over the Shaw trial. Moffett had married and moved to Nebraska by this time. She said she was willing to testify, and was scheduled for April. She was sent a check for her travel expenses. But two weeks before she was to arrive, Sandra Moffett had a change of heart. She said she would fight the subpoena. County officials would not attempt to enforce the New Orleans order, which was odd since Nebraska and Louisiana had a full extradition compact at the time, and they then announced that their search for the now missing witness was being abandoned. Moffett had fled to Iowa, a state with no extradition agreement with Louisiana.

Also subpoenaed was Sergio Arcacha Smith, a Cuban exile leader in New Orleans with close ties to David Ferrie. He had played an important role in the Houma arms raid. Through Houma, Arcacha was linked to Gordon Novel. He also had ties to Banister and Ward, who had secured an office for him at 544 Camp Street. By the time Garrison requested his extradition, Arcacha was in Dallas and refused to return to New Orleans. He told Garrison he would be interviewed only if members of the Dallas police were present. His attorney, William Colvin, commented, "Garrison is a man who is power mad! ... [He] used the law like a damn club."[18] Garrison refused the offer, but when he tried to have Arcacha extradited, Texas Governor Connally refused—unless the new Texan was promised immunity from civil and criminal action. This was a condition that no responsible DA could possibly agree to.[19]

Gordon Novel's globetrotting dodging of subpoenas has already been mentioned. Still it should be noted that when

Sergio Arcacha Smith, center, arrested in Dallas, April 3, 1967, on Garrison's extradition warrant. At left is Dallas Deputy Sheriff Buddy Walthers.

Gordon Novel, right, with newsmen after his release on bond in Columbus, Ohio, after his arrest on Garrison's extradition warrant.

Garrison requested his return from Ohio, Governor John Rhodes said he would agree only if Novel got the identical promises that Connally had asked for Arcacha.[20] Novel added some conditions of his own, specifying limited areas he would testify about.[21]

It came as no surprise, therefore, that the federal government refused to permit various potential witnesses to testify. Warren DeBrueys, an FBI agent who had shadowed Oswald in New Orleans and then followed him to Dallas, was subpoenaed. He refused to answer on the ground of executive privilege. Agent Regis Kennedy, who had interviewed Ferrie in New Orleans in 1963, was asked to testify. He also pleaded executive privilege.[22]

These were all potentially crucial witnesses. Moffett could have verified and placed certain people—particularly Shaw —at Ferrie's apartment. Arcacha Smith could have linked Oswald, Ferrie, and Banister to the Camp Street address. Novel could have demonstrated the CIA connections of Ferrie and Arcacha. DeBrueys could have offered testimony on

Oswald's suspected status as an FBI informant. Kennedy might have given some insight into the inner workings of the Bureau's 1963 investigation of Ferrie. Their combined resistance leads to the obvious question: Why? Why would they all *refuse* to testify in Garrison's case, especially if they had nothing to help him?

Garrison also ran into trouble with other key witnesses he needed to use to place the conspiracy in the shadow of the Agency, particularly Richard Case Nagell. Nagell had obviously been shaken by his experience with the plotters and his subsequent harsh prison sentence. His first meeting with Garrison was held, at his demand, in the open in Central Park in New York City.[23] Still, Nagell told Garrison he *would* testify for him at the Shaw trial, and he journeyed to New Orleans for an interview. Garrison was impressed by his memory and wanted to put him on the stand, but Nagell added a condition. He would only say that he worked for "an intelligence agency"; he would not specify which. He was fearful of reprisals both because of his secrecy agreement and because of what he was going to disclose. Garrison realized

FBI Agent
Regis Kennedy
leaving the courtroom,
May 17, 1967.

that no matter how important his testimony or how good a witness he was, the defense would use his refusal to be specific to render his testimony meaningless.[24]

Even some of Garrison's staff began to succumb to the pressure. Capping the media onslaught in June, William Gurvich, a former investigator, loudly "quit" after talking to Walter Sheridan. Posing as Garrison's "chief investigator," Gurvich charged that the inquiry had "no basis in fact."[25] He told CBS that unethical practices were going on in the DA's office and there should be a grand jury inquiry of Garrison. This was odd because in April, Gurvich had told reporters that the office had "a strong conspiracy case" and that Russo was a convincing witness.[26] After Gurvich was in fact called before a grand jury in June, the foreman released a statement saying they found his testimony not to merit further investigation. Later, Gurvich claimed that the DA had ordered the beating of two NBC crew members and a raid on the local FBI office with red pepper guns.[27]

The vicious media attacks of the summer did seem to throw Garrison's once smoothly running office off stride. The staff, which had not lost a major case in five years and never had a conviction reversed on appeal, began to make mistakes. When Garrison tried to subpoena Eugene Brading, the California mob man who had been in Dallas during the assassination, his office was given false information by Loren Hall, a shadowy anti-Castro militant who had lied to the FBI during the Warren Commission investigation.[28] Garrison issued a subpoena for a Eugene Bradley instead of Brading. A Eugene Bradley from California promptly responded that he was neither a rightwing nor leftwing extremist. "I don't belong to a thing and I don't know anything about Garrison or the Kennedy affair."[29]

Later, Garrison himself, rattled by the incessant press antics, began to play their game: he would announce important developments in his investigation to offset the effect of another attack. When Garrison learned that an article critical of his case was about to appear in the *New Yorker*, he announced that a foreign intelligence agency had issued a report that agreed with his findings. Later, however, he was honest enough to admit he had made the announcement as a preemptive measure.[30]

Garrison had an unusual problem in administering his office. Once his probe became public, many of the Warren Commission critics, with whose work Garrison was intimately familiar, flocked to New Orleans, offering to help. Garrison, both shorthanded and appreciative, agreed to let them supplement the inquiry. The decision had mixed results. Some good work was produced by these researchers, for example, Harold Weisberg's *Oswald in New Orleans*. But the migration led to two problems. First, there began to be friction between the DA's regular staff and these amateur sleuths, with Garrison caught in the middle. Garrison would spend a lot of time talking to people like Mark Lane, and the conversations and theorizing would detract from the actual preparation of what would be a legally admissible case in court. This difficult task was left to the regular staff of assistants.[31] Second, there began to be rivalries among the researchers who had rushed to New Orleans. One such conflict was between Weisberg and Vincent Salandria.[32] Edward Jay Epstein became so piqued by his treatment that he wrote a book attacking the investigation.[33] This disorganized atmosphere simply made it easier for Garrison to be caricatured by the press and for moles to infiltrate his office. Indeed, it was later revealed that the office had been penetrated by a total of nine CIA agents, who would drop disinformation and then report back to Washington on their successes.[34]

In the face of all these setbacks to the case, why did Garrison choose to proceed against Shaw? With the media buzzsaw affecting his own credibility, with major witnesses passing away, with his inability to extradite other key witnesses, with his office infiltrated, why not just drop a seriously weakened prosecution?

There seem to be several reasons. First, Garrison saw the case as a crusade, with a near-religious obligation to prosecute the murderers of the president. And he still felt that even with the numerous reversals, it was a good enough case to bring to trial.[35]

Strangely, despite vehement claims to the contrary, Garrison always insisted he felt no real animus toward Shaw. He was simply where the evidence led. If Shaw and his lawyers were to beat him in court, that would be tough, but it would not stop him from believing in his discoveries or pursuing his case further down the line.

One of Garrison's most appealing traits was his refusal to become embittered toward those who were, in fact, his enemies. We have seen this in his attitude toward Ferrie. He also showed it toward Dean Andrews, who, after his conviction for perjury, told Garrison his heart condition would prevent his living out his six-month sentence. Garrison arranged the legal paperwork so Andrews would not have to serve his sentence.[36]

Finally, there was the matter of pride. Garrison had spent almost three years not just working on, but living this case. He had put in many seven-day weeks and sixteen-hour days researching it thoroughly. He had dismantled the Warren Report, discovered new evidence and witnesses, and rolled back the camouflage of Oswald's associations in New Orleans. A trial would provide a direct opportunity to present his case. Even in its attenuated form, that would be better than simply being bombarded by the unguided missiles of the press.

But it was to be two years before the opportunity arose and even then he would be denied the best evidence.

12

Anticlimax: The Shaw Trial

Clay Shaw was arrested in March of 1967. He was ar-
raigned on April 5, 1967. His chief counsel, F. Irvin Dymond,
entered a not guilty plea for him and asked for an expeditious
trial so his client would have the opportunity to demonstrate his innocence. He requested 30 days to file pre-trial
motions.

The motions dragged on for twenty more months.[1] The trial
did not begin until January of 1969. Some of the delay was
caused by prosecution motions, but, contrary to lingering
claims that Garrison never really wanted a trial,[2] most of it
was due to the defense attorneys. Moreover, there was a
critical difference between the two sets of pre-trial motions.
Most of the prosecution's motions were to secure evidence
or witnesses. Despite Dymond's original request to expedite
the case, most of the defense motions were meant to delay or
throw out the case.

For instance, in June the defense requested subpoenas for
32 witnesses. Included were Garrison; members of his legal
and investigative staff; businessmen from Truth and Consequences; Albert LaBiche, the foreman of the Orleans Parish
Grand Jury; and the entire grand jury itself.[3] The tactic was
to subpoena many witnesses and much documentary material
and then to file more motions based on anything discovered.
In fact, Dymond subpoenaed the entire grand jury twice.[4] He
also summoned seven criminal court judges. Sometimes, the
defense would file a motion and then not show up to argue
it.[5] Occasionally Dymond would file a motion on the last day

The founders of Truth and Consequences, the private fund set up to help in Garrison's investigation: Willard Robertson, left; Cecil Shilstone, center; and Joseph M. Rault, Jr., February 24, 1967.

of a sitting grand jury, so that the motion would have to be tabled for 30 days until a new grand jury was seated.[6]

The longest delay, the one that postponed the trial for six months, came after the defense had exhausted all local and state pretrial appeals. In the summer of 1968, Dymond filed a petition in federal District Court asking that Shaw's indictment be overturned on the ground that the Warren Report was "legally valid, accurate, binding and controlling upon all courts in the United States."[7]

In July of 1967, Garrison had tried to expedite matters by filing for an early trial date.[8] For one thing, he wanted to stop Phelan and Sheridan from tampering with, intimidating, and making offers to witnesses. But when he saw that the defense was determined to drag out the pre-trial phase, he decided to use the interval to secure more evidence from the government. Here, Ramsey Clark, his nemesis, blocked his path.

After the Attorney General had bungled his first attempt to discredit Garrison's case, he secretly tried another method. Garrison had been trying to secure the original JFK autopsy photos and x-rays to exhibit at the trial. They would form an important part of his case, since, to prove a conspiracy, he had to present evidence against the Warren Report, which maintained there was no conspiracy and that Oswald had acted alone. In 1968, Clark convened a panel of experts— which did not include any of the doctors who had performed the original examinations—to review what was extant of the photos and x-rays. In early 1969, just a few days before he left office and on the eve of the trial, Clark announced that this panel had endorsed the findings of the Warren Report. The panel released its findings, but none of the original evidence on which it was based. And when Garrison again requested the autopsy materials, he was turned down by Clark's Justice Department.[9]

There was, of course, a method to the seemingly endless and frivolous attempts by the defense to delay the trial (they even attempted to subpoena Clark as a witness to support the Warren Report[10]). It was to gain more time for their media allies to spread more doubts about the merits of Garrison's case, all the while rattling the prosecution. Judge Edward Haggerty seemed to realize this when he commented from the bench in 1967:[11]

The key flaw in the system of free press versus free trial is the unchallenged chatter that hits the ... media between the time of the arrest and the time of trial. Elaborate trial rules permit jurors to hear admissible evidence, subject to searching cross-examination; the whole system is subverted when the press, radio and television media fill jurors' heads with inadmissible evidence.

Wise and fair words. But Haggerty did not seem to realize that his admonition was far more constraining for Garrison— isolated and under the judge's nose as he was—than for Shaw's attorneys, whose cooperative friends in politics and the media were not bound by Haggerty's warning. By 1969, Haggerty himself seemed infected by the endless drumbeat.

Judge Edward Haggerty.

One friend of the defense was Aaron Kohn, the managing director of the Metropolitan Crime Commission.[12] This was a private watchdog organization of business interests that kept an eye on the police and the DA's office. Under the influence of *Newsweek* and its point man Hugh Aynesworth, as well as Shaw's defense team, Kohn had sent an ominous letter to Louisiana Attorney General Jack Gremillion urging him to investigate charges of bribery and intimidation in the DA's office. Not content with this, Kohn went to the media and began to denounce Garrison: "What you are looking at is a budding new Huey Long. I'm no longer interested in if he's right. His course is a destructive one."[13] Kohn did not say what Garrison was destroying. And he did not seem to realize how serious it was for the Metropolitan Crime Commission to accuse the DA of such serious transgressions, especially since the grand jury and police department had already investigated the charges and found them false.

The defense also used their friend Dean Andrews. Andrews had stated on the NBC special that the mysterious Clay Bertrand was not Shaw, and that although he knew who Bertrand was, he could not disclose his real name. Later, after Sheridan's special, NBC gave what it said was the name,

Eugene Davis, to the FBI. But when Andrews testified before the Warren Commission, he had stated that he had seen "Bertrand" only a few times. He had known Davis since law school, for 17 years. He had seen him every few months during all that time. Moreover, Davis himself vehemently denied ever using the alias, and when he was separately questioned and investigated by both Garrison and the FBI, they concurred.[14]

This was a good example of how the media coverage delayed the trial and damaged the case. When Shaw's lawyers heard Andrews's new story, they asked for a dismissal because now Shaw could not be Bertrand. The judge had to wait for Davis to be checked out before throwing out the motion.[15] In the meantime, Garrison felt compelled to file perjury charges against Andrews for the games he was playing. He got the perjury conviction, but under Louisiana law a convicted perjurer can still testify at a trial while his conviction is being appealed. Andrews appealed, and Dymond went ahead and used him at the Shaw trial.

But Walter Sheridan had done even more to undermine Garrison's case. A former CIA agent, Jules Ricco Kimble, had been on a mysterious plane flight to Montreal in 1963 with

Eugene Davis phoning his lawyer after Dean Andrews had named him as "Clay Bertrand" on the NBC special.

Dean Andrews,
left, shares a joke
with James Phelan
during the trial,
February 25, 1969.

Ferrie and Shaw. When Sheridan got wind of it, he intimidated Kimble first, into not talking, and then, into skipping
town.[16] Emilio Santana, another important witness (see
Chapter 6), also disappeared. Garrison's investigators felt
that the ubiquitous Sheridan might have reached him also.[17]

The journalistic duo, Phelan and Aynesworth, were both at
the trial, Phelan as a witness for the defense and Aynesworth
to help Shaw's attorneys. This included sandbagging the
prosecution by obtaining its witness list and running background checks to provide information with which the defense
could attack them. By this time, the duo made little pretense
of being journalists. Joined by James Kirkwood, a playwright
with similar prejudices against Garrison,[18] there to do a book
on the trial, they composed a clever limerick that caricatured
the DA:[19]

Cried Big Jim, the world owes me praise,
And I'll get it, come one of these days.
Earl Warren, the dunce,
Solved the killing just once,
But I solved it seventeen ways!

But the worst for Garrison was yet to come. Tom Bethell
had been one of the DA's most important investigators and

researchers, He was an Englishman, an assassination expert, and he had access to all of Garrison's files and his most recent witness list. He had initially admired the DA, but for various reasons, perhaps including the media blitz and the disinformation it was spewing forth, he never believed much in Garrison's case. Secretly, he met with Sal Panzeca, one of Shaw's attorneys, and gave him a witness list he had prepared, with summaries of each witness's expected testimony for the prosecution.[20]

If anything showed Garrison's desire to try this case, it was his response to Bethell's confession.[21] With it, Garrison could have called for a mistrial. He did not. He continued to press forward knowing the defense was lying in wait for him every step of the way. Whether this was nobility, stubbornness, stupidity, or a death wish, I leave to the reader's own conclusion.

The Shaw case posed both tactical and strategic problems. Tactically, the classic way to crack a conspiracy is to isolate one of the conspirators and convince him to talk, either by offering immunity or presenting an overwhelming accumulation of evidence that targets him. This way, the code of silence can be broken. Once one yields, the dominoes fall one by one as the evidence begins to accumulate, and the convictions follow. Shaw understood that with Ferrie, Oswald, and Banister all dead, this tactic would be virtually impossible. As long as Shaw preserved his impeccably respectable exterior and denied everything, the true nature of his background and operations was shielded from Garrison's probing. And as long as his attorneys and the media pummeled Garrison, others would be discouraged from digging further into Shaw's background.[22]

But Garrison made a strategic error here. With Shaw and his attorneys taking a hunkered-down stance, while seeming to be above the fray, the only attack with any hope of success was to overwhelm them with so many witnesses, even minor ones, as to make that stance seem phony. If one could chip away at Shaw's testimony, his image might begin to crack and, along with it, the basic defense strategy. In other words, the "respectable" Clay Shaw would become the issue: his character, his life, his weird associations, his murky service record, his mysterious European jaunts. Who was he *really*? If that line could be crossed, Garrison could go on the offensive, and the wall might come tumbling down.

But Garrison rejected this approach. He wanted to present a streamlined case against Shaw, using a few credible witnesses to expose his alias and his part in the conspiracy. He then hoped to launch a frontal assault against the Warren Report to prove that the assassination was the work of many, not of one man.

It was a mistake. Garrison realized this after the trial when he said, "one of my bad decisions was not to use all of our witnesses."[23] Some of the CIA-linked witnesses like Richard Nagell, Sergio Arcacha Smith, and Gordon Novel may have presented overwhelming problems, but there were other witnesses with no such difficulties. For instance, Garrison never called any witnesses to the Oswald impersonations in and around Dallas. These Dallas witnesses could have provided a link between New Orleans and Dallas, between the genesis of the conspiracy and its completion.

Shaw, right, with one of his attorneys, Edward Wegmann.

The prosecution also chose to minimize the issue of Shaw's homosexuality.[24] New Orleans is one of the centers of gay life and culture in the United States, and many members of its large gay community strongly criticized Garrison's initial revelation of the contents of Shaw's home and the attendant publicity. Otherwise communicative potential witnesses had become close-mouthed. The go-easy strategy was also, perhaps, a humane thing to do considering the mores of the time, but it seriously hurt the State's chances of proving Shaw's use of an alias. Given the prejudices of the establishment and Shaw's straight business ties, his homosexuality would obviously have been a strong motive for using an alias. Garrison even had witnesses in the French Quarter who attested to its use.[25] But they were hesitant to violate Shaw's privacy and Garrison was reluctant to press them or Shaw on the issue.[26] Except for one instance, not initiated by the prosecutor, whenever the point surfaced, it did so in veiled, indirect terms.[27.]

One failure that was not Garrison's fault was his inability to bring in the intelligence community and its ties to the assassination. In May of 1967, Garrison first openly attacked the CIA and accused it of complicity in the crime.[28] But many of the intelligence connections to the case, such as Banister, Ward, and Ferrie, had died, while some, like Novel, had fled, and others, such as FBI agents Kennedy and DeBrueys, initially refused to testify. This weakened the possibility of getting the intelligence community in the dock and really exposing the conspiracy and coverup.

But Garrison did not stop trying. He subpoenaed both the current DCI Richard Helms and former DCI Allen Dulles. To say the least, they would have been interesting witnesses. Helms ignored the subpoena[29]; Dulles had Agency help in resisting his.[30]

Another prosecution error was in not calling enough witnesses to nail down the Shaw-Ferrie relationship. As noted above, Sheridan deprived Garrison of Jules Ricco Kimble, who had flown with the pair to Montreal.[31] Another of Garrison's witnesses had been introduced to Shaw by Ferrie at a bar. He also had the testimony of Raymond Broshears, who had also been introduced to Shaw by Ferrie.[32] On rebuttal, Garrison did call two witnesses, Nicholas and Matilda Tadin, to link the pair and fortify Russo's statements, but there should have been more.

Garrison's attack on the Warren Report was much better than the New Orleans side of the case. He attacked the Report on three levels. First, he called new witnesses or witnesses who had been ignored by the Commission, all of whom attested to crossfire in Dealey Plaza and/or sightings of possible assassins. Second, he demonstrated how one shooter could not have performed the feat attributed to Oswald, because of the timing of the shots and the trajectory of the bullets. And finally, by obtaining the Zapruder film and by cross-examining Dr. Finck, he made public evidence which had never before been revealed, and changed the nature of the case forever.

Garrison himself did not appear often at the trial. He was well aware that he had become the lightning rod in this affair and that everything he did would be examined for deeper political or personal motives. He was caught in a no-win situation: if he argued the case, he would be accused of grandstanding and political ambitions; if he was absent, he would be charged with insincerity and sabotage. He made the State's initial presentation, outlining the case to the jury, and he made the final summation.[33] He questioned few witnesses between.

The lead attorney for the State was young Jim Alcock. One of Garrison's few excellent choices during the trial, Alcock did a good job with the materials available. He knew the nuances of the case, the constitutional issues involved, and his summation, before Garrison's, was simple, direct, and impassioned.

Jim Garrison, left, with Andrew ("Moo Moo") Sciambra, center, and James Alcock, shortly before the trial began.

Alvin Oser, the assistant DA who handled most of the Dealey Plaza testimony, was just as good as Alcock. Amazingly, with the help of Vincent Salandria, he had mastered the technical aspects of the case, *i.e.*, the autopsy report, the ballistics tests, the bullet trajectories, and more. Oser was confident, aggressive, and thoroughly convinced of and schooled in the fallacies of the Report. By the time he delivered his summation, the Warren Report lay in tiny pieces on the courtroom floor.[34]

After a long jury selection process, that entailed more than 1,200 interviews, the trial began on February 6, 1969. Including jury selection, it lasted 39 days.[35] After opening presentations by Garrison and chief defense attorney Dymond, the prosecution led off with what many observers considered their best witnesses: the people from Clinton who had seen Ferrie, Oswald, and Shaw together in late September of 1963. Reeves Morgan, Edward Lee McGehee, and others made strong, simple witnesses. The prosecution bolstered their testimony with two women from Louisiana State Hospital in Jackson, the place where Shaw and Ferrie wanted Oswald to get a job. They testified that Oswald had indeed visited them to inquire about a position and had filled out an application, which they had since discarded.[36]

Next on the stand for the State was Vernon Bundy, who linked Shaw to Oswald. Dymond warmed to the attack on this relatively easy target. Bundy was black, was a drug user, and had a police record, so Dymond scored some points here. But Bundy had a surprise in store for the crusty courtroom veteran. He asked the judge to have the defendant go to the back of the room while Bundy himself sat in an aisle seat. Judge Haggerty agreed, and Vernon Bundy now began his demonstration. He asked Shaw to walk toward him. As Shaw did so, Bundy stared at his feet. When he got close, he stopped, and after a pause, Bundy asked him to repeat the exercise. After the second time, Bundy returned to the witness stand and revealed how he knew he had seen Clay Shaw: "I watched his foot, the way it twisted that day. This is one way I identified this man the next time I saw him."[37] Shaw, in fact, did walk with a slight twist. He explained later how an old war injury to his back had caused this hitch in his gait. The irony was

**Mug shot of
Vernon William Bundy, Jr.,
from a 1959 arrest
in New Orleans.**

that this witness, whose status the defense had tried to belittle, had noticed something telling that no one else had.

The prosecution had quickly reached its zenith. The next witness for the State was a New Yorker named Charles Spiesel.[38] The small, wiry accountant had been in Louisiana, he related, to visit his daughter who attended LSU, when he met Ferrie at a bar.[39] The two then went to visit Clay Shaw at a building in the approximate area where Shaw's home was located. They began drinking, and, testified Spiesel, Ferrie brought up the subject of a possible Kennedy assassination. Spiesel was surprised at this turn in the conversation but he chalked it up to the liquor. Spiesel recalled some talk about a high-powered rifle and a telescopic sight. Shaw had added that Ferrie would have to fly the assassins away after the crime.[40] He closed his direct testimony saying that he never saw Shaw again, though he did run into Ferrie a few times. Ferrie had suggested, he claimed, that Shaw could help set him up in business in New Orleans. Spiesel allegedly called Shaw's office on a few occasions, but those calls were never returned.[41]

At this juncture, Garrison's case blew apart. Armed with the knowledge of who Spiesel was and what he would say through the leaking of Tom Bethell's files, Shaw's defense scored a coup. They had thoroughly researched Spiesel's background and used the results to cut him to ribbons.

Dymond took over, asking the witness if he had tried to sell his story to the media. At first Spiesel resisted, but when Dymond challenged him, he admitted he had discussed the matter with CBS. When the attorney asked how much he was looking for, he replied, "I told him a couple of thousand."[42]

Dymond then asked where Spiesel had stayed in New Orleans during the summer of 1963. He said it had been at a hotel and then two apartments. When asked to name the hotel and the location of the two apartments, Spiesel could not recall.[43]

Now Dymond closed in for the kill. He asked Spiesel if he had noticed anything unusual about David Ferrie. "No," replied the witness. This was amazing because everyone knew what a startling appearance Ferrie had possessed. Spiesel added that he was "fairly well-groomed," and the only unusual thing about his appearance was his rather thin eyebrows.[44] This about a hairless man who glued on a wig and pasted mohair above his eyes.

Dymond then asked Spiesel if he had ever been hypnotized, and Spiesel replied many, many times.[45] When asked by whom, he said it was the New York City Police who had tortured him while he was under hypnosis and made him give up his accounting work.[46] Dymond pursued this, asking if he had had trouble with a communist conspiracy, "people following you and tapping your phones?"[47] Spiesel tried to dodge this, and Dymond then asked if he had fingerprinted his daughter in New York before she left for LSU. Spiesel said he had. Did he also fingerprint her when she returned. Again, the answer was yes. When Dymond asked why he did this, Spiesel replied that he had been hypnotized so often he wanted to be sure it was she when she returned.[48] At this point, Garrison later recalled, "I was swept by a feeling of nausea."[49]

Why Garrison had no inkling of Spiesel's paranoia is a complete mystery. Any careful background probe would have discredited him. Dymond utterly destroyed Spiesel and, along with him, the case against Clay Shaw. Garrison never fully recovered the lost credibility.

Perry Russo, a crucial witness, was next. During his two-and-a-half day ordeal, he admitted that the fateful discussion he overheard may have been just that, just talk, not an actual plan to commit a crime. Russo also said that no one except Ferrie ever told him they had decided to kill the President, and Ferrie told him this in private.[50]

Dymond tried to get Russo to say that he was not sure that the "Bertrand" at the meeting was actually Shaw. Earlier, journalist James Phelan had also tried this on Russo, implying he had actually seen Banister instead of Shaw. But Russo was ready this time. He denied it categorically, "No, that is absolutely false.... I am absolutely sure the defendant is the man who was there."[51]

After two days of grilling, Russo got strained and edgy. His cross-examination ended in a shouting match between the witness, Dymond, Alcock, and the judge. Dymond closed his cross-examination by implying that Russo was mentally ill.[52]

Since the defense had impugned Russo's mental state, Alcock made a motion to read to the jury the testimony of Dr.

Perry Russo outside the criminal court building.

Nicholas Chetta at the preliminary hearing. (Dr. Chetta had died in the interval.) The real reason for bringing in the testimony was to bolster Russo's credibility by showing there was no hanky-panky during the administering of the Sodium Pentothal®. Alcock knew that Phelan would later be put on the stand by the defense to tell his story about Russo. Because of Dymond's references to Russo's mental state, Judge Haggerty allowed the reading of Dr. Chetta's testimony.[53]

When Alcock tried to have Dr. Fatter, who had conducted the hypnosis, accepted as a witness, Dymond objected on the ground that most of what he had to say was hearsay; Judge Haggerty agreed. Alcock argued, with some logic, that this was inconsistent with the ruling on Dr. Chetta's testimony.[54]

After Russo, the most important witnesses relating to Clay Shaw were Richard Jackson and James Hardiman.[55] These two postal employees testified that for a time in 1966, Clay Shaw had redirected his mail to 1414 Chartres Street, home of a friend named Jeff Biddison. There was confusion over just when this had begun, but it ended on September 21 of that year. Jackson had handled the change of address card, whereas Hardiman actually delivered the mail to the house. He said that a few pieces of mail were in fact addressed to a Clem Bertrand at the Chartres house. When Alcock asked if any of the letters were given back because they were wrongly addressed, the letter carrier replied, "No, I don't recall getting any back."[56] This restored some of the lost credibility to Garrison's case, particularly as it related to the alias.

Alvin Oser then presented the prosecution's all-out attack on the Warren Report. It featured a scale model of Dealey Plaza, the Zapruder film shown at various speeds, photos and visual models, and compelling witnesses the Commission ignored. Well prepared by Salandria, Oser was particularly adept at demolishing the testimony of "experts" like Robert Frazier on ballistics and Dr. Finck on the autopsy. Oser got Frazier to admit that the tests conducted by the FBI did not replicate the conditions at Dealey Plaza. They were staged to

Colonel Pierre A. Finck outside the courthouse, February 24, 1969.

produce a desired result, and even then, none of the marksmen could duplicate Oswald's alleged feat.[57]

If Oser was tough on Frazier, he was withering with Finck. Dr. Finck admitted that he did not dissect the neck wound because he was ordered not to do so by the assembled military brass; that he was given false information to prejudice him toward a particular finding; that the autopsy was not completed in 1963; that he did not see the photos until years later, by permission of the military—and then only to coordinate the photos to his prior report. Indeed, the autopsy was a sham. (See Appendix A for excerpts from Dr. Finck's cross-examination on these points.)

Vince Salandria had always suspected as much.[58] This is why he and Garrison wanted those autopsy photos and x-rays at the trial. If that material had been available, if Oser could have led Finck through them one at a time, if the Parkland Hospital doctors had been on hand, the case might have exploded right there. The size and scope of the plot would have been evident through the three differing sets of observations.

The final witnesses during the prosecution's direct case also dealt with Shaw's use of the Bertrand alias. Mrs. Jessie Parker, hostess at the exclusive VIP Room at the New Orleans Airport, said she had seen Shaw sign the guest register as "Clay Bertrand" in 1966. She described his appearance and pointed to his signature in the book. She then pointed to Shaw as the man who signed in. She said she remembered him because of his striking appearance and because very few people used the room. One needed a pass key. A handwriting expert, later disputed by the defense's expert, verified Shaw's writing in the book.[59]

Then came the second and final turning point in the trial. Jackson, Hardiman, and Parker had been good witnesses. The Zapruder film was shocking. Garrison had actually recovered a bit from the Spiesel disaster. To try to clinch the case that Shaw was Bertrand, Garrison called to the stand policeman Aloysius Habighorst.[60] When Shaw was first arrested in March of 1967, Habighorst had handled the booking. Before having him sign the fingerprint card, the officer had routinely

Officer Aloysius
Habighorst at his home
in a family snapshot.

asked if the defendant had ever used an alias. Apparently unsettled by his arrest, Shaw had replied "Clay Bertrand." Habighorst typed this on the card and Shaw signed it. Alcock now wanted to admit both the card and the officer's testimony as evidence into the trial. This seemed powerful, damning evidence because it came right out of Shaw's mouth and hand. It would lend credence to Garrison's claim that Shaw really had called Dean Andrews to defend Oswald, and that Andrews had indeed perjured himself to protect Shaw.

Aloysius Habighorst joined the police force at 21; he was a 15-year veteran when he appeared at the Shaw trial.[61] In 1967, at the time of Shaw's arrest, he had been receiving three letters of commendation a year for his work.[62] He had been taking FBI classes in fingerprinting and would often take cards home with him to practice identification techniques.[63] The day after he had booked Shaw, he and his wife, Elsie, were home watching television when they heard a news commentator mention Garrison's contention that Shaw had used the alias Clay Bertrand. Habighorst jumped out of his chair and told his wife that that was just what Shaw had said to him the night before, at the routine booking procedure.[64] He ran to his room and showed her the three copies of Shaw's card, which listed the alias and had Shaw's signature.[65] The alias also appeared on the arrest record.[66]

Habighorst hardly knew Garrison when he went to him with the cards. Garrison realized how critical this was to his case, and, with witnesses disappearing right and left, he placed Habighorst under protective surveillance.[67] Two days before he was to testify, a man called his house and asked Elsie if "Al" was there. She thought this odd, since all her husband's friends called him by his boyhood nickname, "Hotsie." The caller asked when he would be getting off work. She said it would be late that evening and asked if there was any message. The man said no. The next day, Mardi Gras, Garrison decided to take the surveillance off Habighorst since he would be with other officers guarding the parade.

Unexpectedly, however, Habighorst was relieved early, and headed home. As he was driving, a yellow truck pulled out of an alley near his house and tried to ram him.[68] Habighorst suffered facial lacerations in his attempt to avoid the truck.[69]

Dymond would have had a tough time belittling Habighorst, given his performance record. He could hardly have attacked his character. Habighorst came from a religious family, and served still, on occasion, as an altar boy. He had once leapt into a river to rescue a drowning man. He was so well-regarded by his superiors he was used in training films.[70] It would have been difficult for Dymond to convince the jury that Habighorst was perjuring himself to help Garrison or to harm Shaw.[71]

Consequently, he took a different tack. Dymond decided to challenge both Habighorst's testimony and the admission of the card. Haggerty excused the jury. Shaw took the stand and told the judge he had never told Habighorst he used an alias. He also said he had signed a blank card that was filled in later.[72] Shaw's attorneys at the time of the arrest, Sal Panzeca and Edward Wegmann, testified that neither was at Shaw's side at the time of the booking.[73] The defense argued that this

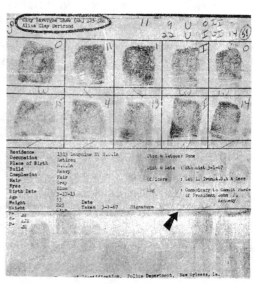

Above, Habighorst on his way to court; right, the fingerprint card with the alias.

violated the *Miranda* and *Escobedo* rules, which require police to inform a suspect of his rights to remain silent and to have an opportunity to consult with an attorney.[74]

Invoking *Miranda* was stretching things, since Shaw had already been read his rights before he was brought to the booking room.[75] As for *Escobedo*, New Orleans police procedure has always required that a suspect's counsel be *nearby* when routine booking was taking place, which was in fact the case at Shaw's booking.[76] This had been standard practice since before *Miranda* and *Escobedo* were decided by the Supreme Court.[77]

The prosecution's protestations fell on deaf ears. Judge Haggerty would not allow the evidence. He held that Shaw's constitutional rights were violated because his attorney was not standing right next to him during his fingerprinting. Habighorst had no right to ask Shaw if he used an alias without Panzeca or Wegmann in his presence.[78] But the judge went further.

He said, "If Officer Habighorst is telling the truth—and I seriously doubt it..."[79]

Alcock leaped out of his chair. His face was red, and his voice cracked with emotion. "Your Honor. Are you ruling on the credibility of Officer Habighorst?"

Peering over his spectacles, Haggerty replied, "No jurors are present."

"But you are passing on the credibility of a witness before the press and the entire world."

"I don't care," Haggerty responded. "The whole world can hear that I do not believe Officer Habighorst. I do not believe Officer Habighorst."

"I demand a mistrial," Alcock shouted. "A judge's unsolicited comment on evidence..."

"Denied," said Haggerty. "I rule this evidence is inadmissible before the jury."

Alcock did not file for a mistrial. Instead he tried to get a 24-hour stay of the judge's ruling from the State Supreme

Court. The motion was denied.[80] The next day he asked Haggerty to reconsider the ruling. Haggerty refused.[81]

If the defense had made a wish list before the trial, they could not have asked for a better witness than Spiesel or a better ruling than Haggerty's exclusion of Habighorst's testimony. Indeed, the judge had now deprived the prosecution of their best hope of linking Shaw to a conspiracy. The jury would not get to pass on the credibility of the officer. The judge had already done so.

Dymond's defense case included Dean Andrews and James Phelan. Andrews changed his testimony yet another time to say that there was no such person as Clay Bertrand. It had all been a figment of his imagination. Alcock was not allowed to bring up Andrews's perjury conviction directly because of the pending appeal,[82] although the defense later mentioned it.

Phelan had been cooperating with Sheridan, Aynesworth, and Shaw's attorneys almost since he arrived in New Orleans. It was only natural that the journalist was happy to testify for Shaw. Phelan was used to attack both Russo's testimony and Sciambra's memorandum of his first interview with Russo in Baton Rouge.[83] But after Dymond took him through his paces, Alcock showed him the obstacle course. Phelan had been on local television, the Sterns' WDSU, and stated that he had a taped interview with Perry Russo in which he contradicted his original Baton Rouge statements to Sciambra. Alcock asked him if he did, indeed, have such a tape. He replied he did not. Alcock then asked him if his statement on television was a lie. Phelan replied diffidently, "If you wish to call it that."[84]

Alcock then asked Phelan about his visit to Russo before he had submitted his *Saturday Evening Post* story. He asked how long he had been with Russo at that time, and Phelan replied more than two hours. Alcock asked him why the very last thing they discussed, literally as he was walking out the door, was the Sciambra memorandum. Phelan said that once he got going, Russo was a talkative young man.[85] But, Alcock asked, if Russo had not mentioned any meeting at Ferrie's apartment, why did he leave that fact out of his article? Phelan replied it was because of space limitations.[86] When Alcock asked Phelan if he had tried to convince Russo that Shaw was really Banister, Phelan agreed. Alcock then asked if Phelan had ever seen Banister. He had not. Then how did he know what the now dead Banister had looked like? Phelan replied that Banister had been described to him by *Sheridan.*[87]

What should have been a bombshell went off right after Phelan stepped down, but it was so subtle that almost no one noticed. Alcock seemed to be tiring and was unable to take advantage of it. The self-confident, clever Phelan had once told Kirkwood that Garrison did not have a bad case *without* Russo, but Garrison needed Russo because he "is the only man on this planet who puts Dave Ferrie and Oswald together, the only one."[88]

This was false on its face. There were witnesses who had seen the pair together in New Orleans from 1956 to 1963. But grant that Phelan believed it. Right after he stepped off the witness stand, the defense called Mrs. Jessie Garner. She had been Oswald's landlady in the summer of 1963 in New Orleans. The defense had called her to say that she had only seen Oswald clean-shaven and neatly dressed. Her testimony was supposed to rebut Russo's testimony that, at Ferrie's party, Leon Oswald had been whiskered and scruffy in appearance. She was shown some photos of Oswald, and with these photos there was a picture of Ferrie. Surprised, she quietly and unexpectedly said that she knew "that man" too. She spoke so softly that almost no one heard her utter the sentence.[89] She added that he was at her house shortly after the assassination.

In the aftermath of the assassination, many government agents had come to her home. But Ferrie was also there. When she realized he was not an agent, she asked him to leave. Incredibly, the prosecution did not press this issue.

Alcock did not even mention it until his summation, and then he made almost nothing of it. But several researchers did talk to Mrs. Garner afterwards. She said that Ferrie had returned to search for his library card.[90] He thought he had given it to Oswald and wanted to retrieve it from his room. Right then, two months after Oswald had left town and immediately after the assassination. So much for Phelan's assurance that "no one on the planet" could put Oswald and Ferrie together. No one except Ferrie himself.

The last defense witness was Shaw himself. He did not have to take the stand, but his attorneys had a good feeling about his performance and the way the trial was proceeding. They wanted a complete vindication, for Shaw to deny all charges and to paint the Garrison case as a slimy sham motivated by the basest political and personal opportunism— a motive so reckless and a DA so driven by the lust for power that he would wreck the life and reputation of a completely innocent citizen.

Shaw did just that. He denied ever knowing Oswald or Ferrie. He denied attending any meeting at Ferrie's apartment. He denied using an alias. He denied any association with the CIA. He even denied the Clinton trip. He said he was a believer in what Jack Kennedy stood for and harbored no ill feeling toward him.[91]

The last to testify were rebuttal witnesses, called by both sides to counter specific testimony already presented. The most important rebuttal testimony in Garrison's favor was delivered by Mr. and Mrs. Nicholas Tadin. They had called the DA after reading that Shaw denied ever knowing David Ferrie. Both testified that in the summer of 1964, they had taken their sixteen-year-old son to Lakefront Airport, to get a flying lesson from Ferrie. Mr. Tadin stated that previously he had seen Clay Shaw around town and knew from the papers who he was. When he and his wife brought their son to the airport, he saw Ferrie emerge from the hangar door with a tall, white-haired man. As they got closer, he recognized the second man as Shaw. As Shaw walked off, Tadin asked Ferrie if he had a new student. "No," he replied. "He's a friend of mine, Clay Shaw. He's in charge of the International Trade Mart."[92] His wife testified to the same incident. She also knew who Shaw was. The last question Alcock asked Matilda Tadin was, "Are you telling the truth?" The woman immediately snapped, "Of course I'm telling the truth."[93]

The trial was now over. Closing arguments were presented. Alcock tried to counter Dymond's admission from Russo that the discussion at Ferrie's had the characteristics of a "bull session." Alcock stated that the "bull session" was carried out precisely on November 22: Oswald was in Dealey Plaza, Shaw had an alibi on the West Coast, and Ferrie made his trip to Texas in case he was needed as a getaway pilot.[94] Alcock also accused Shaw of lying in the face of the number and credibility of the Clinton witnesses.[95] Oser went through the impossibility of any single person performing the feat of marksmanship achieved during the assassination. He insisted that there must have been at least three assassins in Dealey Plaza. And that, he concluded, brought us to a conspiracy and David Ferrie's "triangulation of fire" concept at the meeting at his apartment.[96]

Dymond cast doubt on all the prosecution witnesses, even the Tadins and the people from Clinton. He said it was ludicrous to think that someone as well-known as Shaw would really attempt to use an alias. He added that much of Garrison's entire theory came from the mind of Dean Andrews, who had only once told the truth—when on the stand in this case. Could they really convict Shaw on such questionable testimony?[97]

Garrison spoke last and bitterly attacked the testimony of Frazier and Finck to illustrate what a colossal fraud the Warren Report was. He tried to get the jury to be courageous enough to overrule the experts and the Report and to begin to tell the truth about the assassination.[98]

The four summations began at about 2:30 p.m. Friday afteroon, February 28. They ended about 11:30 p.m. that night.[99] The judge charged the jury and they went in to deliberate. The jurors asked the two alternates to vote and leave their ballots with a deputy. Interestingly, they both voted guilty.[100] The jurors who counted did not see it that way. In an hour, a not-guilty verdict was returned.[101] Thus ended the only trial ever conducted for the murder of John F. Kennedy.

In addition to the many witnesses who link Shaw and Ferrle, there is some photographic evidence. The two snapshots at the top appeared in the May 1967 issue of *The Councilor*, a rightwing newsletter published in Shreveport, Louisiana. They are purportedly from a 1949 New Orleans house party attended by the staff and friends of WDSU. The man standing in the center of the photo on the left, and second from the right, clowning with a mop on his head, is undoubtedly Clay Shaw, an old friend of the owners of WDSU, the Sterns. It appears that the man second from the left in the first photo and on the left in the second photo is David Ferrle. In the two photos below, which appeared in a later issue of *The Councilor*, Ferrle's mug shot can be compared to a blow-up from the first photo. The resemblance is compelling.

Following the verdict, Garrison filed perjury charges against Shaw for denying that he ever knew Ferrie. In light of the Clinton witnesses and the Tadins, Garrison seemed to have a good case.

Shaw's attorneys petitioned the federal courts to intercede in the perjury action, unusual because the federal judiciary does not often interfere in state prosecutions.[102] But because of its notoriety, this was an exception. In fact, the court decided, the charge placed Shaw in double jeopardy. The U.S. District Court ordered the DA not to prosecute Shaw. Garrison was reviled in the press. Editorials demanded his resignation.[103] Clay Shaw was finally home free.

13

Long Time Coming

Sometimes it takes a while for the truth to work its way out. In this case, the truth was like an underground stream that was always there but took years to burst through the earth, first going sideways, then diagonally, then bubbling up to the surface and cracking through, first as a rivulet, then a creek, and finally a river. And as in the Chinese proverb, Garrison was on shore to see the bodies of his slain enemies being carried away by the current.

The first myth to die was that of Clay Shaw. It began to crack in 1969, just too late for the trial. One of the problems the jury had with Garrison's case was the question of Shaw's motivation. They could not fathom how such an appealing man, such a pillar of civic pride, such a cultivated play-wright, could have a part in a plot to kill President Kennedy. Shaw added to this quandary by proclaiming to all who would listen that he admired Kennedy. When a journalist would interview him and ask about his political leanings, he would inevitably reply matter-of-factly, "I suppose I'd describe myself as a Wilsonian-FDR-Kennedy liberal."[1] Sure enough, like trained seals, Shaw's champions took his word for it, and the question of motive became the pivotal hole in Garrison's case.

Garrison was aware of this, and it was why he needed Gordon Novel, Richard Nagell, Sergio Arcacha Smith, and, finally, Dave Ferrie, at the trial. Without them, he had no intelligence connections to Shaw and no credible motivation.

Without that connection, the press, public, and jury would accept Shaw's Kennedy-liberal line.

But America is a parochial country with a lack of understanding of the dynamics of world history. The mainstream media can keep the populace isolated from foreign opinion. Indeed, few were aware that the international press was not swallowing Shaw's story. If the American media had investigated Shaw with half the interest they showed in Garrison, his smooth façade might have cracked sooner. Sometime in 1963 or 1964, Clay Shaw took a small but brilliantly illuminating step. In the *Who's Who in the Southwest* for 1963-64, there is a rather long entry for Shaw. In fact, in the preceding years his name and entry appear regularly.[1] But in the 1965-66 edition his name is missing,[2] never to appear again. No reporter in the entire two-year period of Shaw's arrest and trial ever noted this curious fact. Why had Shaw withdrawn his entry?

There were two reasons. The first relates to one brief item in Shaw's long resumé: he was listed as a member of the Board of Directors of a company called Permindex. The saga of Permindex and its parent company Centro Mondiale Commerciale (CMC), and their relations to director Clay Shaw through his International Trade Mart would have belied his image as an ordinary businessman and his pose as a Kennedy liberal.

According to a series of articles in Swiss, Canadian, and Italian newspapers, both entities were suspected of being CIA fronts in Europe, with reactionary politics and reactionary leaders on their boards.

The origins of Permindex and the CMC lie in Switzerland in 1956. On December 28, Ferenc Nagy, former premier of Hungary, announced his intent to form a "permanent industrial exhibition" named Permindex, in Basel.[3]

Nagy's past was suspect. Before Hungary became communist, he was accused of plotting a coup within the then

**Ferenc Nagy when
Prime Minister of
Hungary, 1946.**

government. Shortly afterwards, while on vacation in Switzerland in 1947, he phoned in his resignation to Budapest, while arranging his future finances and politics.[4] From Europe, Nagy went to the United States,[5] but he never stopped meddling in European affairs and never lost his interest in rightwing European politics.

After his announcement in December 1956, Nagy outlined a large, three-part construction project to include a trade center, a hotel, and an office center.[6] He was unwilling to reveal the people and firms involved in financing the project, and denied any American backing. But he dropped the name of J. Henry Schroder, a New York banker. Schroder denied having anything to do with the enterprise.[7] Nagy then mentioned Hans Seligman, a Swiss banker.[8] This generated some controversy, not only because Seligman's bank was not a major house, but also because he had been accused by both the U.S. and the U.K. of cooperating with fascists during World War II.[9] Things got worse when it was discovered that George Mantello was also involved.[10] Mantello's real name was George Mandel. His name brought about attacks in the Swiss papers against Permindex, its organizers, and the Swiss government. The *Arbeiter-Zeitung* accused Mandel of being a gold profiteer during the war and of working the Jewish refugee racket. He had done both while holding Salvadoran citizenship and acting as secretary at the El Salvador Consulate in Geneva. Mandel was a naturalized Swiss citizen of Eastern European origin, who had aided Nagy in his flight from Hungary and helped him get established in America.[11]

The combination of proto-fascist directors and murky financing led to an outburst of editorial attacks against Permindex. But the pressure did not induce Nagy to be more forthcoming about the source of his funds. The enterprise began to lose both public support and government approval.

At this point, two things happened. In April of 1957, two local officials interested in getting Permindex approved went to New Orleans to visit the International Trade Mart.[12] By the next year, the directors of Permindex decided to move their company to Italy. The same people were involved: Nagy, Mandel, and Seligman, with one addition, Clay Shaw.[13] Shaw later became associated with CMC, which had been formed in 1961 by reputed former OSS operative Major Louis Bloomfield.[14] Curiously, CMC also moved to Rome, the next year.[15]

Nagy was on the CMC board. Another director was Gutierrez di Spadaforo, a wealthy Italian with considerable interests in oil and the arms trade. He had worked in Benito Mussolini's fascist administration, and was related through marriage to Hjalmar Schacht, the notorious economic wizard whose fiscal policies had financed Hitler's Third Reich and who was tried at Nuremburg for war crimes, though later released. Another director was Giuseppe Zigiotti, president of the Fascist National Association for Militia Arms.

CMC's board was representative of the paramilitary right in Europe. It formed a small cross-section of the aging royalists with whom Shaw liked to hobnob on his European jaunts and whose names and phone numbers were kept in his address book.[16] The organization was described by one writer as "a shell of superficiality ... composed of channels through which money flowed back and forth, with no one knowing the sources or the destination of the liquid assets."[17]

In 1967, the Canadian newspaper *Le Devoir*, following up on an extraordinary exposé of CMC that had just appeared in Italy, noted:[18]

[H]ere is where the affair assumes stranger and stranger characteristics. It has just been learned that the name of Clay Shaw was found among that of the eleven directors of a company, which up until 1962 had its headquarters in Montreal ... in Rome it is known as the Centro Mondiale de Commerciale....

In Italy, when the papers—both the liberal *Paesa Sera* and the conservative *De La Sera*—exposed CMC's personnel, practices, and policies *again*, as in Switzerland, the company was swept out of the country. It then found corporate headquarters more sympathetic to its fascist leanings in Johannesburg, South Africa.[19]

CMC was described in some detail in the series of articles in *Paesa Sera* that led to its expulsion from Italy. Here are two excerpts:[20]

Among its possible involvements is that the Centro was a creature of the CIA ... set up as a cover for the transfer of CIA ... funds in Italy for illegal political-espionage activities. It still remains to clear up the presence on the administrative board of the CMC of Mr. Clay Shaw....

It is a fact that the CMC is nevertheless the point of contact for a number of persons who, in certain respects, have ties whose common denominator is an anti-communism so strong that it would swallow up all those in the world who have fought for decent relations between East and West, including Kennedy.

Permindex was of the same order. Reportedly, it was incorporated in 1958 by Bloomfield, then residing in Montreal, and Nagy. Both Bloomfield and Nagy were on the board of Permindex along with Shaw. The Italian press revealed that it had been accused of channeling funds to the Secret Army Organization (OAS), a clandestine paramilitary group opposed to President de Gaulle's support for Algerian independence.[21] Later, the OAS attempted to assassinate de Gaulle.[22]

This is intriguing, to say the least. First, we saw earlier that Kennedy had been one of the leading American sympathizers with Algerian independence.[23] Second, in the 1961 Houma arms raid (see Chapter 3), the arms heisted and then transported to Guy Banister's office were CIA-stockpiled weapons on loan to the OAS.[24] Third, in tracing the money used to finance the de Gaulle assassination plots, French intelligence discovered that about $200,000 in secret funds had been sent to Permindex accounts in the Banque de la Credit Internationale. In 1962, Guy Banister had dispatched to Paris a lawyer friend, Maurice Gatlin, a member of Banister's Anti-Communist League of the Caribbean, with a suitcase full of money for the OAS, reportedly around $200,000.[25] Finally, the French authorities accused the CIA of encouraging French generals to try to get rid of de Gaulle, a charge the Agency has never convincingly denied.[26]

What makes the Permindex connection even more fascinating is that four of its directors are knit into the events in Dallas or surrounding the assassination. Besides Shaw, there is Nagy, who lived in Dallas at the time.[27] Jean DeMenil of Schlumberger Corporation, which owned the ammunition dump at Houma raided by Ferrie and Novel was also on the board. Another director was Paul Raigorodsky, a millionaire Texas oilman and a prominent figure in the Dallas White Russian community, who was a friend of George DeMohrenschildt and a director of the Tolstoy Foundation, a CIA front that helped Eastern European exiles get to America.[28] The Tolstoy Foundation, which aimed to use those exiles against the Soviet Union, was the brainchild of Reinhard Gehlen.[29]

How did Shaw get involved with this bunch? Why would a "Wilsonian-FDR-Kennedy liberal" serve on boards with groups of paramilitary, rightwing fascists involved with political assassinations? In 1977, a CIA document disclosed Shaw's long association with the Agency[30] (Shaw died in 1974). This document had been prepared in 1967 in response to queries by Ramsey Clark and the Justice Department, which was nervous about Garrison's investigation and what it might reveal about Shaw. The document disclosed his ties to the Agency during his tenure at the International Trade Mart and went even further.

Shaw had been a CIA contact as far back as 1949. According to Fletcher Prouty, the Agency favors using people in the import-export business because it allows them to fly around the world making contacts while having a legitimate commercial cover.[31] Shaw was filing reports from countries like East Germany, Czechoslovakia, Peru, Argentina, and Nicaragua. Between 1949 and 1956, Shaw filed thirty reports with the Agency.

And why did he begin filing those reports? Because there is evidence that during World War II, Shaw, like Bloomfield, was in the OSS (he may have been liaison officer to the headquarters of Winston Churchill).[32]

This leads to the second reason Shaw had to expunge his entry after the 1963-64 *Who's Who*. It also included the fact that he was aide-de-camp to General Charles Thrasher, and then later Deputy Chief of Staff of the Oise Section in France. (Thrasher was commanding officer of the Oise Section.[33]) According to Jim Marrs, Thrasher was involved in the transfer of Nazi prisoners and war criminals at the end of the war.[34] In his 1991 book, *Other Losses*, James Bacque confirms this.[35] Shaw was thus probably involved in those transfers.

There are three other unsubstantiated reports[36] that Thrasher was involved in Operation Paper Clip, an adjunct to Allen Dulles's Gehlen Operation (see Chapter 1). At the end of

May 21, 1945: The Nazl's V-2 rocket team surrenders to the U.S. Army. Walter Dornberger, left, In hat, and Werner von Braun, right, arm In cast.

World War II, the Nazi scientists and administrators at the Peenemünde rocket center on the Baltic coast, fearing capture by the Russians, fled south and decided to surrender to the more friendly Americans.[37] The Americans were all too happy to accommodate them. Two of the group were Werner von Braun and Walter Dornberger.[38] Dornberger ran the center, which used slave labor from the nearby Dora concentration camp.[39] He, like Gehlen, should have been tried at Nuremburg. But as Dulles with Gehlen, and McCloy with Krupp, Paper Clip allowed Dornberger to be smuggled into America. What was Dornberger in November of 1963? Overall supervisor of classified projects for Bell Aerospace, the division for which Michael Paine worked at Bell Helicopter in Dallas.[40] And when von Braun deconstructed his V-2 rocket for U.S. scientists after the end of the war as part of his Paper Clip deal, where did it come to port? New Orleans, just before Thrasher's deputy, Clay Shaw, co-founded the Trade Mart there.[41]

After the war, Shaw not only served on the boards of protofascist business organizations; he also maintained social ties with European monarchists, fascists, and intelligence agents. He knew Hjalmar Schacht not only through the CMC board, but personally, and liked him.[42] He was associated with the Borghese family, which contemplated a fascist coup in Italy with the aid of Otto Skorzeny, a former SS officer and another Nazi smuggled out of danger by the OSS, this time by James Jesus Angleton.[43] A British intelligence newsletter has reported that some of Shaw's friends in England had intelligence backgrounds.[44]

Even in New Orleans, Shaw's business and personal relationships appear shadowy and tied to the right wing. Shaw was a friend of Alton Ochsner, a wealthy doctor and a notorious backer of reactionary causes. Ochsner was a friend of Henri Debayle, personal physician to Nicaraguan dictator Anastasio Somoza García, and a relative of Somoza's wife.[45] Both Debayle and Somoza served on Guy Banister's Anti-Communist League of the Caribbean (see Chapter 4), a conduit for Agency funds to counter-revolutionary causes in that

Alton Ochsner, right, and William ("Wild Bill") Donovan, former head of the OSS, elected officers of the American Cancer Society, 1949.

area.[46] Ochsner was also a director of the Information Council of the Americas (INCA), a rightwing communications center that produced tapes for radio broadcast.[47] It was a block and a half from the Trade Mart. William Zetzmann, a former president of the Trade Mart, was also on the board and was a heavy contributor.[48] William Reily of Reily Coffee Company, where Oswald worked that summer, also donated funds.[49] Together, INCA, Shaw, and the Agency figure in a strange charade Oswald performed in New Orleans.

On August 9, 1963, Oswald was involved in an incident with an anti-Castro activist, Carlos Bringuier, on Canal Street about two blocks from the Trade Mart.[50] Oswald had approached Bringuier earlier as if he were an anti-Castro sympathizer. Yet within days he was passing out FPCC literature in proximity to Bringuier, who found out about it and confronted Oswald. Oswald invited him to punch him; the police intervened; the pair went to the station. Bringuier got off, but Oswald pleaded guilty to disturbing the peace. A

Left, Oswald hawking his "Hands Off Cuba" leaflet In New Orleans; right, Carlos Bringuier In 1967.

week later, August 16, he was back again, leafleting in front of the Trade Mart.[51] Strangely, WDSU sent a camera crew out to record this. The next day, Bringuier and George Butler of INCA debated Oswald at a local radio station. After a phone tip from Washington,[52] they got Oswald to admit he had defected to the Soviet Union. Oswald later went to WDSU-TV and admitted on film that he was a Marxist.[53]

Would an American trying to create goodwill toward Castro do such a thing? These incidents all have more than a touch of staging about them. Both Butler and Bringuier had Agency ties through the anti-Castro network in New Orleans.[54] Although Shaw maintained that he did not even know Oswald was in front of the Trade Mart on the 16th,[55] there is a photograph of Shaw going to work that day, and as he approaches the building he is looking at Oswald and Oswald is looking at him.[56]

There are two major reasons it all seems staged. First, as Anthony Summers discovered, Oswald wrote a letter about the confrontation five days *before* it happened; second, there is a very interesting chronology surrounding one of the pamphlets Oswald was passing out that week, entitled "The Crime Against Cuba."[57]

This pamphlet was written by a well-known New York writer and peace activist, Corliss Lamont. The pamphlet, like other material distributed by Oswald (see Chapter 4), had the address "544 Camp Street" stamped on it. But unlike the other literature, this was not a simple flyer printed by Oswald himself in New Orleans. It was published in New York City and distributed for Lamont through Basic Pamphlets. One could order copies by mail at ten cents each or 15 for a dollar.

What is most intriguing is that this pamphlet, which attacked the Bay of Pigs invasion, was written and published in June 1961. By December of that year, it had already gone through four printings, each noted on the second page. What Summers did not realize was that the copy Oswald was handing out in August 1963 was not the latest edition then current, but the *first*, published—and sold out—when Oswald was in the Soviet Union. Fortuitously, Lamont—who is now 90 years old and still politically active—saved a photocopy of a most interesting bulk order for 45 copies of the first edition, mailed from Washington June 29, 1961, and received and filled the next day. It was not, of course, from Oswald; it was not from Guy Banister; it was from the Central Intelligence Agency itself.

*...... ....
Columbia University, Cornell, Harvard and the New School for Social Research, and is now lecturing and writing extensively about the causes in which he believes.*

*Copyright 1961 by Basic Pamphlets
First printing, June 1961
Mary Redmer, Editor*

Columbia University, Cornell, Harvard and the New School for Social Research, and is now lecturing and writing extensively about the causes in which he believes.

*Copyright 1961 by Basic Pamphlets
First printing, June 1961
Fourth printing, December 1961
Mary Redmer, Editor*

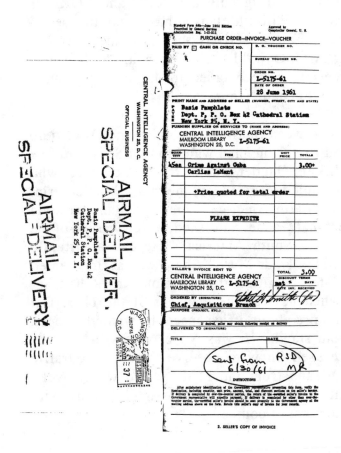

Top left, the second page of the first edition of Lamont's pamphlet, which Oswald was leafleting in August 1963 (also reproduced as WCT Exhibit 3120). Top right, the same page of the fourth printing of December 1961. Left, the envelope and order form from the CIA for 45 copies of the first printing, ordered June 28, 1961, mailed June 29, and filled June 30.

This strange ballet gains some clarity when one reflects on
the other Shaw-Oswald public appearance, in Clinton. As
noted earlier, there was a voter registration drive taking place
in Clinton at the time. Shaw and Ferrie seem to have had two
aims in bringing Oswald: first, to try to set up the "oddball"
scapegoat by placing him at a sanitarium; and second, to try
to monitor the voter registration drive set up there by the
militant Congress of Racial Equality (CORE). The Trade
Mart incident throws more light on this, because one of the
Agency's—and the Bureau's—functions in the 1960s was to
monitor and infiltrate leftwing organizations. By carefully
planning an incident to get himself exposed as a "Marxist"
on both radio and television, Oswald, with help from Shaw
and Ferrie, was discrediting both the FPCC and CORE as
communist fronts. As Philip Melanson has noted, this seemingly subversive espionage activity seems to have been Oswald's specialty. After Oswald's return from his "defection,"
the Agency seems to have decided to use his communist
credentials on the domestic front.

The connections between Shaw, the Agency, and Oswald do
not end here. Ted Brent, the man who brought Shaw into the
ITM,[58] knew William Gaudet, one of the CIA contacts who
allegedly accompanied Oswald on the hazy Mexico trip.
Brent subsidized "Latin America Report," a Banister-style
propaganda sheet that Gaudet published, which warned of the
communist threat in South America.[59] He had a virtually
rent-free office in the Trade Mart.[60] Shaw, who at first denied
knowing him, later admitted that Gordon Novel had approached him when he was the manager of the ITM. But
Novel did not inquire about office space; he wanted to open
up a "refreshment stand."[61] It was Novel who said that the
CIA might have used Shaw to observe the flow of traffic
through New Orleans from the ITM.[62] Who was Novel's
representative in his refreshment stand negotiations with
Shaw? Dean Andrews, of course.[63]

Shaw was found not guilty, and considering the Spiesel testimony and the Habighorst ruling, that verdict was understandable. But if the many facets of Shaw's life that were hidden at the time—his wartime activities with Thrasher, his CIA contact work, his roles in Permindex and CMC—if these had been aired, a different portrait would have emerged. Shaw's testimony seems demonstrably false; he perjured himself on at least four salient points.[64] Why would an innocent man risk 20 years in prison?[65]

Reflecting on Shaw's life, he is one of the most complex and unexplored people connected to the Kennedy case. Studying his life and career chronologically, one finds that there were really three Clay Shaws. The first was Shaw the young man. He was glib and affable, and developed a literary bent in high school that never left him.[66] He wrote four plays in the 1930s, one of which—*Submerged*—was often performed.[67] Later in that decade, Shaw emigrated to New York and became a Western Union executive. He did this for three years before turning to public relations and serving as an actors' agent. (While with Western Union, he requested to be placed in the theater district.)

**Clay Shaw
In the early 1950s.**

His military service was a crossroads. When he returned to New York after the war, many of his friends were gone and his professional contacts has disappeared. He returned to New Orleans, where an old high school friend, Ted Brent, was impressed by his public relations skills. ("He could sell a refrigerator to an eskimo," Shaw's cousin told me.) Brent brought him into his new venture, the International Trade Mart.[68] By 1947, Shaw was an integral part of the ITM. Within two years, he had his part in the reorganized CIA, first as a commercial contact and then, in 1957, as a representative on the boards of two reactionary organizations.

From here to the end of his life, there seem to have been two Shaws. On the one hand, overtly, there was the charming, outgoing, *bon vivant*—a public-spirited citizen who worked for the restoration of the French Quarter, brought new business to New Orleans, and hobnobbed with New Orleans high society. The other, covert, Shaw was both a closet homosexual and a secret neo-fascist, friend and colleague of extreme rightwingers and CIA operatives, a part of the Agency's overseas anticommunist crusades. Henry Hurt has argued[69] (and Gordon Novel hinted) that Shaw was a "deep cover" agent ever since the war. This might explain why it was Shaw who introduced Charles Cabell at a gathering of the Foreign Policy Association in New Orleans in May 1961, just a month after the Bay of Pigs debacle.[70] It was Cabell who tried to press Kennedy to send in the U.S. Air Force when the beach landing was collapsing. It might also explain why Richard Helms began daily meetings at CIA headquarters in 1969 with questions like, "How is the Shaw trial going? Are we giving them all the help they need? Is everything going all right down there?"[71]

From all this, it seems fair to conclude that even if Shaw was not in on the planning stages of the plot—and, as we shall see, there is evidence that he was—he likely knew about its formation. As Garrison came to conclude, Shaw was a minor operative in a major operation, or, as he put it, "I had stumbled across the big toe of someone who was involved in one of the biggest crimes in history."[72]

In 1964, then DCI John McCone testified categorically to the Warren Commission:[73]

> My examination has resulted in the conclusion that Lee Harvey Oswald was not an agent, employee, or informant of the Central Intelligence Agency. The Agency never contacted him, interviewed him, talked with him, or received or solicited any reports or information from him, or communicated with him directly in any other manner.

Later, Richard Helms, McCone's assistant and soon to be DCI himself, testified to the same effect. McCone may have been misled, or kept out of the information loop so he could maintain plausible deniability. Considering Helms's subsequent and famous perjury conviction,[74] he certainly could have been lying.

In 1976, a CIA document was released that noted Agency interest in recruiting Oswald.[75] The document suggested that

Richard McGarrah Helms, Deputy Director for Plans, 1962-1965; Deputy Director, 1965-1966; Director of Central Intelligence, 1966-1973.

interviews should be held with him through the Domestic Contacts Division. Later, the Agency revealed it had a "201" (or personnel) file on Oswald.[76] Some commentators, even former CIA employees, have stated that a 201 file would strongly suggest that Oswald was an agent.[77] Other credible observers deny this.[78] Whatever the truth, the file the Agency had on Oswald was voluminous.[79] It began with documents from 1959, the year of his "defection," although the Agency says the file was opened in 1960.[80] The file itself contains 1,196 documents, some of them hundreds of pages long. Of these, more than two hundred are still classified, almost 30 years after his death. Many of those released are heavily censored.

But few informed observers believe these files comprise the definitive account of Oswald's association with the CIA. As Fletcher Prouty told Anthony Summers:[81]

> Lee Oswald was not an ordinary Marine. He was a Marine on a cover assignment.... It is obvious that much of the material in the Oswald cover file is wrong. It could be human error, though I doubt it, or it could be some kind of obfuscation. There are thousands of people who have had such files—that is, life records—done, and it is all mixed up....

With someone whose exposure could have done such damage to the Agency as Oswald, one can bet the file was "all mixed up."

There is another curious aspect of Oswald's relationship to U.S. intelligence. After his apprehension, the only alias the Dallas police made public was that of O.H. Lee, the name given to his landlady in Oak Cliff.[82] Although the Dallas police later said they had, within hours, taken from Oswald an ID card with the name "Hidell" on it, it was not released to the media until the next day, *after* the discovery of a mail order in that name for the Carcano.[83] Members of the Military

Intelligence Group received a mysterious call that day, about the Hidell name. They looked for it in their files[84] and found it cross-referenced to Oswald. The cross-referenced file had been opened in the summer of 1963.[85] But when the Warren Commission asked for any Army files on Oswald, they were never shown this one. When the HSCA asked for it, they found it had been destroyed, as a matter of "routine."[86]

The best discussion to date of Oswald's intelligence role is the 1990 book, *Spy Saga,* by Philip Melanson. Of the many odd incidents related in this volume, perhaps the most telling is that on his trip to Mexico, after leaving New Orleans for Dallas, Oswald was shadowed by two to three intelligence agents.[87] (As we will see in the next chapter, if Oswald *did* go to Mexico, he was heavily chaperoned.)

In a bit of understatement, Garrison wrote in 1988, "It would certainly have helped our case against Shaw to have been able to link him definitively with the CIA."[88] Not to mention Oswald. If any of this information had come out in 1969, a plausible motive for Shaw's involvement could have been discernible and Garrison's case would have been on solid ground. The decorative wall of respectability so carefully constructed by Shaw and his lawyers could have been shattered, and the verdict might well have been different.

In 1975, the second myth surrounding the assassination, that the CIA and the FBI had cooperated with the Warren Commission, began to collapse. In January of that year, the Rockefeller Commission was created. Its expressed purpose was to investigate unlawful CIA activities inside the United States. Some of its discoveries were shocking. The CIA had intercepted and opened U.S. mail from 1953 to 1973. A domestic spying operation against Vietnam dissidents—Operation CHAOS—had begun in 1967 and continued to 1974. The Agency created and implemented a foreign assassination group called "Executive Action" and it had a hand in plots against Salvador Allende of Chile, Patrice Lumumba of the

Congo, Rafael Trujillo of the Dominican Republic, and, of course, Fidel Castro. Devastatingly, the Commission unearthed the infamous use by the Agency of the Mafia in the early plots to kill Castro.[89]

This knowledge, however, proved too much for the Commission members. They decided not to include a draft of the chapter on assassinations in their report. It is not clear why, but as its Executive Director David Belin—staff lawyer for and still a key defender of the Warren Commission—has written, "The ramifications of an Agency out of control were very grave."[90]

The job of truly exposing this out-of-control Agency fell to the Senate Special Committee on Governmental Operations headed by Senator Frank Church of Idaho. The Church Committee membership included such luminaries as Walter Mondale, Barry Goldwater, and Gary Hart. The Committee's multi-volume Final Report became one of the most sensational and scathing documents ever issued by a congressional committee overseeing a government agency. It was so troubling that it led to the creation of Intelligence Oversight Committees in both houses of Congress.

The Final Report devoted an entire volume to the performance of intelligence agencies in relation to the JFK assassination.[91] In it, almost every aspect of the association between both the Bureau and Agency on one side, and the Warren Commission on the other, is scored. Whole areas of overwhelming importance were kept from the Commissioners, so that any chance of uncovering ties between the principals and any intelligence or underworld bodies was almost impossible.

Some key revelations of this extraordinary report include:

•The CIA attempts to assassinate Castro were never revealed to the Warren Commission.[92]

•The CIA realized that Castro knew of the plots, yet this was never disclosed to the Commission.[93]

•The FBI never investigated the Cuban exile groups in New Orleans and their possible connections to Oswald.[94]

•J. Edgar Hoover had a deep antipathy toward the Commission. After the Report was released, "Hoover asked for all derogatory material on Warren Commission members and staff contained in FBI files."[95]

•The Agency deliberately covered up the true facts about Oswald's alleged trip to Mexico.[96]

•Within hours of the assassination, Hoover used his muscle to issue a report incriminating Oswald.[97]

•Hoover's leaks to the press about the FBI investigation were meant to shut off the possibility of an independent inquiry.[98]

Two members of the Committee, Colorado Democrat Gary Hart and Pennsylvania Republican Richard Schweiker, had access to many classified intelligence files. Both of the Senators came away from them enlightened, angered, and alarmed.[99]

At first, Hart was reluctant to reopen wounds from 1963. But, appalled at what he had learned and fed up with the Agency's stonewalling, he finally spoke out. Commenting on Oswald's summer in New Orleans, he called for further inquiry into "who Oswald really was—who did he know? What affiliation did he have in the Cuban network? Was his public identification with the left a cover for a connection with the anti-Castro right wing?"[100]

Hart went on to declare that, in his opinion, Oswald was quite a sophisticated operator, bright enough to act as a double agent.[101]

Schweiker was even more forthright: "Either we trained and sent him [Oswald] to Russia, and they went along and pretended they didn't know to fake us out, or in fact, they inculcated him and sent him back here and were trying to fake us out that way."[102]

In 1978, Schweiker went even further and stated that the Warren Commission had collapsed. It was set up to numb the public in order for a huge coverup to be enacted.[103] He then focused on Oswald's role in that charade:[104]

I think that by playing a pro-Cuban role on the one hand and associating with anti-Castro Cubans on the other, Oswald was playing out an intelligence role. This gets back to him being an agent or double agent.... All the fingerprints I found during my eighteen months on the Senate Select Committee point to Oswald being a product of, and interacting with, the intelligence community.

This quote could have been taken from any of several interviews given by Jim Garrison circa 1967. It took eleven years and a two-year investigation to convince a Senate committee that, in essence, Garrison was right and the Warren Commission, with their farcical tales of Oswald walking through the park shooting birds with his rifle, was wrong.

Almost immediately after the Church Committee released its report in May of 1976, the House of Representatives voted to create the House Select Committee on Assassinations (HSCA).[105]

The Church Committee had not investigated the actual circumstances of the assassination. It had confined itself to the performance of the intelligence agencies in response to that event. But its findings were so sobering that it opened up a Pandora's Box of doubt as to the validity of the official findings.

Also at that time, assassination researcher and photographic expert Robert Groden was showing his optically enhanced copy of the Zapruder film on television and college campuses.[106] Congressman Thomas Downing (Dem.-Va.) was impressed by it and sponsored a bill to create a committee to reinvestigate the events surrounding the shooting. Downing did not run for reelection in 1976, and, when his bill passed, the chairmanship went to Representative Henry Gonzalez of Texas, who happened to have been in the motorcade through Dallas on November 22, 1963.

Almost immediately, Gonzalez became embroiled in a vicious argument over money, methodology, and power with Richard A. Sprague, his chief counsel. Their relationship deteriorated to the point where Gonzalez tried to fire Sprague. In one instance, Sprague literally locked himself in his office and refused to leave while rallying members of the Select Committee to his cause.[107] Angered and embarrassed, Gonzalez resigned. The probe seemed on the verge of collapse before it began.[108]

A compromise was reached, and Representative Louis Stokes of Ohio took command in March 1977. Sprague agreed to step down, and he was replaced by Cornell University law professor Robert Blakey, a specialist on Mob influence in American life and author of several laws meant to combat that influence. The HSCA had wasted almost a year on internal bickering and finding a counsel. It now had new leadership on both the political and legal/investigatory sides.

In retrospect, the new leaders were quite a mixed bag. Downing and Gonzalez had been convinced that the Warren

**Representative
Louis Stokes, left,
with G. Robert Blakey.**

Commission was wrong in both procedure and conclusions, and they were both familiar with the literature in the field. Sprague was new to the field, but seemed to have had an open mind and been willing to follow the trail of evidence wherever it led. This was not the case with Stokes and Blakey. Neither man had a broad background or familiarity with the case. Far from being open-minded, Blakey seemed to look on many of the writers and researchers in the field as kooks and scholars of witchcraft and demonology. Consequently, it took both men quite a while to get up to speed, acquainting themselves with the reputable literature and scholars in the field.

Blakey and Stokes quickly revealed two hallmarks of their working methods. First, as with the Warren Commission, most of their hearings were held behind closed doors. Second, Blakey placed a great belief in what he termed "scientific evidence." He divided the inquiry into several areas of study, *e.g.*, photographic evidence, medical evidence, ballistics, etc. He then appointed large panels of experts to oversee those areas and to come to collective conclusions by vote.

Superficially, this approach had some appeal. Who could argue with a purely scientific probe into a complex event? But often these panels expressed their opinions in pseudo-scientific gobbledygook in order to endorse preconceived theses. Many of these men were new to the case and they had a predisposition to abide by the existing official line. Blakey and Stokes did nothing to discourage this predilection, in contrast to Garrison, who often coaxed his young staff into spontaneous brainstorming sessions. Indeed, this explained why these scientifically minded experts ended up affirming the demonstrably unscientific single-bullet theory.

Two examples reveal the shallowness of Blakey's approach. Robert Groden was allowed to appear before the Committee to present some of his photographic discoveries. During his presentation, he pointed out in films from Dealey Plaza a man he felt was Joseph Milteer.[109] Milteer, mentioned in Chapter 6, was caught on audio tape predicting that Kennedy would soon be shot with a rifle from an office building. He was obviously a strong suspect in the assassination. He belonged to several powerful racist groups, among them the Ku Klux Klan. He was independently wealthy. He knew others who wished JFK dead.[110] The man who recorded Milteer's talk was William Somersett, an informer for the FBI and the Miami Police. On November 22, Somersett received a call from Milteer, saying he was in Dallas, that JFK was there that day, and that he would never be in Miami again.[111]

This was a strong indication that Milteer was somehow part of a Dallas conspiracy, but the Committee did not want to hear of it. They set about to disprove Milteer's presence in Groden's films. In some tortured reasoning, they tried to show the man could not be Milteer because he was too short. In fact, faulty mathematical premises, as later disclosed, made everyone seem shorter than they were.[112]

Blakey himself furnished another example of HSCA "scientific method." The Committee was having difficulty explaining the rapid firing sequence during the assassination. They were trying to aim and fire each round of the Mannlicher-Carcano in even less time than the 2.3 seconds achieved by the FBI in 1964. When none of the marksmen used by the Committee could accomplish this, Blakey told them to discard the telescopic sight, to just line up the target and fire. This still was not fast enough. But Blakey did not accept the obvious fact that if these marksmen could not do it, then Oswald certainly could not either. He took a rifle and began firing from the hip, without even aiming the weapon.[113] If necessary, Blakey was quite ready to disregard "scientific method," common sense, and honesty.

There was one piece of new evidence that even Blakey and the Committee found so convincing they had to drop the Warren Commission axe they had been grinding. This evidence led to the slaying of a third myth: that a lone gunman had assassinated John Kennedy, that there was no conspiracy.

The Zapruder film has always provided powerful evidence of a sniper shot from the front of the motorcade, from the grassy knoll. Unfortunately, Zapruder's camera was silent, so one could not synchronize the sounds of the shots with the pictures to pinpoint an exact timing sequence that would help in locating the direction of the shots. To fill this gap, Mary Farrell, Gary Mack, and other researchers alerted the HSCA to the existence of a tape recording of the Dallas Police's radio transmissions from Dealey Plaza at the time of the assassination.[114]

In the late spring of 1978, the tape was submitted to Dr. James Barger, chief acoustical scientist for the firm of Bolt, Beranek, and Newman. Dr. Barger had done acoustical research for the Navy in the field of submarine sonar detection. He had been involved in determining the source of gunfire from tapes of the tragic 1970 Kent State shootings, when antiwar protesters were shot down by National Guardsmen. Barger's analysis differed from earlier work done on the tapes by Bell Telephone Acoustics for the Warren Commission, which had been done just to sort out message and movement.[115] But both analyses indicated that there were six distinctive "non-voiced" noises on the tape. Dr. Barger tested the soundwaves he discovered against the following criteria: Did they occur during the time frame of the assassination? Do the shots occur during the time frame indicated by the Zapruder film? Do the patterns resemble waves of gunfire as they would pass through the transmission systems used by the Dallas Police radio network?[116]

Barger found that all six soundwaves passed the tests. On the basis of his preliminary work, he found a 50-50 chance there was a sniper firing from the direction of the grassy knoll.

Blakey and the Committee required more certainty. They submitted Barger's findings to another team of scientists, Professor Mark Weiss and his associate Ernest Aschkenasy.

After two months of more refined testing, the pair presented their conclusions to the HSCA in dramatic public testimony. On December 29, 1978, they stated that there was a 95 percent probability of a second assassin firing from the knoll. Barger was called in to go over their findings. He concurred.[117]

To test whether or not the sounds on the tape were authentic, the HSCA had sent a team of riflemen out to simulate rifle fire in Dealey Plaza and to tape it on devices similar to Dallas Police equipment. But here crucial scientific evidence was compromised by politics. All three teams of scientists had found six supersonic rifleshots on the tape. Yet, the HSCA Final Report stated:[118]

Accordingly, impulses one and six on the dispatch tape did not pass the most rigorous acoustical test and were deemed not to have been caused by gunfire from the Texas School Book Depository or Grassy Knoll.

Just what did "did not pass" mean? The riflemen were ordered to shoot from *only* the book depository and the grassy knoll area. If test shots had been fired from, say, the Dal-Tex Building, the impulses and echo patterns might have matched. After all, the impulses could only be gunshots.[119] "Did not pass" simply meant they were not fired from two particular locations. Indeed, in all likelihood, there were six shots from three directions, or as David Ferrie had put it, a "triangulation of fire" (see Chapter 9).[120]

The timing of the shots also fits a pattern of multiple assassins. They are bunched very close together on the tape, some of them occurring less than one second after the previous shot.[121] If the HSCA had recognized *both* these facts—six soundwaves *and* the close timing sequence—they would have had to conclude there were two, or more likely, three snipers.[122] This was too bold for Blakey and Stokes. They eliminated two shots by testing only two firing locations, and they solved the firing sequence problem by dredging up Arlen Specter's discredited single-bullet theory.

The Committee also flouted scientific method when the sound recordings were synchronized with the Zapruder film. Weiss and Aschkenasy worked diligently with Robert Groden to synchronize the most logical sequence of shots with the proper frames of the Zapruder film. The sequence they came up with was as follows: The first shot was from behind; the second from behind; the third from the right/front; and the fourth from behind.[123]

The three experts believed the fatal head shot matched the shot coming from the front. In Groden's words:[124]

When the fourth shot matched the head shot, no other shots aligned to a verifiable action on the film. But when the third shot was matched up, every other impulse matched an action on the film exactly.

When Groden, Weiss, and Aschkenasy told Blakey this, the chief counsel overruled them. In fact, Groden reports that he was *ordered* by Blakey *not* to express his conclusions to the Committee.[125] The Congressmen were to be told that the fatal shot came from the rear.[126]

But whatever the Committee did with the acoustics evidence, it still pointed to a conspiracy. And armed with this finding, Blakey picked up the second axe he had to grind, namely that the conspiracy was molded by the Mob. The problem with this has always been that, while Oswald has intelligence ties printed all over him, he does not have significant Mob connections, nor does he in any way fit the profile of even a low-level mob operative.

This did not deter Blakey. He decided to use whatever time and money the Committee had left to seek out *any* possible mob ties. Predictably, they were quite weak: The area where Oswald lived when attending high school had a lot of organized crime activity. Oswald's mother worked for a shady lawyer. Dutch Murret, Oswald's uncle, with whom he stayed for a week in New Orleans in the summer of 1963, was a bookie.[127]

Subsequently, Blakey, and later, authors like John Davis and David Scheim, have spun out elaborate but amorphous paradigms to fit the Mafia into Oswald's life and acts.[128]

Blakey's two other published works are also on organized crime. In his preoccupation with mob connections to the JFK assassination, Blakey is like the medical student who, after preparing for an exam by studying the stomach, was asked about the heart, and replied, "The heart lies near the stomach. The stomach is constructed of...."

In the last days of the HSCA inquiry, other investigators were already looking into promising leads. Oddly enough, at that late date in 1978, the Committee was just discovering the significance of the 544 Camp Street address. To them, it served as a crucial intersection of Cuban exiles, intelligence interests, and mob influence. The mob link came from Ferrie's working for an attorney, G. Wray Gill, who was defending Mafia don Carlos Marcello, and had interested Banister in helping Marcello fight deportation.[129]

Still, a constructive new angle was also being developed in those last, frantic days. One of the Committee's best field investigators, Gaeton Fonzi, was pursuing the last phase of the CIA assassination plots against Castro, codenamed AM/LASH.

In September of 1963, the Agency made one last attempt to kill Castro, this time without Mafia help. They used a man close to Castro, Rolando Cubela, who had become disenchanted with the Cuban leader. The Agency learned of this and agreed to supply him with weapons, including a telescopic rifle and a poison fountain pen. This was coordinated with an effort to encourage the more radical anti-Castro groups to attack Soviet ships in Cuban ports.[130]

This is significant because, by late 1963, Kennedy seriously considered a softer line toward Cuba. Secretly, he was moving toward reconciliation.[131] Neither he nor any other high administration official sanctioned these anti-Cuban activities. In these operations, the Agency was acting on its own.

One of the men recruited for these clandestine enterprises was Antonio Veciana, a founder of the radical Cuban exile group Alpha 66. Veciana was tutored by the CIA in guerrilla methods, psychological warfare, organization of cells, counterfeiting Cuban currency, maritime sabotage, and political assassination.[132] In nearly all these efforts, Veciana says that his CIA contact and mentor was a man he knew as Maurice Bishop. (The future Prime Minister of Grenada, with the same name, was a teenager at the time.) Bishop—a code name—recruited him in Havana in 1960, and the two stayed in contact through various South American intrigues until 1973.[133] Bishop, in fact, was involved in the attacks on Soviet ships mentioned above.[134]

Veciana said that Bishop told him it was his intention to cause trouble between Kennedy and the Russians, to negate the pledge JFK had ostensibly made to Khrushchev not to invade Cuba. Bishop felt that:[135]

Kennedy was a man without experience, surrounded by a group of young men who were also inexperienced, with mistaken ideas on how to manage this country.... You had to put Kennedy against the wall in order to force him to make decisions to remove Castro's regime.

This reasoning sounds ominously like that of the CIA officers involved with the Bay of Pigs, Bissell and Cabell, but Bishop went even further. He told Veciana that the best thing for this country would be "that people like Kennedy and his advisers should not be running it."[136]

A few months later, Veciana met Bishop in Dallas, at the downtown Southland Center. Veciana waited for Bishop on the first floor; when he arrived, he was accompanied by a

Antonio Veciana,
head of Alpha 66,
photographed in
Puerto Rico in 1962.

stranger. The three went to the cafeteria, where Bishop asked the stranger to leave. Veciana remembered this as being late August or early September of 1963. After the assassination, Veciana realized the strange man was Oswald. He was adamant on this point; it was Oswald or his double. The time period is difficult to pinpoint. But Oswald's aimless New Orleans itinerary—he was supposed to be looking for a job at the time—allows for the rendezvous.[137]

Veciana never revealed Bishop's true identity. But Fonzi strongly suspected that it was David Atlee Phillips, long-time CIA Latin America specialist, and a key figure in the Bay of Pigs operation.[138]

If Fonzi is right, the story becomes even more intriguing, for after the assassination, Phillips tried strongly to implicate Oswald with Soviet and Cuban contacts, especially during the Mexico trip.[139] Oswald may have made the trip, but it is quite probable that he was impersonated at both the Soviet and Cuban Embassies (see Chapter 14). For instance, Phillips insisted he saw a transcript of taped conversations Oswald had in both embassies, since they were both bugged by the Agency. But, he said, the transcripts were destroyed after he saw them. Phillips also said Oswald called the Soviet Embassy and offered them information if they would pay his way to Russia.[140]

This is consistent with Veciana's statement that, after the assassination, Bishop had asked him if his cousin at the Cuban Embassy in Mexico City would state that he saw Oswald there weeks before.[141]

The scenario fits Bishop's rationale for pressuring JFK as described to Veciana. Now that Kennedy was dead, if Bishop could link Oswald to Cuban and Soviet interests, the campaign against Castro, perhaps ending in American intervention, could be revived to avenge the murder of the President.

If Phillips *was* Bishop, he and Cabell were very possibly the Agency links who authorized the New Orleans-based plot.[142] It was Shaw who introduced Cabell at the conference in New Orleans right after the Bay of Pigs debacle, shortly before Kennedy fired him. After Cabell was fired, he went to work for Howard Hughes and reportedly worked closely with Robert Maheu.[143] Maheu was the Agency contact man with the mob when the CIA first sought out assistance in the Castro death plots in 1960. And it was Cabell, along with

Left, the sketch of "Maurice Bishop" released by the committee; right, David Atlee Phillips.

Allen Dulles, who Bissell says originally authorized these plots.[144] (Then again, Bissell is not a disinterested source.)

Unfortunately, these promising leads did not surface until the Committee's final days. Blakey's last act was to recommend the HSCA findings of a probable conspiracy to the Justice Department. Later, the Justice Department—under Reagan at the time—commissioned a study that tried, unsuccessfully, to discredit the acoustical evidence.[145]

Ultimately, the House probe was unsatisfactory in many ways. It took to task the methods and findings of the Warren Commission in no uncertain terms (see Final Report, p. x); but reservations about its work are best summed up by writer-researcher Carl Oglesby:[146]

This report has serious shortcomings. It pulls its punches. It insinuates much about the Mob and JFK's death which it then says it doesn't really mean. It is alternately confused and dogmatic on the subject of Oswald's motive. It tells us it could not see all the way into the heart of CIA or FBI darkness. Its treatment of the technical evidence in the crucial areas of shot sequencing and medical evidence is shallow and unconvincing.

Chief House investigator Fonzi had similar strong reservations:[147]

There is not one investigator—not one—who served on the Kennedy task force of the Assassinations Committee who honestly feels he took part in an adequate investigation, let alone a "full and complete" one.

The HSCA, led by Blakey, ranged wider than the Warren Commission had. It had more citizen involvement, mainly because it had been created because of public demand. But in two telling ways, its process and its end results resembled those of its predecessor.

First, very few hearings were open to the public.[148] Then, when the investigation ended, many of the files were classified and stored away until the year 2029. But Blakey went beyond even Warren in his quest for secrecy. He made staff members sign secrecy agreements before examining classified files.[149] He also required a non-disclosure agreement, prohibiting staff members and consultants from discussing Committee business with outsiders.[150]

Blakey's cooperation with government agencies extended further. When the HSCA reviewed Oswald's "201" file, 37 memoranda were missing. Blakey accepted the CIA's explanation that they were not really missing; they had just been checked out that day.[151] Then, the CIA was allowed to review preliminary drafts of the Committee's final report.[152] And although Blakey insists that the files hidden away until 2029 are just personnel files, it is hard to see how Edwin Lopez's report on "Oswald in Mexico" (see Chapter 14) qualifies.[153]

Even when Blakey was no longer in charge and published a book on the investigation, he let both the CIA and the FBI review his manuscript.[154] This is the person who, when confronted with skepticism over the Agency's intentions, replied, "You don't think they'd lie to me, do you? I've been working with these people for twenty years."[155] Blakey could say this about the CIA even though the Agency liaison to the HSCA had broken into his office and stolen some of the autopsy materials.[156] And like Gerald Ford with John Stiles, Blakey seems to have been looking toward the future while serving on the Committee. The only man who was not asked to sign a non-disclosure agreement was Richard Billings, the man assigned by Blakey to write large parts of the HSCA Final Report. It was Billings who ended up co-writing Blakey's book.[157]

Before Blakey limited the investigation, Sprague had made two honest and intelligent moves. He hired a number of professional, independent investigators and criminal lawyers with no ties to the federal government. They included Robert Tanenbaum as his Deputy Counsel and Cliff Fenton as chief field investigator.[158] Also, he contacted Garrison and asked for all important data and leads he could give him.[159]

Sprague, Fenton, and Fonzi realized that the Dallas-New Orleans-Miami-Cuban exile corridor was a key element with both Oswald and the assassination. Fenton's team followed up on Garrison's leads and found one that was explosive. A former CIA agent had been involved in a meeting in New Orleans concerning the assassination.[160] He was willing to testify before the Committee. Fenton had made a tape of his testimony, in which he stated that both Shaw and Ferrie were at the meeting.[161] Fenton found the witness convincing and credible. When Sprague left, however, Blakey chose to bury the Fenton report.[162] Fenton, who signed Blakey's non-disclosure agreement, has not made the report, or the tape, public.[163]

It is sad that *Blakey's* HSCA did not consult Garrison. His files could have saved the blinker-eyed Blakey much time, perhaps enough time for Fonzi to solve the mystery of Maurice Bishop.

To read the section of the HSCA Report concerning the Cuban exiles and Oswald's association with them is almost to reread the history of Garrison's case.[164] Some of the topics include: Kennedy and the Bay of Pigs, the Cuban Missile Crisis, militant anti-Castro groups, Agency involvement with these groups, Sylvia Odio, the possibility of a "second Oswald," Oswald's connections to exile groups, Oswald in Clinton, Oswald and Ferrie, Guy Banister and 544 Camp Street, Clay Shaw, Sergio Arcacha Smith, George De Mohrenschildt, and a supplementary report verifying the Rose Cheramie story in all essentials.[165] The Committee also concluded that Ruby's murder of Oswald was not spontaneous and that he likely had help entering the Dallas police station.[166]

Although slightly better than the Warren Report, the new official version was issued so long after the fact—sixteen years—that it was impossible to pinpoint the masterminds of the operation. It came to no definite conclusions. But via the Veciana-Bishop episode, it furthered Garrison's case. And whichever of the probable paths of suspicion one pursues— Cuban exile groups, organized crime, CIA-Mafia plots against Fidel—the guidepost is David Ferrie. The man who unmasked Ferrie is Jim Garrison.

14

The Unmarked Milestone

During the 1970s and 1980s, with the decline of liberalism and the ascension of Reagan-Bush conservatism, it became a cliché in journalism and publishing for writers to pinpoint when "the transformation of America" had begun. Some of the more common choices are the Vietnam War, the 1968 election, the Watergate scandal, and the 1980 election. Some of the books on the subject have indicative titles: *Where Have All the Flowers Gone, Coming Apart, From Camelot to Kent State, Decade of Shocks, In Time of Torment, Something Happened*. The themes addressed are similar, whatever the approach: They concern a rite of passage from a period of youthful optimism, hope, innocence, and achievement to an era of pessimism, greed, corruption, and retrenchment. America had seemingly gone from a time where progress and idealism were commonplace to one in which they were out-moded, old-fashioned, unrealistic. We now live in a period of deep cynicism where debacles like the Savings and Loan scandals and the Iran-Contra affair hardly seem to raise eyebrows.

One can make a good argument for marking the transition at any of the four events mentioned above. The U.S. adventure in Vietnam turned out to be Lyndon Johnson's *bête noire*. It ruined his presidency and overshadowed his Great Society. It split the Democratic Party, which has never really recovered, and led to the 1968 election of Richard Nixon.

Nixon's personal and political machinations led to the Watergate scandals, his virtual impeachment, and the inevitable weakness of his successor, former Warren Commissioner Gerald Ford, who was challenged for the Republican nomination for president by Ronald Reagan in 1976. Seasoned in the 1976 primaries, Reagan ran successfully in 1980.

The transformation was now complete. The New America was a *fait accompli*. We had gone from the Kennedys to the Reagans; from William Douglas to William Rehnquist; from Martin Luther King, Jr. to Michael Milken; from *Lawrence of Arabia* to *Rambo*. Socially, the nation moved from one seemingly committed to experiment, change, and perfection to one of caution, conservatism, and stasis. Young college students no longer vied for openings in John Kennedy's Peace Corps.

Nevertheless, I think the sea change really began earlier. A better argument can be made that the New America was born on November 22, 1963, and that many of the plagues visited on us since can find their roots in the Kennedy assassination and its aftermath.

The first is the use of the "big lie." The American people had been lied to before, but the Warren Report moved this phenomenon to a higher plane. The lie was so big, the attendant praise so lavish, the holes in the story so gaping, that it quickly sparked a countermovement to the official story. Widespread public disbelief in government burgeoned. Indeed, the wave of public skepticism and then cynicism which would sweep through the nation with Vietnam, Watergate, and Iran-Contra, began with the public rejection of the Warren Report. Today it is nearly institutionalized. We have become so accustomed to the big lie that the effect has become numbing. Neither Reagan nor Bush was mortally wounded by the Iran-Contra or S&L fallout. Today, few people believe what the government says or does, and concomitantly few vote. Non-voting has increased in every presidential election since Kennedy's in 1960.[1]

The CIA has also become much more notorious since 1963. It had managed to keep a relatively low profile before the Bay of Pigs. But after the Kennedy assassination, the Agency took part in so many dubious, ill-advised schemes that it was censured twice by Senate committees.[2] CIA involvement in the Operation PHOENIX assassination program in Vietnam, in the overthrow of Salvador Allende in Chile, in the mining of Nicaraguan harbors, in the Iran-Contra scandal and cover-up—all these and more show that even exposures of violations of international law were no obstacle to the bureaucratic growth of the national security apparatus. The CIA is now more entrenched than ever, even though its reason for being, "the communist threat," has all but collapsed.

To a lesser extent, the FBI and especially J. Edgar Hoover were also brought into high relief for the first time in 1963. Hoover was such a uniquely powerful man that it was not until after his death in 1972 that people felt at liberty to criticize him.[3] But once he died, the dam quickly burst.

The Church Committee was the first official body to start to crack his image, and a series of books, the latest and best being Curt Gentry's *J. Edgar Hoover*, has finally exposed the incompetent lunacy and unprecedented power of this man.[4] It is a sorry fifty-year record. Perhaps even worse is the spinelessness of the many politicians, including the Kennedys, who ran up against him but failed to do open battle with him. The Warren Commission might have demanded a competent performance from him. That it did not was one reason for the failure of its Report.

The Kennedy assassination and the Garrison investigation highlighted the shortcomings of the American print and electronic media. Their lack of vigor in seriously investigating the assassination and their gullibility in accepting the Warren Report was staggering. The *New York Times* sanctified the Report by issuing both its own abridged version and a companion volume called *The Witnesses*, which contained excerpts from the testimony of selected witnesses before the Commission.[5] Then with the exposure of the Garrison inquiry in February of 1967, we saw the other side of this eager embrace of the Report: a vicious smear campaign against those who expressed reservations about it.

There seem to be two reasons for this, one political and one cultural. The first is that, as shown above, some publications like the *New York Times* had then and still have a vested interest in seeing the official story prevail.[6] Likewise, the *Washington Post* for years after the assassination had a policy of not reviewing books critical of the Warren Report.

The cultural reason is more complicated and has three aspects. First, as we have seen, in the cases of Aynesworth, Phelan, and Sheridan, these men all had national security axes to grind. They ground them so hard that they rose above the status of journalists to become full participants, almost as much as Shaw, his lawyers, or even Garrison himself. (In Aynesworth's case he was a combatant, getting into a scuffle outside the courtroom.[7])

A second cultural, inbred reason for the media's failure—one that continues to this day—is that many journalists just completely missed the story the first time around and do not like to admit that fact. Indeed, the JFK assassination story is anything but simple. It does not lend itself to the "four-W," pyramid-style, two-column newspaper approach. Neither can justice be done to it in a feature magazine article. Very few newspaper reporters had the time and dedication, and fewer publications were willing to spend the money, to try to get to the bottom of the events in Dealey Plaza. Nor was the cause of investigative journalism served by the intense pressure from the FBI and the White House to blame a lone nut and discard conspiracy hypotheses.

Consequently the media became a focus of "spin-control." The Aynesworth-Phelan-Sheridan nexus pointed to another path for American journalism, one that led communications experts directly into the political arena, and politicians and their advisers into media management. Aynesworth, Phelan, and Sheridan foreshadowed the coming to prominence of men like Roger Ailes, Michael Deaver, and Lee Atwater.[8] It was Deaver who managed the 1980 and 1984 campaigns of Ronald Reagan. Atwater masterminded the stigmatizing 1988 Bush campaign with its blatant race-baiting use of Willie Horton.

A good model for the media's performance in New Orleans from 1967 to 1969 is the recent Tom Wolfe novel *The Bonfire of the Vanities.*[9] In it, no one even asks what the truth is. It does not matter. It has become totally irrelevant to the projection of images and egos.

But the truth does matter; patterns in history do emerge. In the Watergate scandal, some players from the Kennedy assassination saga revisited American history. E. Howard Hunt, Bernard Barker, and Frank Sturgis, all part of the CIA's anti-Castro effort, were back in the news. This time they went to jail. Gordon Novel, the man who defied Garrison's extradition attempts, offered to lend the White House his electronics savvy to erase Nixon's self-incriminating tapes.[10] In 1988, William Casey's "off-the-shelf" covert operations setup was reminiscent of a faction of the Agency that ostensibly broke away after 1962 and decided that JFK was expendable.[11]

Even worse than the loss of truth and perspective is the constant refrain of the unfulfilled promise of a second Kennedy term. When one scans the pages of the *Dallas Morning News* from the week leading up to the assassination, a bittersweet headline appears on the front page of the November 17 issue. Featuring the results of an early Gallup poll for the 1964 presidential race, the figures read: John Kennedy 58 percent, Barry Goldwater 42 percent. It is safe to argue that Kennedy, the experienced candidate, would have run an efficient, smooth campaign, while the unvarnished, hawkish Goldwater would have encountered problems, as he did against Johnson. Barring an extraordinary mistake or scandal,[12] Kennedy would likely have been re-elected.

Would that have made a difference to America? Would Kennedy have been able to ease the strain of the cataclysmic changes that were rocking America and had their seeds in the Eisenhower years? The question is ultimately speculative. (After all, many people voted against Goldwater and for Johnson in 1964 out of fear that Goldwater would get the United States involved in "a land war in Asia.") I am not a JFK hagiographer, but in my view most commentators miss a quite simple fact: Kennedy was not a great president; he just looks good today compared to the competition.

Most historians agree that Eisenhower was ignoring serious and festering problems in his second term, e.g., civil rights, the economy, and education. Kennedy addressed these head-on. Most historians would also agree that of the six presidencies that followed, four were not particularly successful, one—Reagan's—is being seriously reevaluated (because of what may turn out to be disastrous long-term effects on the economy, the environment, and the quality of life in general), and the latest—Bush's—is up in the air. No historian could say those things about JFK. If the Kennedy years were not Camelot—and they were not—they certainly seem to shimmer slightly in retrospect.

Another factor that makes the Kennedy years seem so attractive is the visionary call for idealism that he championed. He was serious about energizing the country out of the Eisenhower doldrums. His primary method was to challenge a sleeping political imagination with a sometimes choppy, sometimes grandiose, but at times quite powerful rhetoric:[13]

I am sick of reading these studies ... which show that the image of America as a vital, forceful society, as it once was under Franklin Roosevelt, has begun to fade. I believe it incumbent upon this generation of Americans to meet the same rendezvous with destiny of which

Franklin Roosevelt spoke in 1936. This country has to do better. This country has to move again. This country has to provide full use of its people and all of its facilities if we are going to win out.

But Kennedy's plea to idealism was not just the use of flowery words to pacify the converted and confound the opposition. JFK was a politician to his fingertips. His rhetoric was used to build and fire a consensus for change so that he would neither be ahead of the curve, nor lag behind, but be right at the cutting edge of reform. For Kennedy was not dewy-eyed about reform.[14] He knew that the populace had to be ready for it. "Great innovations should not be forced on slender majorities," he said.[15]

Kennedy's idealism was tempered by practical political and cultural factors that he always considered. And one of those practical considerations was what the opposition had to offer. In 1960, the other side was offering Richard Nixon. Whereas Kennedy was the politician of unity and idealism, Nixon was the politician of divisiveness and negativism.[16] To hear JFK on Nixon is a good reflection on what has happened to America in the intervening years. Indeed, during the 1960 campaign, as Kennedy grew more accustomed to Nixon's style of campaigning, he privately summed up the candidate quite pithily and succinctly: "He's a filthy, lying son-of-a-bitch, and a very dangerous man."[17] And Kennedy had no affinity for the negative campaigning that Senator Joe McCarthy and Nixon pioneered and which has polluted the political process ever since. During the 1960 Wisconsin primary, for example, a race Kennedy had to win, and in which he was trailing then-Senator Hubert Humphrey, one of his aides suggested a negative attack campaign to ensure victory. Kennedy replied:[18]

I'm winning this thing on my own and if we start exchanging smears the whole campaign will become an issue of credibility. Whose lies do you believe? I'd rather have people make a judgment about who can lead.... If I'm wrong there will be other primaries....

He was right and he won.

Unlike Reagan, Kennedy did not center his idealism on the past. JFK was fluid, with many interests, and always growing. A close observer characterized him early in his career:[19]

He could not be called a natural politician; he was too reserved by nature. To stand by a factory gate and shake hands with the workers was never easy for him.... But he knew what he wanted and he would force himself to do whatever was necessary to achieve it. Throughout the 1952 campaign he became more at ease with strangers, a better public speaker and more confident campaigner.... Kennedy had talent and he worked hard; above all, he was a proud man who took intense pride in every aspect of his work.

He tried to be at the forefront of new ideas. Kennedy was not a scholar-intellectual like Jefferson or Wilson. But he had a quick mind, he learned easily, and he had sound instincts. He was always on the lookout for good advice and he was not too arrogant to follow it. One observer described this trait as "an ability to discern quickly what people had to say that was important to what he was trying to do. He shunned conversations with people about things which they knew very little. He always tried to find a person's area of expertise and to channel conversations in that direction."[20]

In 1963, Kennedy was just hitting his stride in both domestic and foreign policy. Consider his underrated record on the domestic side by 1963: the return of Keynesian economics; the construction of a civil rights bill and its shepherding through the Judiciary Committee; the enforcement of court-ordered integration; federal aid to education; the raising of the minimum wage and expansion of the Fair Labor Standards Act; establishment of the Peace Corps; the beginning of the fight for women's rights and Medicare. The list is only partial.[21] Martin Luther King, Jr., could say about Kennedy's emerging record:[22]

> There were in fact two John Kennedys. One presided in the first two years under pressure of the uncertainty caused by his razor-thin margin of victory. In 1963, a new Kennedy had emerged. He had found that public opinion was not in a rigid mold. He was, at his death, undergoing a transformation from a hesitant leader with unsure goals to a strong figure with deeply appealing objectives.

One of those deeply appealing objectives was ending the Cold War. JFK had outgrown the Cold Warrior mentality that held so many politicians of his time in a viselike grip. We can see today that he was right, that the "Red Scare" was never the threat it was made out to be. It was to a large degree an exaggerated stance assumed for domestic political reasons. To compare Kennedy's speeches on colonialism and Vietnam with those of Johnson is to see the difference between a man confident of his abilities, his perceptions, and the future, and a man who lacks conviction in himself and his vision. LBJ's forte had always been domestic policy and Congress. When the arena changed to foreign policy, especially Southeast Asia, Johnson quickly went from leader to follower to victim. It was not until 1968 that LBJ saw how badly he had been advised and how poorly he had handled the situation. He began to consider withdrawing from Vietnam (even Cold Warrior Dean Acheson told Johnson to "shove Vietnam up your ass"[23]) and ultimately decided not to run in 1968.

Would Kennedy have extricated the United States from Vietnam before the stupid and lamentable slaughter of so many

Americans and Vietnamese, which in turn buried the Democratic Party in the election of 1968? Pioneering work by Peter Dale Scott and L. Fletcher Prouty strongly indicated that withdrawal was Kennedy's intention.[24] If one studies three key Kennedy National Security Action Memoranda (NSAMs) from the period 1961 to 1963, it is hard to deduce that JFK was readying for a long, bloody, air-land war in Southeast Asia.

Since 1961, NSAM 111 had allowed advisers into Vietnam but specifically did not mention combat troops. Kennedy could not justify sending troops into Southeast Asia when he refused to do so at the Bay of Pigs.[25] The crucial year was 1963. On October 11, 1963, JFK issued NSAM 263, a directive that included the withdrawal of 1,000 of the 16,000 advisers then in Vietnam by the end of the year. In fact, at the preliminary announcement of this order, Secretary of Defense Robert McNamara and General Maxwell Taylor reported that in "their judgment the major part of the U.S. military task can be completed by the end of 1965."[26] Yet within four days of JFK's murder, this month-old directive was reversed by NSAM 273—issued by Lyndon Johnson—which not only effectively thwarted the troop withdrawal but, as Scott points out, changed the central objective of U.S. policy there to "win[ning] the contest against the externally directed and supported communist conspiracy."[27] As Scott notes, JFK had refused to issue just such a statement.[28] And as Robert Groden and Harrison Livingstone summed it up: "Not one American was in combat in Vietnam when President Kennedy died, and there was not one more American in all of Indochina when he died than when he became President."[29]

One month after issuing NSAM 273, LBJ told the Joint Chiefs at a cocktail party, "Just get me elected, and then you can have your war."[30] Johnson kept his promise. Less than a year after his election, the U.S. staged the Gulf of Tonkin incident,[31] which LBJ used as a pretext to start the bombing of North Vietnam and to place the Marines on shore at Da Nang. Then, furnished with a blank check from Congress, he began throwing the domino theory in the face of anyone who dissented.[32]

While much of this can be found in the work of Prouty and Scott, it is taken much further in a definitive new work by John Newman, *JFK and Vietnam*.[33] Working from a database of 15,000 government documents recently declassified by Freedom of Information Act requests, Newman makes a strong case that Kennedy meant just what he said in 1963: "The first thing I do when I'm re-elected, I'm going to get the Americans out of Vietnam."[34]

In the wake of the opening of Oliver Stone's *JFK*, this controversy continues to rage.[35]

What of Kennedy's other moves to relax the Cold War? By 1963 Kennedy had opened a back channel to Fidel Castro through U.N. Special Adviser William Attwood and TV commentator Lisa Howard.[36] Castro proved receptive and was responding. After the assassination, Attwood was told by National Security Adviser McGeorge Bundy that "the Cuban exercise would probably be put on ice for a while."[37] Johnson went further. On December 14, 1963, he named a new Assistant for Latin American Affairs, the Texas conservative Thomas Mann. Mann had helped plan the Bay of Pigs operation. Soon after this, LBJ moved to replace those few at the State Department who had spoken out for withdrawal from Vietnam.[38]

On the ultimate Cold War front, the Soviet Union, a similar pattern had occurred. In June of 1963, at American University, Kennedy made one of his most famous speeches on Soviet-American relations and the threat of nuclear war:[39]

[B]oth the United States and its allies, and the Soviet Union and its allies, have a mutually deep interest in a just and genuine peace and in halting the arms race.

Agreements to this end are in the interests of the Soviet Union as well as ours....

In the final analysis, our most basic common link is that we all inhabit this small planet. We all breathe the same air. We all cherish our children's future. And we are all mortal.

These sentiments evinced a watershed event, to which Khrushchev, like Castro, was responsive. On June 20, 1963, the U.S. and the Soviet Union agreed to establish a direct telephone link, or Hot Line, between Washington and Moscow to minimize the chances of nuclear war. By August the first Nuclear Test Ban treaty was signed, another milestone in U.S. foreign policy.[40]

But after Kennedy's death, with the escalation of the Vietnam War and the freeze on any rapprochement with Castro, U.S.-Soviet relations also worsened. In less than three years Kennedy had had two summit meetings with Khrushchev. In five years Johnson met with the Soviet leadership once. No further nuclear arms control was achieved.

These policy reversals all benefited the Pentagon and the CIA. They meant heightened tensions and bigger arms budgets. At the time of his death, JFK was also planning a task force on reorganizing the structure and redesigning the mission of the Agency.[41]

There is certainly a strong case to be made that, in 1963, Kennedy was well on his way to relaxing the Cold War; once reelected, he may well have reversed it.[42] It is important to review the course of Kennedy's foreign policy chronologically, to see the clear departures from Eisenhower's, and how this affected the military-intelligence establishment.

The Bay of Pigs was not the first conflict between JFK and the Agency; there is an earlier precedent. In the summer of 1960, the Congo (now Zaire) won its independence from Belgium. Eisenhower had supported Belgium, while Kennedy had favored independence.[43] A dynamic, socialist leader, Patrice Lumumba, had emerged as the new republic's Prime Minister. His expressed willingness to accept aid from any sources, including communist nations, was anathema to Eisenhower and Director of Central Intelligence Dulles. By August, the DCI was warning of "a communist takeover of the Congo with disastrous consequences ... for the interests of the free world...."[44]

The Agency truly feared Lumumba.[45]

The CIA encouraged reactionary forces to kidnap him. By the next month, the man Eisenhower considered a "Soviet instrument" was a prisoner.[46] Kennedy was backing a U.N. settlement to the dispute, with all political prisoners, including Lumumba, to be freed. The CIA station chief in Leopoldville (now Kinshasa) feared Kennedy's "radical" proposal and began to urge "drastic steps."[47] Dulles ordered Lumumba's assassination as "an urgent and prime objective."[48] But Lumumba somehow escaped.

In November, *after* Kennedy's election, the CIA began to help track him down.[49] He was caught and kept by the current, reactionary government until January 17. Then, less than three days before JFK's inauguration, Lumumba was turned over to a rebel group formally backed by the Agency. He was dead by nightfall. Several years later, John Stockwell spoke with a colleague at the CIA who described his "adventure in Lubumbashi, driving about town after curfew with Patrice Lumumba's body in the trunk of his car, trying to decide what to do with it."[50]

At the same time, Dulles was preparing for the Cuban invasion and presenting it in detail to the President-elect. We have seen how taken aback he was when JFK placed the operation on hold (see Chapter 2). By the end of 1960, perhaps spurred on by these two disagreements, the CIA had prepared its "dossier analysis," or psychological profile, of Kennedy.[51] The aim was to predict his behavior in various circumstances.

The Bay of Pigs caused the first major falling out between Kennedy and both the CIA and the Joint Chiefs of Staff (JCS). As noted, Allen Dulles and Charles Cabell were ousted, and Richard Bissell was reassigned. David Atlee Phillips and E. Howard Hunt remained, but with markedly changed attitudes.[52]

On the heels of the Cuban debacle, there was another crisis, which few commentators have noted. In late April, Secretary of State Dean Rusk was warning Kennedy that Laos could become a communist satellite.[53] The JCS urged the dispatch of 10,000 troops to the Laotian panhandle.[54] But Kennedy rejected the advice and opted for a negotiated cease-fire and settlement.[55]

Thus, in a little more than three months, Kennedy had been at odds with the military-intelligence establishment three times, each involving Third World interventionism. Kennedy was losing faith in and respect for his military and intelligence advisers. He told a friend:[56]

Looking back ... one of the things that appalled me most was the lack of broad judgment by some of the heads of the military services.... For years I've been looking at those rows of ribbons and those four stars and conceding a certain higher qualification not obtained in civilian life. Well ... a lot more attention is going to be given their advice in the future before any action is taken as a result of it. *They wanted a fight and probably calculated that if we committed ourselves part way and started to lose, I would give the OK to pour in whatever was needed.* [Emphasis added.]

The emphasized passage suggests JFK knew he was being misled by his military advisers. Waving a stack of cables at an aide, he said, "If it hadn't been for Cuba, we might be about to intervene in Laos. I might have taken this advice seriously."[57]

The military was equally chagrined. Lyman Lemnitzer, the Chairman of the JCS, "deplored the tendency of the U.S. government to waste time in quibbling over policy." Air Force chief Curtis LeMay complained that there were too many people "in the act and making decisions in areas where they weren't competent." going to war, he said, "is a very serious business and once you made [the] decision that you're going to do that, then you ought to be prepared to do just that."[58]

By mid-May 1961, there were news stories about a shake-up at the JCS,[59] and similar talk about the CIA. But the CIA sent a reminder, Lumumba-style, of their autonomy. Since the Eisenhower years, the Agency had been contemplating the assassination of Rafael Trujillo, dictator of the Dominican Republic, who had been a staunch U.S. ally, but who was getting out of hand and generating sympathy for his leftist opponents.[60] Kennedy sent aide Richard Goodwin to Santo Domingo to advise U.S. Consul Henry Dearborn not to let the U.S. get involved in any assassination attempt. Dearborn thought it was too late, and on May 30, Trujillo was assassinated by a three-man team supplied by the CIA with machine guns.[61]

In June 1961, Kennedy issued three National Security Action Memoranda (NSAMs) aimed at limiting the Agency's covert operations.[62] NSAM-55 turned over all "military-type" peacetime operations to the JCS. NSAM-56 called for the Pentagon to begin addressing its paramilitary abilities around the world. And NSAM-57 defined what sort of paramilitary operations the CIA could continue to carry out. They had to be "wholly covert or disavowable" and small enough for the Agency to handle on its own while *remaining* covert or disavowable. As Mark Lane noted:[63]

These documents, in theory, eliminated the ability of the CIA to wage war. The CIA would not be permitted to initiate any operation requiring greater firepower than that generated by handguns.

The officer who delivered the NSAMs to the Agency, Fletcher Prouty, recalled:[64]

Nothing I had ever been involved in in my entire career had created such an uproar. NSAM-55 stripped the CIA of its cherished covert-operations role, except for small actions. It was an explosive document. The military-industrial complex was not pleased.

Just after placing these tough restrictions on the CIA, Kennedy said no to the JCS once more. In November 1961 everyone—the JCS, State, the Pentagon, Generals Taylor and Lansdale—was urging the President to commit combat troops to Vietnam. Kennedy issued NSAM-111, turning it down, despite all the dire predictions.[65]

The struggle continued through the Cuban Missile Crisis. Kennedy, as we have seen, took the least militant choice and pledged not to invade Cuba and also to dismantle Operation MONGOOSE. But the Central Intelligence Agency was resisting, just as it had in the Congo. As Kennedy was assuring French President de Gaulle that the U.S. had nothing to do with the plots against him (see Chapter 13), the CIA and U.S. NATO generals were encouraging them.[66] And in Laos, after the July 1962 accord, the CIA retreated to Thailand and began a secret war against the neutralist government Kennedy supported.[67]

And finally, in the last days of his life, the President was being seriously thwarted in Vietnam. NSAM-263, on personnel withdrawal, was altered by the JCS, "whittled down to the point that it was meaningless."[68] There was a two-day conference on Vietnam in Honolulu, November 19 and 20; JFK was not there, as he was preparing for his Texas trip. A decision was made to expand covert operations against North

Vietnam; the military told the CIA they could work with them on this.[69]

NSAM-273 was prepared in Washington for Kennedy to sign; he never saw it, as he was already on his way to Dallas. Within days, this version was changed; the directive LBJ signed included offensive U.S. operations against the North, which had not been in the earlier version.[70]

It also authorized naval patrols in the Gulf of Tonkin. These, coupled with a disinformation operation, led in the next year to bombing raids over North Vietnam. With NSAM-273, Johnson leapt over the line Kennedy would not cross. The change in U.S. policy was clear: the U.S. would begin a major offensive, even if the massive introduction of combat troops would take some time. (As John Newman notes, while Kennedy had to disguise his *withdrawal* plan because of the upcoming election, Johnson had to disguise his *escalation* plans for the same reason.[71]) The CIA and the JCS could go forward in Vietnam and in Laos. The new directive required no high-level clearances for Laotian operations and designed a plan for over 2,000 direct U.S. operations against North Vietnam.

It is safe to say that by November 1963, there was an undeclared war between the President and the military-intelligence group. Kennedy was prepared to relax the Cold War, to reorganize the CIA drastically,[72] and to force J. Edgar Hoover into retirement.[73] Kennedy's election posed an especially serious threat to a demoralized Agency.[74] There would be investigations, much deeper and more public than the Bay of Pigs inquiry. The Agency might have to account for its activities—all the way back to Gehlen. The Agency's role in assassinations might come out—even as, unbeknownst to Kennedy, the Agency was subverting his foreign policy by trying to assassinate Castro through the AM/LASH plot.

The month these attempts on Castro's life were being plotted—September 1963—Lee Harvey Oswald was leaving

President Kennedy
with J. Edgar Hoover.

New Orleans. The Warren Report tells us he went to Mexico alone, after his wife left with Ruth Paine for Dallas. The official story says he wanted to make contacts with the Soviet and Cuban Embassies to prepare for another defection. This is what the Report told the American public in 1964.[75]

On September 25, Oswald got a Mexican tourist card with his name as "Lee, Harvey Oswald." He went to Houston and then Laredo, where he crossed the border to Nuevo Laredo. On September 26, he bought a ticket on the Flecha Roja bus line to Mexico City, where he arrived on the 27th and registered at the Hotel del Comercio, room 118. The day he arrived he attempted to get a Cuban visa at their Embassy. He said he intended to go to Cuba for two weeks and thence to the Soviet Union. He was told by an employee, Silvia Duran, a Mexican citizen, to fill out an application.

He then went to the Soviet Embassy, where he spoke to "Kostin," whose real name was Valery Kostikov (according to the CIA, in charge of KGB "liquidation plots"). Oswald was unable to obtain a Soviet visa, though no reason for the denial is given in the Warren Report. He returned to the Cuban Embassy and Ms. Duran called the Soviet Embassy to ask about the status of his request there. They said it would take at least four months to process. Oswald became angry, and when he was told he could not get a temporary visa to visit Cuba while the Soviet application was pending, he began to create a scene. Ms. Duran called the Cuban Consul, Eusebio Azcue, with whom Oswald had a heated argument. Before he left Mexico, he visited both embassies once more, and again failed to get either visa. On September 30, he bought a bus ticket home for October 2. On October 1, he paid his hotel bill. He left Mexico City on October 2, at 6:30 a.m. In Monterrey, he switched buses for the ride to Nuevo Laredo, and crossed the border at about 1:35 p.m., October 3. He arrived in Dallas about 2:20 p.m.

This saga was presented to the Commission largely by the CIA, with some help from the FBI. There were some questions, just on the surface. Marina had asked Lee to buy her a bracelet in Mexico City, but the bracelet she got was made in Japan and probably purchased in Dallas; he did not mail her postcards, he brought them back personally; and he did not buy her the Mexican records she had asked for.[76] According to the maid at the hotel, Oswald left every day around 9:00 a.m. and did not return until about midnight.[77] What did he do for 15 hours a day for one week in a strange city with little money? According to the Report, he watched a bullfight, visited museums, went sightseeing, saw one or two movies, and ate lunch at a nearby restaurant. This is supposed to account for 100 hours.

The only solid evidence, in fact, to support Oswald's presence in Mexico at all was a statement by Ms. Duran that Oswald was at the Cuban Embassy requesting a visa.[78] If Oswald had visited those two embassies, the Commission asked, why did no U.S. agency do anything about it upon his return; after all, this was a former defector. Richard Helms said the information was extremely sensitive, and the Agency refused to show the Commission its cables, dispatches, and other documents which, it said, proved Oswald had been in Mexico.[79]

In March, the Commission requested more details on Oswald's movements and activities.[80] In September, days before the Report was to go to press, the bus tickets were produced, allegedly found in some magazines Oswald had brought back from Mexico.

Although the Commission swallowed this story, Senator Russell raised some interesting points. Why did it take so long to find the tickets? Why did Marina take these magazines to the motel the government had put her in? And why did Lee Oswald keep a *Spanish-language* version of *TV Guide*, when he did not speak the language?

Through FOIA requests and private interviews, the research community completed the investigation the Commission let stand. The first part of the story to be questioned was Oswald's visit to the Cuban Embassy. When Ms. Duran was first questioned by the CIA, it was learned, she apparently told a story they did not like. She was arrested, at CIA request, as involved in an "extremely serious matter which could prejudice U.S. freedom of action on the entire question of Cuban responsibility." She was put in solitary confinement; few Mexican officials were to know of her arrest or of the Agency's role in it. She then signed the statement they wanted and was released after promising not to speak on the subject. But she did speak, and was rearrested; again the Agency role was kept secret.[81]

When Eusebio Azcue finished his tour of duty at the Cuban Embassy in Mexico City, he returned to Havana, where he saw the newsreel footage of Ruby shooting Oswald, which offers a clear view of the victim. According to Azcue (and Duran), the man in the film "in no way resembled" the man he saw at the Embassy. When shown still photos of Oswald, he insisted, "My belief is that this gentleman was not, is not, the person or individual who went to the consulate."[82]

What of the visits to the Soviet Embassy? The CIA claimed it had tape recordings of Oswald calling the Embassy, some of whose phone lines were tapped by the Agency. But there were problems. One of the recorded calls was supposed to be Oswald calling the Soviet Embassy from the Cuban Embassy, but Ms. Duran said *she* made that call. She said Oswald did not use the phone while he was there. Also the man on the phone spoke very poor Russian, although Oswald was fluent in the language.[83]

Years later, when asked by the HSCA to produce the tapes, the CIA said they had been destroyed as a matter of routine, within a week of their creation. Yet Hoover had written a report stating that Bureau agents who had spoken with Oswald in Dallas listened to the tapes and were "of the opinion that the above-referred-to individual was not Lee Harvey Oswald."[84] And if the Agents had listened to them at the end of November, they could not have been destroyed within a week of their creation, which was sometime between September 27 and October 2.

The CIA photograph of "Oswald" outside the Soviet Embassy in Mexico City. The subject of the photo bears no resemblance to Lee Harvey Oswald.

Another piece of evidence placing Oswald at the Soviet Embassy was a photograph of him outside the building, from CIA surveillance cameras recording the comings and goings there. The Hoover memorandum noted above also said that his agents had seen the photographs and again denied they were of Oswald. This report was not furnished to the Commission and Warren did not probe the matter further.[85]

There are also questions about the hotel register. Every name on the September 27 entry list is in the same handwriting *except* Oswald's. Supposedly this is because, on the first night, a guest writes his or her own name down, and on succeeding nights, the hotel clerk writes them in. Yet, eight other guests checked in on September 27, and, on the register for September 28, Oswald's name is again in a unique handwriting. To make it more curious, the handwriting is not the same as that of the signature the previous day.[86]

From all the inconsistencies, a logical question arises. Did Oswald ever actually go to Mexico? The bus line he supposedly traveled on, Flecha Roja, normally kept a manifest for each of its runs. A duplicate copy was kept at Nuevo Laredo while the original went to Mexico City. Four months after the assassination, the FBI arrived in Mexico City to look at the original passenger list. They were told that, within days of the assassination, unnamed "investigators of the Mexican government" had taken it and not returned it. What about the duplicate? That had been taken even *before* by those same mysterious investigators.[87] Needless to say, neither copy was ever returned and the investigators have never been identified.

Did Oswald leave Mexico? According to the Report, he left by the Transportes del Norte bus line. Yet the Mexican border records for October 3 do not show Oswald heading for Dallas by bus, but heading for New Orleans by car.[88]

The Agency was the Commission's chief source for information about Oswald in Mexico. Its Western Hemisphere Division chief at this time was David Atlee Phillips; his office was in Mexico City. The same man strongly suspected of asking Antonio Veciana to get a relative to make incriminating statements about Oswald being at the Cuban Embassy in Mexico City a few weeks before the assassination (see Chapter 13).[89] And who was the temporary Chief of Station for Mexico City in August and September 1963? E. Howard Hunt, who to this day cannot or will not explain where he was or what he was doing on November 22, 1963.[90]

It was Phillips who told the Warren Commission he *knew* Oswald had been in Mexico City in 1963.[91] And Phillips was the Agency's point man for the HSCA on the Mexico City trip. (When he was asked for a copy of the regulation that required the destruction of audio tapes in a week, he said the regulation had also been destroyed.[92])

The Mexico City trip was the cap to the Agency's indictment of Oswald. But it became the undeniable fingerprint demonstrating its own involvement, some would say the noose around its neck. Was Oswald there? Perhaps; but if so, he was chaperoned. Did he do what the Agency said he did? If so, the Agency would have produced the tapes and photos within hours. If he did not go, why was this thin evidentiary trail laid down?

Looking at the overall design of the conspiracy, the Mexico trip is almost fiendishly clever. (In its use of doubles and "babysitters," it fits in with what was going on in Dallas and New Orleans.) It plays upon the irrational Cold War fears of the time, both for the crime and for the coverup. It meshed with the media's gullibility in accepting the patsy served up on a platter. Most of all, it is a perfect example of the use of "false sponsor," red herrings to hide the real perpetrators. Oswald's visits to the Cuban and Soviet Embassies were meant to certify the communist origins of the assassination. Just as the use of Braden and Brown was meant to bring in the Mafia (see Chapter 6).[93] The Soviets, the Cubans, the Mafia—in the public's eye they all had reasons to want to kill the President.

It was a plot that could only have been concocted by minds steeped in espionage and camouflage, in double agents and deep cover, *i.e.*, a Lansdale, a Dulles, a Harvey. The use of Oswald was a masterstroke, one the media would have a field day with: the alienated loner with the leftist cover. His FBI contacts would also motivate Hoover to help in the coverup.

Putting the patsy in the middle of Cold War controversy helped hide the ideology of the plot, on both the operational and strategic levels. Concerning the former, no one looked past the leftist, "loner" cover to question why Oswald was surrounded by rightwingers in both Dallas and New Orleans. As for the latter, the fear of communist backing gave impetus to the foreign policy shifts that were, after all, the motivation for the plot. And considering the swift policy reversals in Vietnam, Laos, and the Caribbean, the risk was well worth the benefits.

Was there no difference between the foreign policies of Kennedy and Johnson, as some insist? I would suggest the differences were the reason for the plot and the key to its success.

A friend of Kennedy's once asked him to read *Seven Days in May*. It was a novel depicting a reactionary military coup

Retired Air
Force Major
General Edward
G. Lansdale,
left, arriving in
Saigon, 1965.

against a moderate president. Kennedy read it in one evening, and his friend asked him if he thought it could ever happen. Kennedy said it was possible:[94]

> If, for example, the country had a young president, and he had a Bay of Pigs.... If there were another Bay of Pigs.... The military would almost feel it was their patriotic duty to stand ready to preserve the integrity of the nation, and only God knows just what segment of the democracy they would be defending if they overthrew the elected establishment.

Kennedy paused, realized he was describing himself, and then added: "But it won't happen on my watch."[95]

He was wrong. It did.

In its willful blindness the Warren Commission ensured that the footprints of the conspirators would remain covered. The crime was then complete; America lost its moral compass; the struggle for the soul of a nation was lost.

15

Homage to Jim Garrison

Earlier in this book, I took a few pages to describe Jim Garrison's life up to the time he became an instant celebrity in 1967. Let us take another look at his life since 1969, when he stepped off the national stage.

In 1969, even after losing the Shaw case, Garrison was easily re-elected DA.[1] In 1971 he was arrested on charges brought by the federal government with the help of a former Garrison employee, Pershing Gervais. The trial did not begin until August of 1973; Garrison represented himself. It turned out that the government's case against him, for allegedly taking kickbacks from pinball machine operators, was manufactured, including falsified audio tapes. Rosemary James, the reporter who first exposed Garrison's investigation in 1967, apparently felt she owed Garrison a favor. She journeyed to Canada in 1972 to interview Gervais, who confessed

A rather bemused Jim Garrison, as the election returns come in confirming his 1969 reelection, even after the Clay Shaw trial.

Garrison, left, with
Pershing Gervais,
November 23, 1964, after
the U.S. Supreme Court
threw out Garrison's
conviction for
defamation, brought by
the New Orleans Criminal
Court Judges he had
sharply criticized for
being soft on crime.

to trying to set up Garrison. Garrison used a transcript of the James interview against Gervais and the government, along with experts who proved the tapes were doctored. He was acquitted. But the publicity, plus the proximity of the November 1973 election, led to his failure to gain a fourth term as DA. In March 1974, shortly before Garrison was due to leave office after 12 years as District Attorney of New Orleans, the federal government, in a rather meanspirited, if not foolish, move, charged him with evading income taxes on the same money he had been accused of taking as kickbacks. Again he defended himself, and again he was acquitted.

Garrison went into private legal practice for four years. He then ran for election as a judge of the Louisiana Fourth Circuit Court of Appeal, won a ten-year term, and was subsequently re-elected. He wrote a novel, *The Star-Spangled Contract*, made a cameo appearance in *The Big Easy*, and wrote two books on the assassination, *A Heritage of Stone* and *On the Trail of the Assassins*. The latter was published

Top: Garrison and his wife, Elizabeth, outside court, September 28, 1973, after he was acquitted of the pinball kickback charges. Bottom: Garrison thanks the members of the jury that acquitted him of federal income tax evasion charges, March 26, 1974. In both cases, he represented himself.

in 1988 and almost immediately optioned by Oliver Stone, director of *Platoon, Salvador,* and *Born on the Fourth of July,* among others.

Garrison's professional experiences center around his military service, the law, and JFK's assassination. Just where were all those dark political ambitions that his critics said were his "real reasons" for reopening the Kennedy assassination?[2] According to these rumors, Garrison lusted to be governor, or senator, or even Vice President. The assassination was just a springboard.

That charge, like most of the others, was a fraud and a subterfuge to distract the eye from the object of the investigation to the investigator himself. In fact, Garrison had always denied it:[3]

> I'd have to be a terribly cynical and corrupt man to place another human being on trial ... just to gratify my political ambitions. But I guess there are a lot of people around the country, especially after NBC's attack, who think that's just the kind of man I am.... This rather saddens me. I'm no Albert Schweitzer but I could never do a thing like that.

He later told an author, late at night, after a long day working on the Kennedy probe:[4]

> This thing, I have to do all the way. They'll have to kill me to stop me. But when it's over ... I want to get away from it.... But politics, I don't want any part of it. It is a dirty business.

This is both sad and ironic. For we can now see that Garrison was so prescient about the Kennedy assassination as to be visionary. His analysis was developed both during and after the Shaw trial. But because of the nature and circumstances of the crime, both the press and the govern-

ment had to brand him a pariah.[5] In fact, to this day he is
mainly referred to as the "discredited Jim Garrison."[6]

It was Garrison who shifted the focus from Dallas to New
Orleans in that summer before the assassination. In doing so
he raised some potent, meaningful questions: What was Oswald doing in New Orleans at just that time? Why did he go?
Who was he associating with? And by seeking to answer
these clear, basic questions, we, like Garrison, begin to see
that the solitary randomness of Oswald's life was not so
solitary, and not at all random. For Oswald was in New
Orleans for the penultimate run-up to the assassination, and
his associations in both cities had defense-intelligence ties
in common.

By centering on New Orleans, Garrison was able to con-
centrate on Oswald's true identity and function. For his
hangout, 544 Camp Street, was not just a hub of rightwing
paramilitary activity run by the former head of the Chicago
FBI office; it was also surrounded by other intelligence
headquarters like the Secret Service, the CIA, and the Office
of Naval Intelligence.[7] This helped peel away the veneer of
"Oswald the pinko" and revealed his likely function as an
intelligence agent.[8]

Writers like Robert Sam Anson and James Phelan have
snickered at one of Garrison's most quoted lines: "The key
to the case is through the looking glass. Black is white. White
is black."[9] But the joke is on them. For Garrison could not
be speaking more plainly. He was simply saying that, among
other deceits, Oswald masqueraded as a communist to camouflage his espionage activities. And once this cover was
penetrated, we were able to see the true identities of those
around Oswald. Guy Banister was not just a private detective.
David Ferrie was not just a pilot and moonlighting investigator. Clay Shaw was not just the distinguished former director
of the Trade Mart. (He had retired in 1965 to return to writing
plays.) George DeMohrenschildt was not just a petrochemi-

cal engineer. The Paines were more than just an estranged couple who spoke Russian and worked in the aerospace business.[10] The list even extends to Spas Raikin, who greeted Oswald on his arrival back in the U.S. from the Soviet Union. Raikin was supposed to be a social worker for the Traveler's Aid Society. But he was also a former secretary of the American Friends of Bolshevik Nations, an anticommunist lobby with extensive ties to the CIA and other intelligence units.[11]

Garrison realized that, with all these people, background was more important that foreground. (And with Oswald and the assassination, the background *was* the foreground.) In photographic terms, what he did was "rack the focus" on the people in the picture. Once we do that, Oswald's strange itinerary after his release from the Marines, his odd personal relationships, and the chain of events during those final months begin to mesh into a strange and dangerous mosaic. A mosaic for murder. It seems impossible not to conclude that Oswald was being set up by DeMohrenschildt, passed on to the Shaw-Ferrie-Banister network, and finally placed with the Paines, who got him his job at the depository.

With these connections finally made, Garrison was able to reach his most significant conclusion. Although early critics of the Warren Report, like Sylvia Meagher and Harold Weisberg, had speculated on the source of the conspiracy, and had recognized the involvement of the Cuban exile community, they could not go any further. Garrison made a quantum leap beyond them and others. He saw the military-intelligence trees in the forest surrounding the assassination. Allen Dulles, that master manipulator, had known that the critics' problem was their inability to do more than attack, even destroy, the Warren Report. They had no viable, fleshed-out alternative to it. "If they've found another assassin," Dulles said, "let them name names and produce their evidence."[12]

Garrison did just that. He took the speculation about conspiracy out of the clouds and placed it right on terra firma. He furnished names, locations, cities, and a time frame. He also provided a plausible political motive. As we have noted, most of the people around Oswald were involved in the intelligence and/or military communities. As we have seen in the previous chapter, recent work by scholars suggests that it was Kennedy's moves toward rapprochement with Castro and Khrushchev plus his proposed disengagement from Vietnam that marked him for a military-intelligence coup. Garrison realized the assassination was an inside job from conception to realization. It was too extensive, intricate, and involved for the Mob either to execute or to cover up. He accused the CIA early, in May of 1967.[13] In July he pinpointed the reason behind JFK's death: Kennedy was trying "to obtain a radical change in our foreign policy."[14] And as early as 1969, Garrison was onto the Vietnam angle of the conspirators.[15]

Even during the failed prosecution of Clay Shaw, Garrison managed some real achievements. In New Orleans, Harold Weisberg revealed to Garrison that he felt grains had been removed not only from the tip of CE 399, but also from its base.[16] This would indicate that the government was fabricating evidence to make grain samples from different locations match, to bolster the single-bullet theory (see Chapter 13, n. 153). When FBI ballistics expert Robert Frazier testified, he affirmed this.[17] Garrison was the first to show the Zapruder film publicly, and he also made copies so other researchers could study it further and show it to the public in order to further their cause. As we have also seen, Dr. Pierre Finck revealed at the trial that the autopsy was not controlled by the doctors, but directed by the military brass (see Appendix A). This was the first indication that the medical evidence and perhaps the body itself were altered in order to cover up the crime.[18]

With these powerful discoveries Garrison managed to help move public opinion. When he began his probe in 1966, about 40 percent of the public disbelieved the Warren Report; by 1969, at the conclusion of the Shaw trial, the figure was up to 66 percent.[19] Since then, it has never dipped below a majority. At jury selection, Shaw's lawyers successfully challenged those prospective jurors who said they did not believe the Warren Report.[20] But after the trial, when the jurors were interviewed, most were convinced that there *had* been a conspiracy, even if Garrison had been unable to link Shaw to it beyond a reasonable doubt.[21]

In the 29 years since the assassination, and the 28 years since the release of the Warren Report, Garrison remains the only prosecutor to obtain an indictment and go to trial on conspiracy charges involving the murder of JFK. The almost perverse solitariness of that act speaks volumes both about Garrison and the reluctance at every level of government to uncover the truth about the assassination. With the exception of the HSCA inquiry into the Bishop-Veciana relationship, Garrison's inquiry remains the only one to produce prime suspects and to place them in a framework in which a conspiracy could be demonstrated. Ferrie's death, however, was a fatal blow to Garrison's chances for success in 1969.[22]

Today there are three major theories to explain the assassination. The first school holds that the conspiracy was a CIA-military coup meant to head off JFK's moves toward ending the Cold War. The second maintains that Kennedy was killed because he and his brother were cracking down too hard on the mob: before he got them, they got him.[23] The third is that organized Cuban exiles did it to avenge their betrayal by Kennedy at the Bay of Pigs, and because of his 1962 pledge not to invade Cuba. Garrison's contribution is formidable: He originated the first theory, thoroughly filled in the last, and even uncovered David Ferrie for the mob-did-it advocates who assail him for the favor.

In essence, Garrison was saying that the intelligence community had gotten out of control. It was not serving American interests. It served nothing but itself and it would strike down anyone, including the President, if he got in its way. John Sparrow has noted the implications:[24]

> If the Warren Commissioners are exposed as merely hapless dupes, other doubts about American history during the last two decades become more pertinent. Was the Rosenberg case also a fraud?... Was the whole U.S. position on the origins of the Cold War fraudulent?

Some of the Warren Commissioners *were* duped—like Cooper, Russell, and Boggs—and they lived to regret it.[25] But some of the Commissioners—like Dulles and McCloy—actually perpetrated its frauds. And they went even further. Because they were part of the founding of the national security state, they felt no compunctions about allying with Nazis: borrowing, pardoning, or granting free entry into American life, members of the ugliest, most insane fascist dream ever fashioned.

Here we see a not-so-subtle dividing line over the assassination of John Kennedy. There are those like Dulles and

CIA Director Allen Dulles
briefing Vice Presidential
nominee Lyndon B. Johnson
in July 1960.

McCloy and Shaw, who had a direct interest in never letting the truth out. Then there are those who sympathized with this attitude, not because they had some involvement, but because they had a stake—sometimes simply personal or emotional—in preserving and protecting the national security apparatus. For America had emerged from the war with its status and role altered. It became a model for and protector of what came to be called the free world. But the image presented in that struggle was, from its inception, a false one, both in its exaggeration and demonization of the "monolithic" Red threat, and in its glowing portrayal of a morally upright United States. The Gehlen deal, which underpinned the image, at the same time undermined the model.

Dulles needed Gehlen's warped and exaggerated view of the Soviet threat to expand and perpetuate the new American security fortress that included: Gehlen, Dornberger, and Paper Clip; Bormann and Odessa; McCloy and the Krupps; the coups and assassinations of the Eisenhower era; the CIA-Mafia ties; the gun-running and dope-trafficking. And all the while, great fortunes were being made in the growing mili-

Reinhard Gehlen in 1972.
He had been appointed
by McCloy to head the foreign
intelligence service of Konrad
Adenauer's West Germany.

John J. McCloy. When he was
asked about the Japanese
Internment policy, he replied,
"Why the Constitution is just a
scrap of paper to me."

tary-industrial complex, which men like Dulles and McCloy
represented in their law firms.[26]

Kennedy was perceived as a serious threat to all these
powerful interests, in his foreign policy changes, his brother's war on the mob, his coming showdown with the Agency.
Garrison's inquiry threatened to expose all these machinations. Aynesworth, Sheridan, Phelan, Helms, Johnson, and
the others all understood what would come out if Garrison
succeeded. That exposure, they were sure, would endanger
America and its well-being. The heat and the light would be
too strong to endure.

Garrison had no such fear. He was not condescending to
the American people. He harbored no such insecurities about
himself or his feelings about his country. In short, he had no
such neofascist sympathies. Dulles, McCloy, and Shaw all
saw the horrors of World War II from the intelligence and
logistics office sidelines. They dealt with their counterparts
from the Third Reich on an official, almost comradely basis.
Garrison saw the results of fascism carried to its extreme at

Dachau. In his confrontation with the Warren Commission and Shaw, Garrison was the true democrat, telling the people the truth and letting them decide for themselves on the basis of the facts. In a January 1968 *Ramparts* article, the DA quoted an ancient maxim: "Let justice be done though the heavens fall."[27] He added, "If we don't fight for the truth now, we may never have another chance." A similar sentiment had been voiced by John Kennedy in the 1960 campaign against Nixon:[28]

> [W]e want the truth with the bark off. The people of the United States want the facts.... There is no responsibility, no burden, no hazards that the United States cannot meet, but it certainly cannot meet those hazards unless the leadership is prepared to tell the truth.

Garrison once stated that Huey Long was wrong when he said that fascism would come to America in the name of antifascism. The DA feared that fascism would come to America in the name of national security.[29] And it would be hard to argue that what occurred in November of 1963 was not—at least in its outline and design—a fascist coup.[30] As noted earlier, that Garrison was attacked so violently by the government and its supporters is some proof of that.

If we look back at Garrison's inquiry with the benefit of hindsight, he reminds us of Dr. Tomas Stockmann, the protagonist of Ibsen's *An Enemy of the People*. In this play, Stockmann is a man in possession of the truth about a public scandal. He chooses, at great personal sacrifice, to speak the truth. The elected officials, who know he is at least partially right, fight him viciously. Ibsen understood that it is usually in the interest of elected officials to keep the people in the dark. In 1967, Garrison was too far out in front, too truthful for those officials. That he accomplished what he did, when he did, with as little as he had, is an achievement in itself.

Jim Garrison in 1991.

At the end of his 1967 *Playboy* interview, Garrison was asked if, considering his ordeal, he regretted reopening the case:[31]

As long as the men who shot John Kennedy ... are walking the streets of America I will continue this investigation.... If it takes me 30 years to nail every one of the assassins, then I will continue this investigation for 30 years. I owe that not only to Jack Kennedy but to my country.

Because of the failure of the Shaw prosecution, Garrison could not nail the assassins in 1967. But time and art have a way of altering perceptions.[32] Garrison, who has a strong interest in literature, would empathize with the theme of Marcel Proust's great novel *Remembrance of Things Past*. We proceed through time as mistakes are made, and then we look back at time through art, and those mistakes are understood and learned from. With the release of Oliver Stone's film *JFK*, Garrison has his Proustian triumph. For the inter-

**Oliver Stone at
Dealey Plaza, April
1991, directing *JFK*.**

vening 25 years have educated us to understand our Dr. Stockmann, even in the face of the renewed, but tired, media attacks.

What the media does not understand is that two things have happened to alter the topography of that debate. First, most of the new evidence over the years supports the idea of a conspiracy. Second, Garrison has proved so prophetic on so many elements that *his* version is now closer to an accepted official story than the Warren Report. The media boys on the bus missed the real story in 1967, and in 1992 they are still fighting the last war.

The rest of us can understand what he was up against back then—the press, the CIA, the Justice Department, the Warren Report, Shaw's clever PR campaign. We can now hope that he receives the accolades and respect that he has so long deserved. We can now see Garrison's place in this long and painful puzzle much more clearly, especially those who lived through it and have tried to sort out what Jack Kennedy's death really meant and what the ensuing debate has really signified. From that perspective, since 1967 there is not a writer or a researcher who has entered the fray who does not owe Garrison more than Garrison owes anyone else. Stone's film begins to repay that debt.

As this book goes to press, Jim Garrison, 70, is deathly ill. He has, he said recently to Bill Schaap and Ellen Ray, no regrets. He lived to see *On the Trail of the Assassins* become a best-seller in a dozen countries. He lived to see *JFK* open around the world to incredibly enthusiastic audiences. "One victory like this," he said, "is enough for any lifetime."

The Ongoing Inquiry

It is the author's hope that this book will encourage those who had not been aware of or involved in this study to do so. Only a public outcry will force the government to release all classified files that have been locked away for decades to come. There are three organizations actively involved in the ongoing research. The first two specialize in archives and exhibits; the third publishes a newsletter:

Assassination Archives and Research Center
James H. Lesar, President
918 F Street, NW, Suite 510
Washington, DC 20004
(202) 393-1917

JFK Assassination Information Center
Larry Howard, Director
West End Marketplace
603 Munger, Suite 310
Dallas, TX 75202
(214) 871-2770

The Third Decade
Jerry Rose, Publisher
State University College
Fredonia, NY 14063
(716) 673-3470

Scenes from *JFK*

Above: The co-stars of *JFK*. Sissy Spacek, Joe Pesci, Tommy Lee Jones, Gary Oldman, Jack Lemmon, Walter Matthau, Ed Asner, Donald Sutherland, Kevin Bacon, and Jim Garrison.

Right: Senator Russell Long (Walter Matthau) tells Jim Garrison (Kevin Costner) he does not believe the Warren Report.

Garrison and
Lou Ivon (Jay
O. Sanders)
Interview
David Ferrie
(Joe Pesci).

Guy Banister
(Ed Asner) meets
with Lee Harvey
Oswald (Gary
Oldman).

Garrison and
Asistant DA Bill
Broussard
(Michael Rooker)
Interview Jack
Martin (Jack
Lemmon).

Garrison gives a
press conference
in his office.

Garrison
meets with
Colonel X
(Donald
Sutherland).

Oswald, Ferrie,
and Jack Ruby
(Brian Doyle
Murray) meet in
a nightclub.

Appendix A

Testimony of
Dr. Pierre Finck

One of the many lacunae in the literature on the Garrison case is the transcript of the Shaw trial. It is not available to the public. At the trial, both sides demanded overnight typed transcripts to use on cross-examination. Regular court staff could not comply, so a private stenography firm—Dietrich and Pickett—was engaged. Writers like John Davis in *Mafia Kingfish* list the transcript at Southeastern Louisiana University in Hammond. When I called there in January of 1992, I was told it was not there. They had only the preliminary hearing and the trial testimony of Perry Russo. The transcript, some of which remains in the form of unreadable stenotype notes, remains the property of Helen Dietrich, and she informed me that the only copies she had provided were to the HSCA and to Oliver Stone, the latter for use in his film.

In my view, the transcript should be published, and perhaps it soon will. But until then, writers and researchers are left with two alternatives. One can journey to New Orleans and read the daily transcripts in the *States-Item* and the *Times-Picayune*, which are not always verbatim. Or one can rely on the summaries presented in books. Until 1988 and the publication of *On the Trail of the Assassins*, both responsible writers like Henry Hurt and irresponsible ones like Robert Sam Anson had to rely on two volumes: Milton Brener's *The*

Garrison Case (1969) and James Kirkwood's *American Grotesque* (1970). Brener was a New Orleans attorney who defended both Layton Martens—a friend of David Ferrie's whose phone number was found in Clay Shaw's address book—and Walter Sheridan. Brener is not above attacking Garrison personally, once referring to him as a "witch hunter" (p. 267).

But Kirkwood's book is by far the lengthiest treatment of the Shaw trial that I know of. Unfortunately, it can be read only with great caution. The author begins his work by comparing Garrison to a Klansman (p. 7). A few pages later the preliminary hearing is likened to the Spanish Inquisition (p. 13). Sure enough, towards the end, Garrison's assistant DAs are equated to guards at the Nazi death camps (p. 595). Kirkwood's animus toward Garrison is matched only by his sympathy for Shaw. In the last 616 of the book's 657 pages, the accused is never called Shaw or Mr. Shaw; only "Clay" or "Clay Shaw."

This bias seriously colors the depiction of the trial. In a rather voluminous book that centers on a court proceeding that took 39 days, the reader would never know that the following witnesses appeared: Wilma Bond, Mr. and Mrs. Philip Willis, Billy Joe Martin, Carolyn Walther, James Simmons, Mr. and Mrs. William Newman, and Mary Moorman. In a book that supposedly centers on the possibility of a New Orleans-related conspiracy, one searches in vain for the name of Gordon Novel.

The list could go on, but perhaps Kirkwood's greatest slighting is to Assistant DA Alvin Oser. With help from Vincent Salandria, Oser conducted the Dealey Plaza portion of the trial. Kirkwood refuses to concede that the prosecution shredded the Warren Report, something the jury agreed had been done. He writes about Oser in otiose, condescending, disparaging terms. He even derides his voice. But Kirkwood fails to note that, in his cross-examination of Dr. Pierre Finck, Oser was making history.

This was the first and only time one of the three Bethesda autopsy doctors was exposed to informed, aggressive, relentless questioning. In my view, it is a milestone in the depiction of the autopsy as not only hapless but sinister. This theme has been furthered in the work of Robert Groden and Harrison Livingstone (*High Treason*) and David Lifton (*Best Evidence*), so much so that, today, the autopsy evidence is one of the most questionable aspects of the official story.

In the following excerpts, I have chosen those that show who really controlled the autopsy and those that reveal some of the dubious practices employed. It should also be noted that Oser concentrated on the shifting location of the head wound, which, to Dr. Finck's dismay, Ramsey Clark's panel had raised four inches, and on the location of the back wound, which, Oser felt, made for a rather dubious trajectory in exiting through the throat.

The transcript appears as typed, with misspellings of names intact. Berkley should be Burkley, Kinney should be Kenney. My thanks and appreciation to Helen Dietrich, with whose kind permission this material is reprinted. (The excerpts are from pp. 46-49, 51-52, 54-57, 92-95, 98-118, 138-141, and 152-159 of the first day, February 24, 1969; and pp. 2-8, and 30-32 of the second day, February 25, 1969.)

BY MR. OSER:
Q When did you all contact the doctors at Parkland Hospital?
THE WITNESS:
A Are you asking me if I contacted a Dr. Parker?
Q No, I asked you when did you all contact the doctors at Parkland Hospital in Dallas, Texas.
A Oh, I did not contact them, Dr. Humes did.
Q And did Dr. Humes relate to you what he learned from these doctors at Parkland?
A Definitely.
Q Do you know when Dr. Humes contacted these doctors at Parkland?
A As far as I know, Dr. Humes called them the morning following the autopsy, as far as I know, Dr. Humes called Dallas on Saturday morning, on the 23rd of November, 1963.
Q Doctor, can you tell me why the delay in contacting the doctors that worked on President Kennedy in Dallas until the next morning after the body was already

removed from the autopsy table?

A I can't explain that. I know that Dr. Humes told me he called them. I cannot give an approximate time. I can give you the reason why he called. As I have stated before, having a wound of entry in the back of the neck, having seen no exit in the front of the neck, nothing from the radiologist who looked at the whole body X-ray films, I have requested as there was no whole bullet remaining in the cadaver of the President, that was a very strong reason for inquiring if there were not another wound in the approximate direction corresponding to that wound of entry in the back of the neck, because in the wound of the head with entry in the back of the head and exit on the right side of the head, I never had any doubt, any question that it was a through-and-through wound of the head with disintegration of the bullet. The difficulty was to have found an entry in the back of the neck and not to have seen an exit corresponding to that entry.

Q This puzzled you at this time, is that right, Doctor?

A Sorry, I don't understand you.

Q This puzzled you at the time, the wound in the back and you couldn't find an exit wound? You were wondering about where this bullet was or where the path was going, were you not?

A Yes.

Q Well, at that particular time, Doctor, why didn't you call the doctors at Parkland or attempt to ascertain what the doctors at Parkland may have done or may have seen while the President's body was still exposed to view on the autopsy table?

A I will remind you that I was not in charge of this autopsy, that I was called—

Q You were a co-author of the report though, weren't you, Doctor?

A Wait. I was called as a consultant to look at these wounds; that doesn't mean I am running the show.

Q Was Dr. Humes running the show?

A Well, I heard Dr. Humes stating that—he said, "Who is in charge here?" and I heard an Army General, I don't remember his name, stating, "I am." You must understand that in those circumstances, there were law enforcement officials, military people with various ranks, and you have to co-ordinate the operation according to directions.

Q But you were one of the three qualified pathologists standing at that autopsy table, were you not, Doctor?

A Yes, I was.

Q Was this Army General a qualified pathologist?

A No.

Q Was he a doctor?

A No, not to my knowledge.

Q Can you give me his name, Colonel?

A No, I can't. I don't remember.

* * *

Q How many other military personnel were present at the autopsy in the autopsy room?

A That autopsy room was quite crowded. It is a small autopsy room, and when you are called in circumstances like that to look at the wound of the President of the United States who is dead, you don't look around too much to ask people for their names and take notes on who they are and how many there are. I did not do so. The room was crowded with military and civilian personnel and federal agents, Secret Service agents, FBI agents, for part of the autopsy, but I cannot give you a precise breakdown as regards the attendance of the people in that autopsy room at Bethesda Naval Hospital.

Q Colonel, did you feel that you had to take orders from this Army General that was there directing the autopsy?

A No, because there were others, there were Admirals.

Q There were Admirals?

A Oh, yes, there were Admirals, and when you are a Lieutenant Colonel in the Army you just follow orders, and at the end of the autopsy we were specifically told—as I recall it, it was by Admiral Kenney, the Surgeon General of the Navy—this is subject to verification—we were specifically told not to discuss the case.

Q You were told not to discuss the case?

A —to discuss the case without coordination with the Attorney General.

* * *

Q Doctor, can you tell me how many photographs were taken of the President's body?

A Some of the photographs were taken in my presence in the autopsy room. I can't give you the exact number, but this information is available.

Q To who, Doctor?

A To you.

Q It is?

A It is a public document.

Q Go ahead. How many?

A I can't give you an exact number of photographs taken or X-rays of the body of the President.

Q Doctor, prior to your writing your report on the autopsy, did you have an occasion to view these photographs of the President that were taken?

A Yes, I did.

Q Doctor, I direct your attention to a report allegedly signed by you on 26 January, 1967.

MR. DYMOND: What part are you talking about?
(Conference between Counsel.)

BY MR. OSER:

Q (Exhibiting document to witness) Doctor, I direct your attention to a report, which I mark for identification "S-67," and I ask you to take a look at this document. Would you take a look at this particular one that I have marked Doctor, and let me know whether it is the same as the one you have before you.

A (Comparing documents) It is.

Q Your answer is that it is, Doctor?

A Yes.

Q And it contains your signature? Am I correct, sir?

A Yes.

(Whereupon, the document referred to by Counsel was duly marked for identification as "Exhibit D-67.")

BY MR. OSER:

Q Doctor, I direct your attention to the first page, the bottom of the last line of the fifth paragraph, which states, "Dr. Finck first saw the photographs on January 20, 1967," and I ask you if you would explain your answer to me, sir, just made, that you saw the photographs prior to writing your autopsy report in 1963.

A I did not say that I had seen the photographs before writing the autopsy report of 1963.

MR. OSER:

May I have my original question read back to the Doctor, please, and his answer. (Whereupon, the aforegoing passage was read back by the Reporter as follows: "**Q** Doctor, prior to your writing your report on the autopsy, did you have an occasion to view these photographs of the President that were taken? "**A** Yes, I did.")

THE WITNESS:

No, I did not, I did not see those photographs before signing my autopsy report. I may have answered "I didn't" and it was transcribed as "I did."

BY MR. OSER:

Q Doctor, did you hear what the stenographer just read you back? That is my question that I propounded to you. Now the question is: Did you see the photographs of President Kennedy before signing your autopsy report.

A That is correct.

Q That is correct?

A I was there when the photographs were taken, but I did not see the photographs of the wounds before I signed the autopsy report. I did not see those photographs in 1963.

Q So what you said before, that you did see the photographs, that was wrong? Is that correct?

A I never said that. It was misunderstood. I said "I did not" or "I didn't." I am very firm on this point that I did not see—

Q Is it, doctor that fact that I showed you the report—

THE COURT:

I think you have covered the matter now.

* * *

Q Can you tell me how the final draft of the autopsy report which you signed along with Commander Humes and Commander Boswell came about? How was that put together?

A We signed that autopsy report, as I remember, on Sunday the 24th of November,

1963, in the office of Admiral Galloway, who was one of the Admirals in charge of the Navy hospital. I had reviewed with Dr. Humes his draft of the autopsy report prior to that time, and, as I recall, the three of us, that is Humes, Boswell and myself, were present at that time in the office of Admiral Galloway on that Sunday, to the best of my recollection.

Q Doctor, I show you from Volume 17, Page 30 through Page 47, and ask you if you would view the contents of those pages.

A Yes, sir. This is Volume 17 of the hearings before the President's Commission on the assassination of President Kennedy. I don't recall seeing Pages 30 through 44. What Dr. Humes and I did, we were discussing the wording of the final autopsy report based on a report he had prepared through the night, I should say through Saturday, in the course of Saturday, the 23rd of November, and he worked on this, and he read over to me what he had prepared. Is Page 45 included in your question?

Q Yes, sir, 45 through 47.

A On Page 45 I recognize the drawing which I see now in the room, and which is labelled in this volume Commission Exhibit 397. I don't recall the timing of seeing this. I have seen this at some time. I don't recall exactly when.

Q The exhibit you are talking about right now, Doctor, Exhibit 397, is this the same exhibit you are talking about reproduced here in State 68, as best you can recall, Doctor?

A As best as I can tell, Page 45 of this volume is a reproduction of the exhibit shown in the courtroom as 68, except that at the bottom it doesn't say "Commission Exhibition 397." I remember that these drawings had been made, and you realize now I am referring to Page 45.

Q Which is the same thing as Exhibit 68, is that right?

A Yes, sir, it is. You will realize the drawings are made ahead of time on work sheets to be used at the time of the autopsy, and that wounds are added to these schematic representations of the front and back of a human body. I know this was involved in the discussions, in the testimony, but I can't give you any timing. As I recall, Dr. Boswell did those and discussed them but I can't recall exactly when I saw them.

Q In other words, when an autopsy descriptive list or sheet is used at an autopsy, it is either used at the time of an autopsy or shortly thereafter as a work sheet somewhere in the autopsy room, is that right, Doctor?

A If State 68 is an autopsy work sheet—well, when it was done by Dr. Boswell I don't know.

Q In referring to State Exhibit 69 and 70, Doctor, these two exhibits were not done then until sometime in March of 1964, is that correct, Doctor?

A I wouldn't know the exact date. The first time as I recall that I saw these exhibits was in March 1964, to the best of my recollection.

Q But you do know, Doctor, you can testify that the photographs and X-rays were not available, to the best of your knowledge, to the illustrator of these exhibits as they were not available to you in March, 1964?

A To the best of my knowledge the X-rays and photographs were not available to the illustrator. I know for sure that they were not available to me, the X-rays and the photographs.

* * *

Q When was the first time you saw the Zapruder film, Doctor?

A As I recall, it was in March 1964, when I returned from Panama and was told I had to testify before the Warren Commission.

Q So at the time you signed and co-authored the autopsy report, which has been marked as S-71 for identification, you had not, as of that time, seen the Zapruder film, is that correct?

A I had not.

Q Doctor, are you familiar in this particular report, S-71, which you co-authored with Commanders Humes and Boswell, with all the evidence upon which the report was based?

A Please repeat your question.

Q Are you familiar with all of the evidence upon which this report was based?

A In the general sense, yes.

Q Doctor, I call your attention to Page 2, under the heading of "Clinical Summary," and ask you to tell me the basis for your statement as part of your clinical summary that three shots were heard.

A Where do you see that, that three shots were heard?

Q The first sentence in the second paragraph of Page 2, the first four words.

A This is the information we had by the time we signed that autopsy report.

Q The information from whom, Doctor?

A There were a lot of people who were asked, I wouldn't know their names. I couldn't list all the people by name.

Q Who told you that three shots were heard? Who told you that?

A As I recall, Admiral Galloway heard from somebody who was present at the scene that three shots had been heard, but I cannot give the details of this.

Q I ask you, did you have an occasion to interview any of the witnesses that were present in Dealey Plaza on November 22, 1963, you yourself, before you wrote this?

A During the autopsy of President Kennedy there were Secret Service Agent Kellerman in that autopsy room. I asked him his name. Admiral Berkley, the personal physician of President Kennedy was present, and there was a third person whose name I don't recall who said to Admiral Galloway, who was there during the autopsy, that three shots had been fired. At the time we wrote this we had this information obtained from people who had been at the scene to the best of my recollection.

Q Did you have any information available, Doctor, from people at the scene who heard four shots?

A From the assassination on I heard conflicting reports regarding the number of shots.

Q I am talking about at the time you all prepared and signed this report, Doctor, before you affixed your signature to this, did you talk to anyone or have any reports available from people who heard four shots at Dealey Plaza on November 22?

A I don't remember any.

Q Did you have any statements or reports available to you from people who heard two shots in Dealey Plaza on November 22 at the time you made this report?

A At the time I made the report I don't recall having a report of two shots.

Q Going further, Doctor, in your autopsy report, it states, "Governor Connally was seriously wounded by this same gunfire." From where did you receive this information?

A I knew it at the time of the autopsy because of the news media who reported the President had been shot and the Governor of Texas had been wounded, as I recall.

Q What did you mean, that Governor Connally was seriously wounded by the same gunfire? What did you mean when you said the same gunfire?

A This is the information we had at the time of the autopsy—correction, at the time we signed the autopsy report, and because the information in the autopsy report may be obtained after the autopsy, and again I can't pinpoint the source of that information.

Q Doctor, I now show you State Exhibit 64, and ask you if you recognize what is depicted in this particular photograph, as being similar to something you have seen before during the investigation of the assassination of President Kennedy?

A This black-and-white reproduction is similar to a bullet that, as best I can remember, I saw for the first time in March 1964.

Q Doctor, speaking of your statement in the autopsy report that Governor Connally was seriously wounded by the same gunfire, is it not a fact that when testifying before the Warren Commission you stated that in your opinion it was impossible for Commission Exhibit 399 to do the same damage to President Kennedy as was done to Governor Connally because there were too many fragments in Governor Connally's wrist? Did you not so testify, sir?

MR. DYMOND:
I object to that question. Nobody has stated the same damage was done to Governor Connally as was done to President Kennedy, and that is what this question asks.

THE COURT:
I think the question was put to the Doctor, did he not make a prior contradictory statement, which is legitimate cross-examination.
Let the question be read back.
(Whereupon, the pending question was read back by the Reporter.)

THE COURT:
I am permitting the question. I overrule your objection.

BY MR. OSER:
Q Will you answer yes or no, Doctor, then you can explain.

A This is a difficult question to answer because there were two bullets striking President Kennedy. I have examined the wounds of President Kennedy and I would say that the bullet seen here is an entire bullet.

Q Is what?

A Is an entire bullet. By an entire bullet, I mean a bullet that did not disintegrate into many fragments.

Q Let me ask you about that in this way—

THE COURT:
Let him finish his answer.

MR. OSER:
I thought he had finished.

THE COURT:
Had you finished your answer?

THE WITNESS:
Yes, sir.

BY MR. OSER:
Q Colonel, let me ask you this way: Speaking of State Exhibit 64, the bullet, I ask you whether or not you testified in front of the Warren Commission that that particular bullet could not have done the damage to Governor Connally as there were too many bullet fragments in Governor Connally's wrist. Did you or did you not answer that in front of the Warren Commission in answer to a question by Mr. Specter? It appears on Page 382 of your testimony of the Warren Report about the middle of the page.
A It reads as follows: "Could that bullet possibly have gone through President Kennedy in 388," Mr. Specter's question. "Through President Kennedy's head—" what is 388?

MR. WILLIAM WEGMANN:
The one on the right.

A (Continuing) "and remain intact in the way you see it now?" "Definitely not." "And could it have been the bullet which inflicted the wound on Governor Connally's right wrist?" "No, for the reason there are too many fragments described in that wrist."

MR. OSER:
Thank you, Doctor, that is the point I am talking about.

BY MR. OSER:
Q Now, referring back to that same paragraph in the clinical summary, in the next sentence you said, "According to newspaper reports (Washington Post November 23, 1963) Bob Jackson, a Dallas 'Times Herald' photographer, said he looked around as he heard the shots and saw a rifle barrel disappearing into a window on an upper floor of the nearby Texas School Book Depository Building." Can you tell me who called that particular newspaper article to your attention?
A Are you referring to Page 979 of the Hearing?
Q No, sir, I am back on your original autopsy report, Page 2.
A I have it.
Q The sentence right after you said that Governor Connally was wounded by the same gunfire.
A What was that sentence?

Q Right after "gunfire."

A "Governor Connally was seriously wounded by the same gunfire." This is part of the autopsy report I signed.

Q Can you tell me who called that particular newspaper article to your attention, and why?

A As I recall, it was Dr. Humes who mentioned this article to me.

Q Colonel, do you customarily take notice of newspaper articles in an autopsy report?

A At times it is done.

Q Therefore, Doctor, am I correct in stating that particular autopsy report signed by you was based partially on hearsay evidence, is that correct? By that I mean evidence received by someone other than you having actual personal knowledge of the thing?

A Having not been at the scene I had to get information from somebody else.

Q Did you have occasion to read a newspaper article of November 22 or 23, which reported there were four to six shots fired and they came from the grassy knoll, being stated by Miss Jean Hill? Did you read that before you made your report?

A I don't recall reading that before I made the report. I may have been aware at that time of conflicting reports as regards the number and the difference in the direction of the shots, but I cannot pinpoint the time.

Q Since you are referring to the Washington Post—

A Would you repeat that?

THE COURT:

Mr. Oser, speak into the microphone, it may help a little bit.

BY MR. OSER:

Q Since you are dealing with the Washington Post article of November 23, 1963, in your autopsy report, I wondered if you had an occasion to either read the article or have it brought to your attention, that one Charles Brehm, one of the spectators close to the Presidential limousine, saw material which appeared to be a sizeable portion of President Kennedy's skull—

MR. DYMOND:

Objection, that is not in evidence.

THE COURT:

This is not a prior contradictory statement, Mr. Oser, is it?

MR. OSER:

I am asking if he took this into account when he—

THE COURT:

Where are you reading from?

MR. OSER:

An article taken out of the Washington Post on the same day as the article by Bob Jackson.

MR. DYMOND:
Your Honor, that has no place in this trial at all.

THE COURT:
Mr. Oser, I think you are enlarging the scope of the prior contradictory statement unless you can allege it was made in the report.

MR. OSER:
I am trying to ascertain what hearsay they used to arrive at in their report.

MR. DYMOND:
If you permit that you will have to permit Counsel to go through every conflicting report that was reported by every alleged eyewitness to the assassination and ask this witness whether they were taken into account. It certainly has no place in this trial and is completely irrelevant to the issues and irrelevant to the credibility and qualifications of the Doctor and irrelevant to the material on which he is testifying.

THE COURT:
I believe that the witness did state a few moments ago that he was not there personally and they did have to accept what Mr. Oser termed as hearsay. I believe the question being put by the District Attorney is to find out what other hearsay evidence they received.

MR. OSER:
That's right.

THE COURT:
Can't you ask a specific question instead of reading the article?

MR. DYMOND:
The thrust of my objection is that we have nothing before The Court to show this was even a bit of hearsay without even asking the Doctor whether he heard it. This is something that is purely out of the files of the District Attorney.

MR. OSER:
Your Honor, the State is attempting to ascertain from the Colonel whether or not he based his conclusions or his autopsy report on any type of hearsay other than that type of hearsay that backed up what the Warren Commission wanted it to be, or the Federal Government. Strike Warren Commission and make it Federal Government.

MR. DYMOND:
Your Honor, what I'm trying to impress on The Court is you have nothing before you to even show there is hearsay evidence to the effect of this statement that has been made by the District Attorney. That is completely outside the scope of the evidence in this case. We don't know any such contention was ever made by anybody.

THE COURT:
If the witness signed part of a three-man report and you referred to the report without using exact words, I would permit it, which you did previously. I think a general question can be asked, did they interview any other person, without saying what those persons said.

BY MR. OSER:
Q Colonel, besides what you referred to in paragraph 2 of the report, were you furnished with any other alleged statements by any of the witnesses in Dealey Plaza, namely the witnesses to the assassination of President Kennedy on November 22?

MR. DYMOND:
Is this question restricted to before he signed the autopsy report?

MR. OSER:
I am asking about at the time he signed the report.

THE COURT:
It is restricted to that period.

BY MR. OSER:
Q Were you furnished statements by anyone else?
A We based the statement on the people who had been at the scene.

THE COURT:
Let me interrupt you a second. You say "we," I presume you mean you and the other two doctors?

THE WITNESS:
Yes, sir.

THE COURT:
Mr. Oser's question is, did you and the other two persons personally interview these people or get it from another source?

THE WITNESS:
I personally talked to Secret Service Agent Kellerman. I personally talked to Admiral Berkley, the personal physician to President Kennedy. I personally talked to Admiral Galloway, who was referred to a third witness present at the scene. There may have been others leading us to the statement that to the best of our knowledge at that time there were three shots fired.

BY MR. OSER:
Q Doctor, speaking of the wound to the throat area of the President as you described it, after this bullet passed through the President's throat in the manner in which you described it, would the President have been able to talk?
A I don't know.

Q Do you have an opinion?

A There are many factors influencing the ability to talk or not to talk after a shot.

Q Did you have an occasion to dissect the track of that particular bullet in the victim as it lay on the autopsy table?

A I did not dissect the track in the neck.

Q Why?

A This leads us into the disclosure of medical records.

MR. OSER:

Your Honor, I would like an answer from the Colonel and I would ask The Court so to direct.

THE COURT:

That is correct, you should answer, Doctor.

THE WITNESS:

We didn't remove the organs of the neck.

BY MR. OSER:

Q Why not, doctor?

A For the reason that we were told to examine the head wounds and that the—

Q Are you saying someone told you not to dissect the track?

THE COURT:

Let him finish his answer.

THE WITNESS:

I was told that the family wanted an examination of the head, as I recall, the head and chest, but the prosecutors in this autopsy didn't remove the organs of the neck, to my recollection.

BY MR. OSER;

Q You have said they did not. I want to know why didn't you as an autopsy pathologist attempt to ascertain the track through the body which you had on the autopsy table in trying to ascertain the cause or causes of death? Why?

A I had the cause of death.

Q Why did you not trace the track of the wound?

A As I recall I didn't remove these organs from the neck.

Q I didn't hear you.

A I examined the wounds but I didn't remove the organs of the neck.

Q You said you didn't do this; I am asking you why didn't [you] do this as a pathologist?

A From what I recall I looked at the trachea, there was a tracheotomy wound the best I can remember, but I didn't dissect or remove these organs.

MR. OSER:

Your Honor, I would ask Your Honor to direct the witness to answer my question.

BY MR. OSER:

Q I will ask you the question one more time: Why did you not dissect the track of the bullet wound that you have described today and you saw at the time of the autopsy at the time you examined the body? Why? I ask you to answer that question.

A As I recall I was told not to but I don't remember by whom.

Q You were told not to but you don't remember by whom?

A Right.

Q Could it have been one of the Admirals or one of the Generals in the room?

A I don't recall.

Q Do you have any particular reason why you cannot recall at this time?

A Because we were told to examine the head and the chest cavity, and that doesn't include the removal of the organs of the neck.

Q You are one of the three autopsy specialists and pathologists at the time, and you saw what you described as an entrance wound in the neck area of the President of the United States who had just been assassinated, and you were only interested in the other wound but not interested in the track through his neck, is that what you are telling me?

A I was interested in the track and I had observed the conditions of bruising between the point of entry in the back of the neck and the point of exit at the front of the neck, which is entirely compatible with the bullet path.

Q But you were told not to go into the area of the neck, is that your testimony?

A From what I recall, yes, but I don't remember by whom.

* * *

Q In referring once again, Colonel to S-67 for identification, the five-page report signed by you in January 1967, can you tell me why this report was prepared?

A Please repeat your question.

Q Can you tell me why this report was prepared, the one you signed in January 1967.

A The purpose of this, as I recall, was to correlate our autopsy report of November 1963, and the X-rays and photographs of the wounds, because we has seen the X-rays at the time of the autopsy but we hadn't seen the photographs in November 1963 or in March 1964, so in 1967 we were asked to look at those X-rays and photographs.

Q By whom were you asked to do this?

THE COURT:
Are you waiting for an answer?

MR. OSER:
Yes.

THE COURT:
I thought you were referring to your notes, Doctor.

MR. OSER:
I asked the witness—

THE COURT:
I heard your question. I was just wanting to know if you were waiting for an answer.

THE WITNESS:
I think I went first to the—I saw these photographs and X-rays to the best of my recollection at the archives of the United States in January 1967, the photographs, for the first time.

THE COURT:
He didn't ask you that question. He wanted to know who asked you to do this. Was that your question?

MR. OSER:
Yes, sir.

THE WITNESS:
As I recall it was Mr. Eardley. There are many names involved in this. I think it was Mr. Eardley at the Department of Justice and I had the authority to go there from the military.

BY MR. OSER:
Q Can you tell me whether or not you were asked to do this summary in January 1967 in regard to a panel review that was going to be done by Mr. William H. Carns, Russell S. Fisher, Mr. Russell H. Morgan and Mr. Alan R. Moritz.
A In January 1967 when I signed S-67, to the best of my recollection, I was not aware of this panel review which took place in 1968, if you are referring to an independent panel review.
Q I am.
A It was composed of W.H. Carns, Russell H. [*sic*] Fisher, Russell H. Morgan and Alan R. Moritz.
Q That is correct, Colonel.
A I don't remember knowing in 1967 that these four names were reviewing the evidence to the best of my recollection.
Q Are you familiar with their work?
A I have read this. I was made aware of this panel review, I had received this panel review in February 1969.

* * *

Q Colonel, can you give me the measurements of the wound in the area of the front of the President's neck that I am pointing to here on State Exhibit 69?
A As I recall, it was given by the Dallas surgeons as approximately five millimeters in diameter.
Q Can you convert approximately five millimeters in diameter to a part of an inch

for me, please?

A Approximately three sixteenths of one inch corresponds to five millimeters.

Q Referring, Colonel, to your Summary Report, State-67 for purposes of identification, which you signed on 26 January, 1967, can you tell me why you did not list the size of the wound that you say is the exit wound in the throat of the President?

A Because I did not, I did not see that wound in the front. I did not, I don't know why it is not there.

Q You say you did not see it?

A I did not see the wound of exit in the skin. I saw a hole of exit in the shirt of the President.

Q But in speaking of the throat area, or skin area of the President, relative to his throat you said it was approximately five millimeters and you later said that Commander Humes received this information from Dallas.

A The wound that was in the front of the neck I obtained that information from Dr. Humes.

Q Therefore would you say, Colonel, that the wound in the back of the neck as you describe it is larger than the wound in the throat area?

MR. DYMOND:
We object to this. First of all, the Doctor testified that these are approximate measurements on wounds in the skin. Secondly, the doctor testified that he never saw the front bullet wound and consequently an answer on that would have to be based on measurements made by someone else, told to someone else, and then included in the report.

MR. OSER:
All the results, if The Court please, from two autopsy reports signed by this witness stating that—I believe he said everything in here is true and correct when I asked him, then I asked him if he wished to change anything in here at the beginning of his testimony and he said no. I'm trying to ascertain what he told Defense Counsel on direct examination, he stated this was an exit wound and I am trying to find out whether the hole in the back is larger than the front and whether or not it is compatible with a wound from this type of bullet.

MR. DYMOND:
If The Court please, the Doctor testified what he based his conclusions on and further testified that he never did see the front wound in the neck and consequently the question is impossible of answer.

THE COURT:
He has testified he is familiar with the information received from Dr. Humes from the surgeons in Dallas, Texas and he knows it was in the report and that the information was communicated to him and he was aware of it. I understand that Mr. Oser's question is whether the entrance wound from the rear was larger than the exit wound, which was the information given by the surgeon in Dallas, Texas.

MR. DYMOND:

Your Honor has consistently ruled throughout the trial that a witness cannot relate what someone else related to him.

THE COURT:

Ordinarily I agree but it was advised to him and he was made cognizant of it when he signed the original report, when he signed the report he either knew that as a fact which was received it from Commander Humes who received it from Dallas. I will permit the question.

You are asking Dr. Finck if from the information he had whether or not the measurements of the alleged entrance wound as you wish to call it, alleged, is not larger than the information received from Dallas of the entrance wound in the front. I will permit you to ask it.

MR. DYMOND:

To which Counsel respectfully objects and reserves a Bill of Exception on the grounds this is hearsay evidence making the entire line of questioning, particularly this question, the answer to the question, the objection and ruling of the Court and the entire record parts of the bill.

MR. OSER:

Could I have the witness answer my question. Will you answer the question.

THE WITNESS:

Please repeat the question.

THE REPORTER:

Question: "Therefore, would you say, Colonel, that the wound in the back of the neck as you described it is larger than the wound in the throat area?"

MR. DYMOND:

Your Honor, that is not the question you stated you were ruling on. You said you were ruling on the question whether it was larger than the information indicated.

MR. OSER:

I will ask that question.

THE WITNESS:

Whether or not it was larger?

BY MR. OSER:

Q Than the information you received from the doctors in Dallas.

MR. DYMOND:

Object now on the ground that he didn't receive the information from the Doctor.

THE COURT:

I just ruled that he signed his name to the report and under that exception I will permit the question. Do you understand the question?

MR. OSER:
Let me ask you again, Doctor—

THE COURT:
No, because then I will have to be ruling on different things if you change the question each time.

MR. OSER:
Then I'll ask that the Court Reporter read the question I asked.

THE REPORTER:
Question: "Therefore, would you say, Colonel, that the wound in the back of the neck as you described it is larger than the wound in the throat area"—then he added the second part of the question, Your Honor, which says, "than the information you received from the doctors in Dallas?"

THE WITNESS:
I don't know 'cause I measured the wound of entry whereas I had no way of measuring the wound of exit and the wound could have been slightly smaller, the same size, or slightly larger because all I have is somebody saying it was approximately 5 millimeters in diameter.

* * *

Q Colonel, I direct your attention to Page 4 of your autopsy report of November 1963, and to the fourth paragraph which states, "The complexity of these fractures and the fragments thus produced tax satisfactory verbal description and are better appreciated in photographs and roentgenograms which are prepared." Now, Colonel, can you tell me and tell the Court how you refer in your autopsy report that the fractures and the fragments are better appreciated in the photographs when you did not see the photographs until January 1967?

MR. DYMOND:
We object to this unless Counsel says better than what. This report indicates a photograph would show them better than they could be described in words.

THE COURT:
You are coming to the aid of a witness unsolicited.

MR. DYMOND:
You cannot compare something to nothing, Your Honor.

THE COURT:
Do you understand the question?
THE WITNESS:
Yes. When there are so many fractures in so many directions producing so many

lines and fragments in the bone, a photograph will be more accurate than descriptions. The photographs were taken but turned over undeveloped to the Secret Service at the time we performed the autopsy, and the photographs were taken, we did not know when these photographs would be processed, this was beyond our control because they had been turned over, exposed, taken in our presence, but the Secret Service took charge of them.

BY MR. OSER:
Q And you didn't see the photographs until January of 1967. Is that correct, Colonel?
A That is correct.
Q Also in your autopsy report on the same page, Page 4, I direct your attention to the last paragraph, the last paragraph under "2," where you said in your report, "The second wound presumably of entry," and now you state in Court that you are positive it was of entry.
A As I recall, it was Admiral Galloway who told us to put that word "presumably."
Q Admiral Galloway?
A Yes.
Q Told you to put that word "presumably"?
A Yes, but this does not change my opinion that this is a wound of entry.
Q Is Admiral Galloway a Pathologist, to your knowledge?
A Admiral Galloway had some training in Pathology. He was the Commanding Officer of the Naval Hospital, as I recall, and at that time, in my mind, this was a wound of entry, it just was suggested to add "presumably" this was.
Q Did he suggest you add anything else to your report, Colonel?
A Not that I recall.
Q Can you give me the name of the General that you said told Dr. Humes not to talk about the autopsy report?
A This was not a General, it was an Admiral.
Q All right, excuse me, the Admiral, can you give me the name of the Admiral?
A Who stated that we were not to discuss the autopsy findings?
Q Yes.
A This was in the autopsy room on the 22nd and 23rd of November, 1963.
Q What was his name?
A Well, there were several people in charge, there were several Admirals, and, as I recall, the Adjutant General of the Navy.
Q Do you have a name, Colonel?
A It was Admiral Kinney, K-i-n-n-e-y, as I recall.
Q Now, can you give me the name then of the General that was in charge of the autopsy, as you testified about?
A Well, there was no General in charge of the autopsy. There were several people, as I have stated before. I heard Dr. Humes state who was in charge here, and he stated that the General answered "I am," it may have been pertaining to operations other than the autopsy, it does not mean the Army General was in charge of the autopsy, but when Dr. Humes asked who was in charge here, it may have been who was in charge of the operations, but not of the autopsy, and by "operations," I mean the over-all supervision.
Q Which includes your report. Does it not?

A Sir?

Q Which includes your report. Does it not?

A No.

Q It does not?

A I would not say so, because the report I signed was signed by two other pathologists and at no time did this Army General say that he would have anything to do with signing this autopsy report.

Q Can you give me the Army General's name?

A I don't remember it.

Q How did you know he was an Army General?

A Because Dr. Humes said so.

Q Was he in uniform?

A I don't remember.

Q Were any of the Admirals or Generals or any of the Military in uniform in that autopsy room?

A Yes.

Q Were there any other Generals in uniform?

A I remember a Brigadier General of the Air Force, but I don't remember his name.

Q Were there any Admirals in uniform in the autopsy room?

A From what I remember, Admiral Galloway was in uniform, Admiral Kinney was in uniform, I don't remember whether or not Admiral Berkley, the President's physician, was in uniform.

* * *

Q Do you know whether or not all of the X-ray films came out or not, to your knowledge?

A To my knowledge, they came out all right.

Q Now, if, Colonel, you viewed the X-ray film of the head or had been viewed by a radiologist, can you tell me why there was no mention in your report of a three-quarter by one-half inch rectangular shaped object in the President's brain?

A No.

Q Can you tell me why there is nothing in your report making mention of metallic substances in the track?

A Before you go to that second question, if I may say something, in that panel review of 1968 there was a rectangular structure and they say it is not identifiable to this panel.

Q If it was there, Colonel, in the X-rays, would you say it was there in the brain at the time of the autopsy?

MR. DYMOND:

What page are you referring to, Doctor, what page are you referring to?

MR. OSER:

The panel of 1968, the pages are not numbered.

THE WITNESS:
That is "S-72."

MR. OSER:
Page 8, Mr. Dymond.

THE WITNESS:
"There can be seen a gray-brown rectangular structure measuring approximately 13 by 20 millimeters, its identity cannot be established by the panel." I don't know what this refers to.

BY MR. OSER:
Q Did you see such at the time of your autopsy, did you see such a substance in the brain of the President?
A I don't remember.

Appendix B

CIA Memoranda

As noted throughout this book, the government launched a series of public attacks against critics of the Warren Report. In his *Playboy* interview, Jim Garrison revealed that his phone was tapped by the FBI. As noted in Chapter 11 (note 15), Dorothy Kilgallen resorted to using pay phones and code names to escape taps. Ramsey Clark loudly attacked Garrison, generally inaccurately (see Chapter 11).

At times the Bureau and the CIA were more insidious. We have seen in Chapter 7 how the Bureau used Gerald Ford as a willing informant to apprise itself of the inside workings of the Warren Commission. The CIA later attacked critics through use of "media assets," *i.e.*, reporters in the press and electronic media whose sympathies coincided with theirs and who could be counted on to cooperate in coordinated attacks on the critics (see Chapter 10). The result would be to discredit and/or defame their targets in the eyes of the public and take the heat off the Warren Report by carefully pulling attention away from its shortcomings by belittling those who pointed them out.

Two CIA memoranda have been partially released through FOIA proceedings. The first document reproduced below is the text of an April 1, 1967, CIA Dispatch instructing officers and agents on how to conduct such a campaign to discredit the Warren Report critics. Although the dispatch stated that it had nine attachments, only two were released with it, one apparently in full, the other in part. Fortunately, the directive at the bottom right hand corner of the first page was not followed. It read: "DESTROY WHEN NO LONGER NEED-ED." The second document reproduced below is a one-page CIA Dispatch from July 19, 1968, dealing specifically with Garrison's investigation.

DISPATCH
To: Chiefs, Certain Stations and Bases
Ref: Countering Criticism of the Warren Report
Date: 4/1/67

1. *Our Concern.* From the day of President Kennedy's assassination on, there has been speculation about the responsibility for his murder. Although this was stemmed for a time by the Warren Commission report (which appeared at the end of September 1964), various writers have now had time to scan the Commission's published report and documents for new pretexts for questioning, and there has been a new wave of books and articles criticizing the commission's findings. In most cases the critics have speculated as to the existence of some kind of conspiracy, and often they have implied that the Commission itself was involved. Presumably as a result of the increasing challenge to the Warren Commission's Report, a public opinion poll recently indicated that 46% of the American public did not think that Oswald acted alone, while more than half of those polled thought that the Commission had left some questions unresolved. Doubtless polls abroad would show similar, or possibly more adverse, results.

2. This trend of opinion is a matter of concern to the U.S. government, including our organization. The members of the Warren Commission were naturally chosen for their integrity, experience, and prominence. They represented both major parties, and they and their staff were deliberately drawn from all sections of the country. Just because of the standing of the Commissioners, efforts to impugn their rectitude and wisdom tend to cast doubt on the whole leadership of American society. Moreover, there seems to be an increasing tendency to hint that President Johnson himself, as the one person who might be said to have benefited, was in some way responsible for the assassination. Innuendo of such seriousness affects not only the individual concerned but also the whole reputation of the American government. Our organization itself is directly involved: among other facts, we contributed information to the investigation. Conspiracy theories have frequently thrown suspicion on our organization, for example by falsely alleging that Lee Harvey Oswald worked for us. The aim of this dispatch is to provide material for countering and discrediting the claims of the conspiracy theorists, so as to inhibit the circulation of such claims in other countries. Background information is supplied in a classified section and in a number of unclassified documents.

3. *Action.* We do *not* recommend that discussion of the assassination question be initiated where it is not already taking place. Where discussion is active, however, addressees are requested:

a. To discuss the publicity problem with liaison and friendly elite contacts (especially politicians and editors), pointing out that the Warren Commission made as thorough an investigation as humanly possible, that the charges of the critics are without serious foundation, and that further speculative discussion only plays into the hands of the opposition. Point out also that parts of the conspiracy talk appear to be deliberately generated by Communist propagandists. Urge them to use their influence to discourage unfounded and irresponsible speculation.

b. To employ propaganda assets to answer and refuse the attacks of the critics. Book reviews and feature articles are particularly appropriate for this purpose. The unclassified attachments to this guidance should provide useful background material for passage to assets. Our play should point out, as applicable, that the critics are (i) wedded to theories adopted before the evidence was in, (ii) politically interested, (iii) financially interested, (iv) hasty and inaccurate in their research, or (v) infatuated with their own theories. In the course of discussions of the whole phenomenon of criticism, a useful strategy may be to single out Epstein's theory for attack, using the attached Fletcher Knebel article and Spectator piece for background. (Although Mark Lane's book is much less convincing than Epstein's and comes off badly where contested by knowledgeable critics, it is also much more difficult to answer as a whole, as one becomes lost in a morass of unrelated details.)

4. In private and media discussion not directed at any particular writer, or in attacking publications which may be yet forthcoming, the following arguments should be useful:

a. No significant new evidence has emerged which the Commission did not consider. The assassination is sometimes compared (e.g., by Joachim Joesten and Bertrand Russell) with the Dreyfus case; however, unlike that case, the attacks on the Warren Commission have produced no new evidence, no new culprits have been convincingly identified, and there is no agreement among the critics. A better parallel, though an imperfect one, might be with the Reichstag fire of 1933, which some competent historians (Fritz Tobias, A.J.P. Taylor, D.C. Watt) now believe was set by Van der Lubbe on his own initiative, without acting for either the Nazis or Communists; the Nazis tried to pin the blame on the Communists, but the latter have been much more successful in convincing the world that the Nazis were to blame.)

b. Critics usually overvalue particular items and ignore others. They tend to place more emphasis on the recollections of individual eyewitnesses (which are less reliable and more divergent—and hence offer more hand-holds for criticism) and less on ballistic, autopsy, and photographic evidence. A close examination of the Commission's records will usually show that the conflicting eyewitness accounts are quoted out of context, or were discarded by the Commission for good and sufficient reason.

c. Conspiracy on the large scale often suggested would be impossible to conceal in the United States, esp. since informants could expect to receive large royalties, etc. Note that Robert Kennedy, Attorney General at the time and John F. Kennedy's brother, would be the last man to overlook or conceal any conspiracy. And as one reviewer pointed out, Congressman Gerald R. Ford would hardly have held his tongue for the sake of the Democratic administration, and Senator Russell would have had every political interest in exposing any misdeeds on the part of Chief Justice Warren. A conspirator moreover would hardly choose a location for a shooting where so much depended on conditions beyond his control: the route, the speed of the cars, the moving target, the risk that the assassin would be discovered. A group of wealthy conspirators could have arranged much more secure conditions.

d. Critics have often been enticed by a form of intellectual pride: they light on some theory and fall in love with it; they also scoff at the Commission because it did not always answer every question with a flat decision one way or the other. Actually, the make-up of the Commission and its staff was an excellent safeguard against over-commitment to any one theory, or against the illicit transformation of probabilities into certainties.

e. Oswald would not have been any sensible person's choice for a co-conspirator. He was a "loner," mixed-up, of questionable reliability and an unknown quantity to any professional intelligence service.

f. As to the charges that the Commission's report was a rush job, it emerged three months after the deadline originally set. But to the degree that the Commission tried to speed up its reporting, this was largely due to the pressure of irresponsible speculation already appearing, in some cases coming from the same critics who, refusing to admit their errors, are now putting out new criticisms.

g. Such vague accusations as that "more than ten people have died mysteriously" can always be explained in some more natural way: e.g., the individuals concerned have for the most part died of natural causes; the commission staff questioned 418 witnesses (the FBI interviewed far more people, conducting 25,000 interviews and reinterviews), and in such a large group, a certain number of deaths are to be expected. (When Penn Jones, one of the originators of the "ten mysterious deaths" line, appeared on television, it emerged that two of the deaths on his list were from heart attacks, one from cancer, one was from a head-on collision on a bridge, and one occurred when a driver drifted into a bridge abutment.)

5. Where possible, counter speculation by encouraging reference to the Commission's Report itself. Open-minded foreign readers should still be impressed by the care, thoroughness, objectivity and speed with which the Commission worked. Reviewers of other books might be encouraged to add to their account the idea that, checking back with the Report itself, they found it far superior to the work of its critics.

Attachment 1
4 January 1967

Background Survey of Books Concerning
the Assassination of President Kennedy

1. (Except where otherwise indicated, the factual data given in paragraphs 1-9 is unclassified.) Some of the authors of recent books on the assassination of President Kennedy (e.g., Joachim Joesten, *Oswald: Assassin or Fall Guy*; Mark Lane, *Rush to Judgment* [*sic*]; Leo Sauvage, *The Oswald Affair: An Examination of the Contradictions and Omissions of the Warren Report*) *had publicly asserted that a conspiracy existed before* the Warren Commission finished its investiga-

tion. Not surprisingly, they immediately bestirred themselves to show that they were right and that the Commission was wrong. Thanks to the mountain of material published by the Commission, some of it conflicting or misleading when read out of context, they have had little difficulty in uncovering items to substantiate their own theories. They have also in some cases obtained new and divergent testimony from witnesses. And they have usually failed to discuss the refutations of their early claims in the Commission's Report, Appendix XII ("Speculations and Rumors"). This Appendix is still a good place to look for material countering the theorists.

2. Some writers appear to have been predisposed to criticism by *anti-American, far-left, or Communist sympathies*. The British "Who Killed Kennedy Committee" includes some of the most persistent and vocal English critics of the United States, e.g., Michael Foot, Kingsley Martin, Kenneth Tynan, and Bertrand Russell. Joachim Joesten has been publicly revealed as a onetime member of the German Communist Party (KDP); a Gestapo document of 8 November 1937 among the German Foreign Ministry files microfilmed in England and now returned to West German custody shows that his party book was numbered 532315 and dated 12 May 1932. (The originals of these files are now available at the West German Foreign Ministry in Bonn; the copy in the U.S. National Archives may be found under the reference T-120, Serial 4918, frames E256482-4. The British Public Records Office should also have a copy.) Joesten's American publisher, Carl Marzani, was once sentence to jail by a federal jury for concealing his Communist Party (CPUSA) membership in order to hold a government job. Available information indicates that Mark Lane was elected Vice Chairman of the New York Council to Abolish the House Un-American Activities Committee on 28 May 1963; he also attended the 8th Congress of the International Association of Democratic Lawyers (an international Communist front organization) in Budapest from 31 March to 5 April 1964, where he expounded his (pre-Report) views on the Kennedy assassination. In his acknowledgments in his book, Lane expresses special thanks to Ralph Schoenman of London "who participated in and supported the work"; Schoenman is of course the expatriate American who has been influencing the aged Bertrand Russell in recent years. (See also para. 10 below on Communist efforts to replay speculation on the assassination.)

3. Another factor has been the *financial reward* obtainable for sensational books. Mark Lane's *Rush to Judgment*, published on 13 August 1966, had sold 85,000 copies by early November and the publishers had printed 140,000 copies by that date, in anticipation of sales to come. The 1 January 1967 *New York Times Book Review* reported the book as at the top of the General category of the best seller list, having been in top position for seven weeks and on the list for 17 weeks. Lane has reportedly appeared on about 175 television and radio programs, and has also given numerous public lectures, all of which serves for advertisement. He has also put together a TV film, and is peddling it to European telecasters; the BBC has purchased rights for a record $45,000. While neither Abraham Zapruder nor William Manchester should be classed with the critics of the Commission we are discussing here, sums paid for the Zapruder film of the assassination ($25,000) and for magazine rights to Manchester's *Death of a President* ($665,000) indicate the money available for material related to the assassination. Some newspapermen (e.g., Sylvan Fox, *The Unanswered Ques-*

tions About President Kennedy's Assassination; Leo Sauvage, *The Oswald Affair*) have published accounts cashing in on their journalistic expertise.

4. Aside from political and financial motives, some people have apparently published accounts *simply because they were burning to give the world their theory*, e.g., Harold Weisberg, in his *Whitewash II*, Penn Jones, Jr., in *Forgive My Grief*, and George C. Thomson in *The Quest for Truth*. Weisberg's book was first published privately, though it is now finally attaining the dignity of commercial publication. Jones' volume was published by the small-town Texas newspaper of which he is the editor, and Thomson's booklet by his own engineering firm. The impact of these books will probably be relatively slight, since their writers will appear to readers to be hysterical or paranoid.

5. A common technique among many of the writers is to *raise as many questions as possible*, while not bothering to work out all the consequences. Herbert Mitgang has written a parody of this approach (his questions actually refer to *Lincoln's* assassination) in "A New Inquiry is Needed," *New York Times Magazine*, 25 December 1966. Mark Lane in particular (who represents himself as Oswald's lawyer) adopts the classic defense attorney's approach of throwing in unrelated details so as to create in the jury's mind a sum of "reasonable doubt." His tendency to wander off into minor details led one observer to comment that whereas a good trial lawyer should have a sure instinct for the jugular vein, Lane's instinct was for the capillaries. His tactics and also his nerve were typified on the occasion when, after getting the Commission to pay his travel expenses back from England, he recounted to that body a sensational (and incredible) story of a Ruby plot, while refusing to name his source. Chief Justice Warren told Lane, "We have every reason to doubt the truthfulness of what you have heretofore told us"—by the standards of legal etiquette, a very stiff rebuke for an attorney.

6. It should be recognized, however, that another kind of criticism has recently emerged, represented by Edward Jay Epstein's *Inquest*. Epstein adopts a *scholarly* tone, and to the casual reader, he presents what appears to be a more coherent, reasoned case than the writers described above.

Epstein has caused people like Richard Rovere and Lord Devlin, previously backers of the Commission's Report, to change their minds. The *New York Times'* daily book reviewer has said that Epstein's work is a "watershed book" which has made it respectable to doubt the Commission's findings. This respectability effect has been enhanced by *Life* magazine's 25 November 1966 issue, which contains an assertion that there is a "reasonable doubt," as well as a republication of frames from the Zapruder film (owned by *Life*), and an interview with Governor Connally, who repeats his belief that he was not struck by the same bullet that struck President Kennedy. (Connally does not, however, agree that there should be another investigation.) Epstein himself has published a new article in the December 1966 issue of *Esquire*, in which he explains away objections to his book. A copy of an early critique of Epstein's views by Fletcher Knebel, published in *Look*, 12 July 1966, and an unclassified, unofficial analysis (by "Spectator") are attached to this dispatch, dealing with specific questions raised by Epstein.

7. Here it should be pointed out that Epstein's competence in research has been greatly exaggerated. Some illustrations are given in the Fletcher Knebel article. As a further specimen, Epstein's book refers (pp. 93-5) to a cropped-down picture of a heavy-set man taken in Mexico City, saying that the Central Intelligence

Agency gave it to the Federal Bureau of Investigation on 18 November 1963, and that the Bureau in turn forwarded it to its Dallas office. Actually, affidavits in the published Warren material (vol. XI, pp. 468-70) show that CIA turned the picture over to the FBI on 22 November 1963. (As a matter of interest, Mark Lane's *Rush to Judgment* claims that the photo was furnished by CIA on the *morning* of 22 November; the fact is that the FBI flew the photo directly from Mexico City to Dallas immediately *after* Oswald's arrest, before Oswald's picture had been published, on the chance it might be Oswald. The reason the photo was cropped was that the background revealed the place where it was taken.) Another example: where Epstein reports (p. 41) that a Secret Service interview report was even withheld from the National Archives, this is untrue: an Archives staff member told one of our officers that Epstein came there and asked for the memorandum. He was told that it was there, but was classified. Indeed, the Archives then notified the Secret Service that there had been a request for the document, and the Secret Service declassified it. But by that time, Epstein (whose preface gives the impression of prolonged archival research) had chosen to finish his searches in the Archives, which had only lasted two days, and had left town. Yet Epstein charges that the Commission was over-hasty in its work.

8. Aside from such failures in research, Epstein and other intellectual critics show symptoms of some of the *love of theorizing and lack of common sense and experience* displayed by Richard H. Popkin, the author of *The Second Oswald*. Because Oswald was reported to have been seen in different places at the same time, a phenomenon not surprising in a sensational case where thousands of real or alleged witnesses were interviewed, Popkin, a professor of philosophy, theorizes that there actually were two Oswalds. At this point, theorizing becomes sort of logico-mathematical game; an exercise in permutations and combinations; as Commission attorney Arlen Specter remarked, "Why not make it three Oswalds? Why stop at two?" Nevertheless, aside from his book, Popkin has been able to publish a summary of his views in *The New York Review of Books*, and there has been replay in the French *Nouvel Observateur*, in Moscow's *New Times*, and in Baku's *Vyshka*. Popkin makes a sensational accusation indirectly, saying that "Western European critics" see Kennedy's assassination as part of a subtle conspiracy attributable to "perhaps even (in rumors I have heard) Kennedy's successor." One Barbara Garson has made the same point in another way by her parody of Shakespeare's "Macbeth" entitled "MacBird," with what was obviously President Kennedy (Ken O Dune) in the role of Duncan, and President Johnson (MacBird) in the role of Macbeth. Miss Garson makes no effort to prove her point; she merely insinuates it. Probably the indirect form of accusation is due to fear of a libel suit.

9. Other books are yet to appear. William Manchester's not-yet-published *The Death of a President* is at this writing being purged of material personally objectionable to Mrs. Kennedy. There are hopeful signs: Jacob Cohen is writing a book which will appear in 1967 under the title *Honest Verdict*, defending the Commission report, and one of the Commission attorneys, Wesley J. Liebeler, is also reportedly writing a book, setting forth both sides. But further criticism will no doubt appear; as the *Washington Post* has pointed out editorially, the recent death of Jack Ruby will probably lead to speculation that he was "silenced" by a conspiracy.

10. The likelihood of further criticism is enhanced by the circumstance that *Communist propagandists seem recently to have stepped up their own campaign* to discredit the Warren Commission. As already noted, Moscow's *New Times* reprinted parts of an article by Richard Popkin (21 and 28 September 1966 issues), and it also gave the Swiss edition of Joesten's latest work an extended, laudatory review in its number for 26 October. *Izvestiya* has also publicized Joesten's book in articles of 18 and 21 October. (In view of this publicity and the Communist background of Joesten and his American publisher, together with Joesten's insistence on pinning the blame on such favorite Communist targets as H.L. Hunt, the FBI and CIA, there seems reason to suspect that Joesten's book and its exploitation are part of a planned Soviet propaganda operation.) Tass, reporting on 5 November on the deposit of autopsy photographs in the National Archives, said that the refusal to give wide public access to them, the disappearance of a number of documents, and the mysterious death of more than 10 people, all make many Americans believe Kennedy was killed as the result of a conspiracy. The radio transmitters of Prague and Warsaw used the anniversary of the assassination to attack the Warren report. The Bulgarian press conducted a campaign on the subject in the second half of October; a Greek Communist newspaper, *Avgi*, placed the blame on CIA on 20 November. Significantly, the start of this stepped-up campaign coincided with a Soviet demand that the U.S. Embassy in Moscow stop distributing the Russian-language edition of the Warren report; *Newsweek* commented (12 September) that the Soviets apparently "did not want mere facts to get in their way."

Attachment 2

The Theories of Mr. Epstein
by Spectator

A recent critic of the Warren Commission Report, Edward Jay Epstein, has attracted widespread attention by contesting the Report's conclusion that, "although it is not necessary to any essential findings of the Commission," President Kennedy and Governor Connally were probably hit successively by the same bullet, the second of three shots fired. In his book, *Inquest*, Epstein maintains (1) that if the two men were not hit by the same bullet, there must have been two assassins, and (2) that there is evidence which strongly suggests that the two men were not hit by the same bullet. He suggests that the Commission's conclusions must be viewed as "expressions of political truth," implying that they are not in fact true, but are only a sort of Pablum for the public,

Epstein's argument that the two men must either have been shot by one bullet or by two assassins rests on a comparison of the minimum time required to operate the bolt on Lee Harvey Oswald's rifle—2.3 seconds—with the timing of the shots as deduced from a movie of the shooting taken by an amateur photographer, Abraham Zapruder. The frames of the movie serve to time the events in the shooting. The film (along with a slow-motion re-enactment of the shooting made on 24 May 1964 on the basis of the film and other pictures and evidence) tends to show that the President was probably not shot before frame 207, when he came out from beneath the cover of an oak tree, and that the Governor was hit not later than frame 240. If this is correct, then the two men would not have been hit longer than 1.8 seconds apart, since Zapruder's film was taken at a speed of 18.3 frames per second. Since Oswald's rifle could not have fired a second shot within 1.8 seconds, Epstein concludes that the victims *must* have been shot by separate weapons—and hence presumably by separate assassins—*unless* they were hit by the same bullet.

Epstein then argues that there is evidence which contradicts the possibility of a shooting by a single bullet. In his book he refers to Federal Bureau of Investigation reports stemming from FBI men present at the Bethesda autopsy on President Kennedy, according to which there was a wound in the back with no point of exit; this means that the bullet which entered Kennedy's back could not later have hit Connally. This information, Epstein notes, flatly contradicts the official autopsy report accepted by the Commission, according to which the bullet presumably entered Kennedy's body just below the neck and exited through the throat. Epstein also publishes photographs of the backs of Kennedy's shirt and coat, showing bullet holes about six inches below the top of the collar, as well as a rough sketch made at the time of the autopsy; these pictures suggest that the entrance wound in the back was too low to be linked to an exit wound in the throat. In his book, Epstein says that if the FBI statements are correct—and he indicates his belief that they are—then the "autopsy findings must have been changed after January 13 [January 13, 1964: the date of the last FBI report stating that the bullet penetrated Kennedy's back for less than a finger-length.]." In short, he implies that the Commission warped and even forged evidence so as to conceal the fact of a conspiracy.

Following the appearance of Epstein's *Inquest*, it was pointed out that on the morning (November 23rd) after the Bethesda autopsy attended by FBI and Secret Service men, the autopsy doctors learned that a neck wound, obliterated by an emergency tracheostomy performed in Dallas, had been seen by the Dallas doctors. (The tracheostomy had been part of the effort to save Kennedy's life.) The FBI men who had only attended the autopsy on the evening of November 22 naturally did not know about this information from Dallas, which led the autopsy doctors to change their conclusions, finally signed by them on November 24. Also, the Treasury Department (which runs the Secret Service) reported that the autopsy report was only forwarded by the Secret Service to the FBI on December 23, 1963. But in a recent article in *Esquire*, Epstein notes that the final FBI report was still issued after the Secret Service had sent the FBI the official autopsy, and he claims that the explanation that the FBI was uninformed "begs the question of how a wound below the shoulder became a wound in the back of the neck." He presses for making the autopsy pictures available, a step which the late President's brother has so far steadfastly resisted on the grounds of taste, though they have been made available to qualified official investigators.

Let us consider Epstein's arguments in the light of information now available:

1. *Epstein's thesis that if the President and the Governor were not hit by the same bullet, there must have been two assassins:*

a. Feeling in the Commission was that the two men were probably hit by the same bullet; however, some members evidently felt that the evidence was not conclusive enough to exclude completely the Governor's belief that he and the

President were hit separately. After all, Connally was one of the most important living witnesses. While not likely, it was *possible* that President Kennedy could have been hit more than 2.3 seconds before Connally. As Arlen Specter, a Commission attorney and a principal adherent of the "one-bullet theory," says, the Zapruder film is two-dimensional and one cannot say exactly when Connally, let alone the President, was hit. The film does not show the President during a crucial period (from about frames 204 to 225) when a sign blocked the view from Zapruder's camera, and before that the figures are distant and rather indistinct. (When *Life* magazine first published frames from the Zapruder film in its special 1963 Assassination Issue, it believed that the pictures showed Kennedy first hit 74 frames before Governor Connally was struck.) The "earliest possible time" used by Epstein is based on the belief that, for an interval before that time, the view of the car from the Book Depository window was probably blocked by the foliage of an oak tree (from frame 166 to frame 207, with a brief glimpse through the leaves at frame 186). In the words of the Commission's Report, "it is unlikely that the assassin would deliberately have shot [at President Kennedy] with a view obstructed by the oak tree when he was about to have a clear opportunity"; *unlikely*, but not impossible. Since Epstein is fond of logical terminology, it might be pointed out that he made an illicit transition from probability to certainty in at least one of his premises.

b. Although Governor Connally believed that he and the President were hit separately, he did not testify that he saw the President hit before he was hit himself; he testified that he heard a first shot and started to turn to see what had happened. His testimony (as the Commission's report says) can therefore be reconciled with the supposition that the first shot missed and the second shot hit both men. However, the Commission did not pretend that the two men could not possibly have been hit separately.

c. The Commission also concluded that all the shots were fired from the sixth floor window of the Depository. The location of the wounds is one major basis for this conclusion. In the room behind the Depository window, Oswald's rifle and three cartridge cases were found, and *all* of the cartridge cases were identified by experts as having been fired by that rifle; no other weapon or cartridge cases were found, and the consensus of the witnesses from the plaza was that there were three shots. If there were other assassins, what happened to their weapons and cartridge cases? How did they escape? Epstein points out that one woman, a Mrs. Walther, not an expert on weapons, thought she saw two men, one with a machine gun, in the window, and that one other witness thought he saw someone else on the sixth floor; this does not sound very convincing, especially when compared with photographs and other witnesses who saw nothing of the kind.

d. The very fact that the Commission did *not* absolutely rule out the possibility that the victims were shot separately shows that its conclusions were not determined by a preconceived theory. Now, Epstein's thesis is not just his own discovery; he relates that one of the Commission lawyers volunteered to him: "To say that they were hit by separate bullets is synonymous with saying that there were two assassins." This thesis was evidently considered by the Commission. If the thesis were completely valid, and if the Commissioners—as Epstein charges—had only been interested in finding "political truth," then the Commission should have flatly adopted the "one-bullet theory," completely rejecting any possibility that the men were hit separately. But while Epstein and the others have a weakness for theorizing, the seven experienced lawyers on the Commission were not committed beforehand to finding either a conspiracy or the absence of one, and they wisely refused to erect a whole logical structure on the slender foundation of a few debatable pieces of evidence.

2. *Epstein's thesis that either the FBI's reports (that the bullet entering the President's back did not exit) were wrong, or the official autopsy report was falsified.*

a. Epstein prefers to believe that the FBI reports are accurate (otherwise, he says, "doubt is cast on the accuracy of the FBI's *entire* investigation") and that the official autopsy report was falsified. Now, as noted above, it has emerged since *Inquest* was written that the FBI witnesses to the autopsy did not know about the information of a throat wound, obtained from Dallas, and that the doctors' autopsy report was not forwarded to the FBI until December 23, 1963. True, this date preceded the date of the FBI's Supplemental Report, January 13, 1964, and that Supplemental Report did not refer to the doctors' report, following instead the version of the earlier FBI reports. But on November 25, 1966, FBI Director J. Edgar Hoover explained that when the FBI submitted its January 13 report, it knew that the Commission would weigh its evidence together with that of other agencies, and it was not incumbent on the FBI to argue the merits of its own version as opposed to that of the doctors. When writing reports for outside use, experienced officials are always cautious about criticizing or even discussing the products of other agencies. (If one is skeptical about this explanation, it would still be much easier to believe that the author(s) of the Supplemental Report had somehow overlooked or not received the autopsy report than to suppose that that report was falsified months after the event. Epstein thinks the Commission staff overlooked Mrs. Walther's report mentioned above, yet he does not consider the possibility that the doctors' autopsy report did not actually reach the desk of the individuals who prepared the Supplemental Report until after they had written— perhaps well before January 13—the draft of page 2 of that report. Such an occurrence would by no means justify a general distrust of the FBI's "*entire* investigation.")

b. With regard to the holes in the shirt and coat, their location can be readily explained by supposing that the President was waving to the crowd, an act which would automatically raise the back of his clothing. And in fact, photographs show the President was waving just before he was shot.

c. As to the location of the hole in the President's back or shoulder, the autopsy films have recently been placed in the National Archives, and were viewed in November 1966 by two of the autopsy directors, who... [The last page released ends here.]

Dispatch
To: Chiefs, Certain Stations and Bases
From: Chief,
Subject: Warren Commission Report: Article on the Investigation Conducted by District Attorney Garrison
Date: 19 July 1968

1. We are forwarding herewith a reprint of the article "A Reporter At Large: Garrison", published in THE NEW YORKER, 13 July, 1968. It was written by Edward Jay Epstein, himself author of a book ("Inquest"), critical of the Warren Commission Report.

2. The wide-spread campaign of adverse criticism of the U.S., most recently again provoked by the assassination of Senator Robert Kennedy, appears to have revived foreign interest in the assassination of his brother, the late President Kennedy, too. The forthcoming trial of Sirhan, accused of the murder of Senator Kennedy, can be expected to cause a new wave of criticism and suspicion against the United States, claiming once more the existence of a sinister "political murder conspiracy". We are sending you the attached article—based either on first-hand observation by the author or on other, identified sources—since it deals with the continuing investigation, conducted by District Attorney Garrison of New Orleans, La. That investigation tends to keep alive speculations about the death of President Kennedy, an alleged "conspiracy", and about the possible involvement of Federal agencies, notably the FBI and CIA.

3. The article is not meant for reprinting in any media. It is forwarded primarily for your information and for the information of all Station personnel concerned. If the Garrison investigation should be cited in your area in the context of renewed anti-U.S. attacks, *you may use the article to brief* interested contacts, especially government and other political leaders, and to demonstrate to assets (which you may assign to counter such attacks) that there is no hard evidence of any such conspiracy. In this context, assets may have to explain to their audiences certain basic facts about the U.S. judicial system, its separation of state and federal courts and the fact that judges and district attorneys in the states are usually elected, not appointed: consequently, D.A. Garrison can continue in office as long as his constituents re-elect him. Even if your assets have to discuss this in order to refute—or at least weaken—anti-U.S. propaganda of sufficiently serious impact, any *personal attacks* upon Garrison (or any other public personality in the U.S.) must be strictly avoided.

Bibliography

Government Reports

Report of the President's Commission on the Assassination of President John F. Kennedy (the *Warren Report*) (Washington: U.S. Government Printing Office, 1964), with accompanying 26 volumes of exhibits and testimony.

U.S. Senate, Select Committee to Study Governmental Operations with Respect to Intelligence Activities, *Final Report, Book Five, The Investigation of the Assassination of President John F. Kennedy: Performance of the Intelligence Agencies*, 94th Congress, 2nd Session, 1976, S. Rpt. 94-755.

U.S. House, Select Committee on Assassinations, *Report*, with twelve accompanying volumes of hearings and appendices (material on Kennedy case as opposed to Martin Luther King, Jr., case) (Washington: U.S. Government Printing Office, 1979), 95th Congress, 2nd Session, 1979, H. Rpt. 1828.

Periodicals

Bethell, Tom, "Conspiracy to End Conspiracies," *National Review*, December 16, 1991.

Brinkley, Alan, "Minister Without Portfolio," *Harper's*, February 1983.

Carpenter, Arthur E., "Social Origins of Anticommunism: The Information Council of the Americas," *Louisiana History*, Spring 1989.

Epstein, Edward Jay, "Who's Afraid of the Warren Report," *Esquire*, December 1966.

Garrison, Jim, interview in *Playboy*, October 1967.

Goldman, David, and Jeffrey Steinberg, "Special Report," *Executive Intelligence Review*, November 14, 1981.

Hilsman, Roger, Letter to the Editor, *New York Times*, January 20, 1992.

Joesten, Joachim, "Highlights and Lessons of the Clay Shaw Trial," *Truth Letter*, June 15, 1969.

Krassner, Paul, "First Edition, Second Edition," *Lies Of Our Times*, Vol. 1, No. 2, February 1990.

Kurtz, Michael, "Lee Harvey Oswald in New Orleans: A Reappraisal," *Louisiana History*, Winter 1980.

Lemann, Nicholas, "The Case Against Jim Garrison," *GQ*, January 1992.

Miller, David, "Who Murdered DeMohrenschildt?" *Yipster Times*, October-November 1977.

Newfield, Jack, "Hoffa Had the Mob Murder JFK," *New York Post*, January 14, 1992.

Newman, John, "The 'Gimmick' in JFK's Withdrawal Plan," *Boston Globe*, January 14, 1992.

Oglesby, Carl, "The Conspiracy That Won't Go Away," *Playboy*, February 1992.

322

——, "Reinhard Gehlen: The Secret Treaty of Fort Hunt," *CovertAction Information Bulletin*, No. 35, Fall 1990.

Phelan, James, "Rush to Judgment in New Orleans," *Saturday Evening Post*, May 6, 1967.

Policoff, Jerry, ed., "The JFK Assassination," special supplement to *Gallery*, July 1979.

Popkin, Richard H., "Garrison's Case," *New York Review of Books*, September 14, 1967.

Powledge, Fred, "Is Garrison Faking?" *The New Republic*, June 17, 1967.

Rose, Jerry D., "Jack Ruby and J.D. Tippit: Coincidence or Conspiracy?" *The Third Decade*, March 1985.

——, "The Trip That Never Was: Oswald in Mexico," *The Third Decade*, July 1985.

Salandria, Vincent, "Warren Report Pt. 1," *Liberation*, January 1965.

——, "Warren Report Pt. 2," *Liberation*, March 1965.

Scott, Peter Dale, "How Allen Dulles and the SS Preserved Each Other," *Covert-Action Information Bulletin*, No. 25, Winter 1986.

Spiegelman, Bob, "A Tale of Two Memos: A Manhattan Project for the Mind," *CovertAction Information Bulletin*, No. 31, Winter 1989.

Stone, Oliver, "Oliver Stone Talks Back," *Premiere*, January 1992.

Time Out, Interview with Tommy Lee Jones, January 18, 1992.

Turner, William, "The Inquest," *Ramparts*, June 1967.

——, "The Garrison Commission," *Ramparts*, January 1968.

Weeks, Anthony Edward, "Late Breaking News on Clay Shaw's United Kingdom Contacts," *Lobster*, November 1990.

Unpublished Manuscripts

Carpenter, Arthur E., "Gateway to the Americas," unpublished dissertation, Tulane University, New Orleans, Louisiana, 1987.

Fensterwald, Bernard, and J. Gary Shaw, "A Possible French Connection," 1981, unpublished essay, furnished by author.

Scott, Peter Dale, "The Dallas Conspiracy," unpublished volume, 1971. Available from Tom Davis Books, Aptos, California.

Tatro, Edgar F., "Clay Shaw and Me," copy supplied by the author.

Torbitt, William, "Nomenclature of an Assassination Cabal," unpublished volume, available from the Mae Brussell Research Center, Santa Cruz, California.

Books

Abel, Elie, *The Missile Crisis* (Philadelphia: Lippincott, 1966).

Acheson, Dean, *Present at the Creation* (New York: W.W. Norton, 1969).

Ambrose, Stephen, *Eisenhower* (New York: Simon and Schuster, 1983).

——, *Eisenhower the President* (New York: Simon and Schuster, 1984).

Anson, Robert Sam, *They've Killed the President* (New York: Bantam, 1975).

Archer, Jules, *The Plot to Seize the White House* (New York: Hawthorn Books, 1973).

Ashman, Charles, *The CIA-Mafia Link* (New York: Manor Books, 1975).

Bacque, James, *Other Losses* (New York: Prima Publishing, 1991).

Belin, David, *Final Disclosure* (New York: Charles Scribner's Sons, 1988).
Bernstein, Barton J., and Allen J. Matusow, *The Truman Administration: A Documentary History* (New York: Harper & Row, 1966).
Bernstein, Irving, *Promises Kept* (New York: Oxford University Press, 1991).
Bethell, Tom, *The Electric Windmill: An Inadvertent Biography* (Washington, Regnery Gateway, 1988).
Blakey, Robert G., and Richard Billings, *The Plot to Kill the President* (New York: New York Times Books, 1981).
Blum, John Morton, *Years of Discord* (New York: W.W. Norton, 1991).
Blum, William, *The CIA: A Forgotten History* (London: Zed Books, 1986).
Blumenthal, Sidney, and Harvey Yazijian, eds., *Government by Gunplay* (New York: New American Library, 1976).
Bower, Thomas, *The Paperclip Conspiracy* (Boston: Little, Brown, 1987).
Brener, Milton E., *The Garrison Case* (New York: Clarkson N. Potter, 1969).
Brussell, Mae, *A Mae Brussell Reader* (Santa Barbara, Calif.: Prevailing Winds Research, 1991).
Buchanan, Thomas G., *Who Killed Kennedy?* (New York: G. P. Putnam's Sons, 1964).
Burnet, Vaughn Davis, *The Presidency of Lyndon Johnson* (Lawrence, Kan.: University of Kansas Press, 1983).
Burns, James MacGregor, *John Kennedy: A Political Profile* (New York: Harcourt, Brace, 1960).
Cook, Blanche Weisen, *The Declassified Eisenhower* (New York: Penguin, 1984).
Currey, Cecil B., *Edward Lansdale* (Boston: Houghton Mifflin, 1988).
David, Jay, ed., *The Weight of the Evidence* (New York: Meredith Press, 1968).
Davis, John H., *Mafia Kingfish* (New York: McGraw-Hill, 1989).
Davison, Jean, *Oswald's Game* (New York: W. W. Norton, 1983).
Eddowes, Michael, *The Oswald File* (New York: Clarkson N. Potter, 1977).
Ellis, Rafaela, *The Central Intelligence Agency* (New York: Chelsea House Publishers, 1988).
Epstein, Edward Jay, *Inquest* (New York: Bantam Books, 1966).
——, *Counterplot* (New York: Viking Books, 1969).
——, *Legend: The Secret World of Lee Harvey Oswald* (New York: Reader's Digest Press/McGraw-Hill, 1978).
Evica, George Michael, *And We Are All Mortal* (Hartford: University of Hartford Press, 1978).
Faenza, Roberto, and Edward Becker, *Il Malafare: Dall'America di Kennedy all'Italia, a Cuba, al Vietnam* (Milan: Mondadoro, 1978).
——, and Marco Fini, *Gli Americani in Italia* (Milan: Feltrinelli, 1976).
Fay, Paul B., Jr., *The Pleasure of His Company* (New York: Harper & Row, 1966).
Fensterwald, Bernard, Jr., with Michael Ewing, *Coincidence or Conspiracy* (New York: Zebra Books, 1977).
Flammonde, Paris, *The Kennedy Conspiracy* (New York: Meredith Press, 1969).
Ford, Gerald R., with John R. Stiles, *Portrait of the Assassin* (New York: Simon and Schuster, 1965).
Garrison, Jim, *A Heritage of Stone* (New York: G. P. Putnam's Sons, 1970).
——, *On the Trail of the Assassins: My Investigation and Prosecution of the Murder of President Kennedy* (New York: Sheridan Square Press, 1988).

Gentry, Curt, *J. Edgar Hoover* (New York: W.W. Norton, 1991).

Goodwin, Richard N., *Remembering America* (Boston: Little, Brown, 1988)

Groden, Robert, and Harrison Livingstone, *High Treason* (New York: Berkley Books, 1990).

Harper, Paul, and Joann Krieg, eds., *John F. Kennedy: The Promise Revisited* (New York: Greenwood Press, 1988).

Hepburn, James, *Farewell America* (Vaduz, Liechtenstein: Frontiers Publishing, 1968).

Hertsgaard, Mark, *On Bended Knee: The Press and the Reagan Presidency* (New York: Farrar Straus Giroux, 1988).

Higham, Charles, *Trading With the Enemy* (New York: Delacorte, 1983).

Hinckle, Warren, and William Turner, *The Fish Is Red* (New York: Harper & Row, 1981).

Höhne, Heinz, and Hermann Zolling, *The General Was a Spy* (New York: Coward, McCann & Geoghegan, 1972).

Hougan, Jim, *Spooks* (New York: William Morrow, 1978).

——, *Secret Agenda* (New York: Random House, 1984).

Hunt, Linda, *Secret Agenda: The United States Government, Nazi Scientists and Project Paperclip, 1945-1990* (New York: St. Martin's Press, 1991).

Hurt, Henry, *Reasonable Doubt* (New York: Holt, Rinehart & Winston, 1985).

Isaacson, Walter, and Evan Thomas, *The Wise Men* (New York: Simon and Schuster, 1986).

Israel, Lee, *Kilgallen* (New York: Dell, 1979).

James, Rosemary, and Jack Wardlaw, *Plot or Politics?* (New Orleans: Pelican Publishing House, 1967).

Jenkins, Roy, *Truman* (New York: Harper and Row, 1986).

Jezer, Marty, *The Dark Ages* (Boston: South End Press, 1982).

Joesten, Joachim, *Oswald: Assassin or Fall Guy?* (New York: Marzani and Munsell, 1964).

——, *The Garrison Enquiry* (London: Peter Dawnay, 1967).

——, *Marina Oswald* (London: Peter Dawnay, 1967).

——, *Oswald: The Truth* (London: Peter Dawnay, 1967).

Johnson, Haynes, *Bay of Pigs* (New York: W.W. Norton, 1964).

Johnson, Lyndon Baines, *The Vantage Point: Perspectives on the Presidency, 1963-1969* (New York: Holt, Rinehart & Winston, 1971).

Jones, Penn, Jr., *Forgive My Grief* (Midlothian, Texas: Midlothian Mirror, 1966).

——, *Forgive My Grief, Vol. II* (Midlothian, Texas: Midlothian Mirror, 1966).

Kaku, Michio, and Daniel Axelrod, *To Win a Nuclear War* (Boston: South End Press, 1987).

Kantor, Seth, *Who Was Jack Ruby?* (New York: Everest House, 1978).

Kennedy, John F., *Why England Slept* (New York: W. Funk, 1940).

Kirkwood, James, *American Grotesque* (New York: Simon and Schuster, 1970).

Krüger, Henrik, *The Great Heroin Coup* (Boston: South End Press, 1980).

Kurtz, Michael, *Crime of the Century* (Knoxville, Tenn.: University of Tennessee Press, 1982).

Lane, Mark, *Rush to Judgment* (New York: Holt, Rinehart & Winston, 1966).

——, *A Citizen's Dissent* (New York: Holt, Rinehart & Winston, 1966; Fawcett Crest, 1967; Dell, 1975).

——, *Plausible Denial* (New York: Thunder's Mouth Press, 1991).

Lasby, Clarence G., *Project Paperclip: German Scientists and the Cold War* (New York: Atheneum, 1971).

Leary, William M., ed., *The Central Intelligence Agency: History and Documents* (University, Alabama: University of Alabama Press, 1984).

Lewis, Richard Warren, and Lawrence Schiller, *The Scavengers and Critics of the Warren Report* (New York: Delacorte, 1967).

Lifton, David S., ed., *Document Addendum to the Warren Report* (El Segundo, Calif.: Sightext Press, 1968).

——, *Best Evidence* (New York: Macmillan, 1980).

Lisagor, Nancy, and Frank Lipsius, *A Law Unto Itself* (New York: Paragon House, 1989).

McCartney, Laton, *Friends in High Places: The Bechtel Story* (New York: Ballantine Books, 1989).

McCoy, Alfred, *The Politics of Heroin*, 2d ed. (New York: Lawrence Hill, 1991).

McMillan, Priscilla Johnson, *Marina and Lee* (New York: Harper & Row, 1977).

Mader, Julius, *Who's Who in CIA* (East Berlin: Julius Mader, 1968).

Manchester, William, *The Death of a President, November 20- November 25, 1963* (New York: Harper & Row, 1967).

Marchetti, Victor, and John D. Marks, *The C.I.A. and the Cult of Intelligence* (New York: Alfred A. Knopf, 1974).

Markmann, Charles, *John F. Kennedy: A Sense of Purpose* (New York: St. Martin's Press, 1961).

Marrs, Jim, *Crossfire: The Plot That Killed Kennedy* (New York: Carrol and Graf, 1989).

Martin, James Stewart, *All Honorable Men* (Boston: Little, Brown, 1950).

Martin, Ralph G., *A Hero for Our Time* (New York: Macmillan, 1983).

Marzani, Carl, *We Can Be Friends* (New York: Topical Books Publishers, 1952).

Meagher, Sylvia, *Subject Index to the Warren Report and Hearings and Exhibits* (New York: Scarecrow Press, 1966).

——, *Accessories After the Fact* (New York: Bobbs-Merrill, 1967).

Melanson, Philip, *Spy Saga* (New York: Praeger, 1990).

Model, Peter, and Robert Groden, *JFK: The Case for Conspiracy* (New York: Manor Books, 1976).

Moldea, Dan E., *The Hoffa Wars* (New York: Paddington Press, 1978).

Morley, Morris H., *Imperial State and Revolution: The United States and Cuba, 1952-1986* (New York: Cambridge University Press, 1987).

Morrow, Robert D., *Betrayal* (Chicago: Henry Regnery Co., 1976).

——, *The Senator Must Die* (Santa Monica, Calif.: Roundtable, 1988).

Navasky, Victor, *Kennedy Justice* (New York: Atheneum, 1971).

Nelson, Michael, ed., *The Elections of 1988* (Washington: CQ Press, 1989).

New York Times, *The Witnesses* (New York: McGraw-Hill and New York Times, 1964).

Newman, John M., *JFK and Vietnam* (New York: Warner Books, 1992).

North, Mark, *Act of Treason* (New York: Carroll and Graf, 1991).

Noyes, Peter, *Legacy of Doubt* (New York: Pinnacle Books, 1973).

O'Ballance, E., *The Red Army* (New York: Praeger, 1964).

Oglesby, Carl, *The Yankee and Cowboy War* (Kansas City, Mo.: Sheed, Andrews and McMeel, 1976).

Oswald, Robert L., with Myrick and Barbara Land, *Lee: A Portrait of Lee Harvey Oswald* (New York: Coward-McCann, 1967).

O'Toole, George, *The Assassination Tapes* (New York: Penthouse Press, 1975).

Parmet, Herbert S., *Jack: The Struggles of John F. Kennedy* (New York: Dial Press, 1980).

——, *J.F.K.: The Presidency of John F. Kennedy* (New York: Dial Press, 1983).

Persons, Albert C., *Bay of Pigs* (Jefferson, N.C.: McFarland Press, 1990).

Phelan, James, *Scandals, Scamps and Scoundrels* (New York: Random House, 1982).

Phillips, Cabell B., *The Truman Presidency* (New York: Macmillan, 1966).

Phillips, David Atlee, *The Night Watch* (New York: Atheneum, 1977).

Popkin, Richard H., *The Second Oswald* (New York: Avon Books, 1966).

Powers, Gary Francis, *Operation Overflight* (New York: Holt Rinehart & Winston, 1970).

Powers, Thomas, *The Man Who Kept the Secrets* (New York: Alfred A. Knopf, 1979).

Prados, John, *Presidents' Secret Wars* (New York: William Morrow, 1986).

Prouty, L. Fletcher, *The Secret Team* (Englewood Cliffs, N.J.: Prentice-Hall, 1973).

Ranelagh, John, *The Agency: The Rise and Decline of the CIA* (New York: Simon and Schuster, 1987).

Reese, Ellen, *General Reinhard Gehlen: The CIA Connection* (Fairfax, Va.: George Mason University Press, 1990).

Reeves, Thomas C., *A Question of Character* (New York: Free Press, 1991).

Roffman, Howard, *Presumed Guilty* (Cranbury, N.J.: Farleigh Dickinson Press, 1975).

Saferstein, Richard, *Forensic Science Handbook* (Englewood Cliffs, N.J.: Prentice-Hall, 1982).

Sauvage, Leo, *The Oswald Affair* (Cleveland: World Publishing Company, 1966).

Scheer, Robert, *Thinking Tuna Fish, Talking Death* (New York: Noonday, 1988).

Scheim, David, *Contract on America* (Silver Spring, Md.: Argyle Press, 1983).

Scott, Peter Dale, *Crime and Cover-Up* (Berkeley, Calif.: Westworks, 1977).

——, Paul L. Hoch, and Russell Stetler, eds., *The Assassinations* (New York: Vintage Books, 1976).

Shaw, J. Gary, with Larry Harris, *Cover-Up* (Cleburne, Tex.: privately published, 1976).

Sheridan, Walter, *The Fall and Rise of Jimmy Hoffa* (New York: Saturday Review Press, 1972).

Simpson, Christopher, *Blowback* (New York: Weidenfeld and Nicolson, 1988).

Smith, Bradley F., *The Shadow Warriors* (New York: Basic Books, 1983).

——, and Elena A. Garossi, *Operation Sunrise: The Secret Surrender* (New York: Basic Books, 1979).

Snow, Lois Wheeler, ed., *Edgar Snow's China* (New York: Random House, 1981).

Sparrow, John, *After the Assassination* (New York: Chilmark Press, 1967).

Stockwell, John, *In Search of Enemies* (New York: W.W. Norton, 1978).

Stone, Oliver, and Zachary Sklar, *JFK: The Book of the Film, A Documented Screenplay* (New York: Applause Books, 1992).

Summers, Anthony, *Conspiracy* (New York: McGraw-Hill, 1980).

Texeira, Ruy A., *Why Americans Don't Vote* (New York: Greenwood Press, 1987).

Theoharis, Athan, *Spying on Americans* (Philadelphia: Temple University Press, 1978).

Thompson, Josiah, *Six Seconds in Dallas* (New York: Bernard Geis Associates, 1967).

Tully, Andrew, *CIA: The Inside Story* (New York: William Morrow, 1962).

Turner, William, *Hoover's FBI: The Man and the Myth* (Los Angeles: Sherbourne Press, 1970).

Weisberg, Harold, *Whitewash* (Vols. I-IV) (Hyattstown, Md.: self-published, 1965, 1966, 1967, 1974 [Vols. I, II]; (New York: Dell, 1966, 1967).

——, *Oswald in New Orleans* (New York: Canyon Books, 1967).

——, *Postmortem* (Hyattstown, Md.: self-published, 1975).

Wilber, Charles G., *Medicolegal Investigation of the President John F. Kennedy Murder* (Springfield, Ill.: Charles G. Thomas, 1978).

Wills, Gary, and Ovid Demaris, *Jack Ruby: The Man Who Killed the Man Who Killed Kennedy* (New York: New American Library, 1967).

Wise, David, *The Politics of Lying* (New York: Random House, 1973).

——, *The American Police State* (New York: Random House, 1976).

——, and Thomas B. Ross, *The Invisible Government* (New York: Random House, 1964).

—— and ——, *The Espionage Establishment* (New York: Random House, 1967).

Wofford, Harris, *Of Kennedys and Kings* (New York: Farrar Straus Giroux, 1980).

Wolfe, Tom, *The Bonfire of the Vanities* (New York: Farrar Straus Giroux, 1987).

Wyden, Peter, *Bay of Pigs: The Untold Story* (New York: Simon and Schuster, 1979).

Endnotes

In the notes which follow, references to the Report of the Warren Commission appear as WR. References to any of the accompanying 26 volumes of testimony and exhibits appear as WCT and the volume number. References to the Senate Select Committee Report on Intelligence, Book Five, which relates to the JFK assassination, are from the abridged version in Lester Sobel, ed., *Three Assassinations* (New York: Facts on File, 1978), Vol. 2. These citations appear as Sobel. References to the Final Report of the House Select Committee on Assassinations appear as HSCR. Citations to the 12 volumes of appendices and hearings appear as HSCH and the volume number.

Books cited in these endnotes are listed by author(s) only, unless an author has written more than one work, in which case titles are added, or, if two authors have the same last name, in which case the full name is given. The full citations to all books appear in the Bibliography.

My descriptions of the Clay Shaw trial come from three main sources: Jim Garrison's *On the Trail of the Assassins*, James Kirkwood's *American Grotesque*, and the extensive daily accounts reported in both New Orleans newspapers, the *States-Item* and the *Times-Picayune*. Where possible, quotations have been checked against the transcribed court record. For the latter, I am grateful to Helen Dietrich, who was the court stenographer at the trial.

I would also like to add here my thanks and appreciation to Bob Spiegelman. Bob was a researcher on the film, *JFK*, with whom I was put in touch by my publishers. He checked the manuscript for omissions and inconsistencies and added much from his files to bolster and support the text. I found his work extraordinary in both quality and value. This section of the book is as much his as it is mine.

Preface
1. *Playboy*, October 1967, p. 59.
2. Nationally televised on ABC-TV's "Goodnight America," March 6, 1975.
3. Anson, see especially Chapter 7, "The Man Who Never Was"; Eddowes. To be fair to Anson, which is more than he has been to Garrison and other Warren Commission critics, his theory is more complicated. It entails three Oswalds: the Marine who did not actually go to the Soviet Union, an imposter for him there, and a different imposter to frame the real Oswald in Dallas. To me, this is as outlandish as Eddowes's theory and more pointless.
4. Three of the more popular books that posit a mob execution of JFK are: Blakey and Billings; Scheim; and Davis.

Chapter 1: The Legacy
1. Britain's request for an American takeover of its imperial role allowed the Truman administration to implement a Cold War policy of American leadership which was long in the planning. The British step-down was a necessary component of American leadership. See Jezer, p. 43.
2. Cabell B. Phillips, pp. 167-168. Acheson became a leading architect of American Cold War policy, a proponent of the view that unlike America, the Soviet Union was not entitled to a postwar sphere of influence over other nations. See Jezer, p. 41.
3. This marked the practical beginning of what *Life* magazine publisher Henry Luce had called for in 1941—"The American Century."
4. In congressional testimony, Acheson described the domino theory in terms of "rotten apples": "Like apples in a barrel infected by one rotten one, the corruption of Greece would infect Iran and all to the East. It would also carry infection to Africa through Asia Minor and Egypt, and to Europe through Italy and France, already threatened by the strongest Communist parties in Western Europe. The Soviet Union was playing one of the greatest gambles in history at minimal cost.... We and we alone were in a position to break up the plan." Acheson, p. 219.
5. Bernstein and Matusow, pp. 182-184.
6. The Marshall Plan was tailored to American export needs and well-based fears of a return to prewar depression conditions. The plan, known as the European Recovery Act, made the U.S. dollar the standard of international trade, provided U.S. companies with significant foreign markets, and integrated European recovery into America's industrial and banking system. Jezer, pp. 45-48.
7. The Plan did not pass easily. Its major corporate and political supporters had to overcome determined opposition from then powerful isolationist, nationalist

Congressmen. The communist takeover in Czechoslovakia (Stalin's response to America's rebuilding West Germany) created the crisis atmosphere necessary for its passage. Jezer, pp. 47-48.

8. "Communist aggression" not only referred to events like the incorporation of Czechoslovakia into the Soviet sphere of influence, but also was used against strong pro-European currents that favored either separate nationalisms or neutralism instead of a forced "choice" between American and Soviet dominated power blocs.

9. Ranelagh, pp. 748-749; and Ellis, p. 37. Before the National Security Act of 1947 and the establishment of the CIA, intelligence functions were served by a National Intelligence Authority and a Central Intelligence Group, both established in 1946 by Truman's directive. A director of Central Intelligence served as a member of both bodies.

Among those who testified as to the kind of organization the CIA should be, Allen Dulles made the most sweeping proposals. Some of his suggestions: The CIA should control its own personnel selection; the Agency should have its own budget supplemented by both State and Defense; the CIA should have exclusive domain over intelligence and sole supervision over all intelligence relations with other countries; and that "official secrets" legislation should be enacted to protect Agency personnel and punish those who breach security. Tully, pp. 10-11. A year later, when the Agency went through a reorganization, Dulles was the chief consultant. Dulles so dominated the creation of the CIA that a friend remarked in 1961, "It doesn't matter who takes Allen's place at CIA, he's given the CIA his imprint. It will be a long time before the CIA will be anything but Allen Dulles's baby." *Ibid.*, p. 34.

10. Ellis, p. 36. Indeed, there was fierce bureaucratic infighting, "probably orchestrated by J. Edgar Hoover." Ranelagh, p. 114.

11. The act denied the CIA any "internal police and security functions," although the term was not defined. Natonal Security Act, Sec. 102(d)(3). In fact, the CIA conducted many domestic operations, some, such as Operation CHAOS against opponents of the Vietnam War, quite extensive.

12. Ellis, p. 37.

13. Prados, p. 21.

14. In one early, major covert operation, the CIA intervened decisively in Italy's 1948 elections to prevent a likely Communist victory. Men like Allen Dulles, James Jesus Angleton, Frank Wisner, and William Colby combined in "a crash program of propaganda, sabotage and secret funding" which was "run out of the [Wall Street law] offices of Allen and John Foster Dulles at Sullivan and Cromwell." Simpson, p. 90.

15. Prados, pp. 15, 40-43.

16. After Chiang Kai-shek's defeat by Mao Tse-tung in 1949, several thousand of his troops remained in Burma perched on China's southern border. There they were regrouped and supported by the CIA as contras for some seven or eight military incursions into Mao's mainland China. While the CIA armed and maintained these forces, they also developed into an opium army that would control the so-called Golden Triangle, the poppy-rich area spanning the borders of Cambodia, Thailand and Burma, which became the world's (and America's) chief supplier of raw opium from the early 1970s to the mid-1980s. See McCoy, pp.

162-192. This may have been the organization that Gary Underhill referred to and that JFK had gotten wind of and would use in his upcoming shake-up of the Agency (see Chapters 3 and 14).

17. The CIA's Taiwan (Nationalist China) station run under hawkish ex-China hand Ray S. Cline, a drinking partner to Nationalist leader Chiang Kai-shek's son, the future head of Taiwan, was the nerve center of CIA anti-China and other Asian operations in the 1950s and early 1960s. Cline became the CIA's Deputy Director of Plans and then headed Georgetown's Center for Strategic and International Studies. See Krüger, p. 138, note 20.

18. Ellis, p. 38.

19. Among those surrendering by design was the top German rocket team, which included the eminent scientist, Dr. Werner von Braun and his superior, General Walter Dornberger. Together they had spearheaded Nazi Germany's V-2 missile effort at the Peenemunde rocketworks and the Dora concentration camp whose inhuman slave labor fueled the program. Brought into America under the top-secret Operation Paperclip, von Braun became NASA's top rocket scientist in the space race and Dornberger became the top official at Bell Aerospace responsible for security and oversight of classified projects. (On Dornberger's relationship to Michael Paine, see Chapter 13.) For more information on Operation Paperclip, see: Bower, Hunt, and Lasby.

20. For the story of Gehlen's surrender, see Höhne and Zolling, pp. 53 *ff*. For general details regarding Gehlen, see Simpson, and Reese. For many of the specifics discussed here, see Scott, "Allen Dulles"; and Oglesby, "Gehlen"

21. During the time of Soviet-American wartime alliance, Dulles was harboring, then implementing, virtually treasonous plans for a postwar anti-Soviet alliance. Dulles conducted his own private negotiations with Nazi General Kurt Wolff for a separate German surrender to Americans in northern Italy, to head off Germany's full-scale surrender to the joint allied command—obviously including Americans and Russians. Dulles's dogged efforts—Operation Sunrise—which he secretly continued despite direct orders to stop them, sowed enormous distrust between the Americans and the British on the one hand, and the Russians who feared a separate surrender deal behind their backs, on the other. See Scott, "Allen Dulles," p. 6, and, generally, Smith and Garossi.

22. According to Scott, "There seems no question that by April 1945, the OSS was recruiting Nazis and fascists to help mobilize against postwar Communism." Scott, "Allen Dulles," p. 14.

23. Oglesby, "Gehlen," pp. 14-15.

24. For a recounting of the deal, see *ibid.*, pp. 13-15. For the escapes of Mengele and Barbie, see Scott, "Allen Dulles," p. 10. A future member of the Warren Commission, John J. McCloy, was U.S. High Commissioner for Germany, and played a role in Klaus Barbie's escape. Brussell, p. 105.

25. As chief of Eastern Front intelligence, Gehlen played a signficant role in what Christopher Simpson calls "one of the most terrible atrocities of the war": namely, "the torture, interrogation and murder by starvation of some 4 million Soviet prisoners of war." Simpson, p. 44.

26. Simpson, p. 53. In light of Allen Dulles's anti-Soviet efforts during wartime, his links, and those of his brother, John Foster Dulles, with German financial interests, before, during, and after the war, bear scrutiny. For consider-

able details, see James Stewart Martin, pp. 67-68; Higham, pp. 22, 112-113.

27. A good brief account of the "selling" of the Cold War to the American public by government and the media is Spiegelman, "A Tale of Two Memos."

28. See Chapters 14 and 15 for further discussion.

29. Ambrose, *Eisenhower*, p. 548; Bernstein and Matusow, pp. 293-295.

30. Ambrose, *Eisenhower the President*, see Chapters 5 and 8, also pp. 210, 214-215; Prados, pp. 133-138 for Sukarno operation. The United States refused in 1954 to sign the Geneva Accords, which technically released it from having to assure free elections under international supervision to unify the country. Legalisms aside, by most accounts Eisenhower and Diem fully expected that the winner would be Ho Chi Minh.

31. William Blum, pp. 174-181; see also Chapter 14.

32. Ambrose, *Eisenhower the President*, p. 556-557.

33. *Ibid.*, p. 557. The Agency's use of the Mafia is not so strange. It took place under the leadership of Allen Dulles, who had no moral qualms about cutting the deal with Gehlen. Truman's 1963 reaction to Dulles's CIA seems almost quaint: There is "something about the way the CIA has been functioning that is casting a shadow over our historic positions and I feel we need to correct it." *New York Times*, April 25, 1966. It was Truman, of course, who sought Dulles's advice at the creation of the Agency in 1947 and during its 1948 reorganization. See note 9, *supra*.

34. Ambrose, *Eisenhower the President*, p. 557. In 1960, President-elect Kennedy was formally briefed by Dulles and Bissell on the upcoming Bay of Pigs invasion. According to ex-CIA agent Robert D. Morrow's account, Kennedy "shocked" Dulles and Bissell (who had expected Nixon to win) by putting a "hold" on the invasion planning pending his own assessment and organization of his administration. Morrow, *The Senator Must Die*, p. 47.

35. Dulles was right. Nixon was so wedded to toppling Castro that after failure of the Bay of Pigs, he reportedly answered Kennedy's request for advice by saying "I would find a proper legal cover and go in." Hinckle and Turner, p. 97.

Chapter 2: Kennedy, the Agency, and Cuba

1. Parmet, *Presidency of JFK*, p. 31.

2. Markmann, p. 26.

3. Parmet, *Struggles of JFK*, pp. 175-180.

4. *Ibid.*, pp. 310, 368.

5. Kaku and Axelrod, p. 11: "In 1961, when President Kennedy suddenly realized that the 'missile gap' was ten to one in favor of the U.S., a secret plan was drafted during the Berlin crisis for a possible surprise attack on the Soviet Union."

6. O'Ballance, p. 199.

7. Parmet, *Presidency of JFK*, pp. 45-46.

8. Kennedy outfoxed Nixon on Cuba. According to ex-CIA agent Robert D. Morrow, JFK had already been briefed on the administration's planning against Castro (by the State Department's William Wieland and leaders of the liberal faction of the Cuban exile community). During their debates, JFK would call for tougher actions, knowing full well that Nixon—who was in office and secretly

the White House case officer for the Bay of Pigs adventure—had to conceal his real position to protect the secrecy of the covert plans. Thus, Nixon had to give the official line: that there would be no U.S. intervention into Cuba, and Kennedy appeared the more national security conscious. Morrow, *The Senator Must Die*, p. 46.

9. Parmet, *Presidency of JFK*, p. 46.

10. *Ibid.*, pp. 46-47.

11. *Ibid.*, pp. 47-48. As noted above (Chapter 1, note 34) (and *supra*, note 8), not knowing that JFK had already been secretly briefed by Wieland and the liberal exiles—Dulles and Bissell were "shocked" by Kennedy's putting a *hold* on the invasion. (Morrow, *The Senator Must Die*, pp. 46-47.) This may be connected to a revelation Jim Garrison found "stunning" in William R. Corson's *The Armies of Ignorance*, that "shortly after Kennedy's election in November 1960 [the same month as the Dulles briefing], the CIA began to put together a 'dossier analysis,' including a psychological profile of the President-elect. Its purpose among other things was to predict the likely positions Kennedy would take if particular sets of conditions arose. The existence of this study was not made public." (Garrison, *On the Trail*, p. 60.)

12. The vehemence of anti-Castro opinion related also to the conjunction of corporate and underworld interests at stake in Cuba and, given Castro's threat of a good example, in Latin America. The stop-Castro lobby included: politicos like Secretary of State Christian Herter and undersecretary C. Douglas Dillon (JFK's Treasury Secretary); Treasury Secretary Robert B. Anderson (ex-Secretary of the Navy and top LBJ backer); CIA heavies like Dulles, Bissell, and Cabell; top CIA operatives like E. Howard Hunt and David Phillips; master lobbyist and LBJ intimate Tommy "The Cork" Corcoran of United Fruit Company; top Mafiosi like Santos Trafficante, Meyer Lansky and Carlos Marcello; and outgoing White House Bay of Pigs case officer Richard M. Nixon. Corporate entities with great stakes in Cuba included: the Rockefellers' Standard Oil, Texaco and Shell (whose refineries were eventually expropriated); the Cabot's United Fruit Company (already instrumental in the overthrow of Arbenz in 1954); and a host of cattle ranches, agricultural, sugar and mining interests including Joseph Kennedy's own Coca Cola bottling plant. See Morley, Chapters 2 and 4.

Out of the potent confluence of U.S. interests in Cuba—including the Agency, business and the Mob—come many of the strange complexities in the JFK assassination. It is plausible that it was a joint effort. But it is the author's—and most researchers'—view that the senior partner was the Agency. The CIA knew the Mob wanted to get rid of Castro and get their gambling operations reinstated. The CIA had no compunctions—as with Gehlen—in using the Mob as an instrument to get rid of Castro. The ideological threat would be removed, big business (as well as the Mob) would be restored to the island, and the Agency would retain a degree of deniability. By 1963, after JFK pulled the plug on Operation MONGOOSE, the operation could well have been turned on him.

13. As Eisenhower said of the Vietnam of 1954-5: You have "what you would call the 'falling domino principle.' You have a row of dominos set up, you knock over the first one, and what will happen to the last one is the certainty that it will go over very quickly. So you could have the beginning of a disintegration that would have the most profound influences." Quoted in Jezer, p. 64.

14. More than any other country in World War II, the Soviet Union suffered unprecedented destruction of its people and economy from the German invasion: over 20 million Soviets, and one-third of its total wealth and infrastructure destroyed.

15. Not only "by itself," but against Stalin's express policy. Stalin had long tried to control, curb, even destroy any independent Chinese communism. Indeed, when WWII ended, Stalin signed the Sino-Soviet Treaty of 1945 with Mao's sworn enemy Chiang Kai-shek promising to aid Chiang's troops exclusively and to recognize Chiang's authority even in an area like Manchuria where neither he nor the U.S. then had any forces. Stalin's position was for Mao to at most, accept a junior role in a government under Chiang Kai-shek—definitely not to pursue victory in a civil war. Snow, pp. 227-228.

16. Ambrose, *Eisenhower the President*, p. 183.

17. *Ibid.*, p. 197.

18. *Ibid.*, p. 236. In 1955, the Communist Chinese began to shell two offshore islands, Quemoy and Matsu, which were still run and occupied by Nationalist Chinese troops under Chiang Kai-shek. This caused a brief crisis which not only did the Russians refuse to fuel, but which Communist minister Chou En-lai finally resolved by giving up the islands to the Nationalists.

19. Ambrose, *Eisenhower the President*, p. 180.

20. In the early 1950s, the Democrats were pilloried for having "lost China."

21. Some of the more courageous include scholars such as Noam Chomsky, William Appleman Williams, Bertrand Russell, and Peter Dale Scott; politicians like Senators Wayne Morse, Ernest Gruening, Mike Gravel, and William Fulbright; and independent journalists like I.F. Stone and George Seldes.

22. Kennedy, *Why England Slept*.

23. Parmet, *Struggles of JFK*, p. 226.

24. JFK's nascent moves toward peaceful co-existence and détente with the Soviets may have had their roots in FDR's wartime alliance with the Soviets against the Nazis and his vision of postwar cooperation. See Marzani.

25. Parmet, *Struggles of JFK*, pp. 284-285.

26. It is ironic and frightening to note that Kennedy's interest in Algeria and Vietnam intersects with that of French President Charles de Gaulle. De Gaulle was the target of several assassination attempts because of his support of Algerian independence between 1961 and 1964. By late 1963, he had made several overtures to JFK to discuss the creation of a neutral, re-unified Vietnam. In many ways, JFK and de Gaulle were anathema to hard-line Cold Warrior élites in America and Europe. In fact when JFK was murdered, de Gaulle and he were slated to meet in February 1964 on issues like Vietnam. Also, both men violently crossed paths with Permindex, a quasi-business front with CIA ties used for channeling funds for nefarious, extralegal activities like political assassination. (See Chapter 13.)

27. Parmet, *Struggles of JFK*, p. 407.

28. Parmet, *Presidency of JFK*, p. 333.

29. Ambrose, *Eisenhower the President*, pp. 655-665.

30. Tully, pp. 251-252.

31. On the scale and preparations for the Bay of Pigs, see Hinckle and Turner, pp. 61-85.

32. Prados, pp. 183, 188-189, 191.

33. This account is taken from Prados, Chapter XI, pp. 194-207.

34. Based on congressional testimony of ex-CIA employee James B. Wilcott, Hinckle and Turner argue in *The Fish Is Red* (pp. 80-81, 88) that the so-called diversionary landing at Guantanamo Bay was not necessarily a diversion at all. Rather, the original invasion plans were changed to incorporate a ruse whereby exile commandos dressed up as Castro's soldiers would stage a fake offensive attack on America's Guantanamo Naval Base, thereby provoking direct U.S. retaliation by way of direct intervention. The provocation would put so much pressure on JFK to intervene that it would have been political suicide for him to have refused. However, the commando leader, sensing after two attempts that Castro's people were awaiting the landing, aborted the mission, refusing orders to proceed. In Hinckle and Turner's words, "The CIA had lost its planned excuse to send in the Marines, who were aboard ship nearby."

35. *The Fish Is Red* also contains a detailed discussion of the critical nature of the debate over whether JFK "canceled" the Bay of Pigs air strikes or "refused to authorize them" (pp. 85-95).

36. Hinckle and Turner, p. 95.

37. *Ibid.*, pp. 71, ff.

38. *Ibid.*, pp. 75-77. The authors postulate that the plot never came to fruition because Hunt was preoccupied with the Agency's fig leaf of plausible denial and was unaware that the Mob had chosen one of his recruits, Antonio Varona, for the mission. Hunt kept Varona under wraps—first in New York, then in Miami—until the invasion looked like a success. Of course it never did, and Varona could not act.

39. *Ibid.* For JFK's lack of knowledge about the plots, see p. 71. For his lack of knowledge about the landing, see p. 81.

40. *New York Times*, April 25, 1966, p. 20.

41. McCone was DCI from November 29, 1961, to April 28, 1965. Prior to his appointment he was a California shipbuilder, member of the President's Air Policy Commission, deputy to the Secretary of Defense, Undersecretary of the Air Force, and Chairman of the Atomic Energy Commission. He was also a co-founder of the massive Bechtel Corporation. Ranelagh, p. 730; McCartney, *passim*, especially pp. 52-138.

42. Hinckle and Turner, p. 112.

43. *Ibid.*, pp. 112-123.

44. Operation MONGOOSE was headquartered on the remote South Campus of the University of Miami, a former Naval Air Station. While it lasted, the Miami station, JM-WAVE, became the largest CIA station in the world. and, based on U.S. soil, arguably in violation of the CIA's charter proscribing domestic operations. According to Hinckle and Turner, it operated on a budget of well over $500 million a year, employing between 600 and 700 American personnel. Its case officers controlled upwards of 3,000 Cubans and recruited steadily from Cuban refugees arriving in the U.S. at the rate of some 1,000 per month. It also operated through the cover of 55 dummy corporations and proprietary companies.

The station chief was Theodore Shackley, a protégé of future DCI William Colby. Today, Shackley is the principal target of the campaign to secure convictions of the Iran-Contra plotters. Shackley went from JM-WAVE to Southeast

Asia.

Another MONGOOSE-related figure is counter-insurgency genius General Edward G. Lansdale, who was the Pentagon-based administrator-overseer of this joint Pentagon-CIA project. Oliver Stone's film, *JFK*, suggests that Lansdale may have been a coordinator of the assassination operation.

For accounts of Operation MONGOOSE, see Parmet, *Presidency of JFK*, pp. 214-221; Church Committee Report pp. 139-190; Hinckle and Turner, pp. 111-126; Prados, pp. 211-214; Ranelagh, pp. 383-390; Curry, pp. 240-251.

45. Kennedy's knowledge of the Castro plots is not crystal clear. It can only be assumed. I believe that Bobby did not tell him. In two conversations, one with his friend Senator George Smathers (Dem.-Fla.) and the other with journalist Tad Szulc, Kennedy expressed strong opposition to doing away with Castro. See Parmet, *Presidency of JFK*, pp. 214-217, and Belin, pp. 112-126, for a sampling of different views.

46. For an account of the missile crisis, see Parmet, *Presidency of JFK*, Chapter 12, pp. 277-300.

47. Isaacson and Thomas, p. 630 for the quote; pp. 619-630 for another account of the missile crisis.

48. JFK's ill-considered all-out welcome for returning Bay of Pigs veterans at a packed Orange Bowl, a month after the Missile Crisis, added to the bitter feeling harbored against him in Miami's large exile community. It appeared that JFK was backing, indeed hinting at a forthcoming second invasion. Thus his subsequent moves curtailing the anti-Castro activities of quasi-independent and CIA-backed militant groups made it appear that he had betrayed an implicit promise to invade. Hinckle and Turner, p. 152.

Chapter 3: New Orleans

1. The Cheramie account is from HSCH X, pp. 199-205; and Morrow, *Betrayal*, pp. 196-98. For her strange death, see Marrs, p. 402.

2. The Martin-Banister account is from Garrison, *On the Trail*, pp. 4-5.

3. There, according to ex-CIA agent Robert Morrow, Banister was boss to Robert Maheu, later CIA-Mob interface in their joint attempts to assassinate Fidel Castro. Morrow, *The Senator Must Die*, p. 59.

4. Details about Underhill's arrival at the Fitzsimmonses' are from a letter by Robert Fitzsimmons to John Donovan, June 21, 1964.

5. The conversation between Underhill and Charlene Fitzsimmons is reconstructed from the above letter and a letter from Mr. Fitzsimmons to Jim Garrison, May 3, 1968. Friends' opinions of Underhill's "rational and objective" demeanor are found in Turner, "Inquest," p. 29.

6. Underhill's background is taken from the Fitzsimmons letter to Donovan and a Donovan letter to Jim Garrison dated April 29, 1967; also Turner, "Inquest," pp. 28-29.

7. Underhill's influence on Luce is noted in an internal *Ramparts* magazine memorandum by Edward Cohen dated May 15, 1966. The magazine researched Underhill for its two articles on the Garrison inquiry, one in June of 1967 and one in January of 1968.

8. Turner, "Inquest," p. 28; also Fitzsimmons's letter to Garrison, Donovan

letter to Garrison, and *Ramparts* memorandum by Cohen dated June 21, 1966.
9. Cohen memorandum, May 15, 1966.
10. For Brynes's long relationship with Underhill, see Donovan letter to Garrison.
11. Cohen memorandum, May 15, 1966.
12. *Ibid.*; also Turner, "Inquest," p. 29.
13. *Ibid.*; Cohen memorandum.
14. The Andrews account is from WCH XI, pp. 325-39.
15. The Clinton account is from Garrison, *On the Trail*, pp. 105-8.
16. The witnesses who identified Shaw did so both at his trial and at the HSCA hearings a decade later. Oswald's presence here further supports his profile as someone now involved in domestic intelligence operations. See Melanson, pp. 45-46.
17. An example of Dulles's suppression of input is his burying of CIA Inspector General Lyman Kirkpatrick's report in the Agency archives, Hinckle and Turner, p. 99. A sample of how harsh that report was is in Wyden, pp. 322-324. For an overview of the whitewash, see Prados, pp. 208-9. A measure of RFK's enthusiasm for Operation MONGOOSE is in Parmet, *Presidency of JFK*, p. 221.
18. See Chapter 2, note 44.
19. Hinckle and Turner, p. 198-203.
20. Oglesby, *Yankee*, p. 74; Hinckle and Turner, p. 207.
21. Popkin, "Garrison's Case," p. 28.
22. *Ibid.*
23. Garrison, *On the Trail*, p. 40; Hinckle and Turner, p. 204.
24. Popkin, "Garrison's Case," p. 18.
25. Oglesby, *Yankee*, pp. 74, 106; Hinckle and Turner, pp. 200-202.
26. Hinckle and Turner, pp. 199-200.
27. *Ibid.* Henry Luce's *Time-Life* empire waged a secret, private war on Cuba, spending upwards of $250,000 in secret financing and covering (in *Time* and *Life*) commando raids against Cuba. See Hinckle and Turner, pp. 164-68.
28. Kirkwood, p. 263.

Chapter 4: Witches' Brew

1. Key details of Oswald's portrait—a previously "unknown" person—were uncannily and instantly provided to reporters the afternoon of the murder by the *Miami News*'s Pulitzer Prize winner, Hal Hendrix. We know this from reporter Seth Kantor who was able to pry loose a suppressed FBI document that recorded his phone calls to Hendrix that afternoon. Hendrix was known to his colleagues as "The Spook" because of his phenomenal access to intelligence sources. He uncannily "exposed" the 1965 Dominican invasion 24 hours before it occurred and, reportedly, had links to a CIA source at Homestead Air Force Base, south of Miami. Summers, pp. 134-35.
2. Hurt, p. 19.
3. One of Oswald's legal requests (in the presence of a Secret Service agent) was for New York lawyer John Abt (recently deceased), closely linked to the Communist Party. This, presumably, remained in keeping with his "left profile," which he doubtless soon realized had made him the "patsy." Oswald's attempt to

contact Abt failed, as Abt was away from home that weekend. At that point, Oswald may have expected to be rescued from his plight and kept to his leftist posture. Summers, pp. 130-31.

4. Another image is, of course, the photo of Oswald with a rifle that appeared on the cover of *Life* magazine, February 21, 1964. This photo is very likely forged. For analyses, see Melanson, pp. 117-118; Meagher, *Accessories*, pp. 200-210; and Summers, pp. 94-99.

5. It was founded by Lyle Stuart, the book publisher.

6. Interestingly, a July 5, 1947, supplement to the *New Orleans States-Item* and the *New Orleans Times-Picayune* has a full-page ad (p. 72) introducing and boosting Clay Shaw's Trade Mart. The ad, taken out by the Camp Street Improvement Association, lists all establishments, block by block, number by number, on Camp Street, except one. The only missing number on Block 5 is 544.

7. WR, p. 744.

8. Weisberg, *Oswald*, p. 335.

9. *Ibid.*, p. 331.

10. For a discussion of Oswald's critical activities in this neighborhood, see Chapter 13.

11. Banister's history is taken from Hinckle and Turner, pp. 203-5, and Hurt, pp. 289-90.

12. The incident may have been to create a reason for Banister to move into "private practice" to engage in top-secret anti-Castro operations.

13. Hinckle and Turner, p. 205.

14. Garrison, *On the Trail*, pp. 37-38. Banister's files remain classified—or lost—to this day and (along with the still classified HSCA, FBI, CIA, and Warren Commission files) remain a potentially crucial source of evidence to help resolve the case.

15. *Ibid.*, p. 41.

16. Weisberg, *Oswald*, p. 332.

17. Hinckle and Turner, pp. 208-9.

18. Summers, pp. 323-25. Besides Delphine Roberts, Adrian Alba, who managed the Crescent City Garage next to Oswald's Wm. Reily Coffee workplace, told the HSCA that he often saw Oswald eating in the ground floor restaurant at 544 Camp. The restaurant had a back staircase to the upper office floors. Summers, p. 325.

19. Ferrie's history is from Flammonde, pp. 18-43; and Melanson, pp. 39-53.

20. Weisberg, *Oswald*, p. 198.

21. Kirkwood, p. 264.

22. Hinckle and Turner, p. 269.

23. Melanson, pp. 42-43.

24. Marrs, p. 99. See the testimony of Edward Voebel, Oswald's close friend at the time, for another view of his apolitical attitude at that time. WCT VIII, p. 10.

25. WR, p. 681.

26. Weisberg, *Oswald*, pp. 331-32.

27. Melanson, p. 40.

28. Weisberg, *Oswald*, pp. 195-97.

29. Melanson, p. 51.

30. Hurt, p. 399. This startling incident not only reveals Banister's knowledge

of Oswald, but also marks a strange confluence of names and revelations quite early in this story, actually before the Bay of Pigs. For Banister probably knew of Oswald not just through Ferrie, but also through his FBI connections. J. Edgar Hoover issued a memo requesting information on Oswald in 1960 because someone had possibly been using his birth certificate. Summers, p. 409. The name "Moore" may also be significant. George DeMohrenschildt, who, as we shall see, figures prominently with Oswald in Dallas, told the Warren Commission of having discussed Oswald with a J. Walton Moore. Moore, a CIA employee, acknowledged contacts with DeMohrenschildt through the fall of 1961, but denied any talk of Oswald. Summers, pp. 227-228. To make this all the more eerie, as Garrison notes in *On the Trail* (p. 60), the CIA had prepared a dossier analysis of Kennedy as early as late 1960, perhaps in response to his caution concerning the Bay of Pigs invasion expressed to Dulles at the November 18 briefing. Very early, the associations of Oswald in Dallas, and JFK as a probable enemy of the Agency, were being marked.

Chapter 5: A Question of Motive

1. The basic details of Oswald's life are culled from WR, pp. 669-725.

2. Marguerite Oswald's husband's divorce lawyer had been Fred Korth, an LBJ crony who replaced John Connally as Navy Secretary in 1962. He was also a Bell Aerospace Director from 1961 to 1962. It was at Bell that Walter Dornberger supervised Michael Paine. (See Chapter 1, note 19.) Korth was forced by Kennedy to resign in October 1963 over his role in the TFX scandal. This was the first time in the Kennedy Administration that the position of Secretary of the Navy was not in the hands of a Texan. The TFX hearings, scheduled to begin the week after the assassination, had the potential to destroy LBJ. After Johnson became president, they were postponed for nine years. See Scott, "Dallas Conspiracy," *passim.*

3. He reportedly attempted suicide, but had only a superficial scar on his left wrist.

4. Astonishingly, his return to the U.S. was easy. See Meagher, *Accessories*, pp. 332-333.

5. When Oswald left for New Orleans, his family moved to Irving, Texas, to live with Ruth Paine. Within three weeks, his family joined him in New Orleans. For more on the Paines, see Chapter 6.

6. Weisberg, *Whitewash*, pp. 133-135, 137.

7. WR, p. 379. Oswald was supposed to have undergone a psychiatric examination in the Soviet Union after a highly suspicious suicide attempt after his renunciation of U.S. citizenship and request for Soviet citizenship were both questioned and delayed by Moscow authorities. Most commentators agree that his stay in a mental hospital was a ruse for Soviet intelligence to interrogate him before granting him residency. But even then, they would not trust him in the capital. They shipped him to Minsk, 450 miles away. Summers, pp. 184-185; Melanson, pp. 14-15.

8. WR, p. 407.

9. WR, p. 423.

10. Belin, p. 204. This is one of Belin's few perspicacious statements.

11. Melanson, pp. 42-43.

12. Marrs, p. 105; see also Melanson, p. 12, and Summers, p. 155, for Rankin's reference to Monterey.

13. Marrs, p. 105; see also Summers, p. 155, for Oswald's quick mastery of the language.

14. Prados, p. 69.

15. Hinckle and Turner, p. 220; Weisberg, *Oswald*, p. 91.

16. U-2 pilot Gary Francis Powers has suggested that Oswald, who defected only six months earlier and was likely familiar with the U-2 and its radar, may have helped in the downing of his May 1, 1960, overflight—an event which wrecked the upcoming summit and aborted a growing thaw in superpower relations. Gary Francis Powers, p. 358.

17. Such defections had been rare, at least since the 1930s. Yet Oswald's was the sixth defection to the U.S.S.R. since June of 1959, and was followed shortly by two more. At least three of the eight defectors, including Oswald, had apparent military or intelligence backgrounds. Scott, "Dallas Conspiracy," pp. ii, 10-12.

18. Hinckle and Turner, p. 220. Oswald's defection and entry into the U.S.S.R., and his departure, were both handled by U.S. Moscow Embassy Consul Richard E. Snyder. Snyder was, in his own words, "the sole officer handling the Oswald case." (Melanson, pp. 16-19.) Snyder sent Oswald his passport, months before his return, and processed Oswald and Marina's exit from the Soviet Union as well. CIA document #609-786 says that Snyder joined the CIA in 1949. According to a CIA memo, on September 26, 1950, Snyder resigned from the CIA to work for the High Commissioner's Office in Germany. (Melanson, p. 135.) Julius Mader's 1968 *Who's Who in CIA*, published in East Germany, lists Snyder as still in the Agency. In any event, the High Commissioner, whom he either worked for or used as a cover, was future Warren Commissioner John McCloy.

19. Summers, p. 230.

20. *Ibid.*, p. 231.

21. *Ibid.*

22. Melanson, pp. 83-85.

23. Summers, p. 313.

24. *Ibid.*, p. 312.

25. *Ibid.*, p. 313.

26. Garrison, *On the Trail*, pp. 115-116. Reily was a backer of the Cuban Revolutionary Council, which was organized by E. Howard Hunt, who figures prominently with David Phillips in this affair (Scott, *Crime and Cover-Up*, p. 15). Hunt knew Banister since they worked out of the same offices in New Orleans ("The JFK Conspiracy," broadcast April 15, 1992). It is quite probable that the transfers to NASA were orchestrated by the pair so those employees would not reveal the strange work habits of Oswald that summer. It should also be noted that Banister may have known Hunt and Phillips from the Anti-Communist League of the Caribbean's role in the CIA's 1954 ouster of Arbenz in Guatemala, in which Hunt and Phillips were prime movers (Turner, "Inquest," p. 19).

27. In a new book to be self-published this year, Gary Savage's *JFK: First Day Evidence*, there is a photo of the Minox on the floor of the Dallas police property room.

28. Summers, p. 231.
29. *Ibid.*
30. *Dallas Morning News*, June 15, 1978.
31. Summers, p. 231; Melanson, p. 83.

Chapter 6: The Regicide Succeeds

1. See generally, on the "second Oswalds": Weisberg, *Whitewash*, pp. 141-146; Melanson, pp. 105-115; and Summers, pp. 393-418.
2. Melanson, p. 106.
3. Popkin, *The Second Oswald*, p. 74.
4. Melanson, p. 106. See also, WR, pp. 321-324; HSCR, pp. 137-39; Summers, pp. 411-418; Meagher, *Accessories*, pp. 376-387.
5. Popkin, *The Second Oswald*, p. 64; Meagher, *Accessories*, p. 351.
6. Popkin, *The Second Oswald*, p. 86; Meagher, *Accessories*, pp. 370-372.
7. Meagher, *Accessories*, p. 367; Morrow, *Betrayal*, p. 181.
8. Meagher, *Accessories*, p. 367; Popkin, *The Second Oswald*, p. 83.
9. Belin, p. 1; Kantor, p. 34.
10. Melanson, p. 106; Popkin, *The Second Oswald*, p. 65; WR, p. 324.
11. Weisberg, *Whitewash*, p. 270; Meagher, *Accessories*, p. 352; Thompson, pp. 243, 247-248.
12. On the motorcade route, see Hepburn, pp. 351-352, Groden and Livingstone, pp. 152, 155, 236.
13. Epstein, *Legend*, p. 185. DeMohrenschildt was suspected of being a Nazi spy during the war. If so, he may have been working for Gehlen; Evica, p. 292.
14. Epstein, *Legend*, p. 206.
15. Joesten, *Marina*, p. 72 n.
16. *Ibid.*, p. 87.
17. *Ibid.*
18. Scott, *The Dallas Conspiracy*, p. IV-4; Hepburn, Appendix 1, No. 687. See Garrison, *On the Trail*, p. 63, for a discussion of the classified Paine documents.
19. Quoted in Joesten, *Marina*, p. 91.
20. *Ibid.*, p. 140.
21. Joesten, *Oswald: The Truth*, p. 67.
22. *Ibid.* The Paines have never been adequately investigated or questioned. As Ruth Paine befriended Marina, her estranged husband befriended Lee. He accompanied him to various functions, including an ACLU meeting. Melanson, pp. 55-56. The day of the assassination, when detectives came to her house, she greeted them with, "I've been expecting you to come out. Come right in." She added, "Just as soon as I heard the shooting happened I knew there would be someone out." WCT VII, p. 229. When she discovered they had no search warrant, she said one would not be necessary and they could search the house anytime they wanted. See Weisberg, *Whitewash*, p. 81; and WCT VII, p. 193. Once they were inside, she suggested they look in the garage where the blanket containing Oswald's rifle was located. When the detectives returned the next day, she and her now reconciled husband Michael voluntarily showed them more of Oswald's effects. The couple then left to go shopping, leaving the police with the run of the house for more than two hours. Weisberg, *ibid.*; and WCT VII, p. 209.

The Paines, like most of the "Marxist" Oswald's friends, were members of Dallas's rabidly anticommunist White Russian community. The faction had ties to both the Tolstoy Foundation and the Russian Orthodox Church, which were both backed by the CIA. Melanson, p. 79. Michael Paine's brother was employed by the Agency for International Development (AID), an organization with extensive CIA links. Ruth Paine's father was a retired AID employee. Melanson, p. 80. On November 23, in a phone conversation with his "estranged" wife, Michael Paine stated that although he felt sure Oswald had shot Kennedy, he did not feel Oswald was responsible. He then added, "We both know who is responsible." Summers, pp. 132-133.

There are two more provocative Ruth Paine statements. At her Warren Commission appearance, she said that when she first heard about the assassination on television, she immediately told Marina that it occurred right outside the depository where Lee worked. Yet she thought he worked at the *warehouse*, which is blocks away from Dealey Plaza. WCT I, p. 74; WCT III, p. 36. Finally, although she and George DeMohrenschildt testified that she met Oswald in 1963, Researcher Michael Levy has unearthed a Navy Department document which reports that Ruth Paine was requesting information about the family of Lee Harvey Oswald in 1957.

23. A comprehensive look at Jack Ruby's gunrunning is in Jim Marrs, *Crossfire*, pp. 399-401.

24. Kantor, p. 138.

25. Hurt, pp. 401-5.

26. Kantor, p. 15.

27. See Hurt, p. 404. Harvey also headed ZR/RIFLE, a part of Operation MONGOOSE. See Chapter 14, note 11.

28. Ruby was allegedly always in debt to the mob. Those connections are discussed in Marrs, pp. 391-400; and Carl Ogelsby's afterword to Garrison, *On the Trail.*

29. On Nancy Perrin Rich, see Meagher, *Accessories*, pp. 385-386.

30. WCT XIV, p. 349.

31. Kantor, Chapter 8, *passim.*

32. *Ibid.*, p. 139. Kantor believes Ruby was in Havana for the gunrunning purposes that Rich's testimony indicated.

33. *Ibid.*

34. Flammonde, p. 167.

35. Morrow, *Betrayal*, p. 181.

36. The Warren Report says Lt. Day of the Dallas Police Department got a partial palmprint, identified as Oswald's, from the underside of the rifle's barrel just before it was sent to the FBI. But the FBI found no trace of the print when the rifle arrived. A week later, there was a report of a palmprint. (As *JFK* suggests, this could have been lifted from Oswald's corpse.) Moreover, nitrate/paraffin tests showed negative for Oswald's cheek (positive would have indicated a rifle shot), though positive for his hands (which could, however, come from urine, bleach, matches, even playing cards). The Commission found the tests inconclusive. WCT III, p. 395.

37. WR, p. 29.

38. WCT X, pp. 370-371.

39. Weisberg, *Whitewash*, pp. 71-72.

40. Summers, pp. 428-430.

41. Summers, pp. 429-430, 614-615, note 499.

42. Hurt, pp. 410-411; Jones, *Forgive II*, pp. 39-42.

43. Hurt, p. 411.

44. Jones, *Forgive I*, p. 40.

45. *Ibid.*

46. Weisberg, *Whitewash*, pp. 63-64. For a discussion of the evidence that there was no rifle inside the package, see Summers, pp. 101-2.

47. Meagher, *Accessories*, pp. 37-38.

48. *Four Days*, published by United Press International and American Heritage Magazine (New York: American Heritage Publishing Company, 1964), p. 9.

49. Belin, pp. 1-2; WR, pp. 19-20, 48; Lyndon B. Johnson, p. 6.

50. *Four Days*, p. 9.

51. WR, p. 143.

52. Scott, Hoch, and Stetler, p. 244. As we shall see, Givens's story was very likely forced on him by the Dallas police and the Commission.

53. Meagher, *Accessories*, pp. 225-26.

54. *Ibid.*; Thompson, p. 180.

55. Williams's testimony appears in the Commission hearings in Volume III, p. 173. The best discussions of Oswald's alibi appear in Sauvage, pp. 19-35; and Roffman, pp. 201-23.

56. Both the 120-degree turn and the accompanying slowdown violated normal Secret Service practice and regulations. Marrs, p. 11, Groden, pp. 151-153, 155-157. Marrs notes that, according to book depository superintendent Roy Truly, the turn was so tight that the limo almost hit the curb. The Zapruder film shows a police motorcycle at the right of JFK's limousine peel off from the procession and head along the right side of the depository. The prolonged, startled gaze of another motorcycle cop to the right of the car is also evident. This move could have been to open up more room to the right side of the car for shots from the direction of the grassy knoll.

57. Mrs. Connally's and her husband's quotes are from WCT IV, p. 147. And see Marrs, p. 11.

58. This is the likely moment of bullet-entry through JFK's throat, as soon reported by the doctors at Parkland Hospital. The reports of throat *entry* wounds are, of course, totally inconsistent with the Warren Report.

59. Both Kellerman quotes from WCT II, pp. 73-74.

60. By some accounts the motorcade actually *slowed* for five seconds (after Connally noticed a shot) as the shooting ensued (Summers, p. 37) and the limousine's brake lights went on as the fatal shot was being fired (Marrs, p. 12).

61. WCT V, p. 180.

62. Arts and Entertainment Network five-part special, September and October 1991, testimony of John Connally.

63. WR, p. 55.

64. Thompson, p. 122.

65. *Ibid.*, p. 122.

66. *Ibid.*, pp. 124-125.

67. Meagher, *Accessories*, p. 25.

68. Weisberg, *Whitewash*, p. 77.

69. Baker's initial report was that he "saw a man in the lunchroom drinking a Coke." This meant Oswald had the time to buy the Coke, a detail which further undermines the Warren Report. In an extremely brief time, Oswald would have had to shoot JFK from the sixth floor, get down to the lunchroom, buy a Coke, and be nonchalantly sipping the Coke, when met by Truly and Baker. Summers, pp. 550-551, note 29.

70. A good summary account of the Truly-Baker incident is found in Marrs, p. 51. See also Roffman, p. 201 ff.; Meagher, *Accessories*, p. 70 ff.; and HSCR, p. 601, note 123.

71. WR, p. 79.

72. Thompson, p. 242.

73. See Marrs, pp. 329-330, and Hurt, pp. 119-120.

74. Thompson, p. 243.

75. *Ibid.*

76. See Hurt, photos between pp. 138-39, and Garrison, *On the Trail*, photo before p. 190. Craig, who was perhaps too credible and honest for his own good, was driven from the police force, abandoned by his wife and, on May 15, 1975, at the age of 39, was killed by a rifle bullet in a death ruled a suicide. Marrs, p. 332.

77. Different accounts claim that Oswald went home by foot, by bus, by taxi or some combination of the three.

78. WR, p. 163.

79. Meagher, *Accessories*, p. 260.

80. *Ibid.*, pp. 261-64.

81. *Ibid.*; Hurt, pp. 144-145.

82. The Warren Report account (p. 44) claims that Howard L. Brennan gave Dallas police the description before the dispatch. But Brennan's testimony indicates he gave the description to Secret Service Agent Forrest Sorrels who was at Parkland Hospital and did not return to Dealey Plaza until 12:55, obviously after the dispatch went out.

83. Kantor, pp. 207-209.

84. *Ibid.*, p. 204.

85. Hurt, p. 164.

86. *Ibid.*

87. Kantor, pp. 56-57; Lane, *Rush to Judgment*, pp. 232-235, 288.

88. Hurt, p. 164. The connections between Ruby, Tippit, and his murder do not end here. Jerry Rose pointed out two others: First, Tippit had a moonlighting job as a security guard at a restaurant called Austin's Barbecue, a place Ruby frequented. Second, Ruby's address book contained a phone number that was one digit away from Tippit's unlisted number. Ruby's employee and friend, Larry Crafard, explained the number as belonging to a woman who tried to get a job at Ruby's Carousel Club. The problem is that the woman lived in Carrollton, well north of Dallas, which would make the exchange wrong. Rose, "Ruby and Tippit," *passim.*

89. The Warren Commission should have checked out Olsen more carefully. Author George O'Toole did. In his book *The Assassination Tapes*, he revealed that there is no estate in the area of Oak Cliff described. Further, Olsen could not

remember the name of the owner, the "estate's" precise location, or the name of the officer for whom he was substituting. Olsen skipped town with his police-woman wife (who used to work for Ruby) right after the assassination. See O'Toole, pp. 16-17.

90. Meagher, *Accessories*, pp. 263-264; Kantor, pp. 48-49.

91. Meagher, *Accessories*, pp. 269-270.

92. *Ibid.*

93. Kantor, pp. 99-107. See also Marrs, pp. 391-400, for details of Ruby's mob ties. For a good overview of Ruby, see Hurt, Chapter 8, *passim*.

94. Kantor, pp. 56-57, 109-110.

95. *Ibid.*, p. 37.

96. Kantor, p. 37; Garrison, *On the Trail*, pp. 111-113. The evidence of a Mexico trip is murky at best. The report on the subject by Edwin Lopez for the House Select Committee on Assassinations remains classified. See Melanson, pp. 103-104.

97. Kantor, pp. 28-32.

98. *Ibid.*, pp. 33-35.

99. *Ibid.*, p. 36.

100. *Ibid.*, p. 38.

101. Jones, *Forgive II*, pp. 109-110.

102. Kantor, pp. 45-48. Wade called the group "The Free Cuba Movement." Ruby corrected him with the "Fair Play for Cuba Committee." The former was an anti-Castro group while Oswald's was pro-Castro. Ruby knew the difference. His comment protected a CIA front while it kept Oswald's image that of a leftist. Three members of the Free Cuba group in Dallas were Loren Hall, Laurence Howard, Jr., and William Seymour. Hall told J. Edgar Hoover (falsely) that it was those three who went to Sylvia Odio's house shortly before the assassination. The meeting place of the group was 3128 Harlendale in the Oak Cliff section of Dallas. According to policeman Buddy Walthers, an informant told him that Oswald was reported to have been at one of the meetings. The group moved from that house a week before the assassination. Turner, "Inquest," p. 25.

103. Kantor, p. 52.

104. *Ibid.*, pp. 53, 57.

105. *Ibid.*, pp. 60-61.

106. There is much provocative speculation and conflicting evidence about how Ruby got into the basement. The House Select Committee on Assassinations said it was "improbable" he got in without assistance. See Summers, pp. 458-459; Scott, "Dallas Conspiracy," pp. v, 8-18.

107. Marrs, pp. 423-424.

108. Melanson, p. 42.

109. *Ibid.*; Garrison, *On the Trail*, p. 8.

110. Marrs, pp. 99-100. See also Hurt, pp. 302-303.

111. Morrow, *The Senator Must Die*, pp. 84-85.

112. Garrison, *Playboy*, p. 165.

113. It might be that Shaw wanted to outflank Oswald's call to John Abt. See Chapter 4, note 3.

Chapter 7: The Official Story

1. For one thing, official Washington wanted to preempt the hard right wing, which was using the notion of an assassination by the pro-Cuban/pro-Soviet Oswald to whip up public demand for direct U.S. intervention against Cuba, and a confrontation with the Soviets. See Marrs, pp. 459-460. See Hoover's November 25th memo to LBJ aide Walter Jenkins on Deputy Attorney General Nicholas Katzenbach's idea for a Presidential Commission and Katzenbach's memo to LBJ aide Bill Moyers outlining his thoughts on a subsequent Commission's investigation. *Ibid.*

2. Kantor, pp. 78-79.

3. *Ibid.*, p. 79.

4. *Ibid.* Roffman, p. 74. Less than two hours after Oswald's death, FBI Director J. Edgar Hoover telephoned the White House with the following message for President Johnson: "The thing I am most concerned about ... is having something issued so we can convince the public that Oswald is the real assassin." Hurt, p. 19. Dallas Assistant DA Bill Alexander issued his own snap conclusion. Fanning the flames of immediate military confrontation with Cuba and the Soviets, the Birchite DA talked of charging Oswald with murdering the President "as part of an international Communist conspiracy." (Summers, p. 434.) One of the Commission's political functions was to corral and neutralize ultra-right pronouncements and agendas such as Alexander's.

5. Earl Warren's reputation as a distinguished jurist is quite different from his prior record as a politician. Warren, like future Commissioner John McCloy, participated in and defended the program to incarcerate Japanese-Americans in concentration camps during World War II. He was Thomas Dewey's running mate on the 1948 Republican presidential ticket, whose campaign adviser was future DCI and Warren Commissioner, Allen Dulles. Dewey promised to make Dulles DCI if he won, but Dewey lost to Truman. According to Mark Lane, "each of the Commission members was opposed to the notion that he [Warren, as Chief Justice] should serve [on the Commission], with the exception of Allen Dulles." See Lane, *Plausible Denial*, pp.39-53. For information on Dulles and Dewey, see Morrow, *The Senator Must Die*, pp. 4-5; author interview with John Judge, December 14, 1991.

6. Lyndon B. Johnson, p. 27; Lane, *Plausible Denial*, pp. 41-42.

7. Epstein, *Inquest*, p. 15.

8. *New York Times*, February 5, 1964. To show how thoroughly Warren had been coopted, consider this exchange between Warren and Jack Ruby in the Dallas jail, a meeting which Ruby had to request (WCT V, p. 196):

Ruby: "I can't say it here, with authenticity, with sincerity of truth of everything and why my act was committed, but it can't be said here.... It's got to be said amongst people of the highest authority that would give me the benefit of the doubt. And following that, immediately give me the lie detector test after I do make the statement. Chairman Warren, if you felt that your life was in danger at the moment, how would you feel? Wouldn't you be reluctant to go on speaking, even though you request me to do so?" [Ruby is referring to his request to be transferred to Washington so he could speak freely, a request repeatedly denied by Warren.]

Warren: "I think I might have some reluctance if I was in your position, yes; I think I would. I think I would figure it out very carefully as to whether it would endanger me or not. If you think that anything I am doing or anything that I am asking you is endangering you in any way, shape or form, I want you to feel absolutely free to say that the interview is over."

Warren was inviting the last known member of the conspiracy to shut his mouth.

9. Shaw and Harris, p. 216.
10. *Ibid.*
11. *Ibid.*
12. "The JFK Assassination: What About the Evidence," *Washington Post,* December 24, 1991.
13. Lane, *Plausible Denial,* p. 43n.
14. Shaw and Harris, p. 216. The authors make a strong case that Ford also perjured himself at his vice-presidential confirmation hearings. When asked if he used classified documents in the writing of *Portrait of the Assassin,* Ford replied that all the information he used was either in the Report or in the accompanying 26 volumes. This is false. There is material in the first chapter of the book—the transcript of a meeting in which the Commission was told of a report that Oswald might have been an FBI informant—which was not declassified until 1974, eight years after the book's publication.
15. The details that follow on McCloy are from Brinkley, pp. 31-46. The reference to "banana republic" is from Epstein, *Inquest,* p. 33; the reference to McCloy's comment to Ophuls is from author's interview with John Judge, December 14, 1991.
16. Brinkley, pp. 43-44. Like less than 12 percent of the public, McCloy did not "have any doubts about" the Warren Report.
17. Lifton, *Addendum,* pp. 89-90.
18. Belin, p. 173; Summers, p. 263.
19. Epstein, *Inquest,* p. 78.
20. WCT IV, pp. 325-332.
21. Evica, p. 18.
22. Epstein, *Inquest,* p. 152.
23. *Ibid.,* p. 150. In fact, trouble brewed near the Commissioners' apparently placid surface agreement. Congressman Boggs had "strong doubts" about the magic bullet theory. Senator Cooper told Summers in 1978 that he was in fact "unconvinced." Senator Russell did not at the time wish to sign a report that had both JFK and Connally hit by the same bullet; Russell requested a footnote in the report to indicate his dissent, but Warren refused. Years later, reports Summers, Russell denied that any lone man could have done the reported shooting and he believed there had been a conspiracy. Interestingly, Jim Marrs's *Crossfire* lists Boggs amongst the suspicious case-related deaths, noting that Boggs disappeared in an Alaskan plane flight in 1972 after he "began to publicly express doubts about findings." Marrs, p. 562.
24. Epstein, *Inquest,* p. 100.
25. This fact was discovered by independent researcher John Judge while inspecting documents at the National Archives. Judge states that internal documents show even the staff thought Winnaker's conclusions were strained. It is also noted in "The Nazi Connection to the John F. Kennedy Assassination," in

Brussell, p. 118. Judge interview, December 14, 1991.

26. We do not know how those counsel and staff members were selected. According to David Lifton's *Document Addendum to the Warren Report*, the transcript of the first meeting, at which this was discussed, is classified (pp. 45-46). Also, the Commissioners questioned whether they should have subpoena power (pp. 37-40). Finally, some even questioned whether they should hear witnesses themselves or let the FBI conduct all interviews (p. 41).

27. And was later to become Corporation Counsel of the City of New York. As chief counsel, Rankin's was the key position (in terms of power and sensitivity) on the Commission, the sole point of contact between the staff and Commission members, and the overseer of the final report.

28. Kantor, pp. 81-82.

29. The overlaps with Watergate are extraordinary. In addition to Jenner and Shaffer, LBJ first approached Warren to head the Commission through his emissary, Archibald Cox, the first Watergate special prosecutor (fired by Nixon in the Saturday Night Massacre). And Texas lawyer Leon Jaworski, a Commission staff lawyer, became Cox's replacement as Watergate special prosecutor.

30. In 1974, David Belin became the Executive Director of Vice President Rockefeller's Commission on the CIA, authorized by President Ford essentially as a damage-control operation designed to head off and neutralize congressional probes of the CIA's nefarious activities as they came to light in the mid-1970s.

Two things Belin tried to demonstrate in the JFK assassination section of the Report were that Kennedy's backward head movement could be explained by the "jet effect," and that E. Howard Hunt could not have been in Dealey Plaza that day because he was in Washington with his family. The "jet effect," which posits that, under certain circumstances, an independent object when shot may move in the direction of the shot rather than away from it, has been seriously questioned by many experts as inapplicable to a head attached to a body. The second premise was brought into serious question by Mark Lane in the 1985 trial described in *Plausible Denial*.

31. Specter was one of Judge Clarence Thomas's primary defenders against sexual harassment charges by Anita Hill in the Senate's 1991 Supreme Court confirmation hearings.

32. Kantor, p. 89.

33. Weisberg, *Whitewash II*, pp. 21-24.

34. Roffman, p. 74. The basic evidence against Oswald used by the Dallas police and others has always been: the Mannlicher-Carcano was found near the sixth flooor window; he ordered the rifle through an alias: and the rifle was sent to his post office box. All three are questionable. Evica makes a convincing case that a Mauser, not a Carcano, was found in the depository (pp. 1-26). O'Toole notes that the mail order form for the rifle was not found until Oswald's forged ID was established (pp. 157-167). And Meagher points out that someone was mailing incriminating articles, like a brown paper bag, to the Irving post office around the time of the assassination (*Accessories*, pp. 63-64).

35. Roffman, p. 75. The Dallas police were determined to maintain Oswald's image as an isolated, aimless killer. At Jack Ruby's 1964 trial, there were several witnesses who claimed to have seen the two together; none was called. Wade reasoned, "Testimony from these witnesses would have made worldwide head-

lines. And if jurors had believed the testimony, it would have provided a motive for the slaying of Oswald." *Fort Worth Star-Telegram*, March 18, 1964.

36. Groden and Livingstone, pp. 24, 266; Summers, p. 42. According to the Arts and Entertainment special (see Chapter 6, n. 62), before a gun was pulled, very abusive language was first used. When the Texas authorities still refused to give up the body, a federal agent threatened to bowl over hospital personnel with the casket.

37. Within a few hours of Oswald's arrest, Hoover had Oswald's rifle and the bullet fragments flown to Washington aboard an Air Force jet. "FBI laboratory technicians immediately began intensive ballistics and fingerprint tests on the rifle and slugs." North, p. 412. A 1976 Senate Select Committee report states, "Almost immediately after the assassination, Director Hoover, the Justice Department and the White House 'exerted pressure' on senior Bureau officials to complete their investigation and issue a factual report supportng the conclusion that Oswald was the lone assassin." Hurt, p. 19. By 5:15 (EST)—some two and a half hours after Oswald's arrest and two hours before Oswald is charged with killing Tippit (at 7:15)—Hoover had already written an internal memo stating that Oswald was probably JFK's killer. North, p. 411.

38. Roffman, p. 78.

39. Abridged versions of both reports are in Epstein, *Inquest* pp. 157-204.

40. Roffman, p. 78.

41. See Epstein, *Inquest, supra*, note 39..

42. Seventeen Secret Service agents, though formally on duty for 24 hours, were breaking the rules by drinking (at least beyond 3 a.m. and some as late as 5 a.m.) at a Fort Worth bar owned and operated by Pat Kirkwood, who has stated that Oswald had washed glasses in the bar, and that Ruby was nearly a Friday nite regular. One of Kirkwood's close friends was gambler Lewis McWillie, a very close friend of Jack Ruby's who had further mob ties going back to Meyer Lansky's empire in pre-Castro Cuba. Groden and Livingstone, pp. 149-150; Hepburn, p. 300.

43. Hurt, p. 28.

44. Roffman, p. 81.

45. *Ibid.*, p. 261.

46. Physics experiments conducted in 1976 by Nobel laureate Luis Alvarez have been recently invoked to neutralize what the Zapruder film shows: By firing rifle shots at taped melons that sit freely atop a stand, its results purport to show that, for some reason, some melons recoil backwards towards the shooter, a counter-intuitive result. Publicized by PBS's 1988 and 1991 *Nova* special, narrated by Walter Cronkite, the experiment purportedly shows the *possibility* that, by analogy, JFK too could have fallen backwards after being shot from behind. Whether or not shooting melons is a legitimate simulation of a head attached to a body in a moving vehicle, this argument cannot discredit the testimony of 52 witnesses who state that shots came from the grassy knoll and the rush of many spectators to that area.

47. Roffman, p. 261.

48. Jackie Kennedy's "choice" of Bethesda for the autopsy was not as free as some accounts suggest. For example, there was nothing legal, automatic or medically desirable about situating the autopsy in a military as opposed to a

civilian hospital. William Manchester's reconstruction reports that JFK's doctor, Admiral George Burkley, kneeling in the aisle of Air Force One, told the traumatized Jackie that "security reasons" required that the hospital be military. Then he said the option lay between Bethesda (Navy) and Walter Reed (Army). As Manchester recounts: " 'Of course, the President was in the Navy,' he [Burkley] said softly. 'Of course,' said Jacqueline Kennedy. 'Bethesda.' " Manchester, pp. 349-350.

49. Details of the atmosphere at the autopsy are from Hurt, p. 35. According to the FBI report by Agents Sibert and O'Neill (see *infra*, note 51), those in attendance at the Bethesda autopsy were Secret Service (Greer, Kellerman and O'Leary), FBI men (Sibert and O'Neill) and the rest, the great majority, military. There was no civilian involvement in the autopsy. Recorded Navy attendees included Admiral Burkley (JFK's doctor), Admiral Holloway (Bethesda Commander), Commander Humes (Chief Bethesda Pathologist and conductor of the autopsy), Capt. Stoner (Commander of Bethesda Medical School), Capt. Boswell (autopsist), and Capt. Osborne (Bethesda Chief of Surgery). Not mentioned in the report, but placed at the scene by Dr. Finck, was Admiral Kenney. Recorded Army attendees included Lt. Col. Finck (autopsist) and Maj. Gen. Wehle (Chief of U.S. Military District, Washington). And from the Air Force, Brig. Gen. Godfrey McHugh (JFK's Military Aide). (The Sibert-O'Neill Report is reprinted in Weisberg, *Postmortem*, pp. 532-534.)

50. The following autopsy analysis is from Hurt, Chapter 3, *passim.*

51. In 1975, researcher Michael Levy discovered an FBI document written by Agents Francis O'Neill and James Sibert—both present at the autopsy—which was a receipt for a "missile" taken from Kennedy's body. The document is dated November 22, 1963. If one counts this bullet, CE 399, the one that struck James Tague, the fragments, and the bullet that struck a traffic sign (Buchanan, p. 93; Lane, *Rush to Judgment*, p. 57—the sign disappeared so it could not be examined for traces), the sum is at least four, perhaps five, bullets. This depends on whether the fragments match either CE 399 or the Sibert-O'Neill "missile." Either way, the Warren Report concluded definitively that only three bullets were fired.

52. *New York Times* columnist Anthony Lewis recently claimed (January 9, 1992, p. A23) that the Commission found that Oswald could have fired two bullets that hit JFK *before* or *after* shooting the one that missed James Tague. This is not true.

53. Hurt, p. 35.

54. Thompson, p. 69.

55. There was some debate over this inside the Commission, but in the end, they chose the second alternative. Revealingly, no one threatened to resign over this all-important evidentiary point, as Boggs had over the appointment of Olney. Nevertheless, "not a single witness to the shooting ever suggested that both JFK and Connally were hit by the same bullet, and in fact all of the witnesses in Dealey Plaza who had anything to say about it indicated that the victims were hit by separate bullets." Groden and Livingstone, p. 67. And, as noted earlier, three Commissioners had real problems with the magic bullet theory. See *supra*, note 23. Groden believes that they were "overwhelmed by the CIA-connected persons on the panel," Dulles, McCloy and Ford. Groden and Livingstone, p. 67.

56. WCT VI, pp. 128-134.

57. The bullet tests are described in Roffmann, pp. 137-142.

58. Note that the murder rifle was first announced to be a Mauser, not a Mannlicher-Carcano. See Evica, p. 15 ff.

59. Seth Kantor's and Wilma Tice's testimony are in Jones, *Forgive II*, pp. 98-100.

60. The cartridge analysis is from Kurtz, *Crime of the Century*, pp. 50-54.

61. On the inconclusive nitrate tests, see Chapter 6, note 36.

62. But this was done not with the actual Mannlicher-Carcano. Why? Because when the marksmen tested it, they said the bolt was too difficult to work, the trigger pull was a "two-stage operation" that threw off their aim, the scope was off, and the firing pin was worn and rusty. The weapon was so unreliable that these masters could not practice with it for fear that pulling the trigger would break the firing pin. See O'Toole, pp. 27-28.

63. Weisberg, *Whitewash*, pp. 69-70; Lane, *Rush to Judgment*, pp. 125-130. Oswald's supposed feat is even more incredible. According to photos taken from inside and outside the depository, the window he was shooting from was raised only about 15 inches, and the space from the window to the barricade of boxes he supposedly set up behind himself was about 20 inches, a rather cramped space from which to fire the rifle accurately.

64. Weisberg, *Whitewash*, p. 69; Lane, *Rush to Judgment*, p. 127.

65. WR, pp. 681-682.

66. Roffman, pp. 233-247.

67. WR, p. 195.

68. Roffman, p. 71.

69. "The Other Witnesses" in David, pp. 189-190.

70. Hurt, p. 145. Jerry Rose lists some revealing facts about some of the witnesses to the Tippit murder. Helen Markham had to know Ruby, since she was a waitress at the Eatwell Cafe, one of his favorite hangouts. Also, Joyce McDonald, a stripper for Ruby, once lived at the same two-floor flat where Markham lived at the time of the shooting. McDonald's ex-husband lived a few doors from William Scoggins, the cab driver who was also at the scene of the shooting. Just before arriving at the scene, Scoggins had delivered a fare a few doors from the residence of Harry Olsen and Kay Coleman, the police couple who had talked at length to Ruby the night of the assassination (see Chapter 6). Coleman had also worked for Ruby as a stripper. Finally, the phone numbers of two witnesses who said they saw Oswald running from the scene, sisters-in-law Virginia and Barbara Davis, were in Ruby's address book, under the name Leona Miller. No one has discovered who Leona Miller was.

Rose concludes from all this that Ruby may not only have controlled the Tippit encounter with the suspect, but also the "witnesses" to it. It is an interesting proposition. See Rose, "Jack Ruby and J.D. Tippit," pp. 19-20.

71. Hurt, p. 148.

72. WCT III, p. 304.

73. *Ibid.*

74. Lane, *Rush to Judgment*, pp. 183-186.

75. *Ibid.*, pp. 191-193; Hurt, pp. 149-150; Marrs, p. 341.

76. Lane, *Rush to Judgment*, p. 167.

77. Hurt, pp. 151-157. Hurt also notes that, at the Tippit murder scene, Officer

J.M. Poe was ordered to scratch his initials into the cartridge shells to provide a verifiable chain of custody. Poe, who had an excellent reputation as a Dallas homicide detective, told the FBI he had marked the shells as instructed. He later told a researcher that he could not think of another instance in three decades of service when he had failed to mark evidence properly. Yet the shells presented to the Warren Commission as those from the scene of Tippit's murder do not contain Poe's markings.

78. David Lifton in his book and video *Best Evidence*, garners eyewitness testimony that JFK's body left Parkland Hospital inside the bronze ceremonial casket wrapped in a sheet, whereas it arrived at the Bethesda Hospital autopsy room in a plain, gray military-style shipping casket inside a black zippered body bag. He also found a Bethesda x-ray technician who had apparently processed JFK's x-rays before the ceremonial coffin, ostensibly bearing JFK's corpse, had arrived at Bethesda! There is considerable *prima facie* evidence of foul play in the handling and possible alteration of JFK's body—while in military custody—somewhere between the Dallas takeoff and the Bethesda autopsy. See *Best Evidence, passim*; and Marrs, pp. 373-378.

79. Meagher, *Accessories*, pp. 238-241.

80. *Ibid.*, pp. 65-69. The case cited is that of Charles Givens. Originally, in November of 1963, Givens had stated that he left the sixth floor at 11:30 and then went to lunch. Lt. Jack Revill knew Givens and was aware he had been brought up on drug charges before. Meagher makes a strong case both in her book and in a *Texas Observer* article ("The Curious Testimony of Mr. Givens," August 13, 1971) that Revill and the FBI intimidated Givens into changing his original statement when he was interviewed for Belin. Belin should have been aware of this change, because he was familiar with Givens's original story. But now, in April of 1964, Givens said that he forgot his cigarettes and went *back upstairs* at 11:55 and saw Oswald on the sixth floor. the Report used his testimony to say that he was the last person to see Oswald in the building, thus ignoring the statements of Eddie Piper and Carolyn Arnold (see Chapter 6). In that same issue of the *Texas Observer*, Belin replied to Meagher without ever confronting the matter of Givens's original testimony and admitted that he never questioned Givens on the discrepancy. When Meagher sent both articles to the *New York Times*, it reprinted Belin's piece, but not Meagher's. They let Belin revise the piece, and entitled it, "The Warren Commission Was Right." This was on the eighth anniversary of Kennedy's death, November 22, 1971.

81. Weisberg, *Oswald*, pp. 35-36.

82. WCT VI, p. 392.

83. Weisberg, *Whitewash*, p. 53; Meagher, *Accessories*, p. 83.

84. See Belin, Chapters 7, 29, 30; Liebeler was Epstein's chief source for *Inquest*; Boggs and Russell had difficulty with the single-bullet theory. When the Report was near collapse in 1967 they voiced their reservations publicly.

85. Burnet, pp. 20-21.

Chapter 8: Like a House of Cards

1. On the motorcade route, see Joesten, *Oswald: Assassin or Fall Guy*, pp. 17-23. On the throat wound, see *ibid.*, pp. 93, 96. On the Mauser, see Buchanan,

pp. 118-119. The Commission was also deceptive with Joesten. They wrote him that his materials would not go beyond the Commission files. Rankin's letter to that effect is the frontispiece to *Oswald: Assassin or Fall Guy*.

2. Buchanan, especially pp. 33-51.

3. *Ibid.*, pp. 161-170.

4. Joesten, *Oswald: Assassin or Fall Guy*, pp. 8-9.

5. *Ibid.*, pp. 9-11.

6. Lane, *Plausible Denial*, pp. 44n, 71-74. And see Appendix B.

7. Salandria, "Warren Report Pt. 1" and "Warren Report Pt. 2."

8. See *Esquire*, December 1966; *Saturday Evening Post*, January 14, 1967.

9. The exact quote given to the staff by Rankin at the first full meeting was, "Truth is your only client." Epstein, *Inquest*, p. 15.

10. O'Toole, p. 106.

11. *Ibid.*

12. *Ibid.*

13. *Ibid.*; Epstein, *Inquest*, pp. 33-40.

14. Epstein, *Inquest*, pp. 4-6.

15. O'Toole, p. 107.

16. Epstein, *Inquest*, Chapter 10, pp. 148-154.

17. Lane, *Plausible Denial*, pp. 335-360, for the article; see p. 21 for Mrs. Oswald's contact with him.

18. Lane, *Rush to Judgment*, Chapters 14 and 15, *passim*.

19. *Ibid.*, Chapter 2, p. 36, for the quote, and *passim* for witness breakdown.

20. Lane contributed greatly to public awareness by going on a nationwide lecture tour to protest the Warren Report. Later he joined with filmmaker Emile De Antonio to make the documentary *Rush to Judgment*. For a discussion of these activities, see Lane, *Citizen's Dissent*.

21. For Weisberg's struggle to get the book published, se? the Preface to *Whitewash*.

22. Weisberg, *Whitewash*, Chapter 4, *passim*.

23. *Ibid.*, pp. 37-39.

24. *Ibid.*, pp. 55-56.

25. *Ibid.*, Chapter 7, *passim*.

26. Popkin, *The Second Oswald*, Chapters 2 and 3.

27. *Ibid.*, Chapter 4, *passim*.

28. *Ibid.*, Chapters 7 and 8, *passim*.

29. *Ibid.*, pp. 91-98.

30. *Life* purchased the Zapruder film and salted it away from the public for nearly six years, until Garrison's successful subpoena in 1969. Though legal, *Life*'s actions seem in retrospect an obstruction of the public's right to know and to have access to its real history. When *Life* published frames of the Zapruder film, it presented two of them in an incorrect sequence making it appear that the fatal shot struck JFK from behind, rather than in the front, an "error" that was repeated by the Warren Commission. Also, as noted in Chapter 4, note 4, the cover of its February 21, 1964, issue bore the dubious photo of Oswald. For details of the Luce empire's conflicts with Kennedy, see Hinckle and Turner, pp. 164-68. And, on *Life* publisher C.D. Jackson's Cold Warrior activities, see Cook.

31. Thompson, Chapter 5, especially pp. 86-111.

32. *Ibid.*, pp. 244-248.

33. Meagher, *Subject Index.*

34. Harris poll quoted in Flammonde, p. 298.

35. *Ramparts*, November 1966; *Life*, November 25, 1966; *Esquire*, December 1966; *Saturday Evening Post*, January 14, 1967.

Chapter 9: New Orleans Redux

1. Garrison, *On the Trail*, p. 7.

2. *Ibid.*

3. Melanson, p. 42; Garrison, *On the Trail*, pp. 7-8.

4. Turner, "Garrison Commission," p. 47.

5. Garrison, *On the Trail*, p. 13.

6. Garrison, *Playboy*, p. 74.

7. Biographical details are from Flammonde, Chapter 1, and Garrison, *On the Trail*, pp. 9-11.

8. Flammonde, p. 9.

9. *Ibid.*, p. 10.

10. *Ibid.*

11. Early in the investigation, Garrison's probe won support from a group of some 50 private New Orleans citizens and businessmen called "Truth and Consequences of New Orleans, Inc.," which raised money and supplemented the limited public funds available to sustain Garrison's efforts. One member was the New Orleans oilman, Joseph M. Rualt, who accompanied Garrison and Senator Russell Long on the November 1966 plane flight when they discussed the flaws of the Warren Report.

12. WCT XI, pp. 325-39.

13. Popkin, "Garrison's Case," p. 26. Andrews's testimony about encountering Oswald is also corroborated three times: by Springer, by Davis, and by a Secret Service interview November 25, 1963. He could not have been aware of so many facts about Lee and Marina unless Oswald had revealed them to him at an earlier date. Meagher, *Accessories*, pp. 375-376.

14. Weisberg, *Oswald*, p. 335.

15. Garrison, *On the Trail*, pp. 37-38. For reference to the Shaw file, see Turner, "Garrison Commission," p. 48.

16. Flammonde, p. 23.

17. Melanson's *Spy Saga* suggests that Oswald's presence in Clinton may have related to the early stages of the illegal CIA domestic espionage program against leftwing groups that by the late 1960s became the full-blown Operations CHAOS and MERRIMAC. It might also have related to the FBI's COINTELPRO program which targeted civil rights activities for infiltration and disruption. See Chapter 13.

18. Melanson, pp. 92-95. The three were William Gaudet, Manuel Parras Rivera, and Albert Osborne. The HSCA Report on Oswald's Mexico trip is classified until 2029. The Mexico trip is discussed in Chapter 14.

19. Garrison, *On the Trail*, pp. 52-56; Melanson, p. 81; Epstein, *Legend*, p. 189.

20. Most of the White Russians brought to the U.S. after the war came via the Tolstoy Foundation which received yearly subsidies from the CIA; in addition,

the Russian Orthodox Church, which had a branch in Dallas, also received CIA funding. Melanson, p. 79.

21. Garrison, *Playboy*, p. 72.

22. WCT IX, p. 208.

23. For a discussion of CIA operations in all of these countries, see William Blum, *passim*. According to some observers, DeMohrenschildt was in Guatemala City at the time of the Bay of Pigs invasion, which was, in part, staged from bases and launch points in Guatemala; and was also in Haiti at the time of an abortive CIA coup against Haitian president-for-life "Papa Doc" Duvalier, who was later assassinated with Agency connivance. Melanson, pp. 78-79.

According to Edward Jay Epstein, in the summer of 1960, DeMohrenschildt and his wife disappeared for nearly a year. They said they were going on an "11,000-mile walking trip from Mexico to South America." This is how they emerged in April of 1961 in Guatemala, two weeks before the invasion began. Epstein, *Legend*, p. 183.

24. WCT IX, p. 316. Jenner asked her if she thought that was strange. She replied, "But he was taking the baby out. He goes with her, and that was his amusement."

25. Marrs, p. 200; Epstein, *Legend*, pp. 181-82. DeMohrenschildt's lawyer, Patrick Russell, stated in 1978 that "I personally have always felt that George was a CIA agent." Also, according to Melanson, his CIA connections included J. Walton Moore, the CIA's Domestic Contact Service officer in Dallas. Melanson, p. 80. On J. Moore, see Chapter 4, note 30.

26. Garrison, *On the Trail*, pp. 55-56.

27. For a possible debriefing of Oswald by DeMohrenschildt upon the former's return from the Soviet Union, see Summers, pp. 226-228. DeMohrenschildt personally introduced the Oswalds to Ruth Paine at a party of Russian-speaking Socony-Mobil oil technicians. See Epstein, *Legend*, pp. 206-207. On the Paines, see Chapter 6, note 22. It appears that DeMohrenschildt stepped off stage before the New Orleans hand-off, but ensured that Oswald would be watched over on his return to Dallas.

28. See Epstein, *Legend*, p. xiv; Summers, p. 499. Summers notes that DeMohrenschildt had revealed an Agency link to the plot on the eve of the HSCA inquiry. In an interview with Jerry Policoff, who covered the HSCA, I learned that DeMohrenschildt was tortured by a mysterious Agency contact who was trying to force him to admit complicity in the plot and in his handling of Oswald. The pressure may have been part of the Agency's "limited hang-out" strategy for the HSCA. It entailed sacrificing the obvious, lower-level operatives to the Committee in the hope it would induce them not to reach any further up the line.

Interestingly, DeMohrenschildt's was only one of several suspicious deaths of scheduled congressional witnesses. Mobster Sam Giancana was found murdered in June 1975, when the Senate Intelligence Committee was preparing to question him. Johnny Roselli, another Mob figure, was found murdered in July 1976 when he was due to appear, a second time, before the same committee. Summers, pp. 502-503. George Michael Evica strongly suggests that DeMohrenschildt came to America in 1939 masquerading as a French intelligence officer while in reality being a Nazi overseas spy. This may have been why he tried to penetrate the OSS in 1942 but reportedly was rebuffed. Evica, pp. 291-300; Epstein, *Legend*, p. 180.

29. The background on Novel is from Flammonde, pp. 96-97.

30. Garrison, *Playboy*, pp. 70, 172; Flammonde notes that Novel had "told a number of friends and intimates he was a CIA operative and will use this role to battle Garrison's charges." Flammonde, p. 101.

31. Flammonde, p. 101. And see Garrison, *On the Trail*, p. 40.

32. Flammonde, p. 101.

33. Novel may have known Shaw because the Houma ammo dump was owned by the Schlumberger Company of France, run by Jean DeMenil of Houston, who, along with Shaw, was a Director of Permindex, a shadowy international company discussed in Chapter 13. Shaw may have been the Agency contact who relayed the order to Novel for the raid. (Garrison *On the Trail*, p. 40.) Or Novel may have known both Shaw and Andrews through a contemplated intelligence operation out of the ITM. See Chapter 13.

34. McLean adjoins Langley, the site of CIA headquarters; Columbus is the location of the Defense Industrial Security Command; and Montreal is the destination of several flights by Shaw and Ferrie and the home of Shaw's Permindex associate, L.M. Bloomfield. See Chapter 13.

Novel repeatedly frustrated Garrison's attempts to extradite him, helped particularly by Ohio Governor James Rhodes. Other governors who denied usually routinely granted extradition requests include Reagan of California (Bradley), Connally of Texas (Arcacha Smith) and Judge John Clark of Nebraska in the Sandra Moffett case.

35. Text of note from Flammonde, pp. 103-104. When the Agency finally came over to his side, Novel became so arrogant he threatened Louisiana officials unless they halted Garrison's investigation. *Baton Rouge State-Times*, June 19, 1967.

36. Oglesby, *Yankee*, p. 109-111.

37. Kantor, p. 76.

38. Garrison, *On the Trail*, p. 183.

39. For details about Nagell, see *ibid.*, pp. 184-186; Turner, "Garrison Commission," pp. 57-58; Morrow, *Betrayal*, pp. 131-132.

40. On the weapons order, see Morrow, *Betrayal*, pp. 125-126; on Ferrie and the weapons, *ibid.*, pp. 84-85.

41. In the many months I have worked on this book, I have come to believe that there was, in fact, high-up Agency involvement, with "plausible denial" shielding the sanctioning of the assassination. This, plus "need to know" limitations on the parceling out of pieces of information helped make the conspiracy difficult to detect. I also believe the Agency was aided by top military brass in the coordination of the operation and in the deliberate sabotage of the autopsy. See the testimony of Pierre Finck, in Chapter 12 and Appendix A.

42. Within the CIA there is a distinction in terminology which is not often perceived by the general public. An employee of the Agency is referred to as an "officer." An outsider, who may be used once or regularly, is referred to as an "agent." Thus, someone like Philip Agee or John Stockwell was never "a CIA agent."

43. The Agency's general distaste for publicity has been used by Garrison's detractors, like Robert Sam Anson, to assert that Garrison could make charges against the CIA without fear of contradiction because of its fear of *unjustly*

arousing suspicion of involvement. (Anson, p. 112.) This ignores the equally possible fear of *justly* arousing suspicion. Indeed, Richard Helms defended his lying to Garrison and saying that the Agency had no relationship to Clay Shaw on the ground that, if Shaw's contract agent status were admitted, people would jump to the untrue conclusion that he had been involved in the assassination. See Garrison, *On the Trail*, p. 234, quoting Marchetti's interview in *True*.

44. Many books have been written on the CIA's domestic operations. See, for example, David Wise's excellent exposés: *The Politics of Lying, The American Police State*, and, with Thomas Ross, *The Espionage Establishment* and *The Invisible Government*; and Athan Theoharis, *Spying on Americans*.

45. The Andrews episode is from Garrison, *On the Trail*, pp. 80-82. Andrews strongly implied that he backpedaled because the FBI wanted him to change his story; WCT XI, p. 334. He even denied knowing what Bertrand looked like, though he had seen him twice; WCT XI, pp. 331, 334.

46. February 24, 1967; the station was WAFB, also on February 24.

47. The Russo episode is from Garrison, *On the Trail*, pp. 151-56.

48. Popkin, "Garrison's Case," p. 25.

49. Much has been made, in arguments against Garrison's case, about the fact that Russo did not mention "Clem Bertrand" in the newspaper interview. But, as Russo later, and repeatedly, explained, he was being questioned about Ferrie and Oswald; no one asked him about the tall, distinguished gentleman, who, in fact, did not say much.

50. Popkin, "Garrison's Case," p. 25. The man Russo said he saw was not clean-shaven. This is why he asked that whiskers be added to the picture. See also Kirkwood, pp. 144-145.

Chapter 10: Inferno

1. Rosemary James remains active as a Garrison detractor to this day, having often appeared on TV to criticize Oliver Stone's basing the film *JFK* on Garrison's character and investigation.

2. Phelan, "Rush to Judgment," p. 22. Garrison was so angered that he went through a three-stage reaction to the James story. First, he issued a statement denying the story, saying it was based on rumor. *Baton-Rouge State-Times*, February 18, 1967. Then he swore at the press, before bursting out with, "I don't have to explain trips to any newspaper." *State-Times*, February 18, 1967. By February 20, he could deny the story no longer and called a press conference to detail how the story had already hindered his investigation. "[W]e were making progress until the newspapers revealed a number of details." He added that he did not plan to make the probe public "until the time came to make arrests." *State-Times*, February 20, 1967. James seems to have been less than honest about her "no comment" remark, which, of course, makes her story about poking around in the vouchers even more suspect.

3. Charles Ward, an assistant DA who did not approve of Garrison's inquiry into the assassination, did not show up for work the day James's story appeared, but he did confirm it. *Baton Rouge State-Times*, February 17, 1967. Ward later ran against Garrison for DA and lost. Ferrie quickly followed up the story by disclosing that he was the target of the probe. Considering that he called inves-

tigator Lou Ivon and told him the story had made him "a dead man" (Garrison, *On the Trail*, p. 138), there seem to be two possible explanations to this contradictory behavior. Either Ferrie was playing a complex game of hide-and-seek with the DA by cooperating with the media and then playing innocent, or he tried to make the best of a bad situation by using the media to his advantage once the investigation was exposed. For Ferrie's disclosures to the media, see Popkin, "Garrison's Case," p. 27; Phelan, *Scandals*, p. 141.

4. Flammonde, pp. 39-40.

5. *Ibid.*, p. 33.

6. Hurt, p. 264.

7. Lardner was quite accommodating to Ferrie. In a newspaper article that appeared in the *New York World-Journal-Tribune*, February 23, 1967, he wrote: "I may have been the last person to see David W. Ferrie alive. While I talked to Ferrie, once interrogated as the "getaway pilot" for a presidential assassin, he said he was convinced there was no plot to kill President Kennedy and that Lee Harvey Oswald was a "loner." Ferrie, one of District Attorney Jim Garrison's prime witnesses in the investigation of Kennedy's assassination, also said he was convinced the investigation would turn out to be a "witch hunt." "This is not a city prone to know what it's doing before it arrests people," he declared. (Quoted in Joesten, *Garrison* pp. 38-39.)

8. Garrison, *On the Trail*, p. 130.

9. The first and last quotes are from Brener, p. 84; the second quote is from Garrison's *Playboy* interview, p. 60; the third quote is from James and Wardlaw, p. 39.

10. Flammonde notes that Garrison was subject to a relentless media barrage that "pyramided, apparently peaking around the week of June 19-26" (p. 315). It is certainly possible that Rosemary James's tip came as part of such a campaign. Indeed, given her own continuing attacks on Garrison, James might indeed have been a participant in it.

11. The Whalen account is from Garrison, *On the Trail*, pp. 122-24.

12. There were other death threats. A caller warned Garrison's then wife Liz, "You have kids—we'll get them on the way to school." (Joesten, *Garrison*, p. 24.)

From researcher Hal Verb I have learned of another death threat. In late 1967, Garrison was in San Francisco attempting to extradite Eugene Hale Brading (see Chapter 11). A man named Richard Wrye was informed by a friend in the Mafia that a contract had just been placed on Garrison at a West Coast meeting. There had been a $10,000 down payment, with a much larger sum to follow. Wrye revealed the plot to Garrison and they both immediately left town. Garrison flew back to New Orleans and Wrye drove there with Tom Sanders, a friend of Verb's and Garrison's. Wrye was questioned by Assistant DA Jim Alcock, but refused to give any details and was released. Author's interviews with Verb, November 17 and 25, 1991.

13. Marrs, pp. 502-503. The contents of Ferrie's apartment at the time of his death were unusual for a private investigator. They included: a blue, 100-lb. aerial bomb, a Springfield rifle, a Remington rifle, an altered-stock .22 rifle, 20 shotgun shells, two Army Signal Corps telephones, one bayonet, one flare gun, a radio transmitter unit, a radio receiver unit, 32 rifle cartridges, 22 blanks, several

cameras, and three rolls of film. *Baton Rouge State-Times*, February 28, 1967.
14. Marrs, pp. 502-503; Garrison, *On the Trail*, pp. 142-143.
15. Flammonde, p. 36.
16. *New Orleans States-Item*, February 22, 1967.
17. See Stone and Sklar. One would think that Ferrie's death could not be more suspicious. But it is. The day before he died, Ferrie had purchased 100 thyroid pills. When his body was discovered, they were gone. Minyard theorizes that if Ferrie was murdered, the killers may have mixed the pills into a solution and forced it down his throat with a tube. One of the contusions is on the inside of the lower lip where the tube may have struck during a struggle. With all these suspicious circumstances, why did Chetta rule as he did? In no one's memory had someone left a suicide note and then died of natural causes. But Chetta apparently wanted to play it safe in the face of the tremendous publicity focused on Ferrie's death. Frank Minyard, interview with the author, January 31, 1992.
18. Ferrie's one-time roommate, Raymond Broshears, said that Ferrie told him, "No matter what happens I will never commit suicide." Flammonde, p. 40.
19. Garrison, *Playboy*, p. 59.
20. Despite the fact that Garrison has been attacked for being anti-gay, Garrison insists he never made a public remark, in court or out, about Shaw's homosexuality. No critic has provided any quotation to the contrary, only veiled accusations. Contrariwise, Garrison has also been accused of being a closet pederast, who has had child molestation charges against him dropped. Here too, there is no evidence whatsoever to support such a claim. But, as Garrison has noted, "It has been my policy not to respond to each of the many canards which have been part of the campaign to discredit my investigation, nor to waste time trying to prove negatives." Garrison, *On the Trail*, p. 288. Interestingly, in the midst of the 1967 media blitz, Garrison predicted that he might be accused of something like child molesting. Garrison, *Playboy*, p. 70.
21. Hurt, p. 281. Some have objected to the scene in *JFK* that depicts Shaw, semi-naked, with gold body paint. But Iris Kelso, a *Times-Picayune* reporter who knew Shaw, told me that she had seen him at a bar in the French Quarter during Mardi Gras in gold body paint, jock strap, and sandals. Interview with the author, February 27, 1992. Interestingly, the bar she saw him at was the Blacksmith Shop, one of Andrews's hangouts; see Garrison, *On the Trail*, p. 83.
22. On the controversy over P.O. Box 19106, see Flammonde, pp. 227-31. Garrison's team determined that, based on a code deployed throughout Oswald's address book, this entry when decoded is Jack Ruby's unlisted Dallas phone number. The entry in Oswald's book was most intriguing, since Dallas did not have post office box numbers that high in 1963. Garrison, *On the Trail*, p. 147.
23. *Ibid.*, p. 148. This ties in with Ferrie's comment to Russo in October 1963, "We will get him and it won't be long." Popkin, "Garrison's Case," p. 28.
24. Flammonde, p. 213.
25. See *Los Angeles Times*, July 14, 1967; *New York Times*, February 24, 1967; *New York Post* quoted in Flammonde, p. 287. The information about the Sterns was obtained through interviews with Iris Kelso, February 27, 1992, and court stenographer Helen Dietrich, January 16, 1992. See also Kirkwood, pp. 111-112, 660.
26. Phelan, *Rush to Judgment*, p. 22.

27. *Baton Rouge Morning Advocate*, February 25, 1967; for the television disclosure on February 24, see Popkin, "Garrison's Case," p. 28; see also Garrison, *On the Trail*, pp. 151-152, 162.

28. David, p. 244.

29. "The J.F.K. Conspiracy," *Newsweek*, May 15, 1967, p. 36.

30. *Ibid.*, p. 40.

31. On May 13, three days before the *Newsweek* piece was published, Aynesworth sent a revealing teletype to President Johnson's press secretary, George Christian. See text at note 44.

32. Garrison, *Playboy*, p. 62.

33. *Newsweek*'s bias continues. When Oliver Stone's *JFK* opened, the magazine's December 23, 1991, cover denounced "The Twisted Truth of 'JFK' " and advised "Why Oliver Stone's New Movie Can't Be Trusted." *Newsweek* is owned by the Washington Post Company; it was the *Washington Post* that printed the first attack on the film, by George Lardner, Jr., in May of 1991, before filming was even completed.

34. Garrison, *On the Trail*, p. 161, note.

35. The account of the documentary is from Flammonde, pp. 300-314; Garrison, *Playboy*, pp. 62-68; and Garrison, *On the Trail*, pp. 165-171.

36. North, pp. 69, 169.

37. Flammonde, pp. 302-303. WDSU, the local NBC affiliate, owned by the Sterns, helped Sheridan produce his special. Richard Townley, a newscaster for that station, helped secure and interview prospective "witnesses" for the show. He seems to have adopted Sheridan's G-man tactics. When Townley talked to Gordon Novel's former wife, Marlene Mancuso, he told her that Garrison was going to be destroyed: "We aren't merely going to discredit the probe—Garrison is going to get a jail sentence." Mancuso was also approached by an intermediary for Shaw's lawyers who said if she did not cooperate with them, they would investigate her, call her into court, and smear her on the stand. Flammonde, pp. 312-313.

38. For details of what happened to Sheridan's "witnesses" after the program aired, see Flammonde, pp. 304-314; Garrison, *On the Trail*, pp. 169-171; Garrison, *Playboy*, pp. 64-68. Anson referred to the charges in this scurrilous "documentary" as if they were true; pp. 115-116. Tom Wicker did the same in his December 15, 1991, *New York Times* attack on *JFK*.

39. Flammonde, pp. 309-11.

40. Garrison, *Playboy*, p. 64.

41. Material on Aynesworth's activities in Dallas are primarily from Joesten, *Garrison*, pp. 100-5.

42. *Ibid.*, pp. 102-104.

43. July 1979, on Dallas PBS affiliate, KERA.

44. The Western Union teletype is dated May 13, 1967, and it includes a "rough draft copy" of the piece that appeared in the May 15 *Newsweek*. The elipses are in the original.

45. Phelan, *Scandals*, p. 174.

46. *Ibid.*, p. 175.

47. *Ibid.*, p. 149.

48. *Ibid.*, pp. 143, 161. In his 1982 piece, Phelan tried to bring into question

Garrison's use of the paraffin test as indicative of Oswald's innocence. (See Chapter 6, n. 36.) He states that it was an outdated test and only showed how backward the Dallas police were. This is slickly disingenuous. Today, the nitrate/paraffin test *is* obsolete because it has been superceded by newer and better technology like electron scanning. But in 1963 it was not. It or the nitrite test was used by every major police department in the country. The scanning test and other methods are more conclusive because there is less possibility of "false traces," *i.e.*, elements besides gunpowder that could leave nitrates on the skin. But Oswald's test detected *no nitrates at all*, so there could not be any false traces. (Interviews with Bill Llewelyn and Leonard Henkhaus of the Scientific Investigation Division of the Los Angeles Police Department, March 3 and 5, 1992.) For a discussion of gunshot-residue testing, see Saferstein, Chapter 11.

49. See Garrison, *On the Trail*, pp. 85-87, for Shaw's use of an alias. Needless to say, Phelan never mentions in his 1982 piece that Shaw was a CIA agent, even though it was written five years after the memorandum on his contact status was declassified and three years after Helms confessed to this status under oath. Perhaps this is because Phelan knew that his friend Robert Maheu was a long-time CIA asset and had ties to Banister through the Chicago FBI office where Banister was SAC. Scott, *Crime and Cover-Up*, p. 66, n. 143.

50. In 1991, when the film *JFK* was announced, Phelan called Perry Russo and told him he had to stop this film. When Russo seemed baffled by this request, Phelan said, "It will make Garrison a champion. A generation of kids will believe it was a conspiracy. Do you know what this will do to the intelligence agencies?" In Phelan's book he implied that Russo took the Fifth Amendment at a preliminary hearing to Shaw's perjury trial because he did not believe in Garrison's case. Russo denies this, saying that by that time, 1971, his life had been ruined by all the publicity from the trial. He told Shaw's lawyers he did not wish to testify for either side any more. To this day, Russo says he uses alternative IDs in some parts of New Orleans. Author's interview with Perry Russo, December 6, 1991.

51. Scott, *Crime and Cover-Up*, pp. 31-32, 63, note 128. Maheu, through Hughes, donated an island for a group of mercenaries called the No Name Group to train for anti-Castro operations (Morrow, *The Senator Must Die*, pp. 17, 20). This group made an alliance with Antonio Veciana's Alpha 66 (*ibid.*, p. 82). This new group trained with Ferrie and was asked by Banister to be the assassination team in Dealey Plaza. Maheu knew Banister from their Chicago FBI days (Evica, p. 208). The Dallas leader of Alpha 66 was Manuel Rodríguez. Both he specifically and Alpha 66 generally were prime suspects of Garrison as the Dallas hit team (Turner, "Inquest," pp. 17, 25; Gary Schoener interview, December 2, 1991). Today, Morrow, Evica, and Mark Lane concur. As for Phelan, see his article in the November 23, 1975, *New York Times Magazine*, entitled "The Assassination That Will Not Die." He calls Kennedy's backward head snap a neuromuscular reaction, defends the single-bullet theory, calls the early Warren Report critics a "housewives' underground," and cites the work of David Belin. That Phelan continues to be taken seriously by good writers like Henry Hurt and respectable periodicals like *The Third Decade*, is a mystery of the Kennedy assassination literature.

52. Sheridan, pp. 5, 166-167; North, p. 69; Navasky, p. 405.

53. Garrison, *On the Trail*, p. 166.

54. Hougan, *Spooks*, p. 124.
55. Navasky, pp. 412-413.
56. Hougan, *Spooks*, p. 124.
57. *Ibid.*
58. *Ibid.*, p. 126.
59. *Ibid.*, p. 128. It is important to recall that RFK had a supervising role in Operation MONGOOSE at this time, which explains his access to the CIA.
60. *Ibid.*, p. 126.
61. *Ibid.*
62. *Ibid.*, p. 129.
63. *Ibid.*, p. 128. Note that the first tarring of Garrison's name with Mob connections, particularly Carlos Marcello, began with a story in the September 8, 1967, issue of *Life*. Not only did Sheridan have ties to the magazine, so did another Shaw ally, reporter David Chandler. Sheridan uses the Marcello tactic in his book, on page 417.
64. The judge's order is in Flammonde, p. 212.
65. Fensterwald, p. 454. Novel was so confident of what the documentary would do to Garrison's credibility he wired this brief message to the DA's office shortly before the broadcast: "Big Jim will shortly be dumped in the White Paper can." *New Orleans Magazine*, July 1967, p. 59.
66. Joesten, *Garrison*, p. 89; Flammonde, p. 104. Garrison was not the first Warren Report critic to be infiltrated by the government. In late 1966, Vincent Salandria, a prominent critic and Philadelphia attorney, encountered a woman named Rita Rollins, who said she was a nurse for a wealthy family in Texas and New Orleans. She said this family had a ranch in Texas on which they had practiced "dry runs" of the assassination. She told him she had searched him out because of his reputation as a leading critic of the Report, and she wanted him to go to Canada with her, where she would produce witnesses.

Salandria asked her many specific questions about the assassination, and she had answers for them all. He called another serious critic and researcher, Sylvia Meagher, who came down from New York. They both questioned the woman, and her responses held up. As Salandria was driving Meagher to the train station, she suggested one more round of queries. This time she asked Rollins questions about her occupation, nursing. Rollins was stymied. Her cover was blown.

Six months later, Salandria found out that the woman's real name was Lulu Belle Holmes and she was an FBI agent who had successfully infiltrated the Peace Movement. The story she was trying to sell Salandria was that Hoover and LBJ had killed Kennedy. The point was presumably to try to make Salandria look silly by having the "witnesses" recant or be exposed as unreliable. The Agency was not alone in their campaign against the critics. (See Appendix B.) Author interview with Vincent Salandria, February 23, 1992.
67. Phelan, *Scandals*, p. 165; Kirkwood, p. 282.
68. Joesten, *Garrison*, p. 134.
69. *Ibid.*, p. 153.
70. Two favorable articles are Turner and Popkin, already noted; Powledge is also favorable.

Chapter 11: The DA Stumbles

1. Garrison, *On the Trail*, p. 139.

2. "The Mob, Part 2," *Life*, September 8, 1967, pp. 94-95. Garrison has been accused of links to mobster Carlos Marcello, whom Attorney General Bobby Kennedy had once deported and for whom David Ferrie had worked, through attorney G. Wray Gill, as a pilot and as an investigator. The charges were first made by Warren Rogers in an August 26, 1969, *Look* article, and reiterated ever since by writers like James Kirkwood and Robert Sam Anson, and Mafia-did-it theorists like David Scheim and John Davis.

The charges imply that Garrison's CIA focus was a smokescreen to protect Marcello (and possibly others like Hoffa and Trafficante). Garrison, though he disdains trying to prove negatives, has stated that he never met Marcello in his life and pointed out that Marcello was the subject of both federal investigations, in which Garrison could not interfere, and local investigations in Jefferson Parish, where Marcello lived, in which Garrison also could not participate. Regarding the repeated allegations that Garrison was a big gambler, he has said that he *never* gambled, and defied anyone to come up with proof that he did. No one could.

3. Popkin, "Garrison's Case," p. 19. Andrews appeared on the NBC show to deny that Clay Shaw was Clay Bertrand, after which NBC narrator Frank McGee intoned that NBC knew the "real" Clay Bertrand and was withholding his identity for his own protection. Andrews was soon pushed to reveal his identity and said Bertrand was New Orleans barkeeper, Eugene C. Davis, who vehemently denied the charges and gave Garrison a sworn statement to that effect. See Flammonde, pp. 307-8.

4. Flammonde, pp. 292-94, 308.

5. Garrison, *Playboy*, p. 70.

6. The media's focus on Garrison's personality to the detriment if not obliteration of specific issues has been true of the 1991-1992 controversy surrounding Oliver Stone and *JFK*.

7. Since 1969, when he left office, Ramsey Clark has evolved into both a strong defender of the rights of defendants, minorities, and underdogs against government oppression, as well as a staunch opponent of American policy commitments like the Vietnam War and most recently, the Desert Storm war against Iraq. For his independent stances, the once establishment figure has earned the enmity of the mainstream press. (See David Margolick's attack in the *New York Times*, June 14, 1991, B15.)

8. *New York Post*, March 2, 1967.

9. *New York Times*, June 3, 1967.

10. *New Orleans Times-Picayune*, May 6, 1967.

11. Accompanied by the ubiquitous Ruth Paine, who was to serve as her very first translator, Marina Oswald was taken incognito by the Secret Service directly to the Inn of the Six Flags in Arlington, Texas. According to Peter Dale Scott's *The Dallas Conspiracy*, this motel was owned by the Great Southwest Corp., a company under the joint ownership and control of Murchison and Rockefeller interests. The manager of the motel, James Martin, immediately became Marina's business manager and negotiated the sale of the world-famous picture showing Oswald with rifle and leftist newspapers aloft. Scott, "Dallas Conspiracy," p.

3-20.

12. Weisberg, *Oswald*, pp. 23-24.

13. Perhaps the most interesting item regarding the Paines is an FBI report, Commission Document 206, of an intercepted call between Ruth's home and Michael's office phones, the day after the assassination: "We both know who is responsible." Summers, p. 549, note 71.

14. Flammonde, p. 19.

15. Marrs, p. 559. The Kilgallen death almost ranks with the Gary Underhill and Rose Cheramie deaths in its eeriness and suggestiveness. Kilgallen was one of the very few nationally known and syndicated columnists who had sharp doubts about the Warren Report and voiced them in her writings. As a result, her phone was tapped. She was reduced to using phone booths and resorting to code names to communicate with other critics like Mark Lane. After her interview with Ruby, but before she could publish her story, she was found dead in her New York home. Eight days after her death, it was announced that she had died of barbiturates and alcohol, but no quantities were given. Her close friend, Mrs. Earl Smith, died two days after Kilgallen; the cause of death was unknown. No notes relating to her explosive story were found. None was found at Mrs. Smith's either. See Jones, *Forgive I*, pp. 12-15; *Fort Worth Star-Telegram*, December 18, 1976.

16. Flammonde, p. 180.

17. Hurt, pp. 147-48.

18. Flammonde, p. 120. At first, Arcacha denied he knew Ferrie. He even said he knew no one who hated Kennedy for the Bay of Pigs failure. The pretense collapsed when his wife told reporters that Ferrie had been at their house the day of the invasion. *Baton Rouge State-Times*, February 27, 1967.

19. Garrison has been criticized for failing to bring into the Shaw trial testimony which would link the CIA and Shaw. He was unable to get Novel, and, as noted below, Nagell would not disclose his Agency ties. Perhaps, if he had negotiated with Arcacha, he might have been able later to get some helpful testimony in the trial. Of course, the CIA had denied to Garrison that it had any material relating to Shaw; he may have suspected the Agency was lying to him, but there was nothing he could do to get any information from them.

20. Flammonde, p. 105.

21. *Ibid.*

22. *Ibid.*, pp. 118, 294. It should be noted that Kennedy relented and did testify about his brief, half-hearted investigation of Clay Bertrand; *New Orleans Times-Picayune*, February 17, 1969.

23. Garrison, *On the Trail*, p. 183.

24. *Ibid.*, p. 229. As Garrison put it, "By the time they finished with Nagell, the jury would have been left with the impression of a crackpot. One such incident, one such discrediting, is all it takes to undo an entire case. I decided that with Nagell we could not take that risk." With the benefit of hindsight, this may have been a significant mistake, since the links to the CIA were critical.

25. *New Orleans States-Item*, June 23, 1967.

26. Popkin, "Garrison's Case," p. 22.

27. *Ibid.* Gurvich may have been an agent. In his *Playboy* interview (p. 68), Garrison says that Gurvich approached him almost two months before the James disclosure—shades of Gordon Novel (see Chapter 10). He offered his services

free of charge and brought Garrison a new color television set. Then, à la Novel, he began speaking with Sheridan and at the same time pumping Garrison for more information. When he left, he took a copy of the witness file and began a national press campaign denouncing Garrison (see note 35, below). Garrison adds that he should have asked more questions of Gurvich when he first walked into his office. How true.

28. Melanson, p. 110; Flammonde, p. 200; Noyes, Chapter 3, *passim.*
29. Flammonde, p. 200.
30. "Jolly Green Giant in Wonderland," *Time*, August 2, 1968, p. 56.
31. Interview with Jim Alcock, November 23, 1991.
32. Interview with researcher Gary Schoener, December 2, 1991.
33. Epstein, *Counterplot.*
34. *Inside Edition*, February 5, 1992. Bill O'Reilly hosted a report from a source familiar with the classified files of the HSCA. (See Chapter 13.)
35. Some commentators, notably Robert Sam Anson, have stated that Garrison really hoped the case would never come to trial. Anson, p. 112. No one I interviewed for this book who had any close association with Garrison at the time concurred. On the contrary, they believe that Garrison thought he was going to get a conviction at least up until the eve of the trial. It was not until then that he realized what the media barrage and the foiled extradition and evidence requests had done to his case. Anson also states that Garrison attacked the CIA only because "they can't afford to answer." He attributed this to a December 30, 1967, *Chicago Tribune* story. The quote is not in the story, which is mostly an interview with William Gurvich, Garrison's turncoat investigator.
36. Garrison, *On the Trail*, p. 243, n.

Chapter 12: Anticlimax: The Shaw Trial

1. Flammonde, p. 213.
2. One who claims Garrison never expected or desired an actual trial is Robert Sam Anson, who states in *They've Killed the President* (p. 126): "Significantly, he [Garrison] thought his case against Shaw would never come to trial and when it did he absented himself from nearly all the proceedings."
3. Flammonde, p. 233.
4. *Ibid.*, p. 239.
5. *Ibid.*, p. 240.
6. *Ibid.*, p. 241.
7. *Ibid.*, pp. 244 ff. At this time, Dymond actually had his picture taken clutching the Warren Report to his chest. Joesten, "Highlights," p. 54. For a complete chronicle of the incredible delaying tactics of the defense, see Flammonde, pp. 233-246.
8. Flammonde, p. 235.
9. Kirkwood, pp. 43, 54.
10. Flammonde, p. 244. When offered the chance, Ramsey Clark in fact refused to join in any case as a plaintiff against Jim Garrison.
11. *Ibid.*, p. 212.
12. The Kohn episode is described in Flammonde, p. 235.
13. *Ibid.*, p. 299.

14. *Ibid.* In his statement to the DA's office on charges that he was Clay Bertrand, Davis characterized them as "utterly and completely false and malicious and damnable." *Ibid.*, p. 308.

15. Popkin, "Garrison's Case," p. 20.

16. Turner, "Garrison Commission," p. 68.

17. Author interview with Lou Ivon, February 19, 1992.

18. James Kirkwood was a playwright who went to New Orleans to cover the Shaw trial and became friends with Clay Shaw. His book, *American Grotesque*, is a scathing denunciation of Garrison for carrying out a homophobic, personal vendetta against Shaw. It also offers a slanted account of the case and courtroom testimony (see Appendix A). Kirkwood went on to write the book for the Pulitzer Prize-winning Broadway hit, *A Chorus Line*.

19. Kirkwood, p. 79.

20. *Ibid.*, pp. 246-47.

21. Bethell's is a curious case. In his writings on the Garrison case in his book *The Electric Windmill* (pp. 60-71), Bethell implied that, *in retrospect*, the inquiry was a dubious one. According to Vincent Salandria (interview, February 23, 1992), this is disingenuous. In early 1967, he and Bethell would have long arguments, well into the night, on the efficacy of the Garrison probe, and Bethell would often side with the Warren Commission findings. Also, in his *National Review* article, December 16, 1991, timed for the release of *JFK*, he stated that he *voluntarily* told Garrison about handing over the witness summaries to Shaw's defense counsel. According to Lou Ivon (interview with author, February 19, 1992), this is not so. There was an internal investigation, and, when confronted with the charge, Bethell fessed up. Milton Brener also noted (p. 252) that Aynesworth got his witness list from the same source as Shaw's lawyers. If this is so, Bethell turned over the list twice, once to the media and once to the defense. With the list, Aynesworth went to Clinton to try to challenge and intimidate those witnesses. Brener, pp. 250-251; Kirkwood, pp. 220-223. One wonders just why Bethell joined Garrison's staff in the first place.

22. In a generally faultless performance, Shaw slipped only once. At a very early press conference he referred to the alleged assassin as "Harvey Lee Oswald." As researchers know, the only instances in which Oswald had been referred to in this way were two cases of Oswald impersonations and in some intelligence files. See Weisberg, *Oswald*, p. 233; and Melanson, pp. 124-25.

23. Kirkwood, p. 491. A letter from a source close to Garrison suggests his reasons for such a tactic may have come from a combination of overconfidence and miscalculation: "Garrison, of course, knew how the American news media would treat the trial, so he did not use many of his witnesses and held back on much of his evidence. His strategy considered the trial to be only one step of many, leading to the conviction of all the assassins and the exposure of the top structure above them. However, the strategy backfired...." Joesten, "Highlights," p. 48.

24. Kirkwood, p. 265. It was glancingly mentioned by Russo when Alcock read Sciambra's memorandum of his testimony into the record. Dymond made the motion; *ibid.*, p. 257.

25. Garrison, *On the Trail*, p. 85. Other witnesses included William Morris, who was introduced to Shaw by Eugene Davis, and Mrs. Jessie Parker, a hostess

in the New Orleans airport VIP room who witnessed Shaw signing the register as "Clay Bertrand." *Ibid.*, p. 86.

26. *Ibid.*
27. See *supra*, n. 24.
28. Joesten, *Garrison*, p. 80.
29. *Ibid.*, p. 81.
30. Policoff, p. 3.
31. Garrison, *On the Trail*, pp. 117-119.
32. Ferrie-Shaw relations from Garrison, *On the Trail*, pp. 117-19.
33. Despite statements to the contrary by critics, some 80 percent of Garrison's stirring summation speech as delivered by Kevin Costner at the end of *JFK* is taken directly from the transcript of Garrison's actual trial summation.
34. Kirkwood is grossly unfair to Oser. See the introduction to Appendix A.
35. On the number of jurors, see the *New Orleans States-Item*, February 5, 1969; on the number of days, see the *New Orleans Times-Picayune*, March 1, 1969. Most prospective jurors were dismissed for one of two reasons: financial duress (jurors were not paid) or bias toward one side or the other.
36. This testimony still held up ten years later when repeated before the House Select Committee on Assassinations. Melanson, p. 45.
37. Kirkwood, p. 228.
38. The Spiesel appearance is described in Kirkwood, pp. 231-242, and Garrison, *On the Trail*, pp. 236-237.
39. Kirkwood, p. 231.
40. *Ibid.*, pp. 231-232.
41. *Ibid.*, p. 232.
42. *Ibid.*, p. 233.
43. *Ibid.*
44. *Ibid.*, p. 235.
45. Garrison, *On the Trail*, p. 236.
46. *Ibid.*, p. 237.
47. *Ibid.*
48. *Ibid.*
49. *Ibid.*
50. Kirkwood, p. 276.
51. Garrison, *On the Trail*, pp. 237-238.
52. Kirkwood, p. 295.
53. *New Orleans States-Item*, February 13, 1969; Kirkwood, pp. 296-298.
54. Kirkwood, pp. 308-309.
55. *Ibid.*, pp. 306-308.
56. *Ibid.*, p. 306.
57. *New Orleans Times-Picayune*, February 23, 1969.
58. Author interview with Vincent Salandria, February 23, 1992.
59. Kirkwood, pp. 348-349.
60. The Habighorst episode is in Kirkwood, pp. 353-359; and Garrison, *On the Trail*, pp. 145, 159, 242-243.
61. Author interview with Habighorst's widow, Elsie, February 23, 1992.
62. In Elsie Habighorst's possession. She has sent the author samples.
63. Habighorst interview. Habighorst's captain confirmed this.

64. *Ibid.*
65. See accompanying illustration. These are the cards taken home by Habig-horst and later given by him to Garrison.
66. Hurt, p. 275.
67. Habighorst interview.
68. *Ibid.*
69. See accompanying photo from the front page of the *New Orleans Times-Picayune*, February 20, 1969.
70. Habighorst interview.
71. Habighorst was the kind of policeman who brought home stray animals and lost children; he would make phone calls until he located the pet's owners and the children's parents. Letter from Habighorst's daughter, Karla Kemp, to the author, February 27, 1992.
72. *New Orleans Times-Picayune*, February 20, 1969.
73. *Ibid.*
74. *Ibid.*
75. Author interview with Lou Ivon, February 19, 1992.
76. *New Orleans Times-Picayune*, February 20, 1969.
77. *Ibid.*; see also Garrison, *On the Trail*, p. 242.
78. *New Orleans Times-Picayune*, February 20, 1969.
79. Colloquy from *New Orleans Times-Picayune*, February 20, 1969.
80. Garrison, *On the Trail*, p. 242. Haggerty himself seemed confused by his decision. The day after he made it, when Alcock asked him to reconsider, he based his continued stance on *Miranda*, not *Escobedo*. Yet, the day before, when it was explained that Shaw had his rights read to him *before* Habighorst interviewed him, Haggerty seemed to base his ruling on *Escobedo*. See Kirkwood, p. 360.
81. *New Orleans Times-Picayune*, February 21, 1969. Habighorst took Hag-gerty's rebuke hard. He could not understand why his word was being questioned. Within a year of the trial, he retired from the force, and became a private investigator. When his vision began to fail, he became a steamship dispatcher out of his home. In 1980, he died of a heart attack, aged 47.
   When I asked William Wegmann about Judge Haggerty's hostility to Habig-horst's testimony, he referred me to Irvin Dymond. When I took it up with Dymond, he told me Haggerty knew Habighorst because he grew up in the same neighborhood as the judge's family. This is correct, but Haggerty may have made a grave error. Habighorst had two uncles who lived within two blocks of Hag-gerty. When they got in trouble, they asked Haggerty to bail them out. But Habighorst himself lived *two miles* from Haggerty and had no such history of run-ins with the law. Wegmann interview, February 18, 1992; Dymond interview, February 20, 1992; Elsie Habighorst interview, February 29, 1992.
   Haggerty's attitude is even more odd in light of the fact that he did not believe Shaw. In an interview he did for a New Orleans documentary filmmaker shortly before he died, Haggerty said he thought "Shaw lied through his teeth" at the trial, that he did "a con job on the jury." The documentary, "He Must Have Something," by Stephen Tyler, was broadcast on WLAE-TV, February 9, 1992.
82. *New Orleans Times-Picayune,* February 26, 1969; Popkin, "Garrison's Case," p. 20. By this time, Andrews had been willingly coopted by the defense. On the day he testified, he was accompanied to court by Phelan. (See photo, front

page, *New Orleans Times-Picayune*, February 26, 1969.) It should be recalled that Andrews's original testimony about the Bertrand call, as well as his saying he feared for his life if he revealed the information, were corroborated by three sources. He told it to Mark Lane before he told it to Garrison, and he told it to Anthony Summers after he had told it to Garrison. See Turner, "Inquest," p. 24; Summers, p. 340. The fear explains why he would rather commit perjury than divulge Bertrand's real name.

83. Kirkwood, p. 399.

84. *New Orleans Times-Picayune*, February 27, 1969.

85. *Ibid.*

86. *Ibid.*

87. *Ibid.* Early in the trial, one of the Clinton witnesses, Harry Palmer, revealed that he had known Banister *before* the Clinton trip. When asked if Banister was with Ferrie and Oswald that day, Palmer said no. *New Orleans Times-Picayune*, February 7, 1969. Coupled with the sheriff's testimony about his conversation with the driver of the car (see Chapter 3), can there be any doubt the third man was Shaw? Since the trial transcript has never been published or made public, the Aynesworth-Phelan-Sheridan disinformation machine has kept this piece of propaganda alive to this day. It has led good researchers like Henry Hurt, Philip Melanson, and Anthony Summers to swallow this canard about Banister being in Clinton. Clearly the Clinton witnesses were compelling, which is why Aynesworth tried to intimidate them (see note 21, *supra*), and why, when he failed, Sheridan and Phelan created this concoction.

88. Kirkwood, p. 173.

89. *Ibid.*, pp. 400-401.

90. Marrs, p. 100.

91. Shaw's testimony is from the trial transcript and *New Orleans Times-Picayune*, February 28, 1969.

92. *New Orleans States-Item*, February 28, 1969.

93. Kirkwood, p. 420.

94. *New Orleans Times-Picayune*, March 1, 1969.

95. *Ibid.*

96. *Ibid.*

97. Kirkwood, pp. 454-460.

98. *New Orleans Times-Picayune*, March 1, 1969.

99. *Ibid.*

100. Kirkwood, p. 462.

101. Robert Sam Anson writes (p. 118) that when the jury brought in the verdict, the foreman almost shouted, "Not guilty." But, in fact, the foreman hands a *written* verdict to the judge, who reads it silently and passes it to the bailiff, in this case George Sullivan, who read the verdict in a normal tone of voice. *New Orleans Times-Picayune*, March 2, 1969. Anson's credibility can be judged by this fantastic statement (p. 117): "One would-be witness for the state appeared in court clad in a toga, and, when asked his identity, calmly replied 'Julius Caesar.'" It did not happen. But, like Aynesworth, Phelan, and Sheridan, Anson did not let reality get in the way of his hatchet.

102. Garrison, *On the Trail*, p. 253.

103. Kirkwood, p. 471; Garrison, *On the Trail*, p. 146. Despite the outcry from

certain quarters, Garrison was reelected District Attorney *after* the Shaw trial.

Chapter 13: Long Time Coming

1. Kirkwood, p. 17; Flammonde, p. 211.

2. Marrs, p. 499.

3. The material on Permindex in Switzerland is based on a series of previously classified State Department documents obtained through a Freedom of Information Act request by Bud Fensterwald in November 1982. The date of this particular memorandum is January 2, 1957. This means that almost immediately after Nagy's announcement, the American Consulate in Basel was dispatching reports on Permindex to Washington. If it were merely a trade organization, what was the need to report on it within a few days of the announcement of its formation, long before it was actually established?

4. Flammonde, p. 217.

5. *Ibid.*

6. State Department memorandum, January 15, 1957.

7. *Ibid.*, October 8, 1957. Nagy's slip and Schroder's quick denial should have flagged the attention of anyone privy both to the machinations of the CIA and to the career of Allen Dulles. When Dulles's law firm—Sullivan and Cromwell—was still dealing with the Nazis in the late 1930s, the bank he used was Schroder's (see Higham, p. 22). When Dulles became DCI, the same bank was a repository for a $50 million contingency fund he controlled. Schroder was a welcome conduit because his bank benefitted from the CIA coups in Iran (1953) and Guatemala (1954) (see Hinckle and Turner, p. 79). For a fascinating history of Dulles's career and his incredibly extensive dealings with big business and government power, see Lisagor and Lipsius, *passim*. For a look at how the Dulles brothers worked with the Nazis, see Chapter 8. To see how Sullivan and Cromwell benefitted from the war effort, see Chapter 9.

8. *Ibid.*, January 15, 1957.

9. *Ibid.*, February 1, 1957, and November 7, 1958.

10. *Ibid.*, January 15, 1957.

11. *Ibid.*, April 9, 1958. Mandel threatened to sue *Arbeiter-Zeitung* for libel. He then dropped the idea. The editors commented, "Too bad. We would have heard some great things at the trial." Flammonde, p. 216.

12. State Department memorandum, April 9, 1958. This document is partly censored, in the section dealing with the visit inside the ITM.

13. State Department memoranda, July 18, 1958, and November 7, 1958. Information about the visit to New Orleans is censored, but Shaw is mentioned as a board member of Permindex.

14. Flammonde, p. 219; Garrison, *On the Trail*, p. 87.

15. *Ibid.*, p. 215.

16. *Ibid.*, p. 224; Garrison, *On the Trail*, p. 146. There is a facsimile of the book at the Assassinations Archives and Research Center in Washington.

17. Flammonde, p. 216.

18. *Le Devoir*, March 16, 1967, quoted in Flammonde, p. 218.

19. Flammonde, p. 219. One of the directors of CMC, Mario Ceravalo, innocently asked for an accounting of its activities. When he got no response, he

resigned and asked that the company be liquidated. He wrote a letter to *Paesa Sera* in March 1967. He said he resigned because "it was no longer possible to understand the sources of great sums of money obtained abroad by Mr. Mantello, and the real destination of the money." *Ibid.*, p. 220. When author Paris Flammonde called the Italian consul in New York to inquire about CMC, he did not receive an answer the first three times he called. The fourth time the answer was, "Try the American Embassy [in Rome], I can't help you any further." *Ibid.*, p. 224.

20. Both quotes are in Flammonde, p. 221. The *Paesa Sera* series ran on March 4, 11, 12, 14, 16, and 18, 1967. See also Faenza and Becker, pp. 128, 321, 326, 330, 389; and see Faenza and Fini, *passim.*

21. Flammonde, p. 221; and Garrison, *On the Trail*, pp. 89-90. When Bud Fensterwald tried to obtain all Agency documents concerning Permindex, he was told that the CIA had only one Agency-originated document, relating to Permindex when it was in Basel. They would not release it for reasons of national security and to protect sources. CIA letter to Fensterwald, March 30, 1983.

22. CMC and Permindex appear linked to the shadowy "stay-behind" operations launched by the OSS/CIA and allied groups after World War II to serve as fronts to attack leftist groups. A major component of this terror network appears to have been Operation Gladio, based in Italy. Some of these groups were set up by former OSS and CIA operative James Jesus Angleton. Following Dulles's lead he began them before the war was over. For a discussion of Gladio, see Edward S. Herman, "Hiding Western Terror," *Lies Of Our Times*, Number 18 (June 1991), pp. 21-22.

One of the assassination attempts against de Gaulle was the subject of the film *Day of the Jackal*. Reinhard Gehlen, then chief of West German Intelligence, supported the OAS in its bitter conflict with de Gaulle.

23. See Chapter 2. Gary Shaw and Bud Fensterwald have explored the possibility of OAS involvement in the assassination. In a 1981 paper, "A Possible French Connection," they revealed that OAS terrorist Jean Souetre was reportedly in Dallas on November 22, 1963. So was fellow OAS renegade Michel Roux. Souetre denies it and says a French intelligence agent Michel Mertz may have been there using his name. The FBI actually questioned a Dr. Alderson of Houston who knew Souetre from his military service in France. The agent implied that Souetre may have been a suspect in the assassination.

Souetre is interesting because the OAS tried to kill French President de Gaulle numerous times during the Algerian War, and they hated Kennedy also, for his support of Algerian independence. If Souetre, Roux, or Mertz were not involved in the plot, they may have been called to Dallas to serve as one of the "false fronts" that figure so clearly in the conspiracy. See Chapter 14 for a discussion of this phenomenon. See also, Garrison, *On the Trail*, pp. 283-289. For a summary of the Shaw-Fensterwald essay, see Hurt, pp. 414-419.

24. Garrison, *On the Trail*, p. 90.

25. Marrs, pp. 499-500. Gatlin, as Garrison was to discover, was later thrown or fell from a Panama hotel window or balcony.

Paris Flammonde was one of the first to unearth the details of Shaw's connections to Permindex and CMC. He was in contact with Garrison throughout the period from Shaw's arrest through the trial. I asked him why the DA did not use this material at the trial. He replied that Garrison believed it did not touch directly on the Dallas-New Orleans events. This is questionable, but even so, Shaw's European connections would have had some effect on his carefully constructed image. Author interview with Flammonde, February 9, 1992.

26. Tully, Chapter 4, *passim.*

27. Garrison, *On the Trail,* p. 89; Brussell, p. 109.

28. Evica, p. 296.

29. Brussell, p. 104.

30. Hurt, p. 282. The memo, entitled "Garrison Investigation: Queries from Justice Department," September 28, 1967, is noted in Hurt, p. 495, n. 110.

31. Prouty, pp. 337-39.

32. Marrs, p. 498. Flammonde mentions Shaw at Churchill's headquarters on p. 76. He was actually dining there.

33. Bacque, p. 92.

34. Author interview with Jim Marrs, December 15, 1991.

35. Bacque, pp. 92, 96.

36. The reports are Torbitt, *Executive Intelligence Review,* and Miller. To this day, many of the documents on Paper Clip are classified, as writers like Linda Hunt have discovered. This is why Shaw's involvement in the von Braun and Dornberger transfers must remain conditional. Many OSS files are being declassified, but none on Thrasher or Shaw has been released. Unfortunately, as I learned from John Taylor, the chief OSS archivist at the National Archives, the CIA has the final say on OSS declassifications. Shaw's military files—not the same as the OSS files—were subpoenaed by Garrison before the trial. When the government released them, they gave them to the defense, which summarized them in a three-page press release.

37. Lasby, pp. 30-37.

38. *Ibid.*

39. Author interview with Jim Marrs, December 15, 1991; Simpson, pp. 28-30.

40. Bell Aerospace roster of corporate officials, in *Standard and Poor's 1963*; Brussell, p. 113.

41. The *JFK* research notes of Bob Spiegelman.

42. Brussell, p. 108-109. Schacht's subsequent jail sentence was voided by McCloy, Simpson, p. 251.

43. Brussell, pp. 108-109. Principessa Marcella Borghese's name and address appear in Shaw's address book, which is available at the Assassination Archives and Research Center in Washington.

44. Weeks, pp. 13-23.

45. Author interview with Arthur Carpenter, January 22, 1992.

46. Turner, "Garrison Commission," p. 48.

47. Carpenter, "Social Origins," p. 48.

48. *Ibid.*

49. *Ibid.*

50. Melanson, p. 66; Summers, pp. 300-308.

51. Melanson, p. 66.

52. *Ibid.,* p. 68.

53. Weisberg, *Whitewash,* p. 148. See also, Hinckle and Turner, p. 207. Garrison grew so suspicious of INCA that a rumor started that a subpoena might be

issued for its records. When he heard of this, with Ochsner's knowledge Butler had the records shipped to Los Angeles under lock and key. In May 1967, Alton Ochsner attacked Garrison and his investigation, calling Mark Lane a communist and a sex deviate. He said Garrison was an unstable nut who was being led on by Lane and Harold Weisberg. Carpenter, "Social Origins," pp. 136-138.

54. Melanson, p. 67.

55. Shaw testimony, trial transcript.

56. Model and Groden, p. 77. The incident is depicted in *JFK*.

57. Summers, pp. 315-317.

58. Author interview with Arthur Carpenter, January 22, 1992.

59. Carpenter, "Gateway," p. 172.

60. *Ibid.*

61. Shaw testimony, trial transcript.

62. *New Orleans States-Item*, April 25, 1967.

63. Shaw testimony, trial transcript. Could there be anything more suspicious than links between Shaw, the Agency, and the ITM? Researcher Gary Schoener sent me a document from Garrison's files, dated May 27, 1969, in which it is revealed that not only did Oswald leave for the Soviet Union in 1959 from New Orleans, but he purchased his ticket at the ITM and registered as an import-export agent. If one adds these facts to the 1957 report (see Chapter 6, n. 22) about Ruth Paine's interest in writing the Oswald family and Ferrie's acquaintance with Oswald in 1956 through the Civil Air Patrol, Michael Levy's theory about Oswald becomes provocative. Levy postulates that Oswald's profile was attractive to the Company quite early. He was spotted *before* his military service, and when he returned from the Soviet Union he was deposited with the people in Dallas and New Orleans who knew of him early on. Levy unearthed the 1957 report about Ruth Paine and has done important work through the Freedom of Information Act.

64. Shaw clearly lied when he denied being associated with the CIA. He also denied knowing Ferrie. Considering the photos of the two together, the testimony of the Clinton witnesses, the Tadins, two FBI reports (March 5 and 21, 1967) linking the two, Jules Kimble, and the other witnesses Garrison gathered, Shaw's denial is simply not credible. Even his friends and family no longer make this assertion. Shaw denied he used an alias, yet Garrison found three acquaintances in the French Quarter who knew Shaw as Bertrand. There is Jessie Garner's trial testimony, Russo's testimony, and Habighorst's testimony and fingerprint cards. There are also two sources in a March 2, 1967, FBI report who said the same. Finally, did Shaw know Oswald? He denied it at the trial. In the face of the Clinton witnesses and the corroborating testimony of the nurses at Jackson hospital, plus the testimony of Russo and Bundy, and the incident in front of the Trade Mart, this is also less than credible. In an interview with Vincent Salandria, he revealed to me that a psychiatrist who treated a friend of Shaw's told him he saw Oswald at Shaw's house.

There are two other curious aspects of Shaw's testimony, one in relation to Ferrie, one to Oswald. Shaw admitted on the stand that he knew Layton Martens. He could not deny it since the name was in his address book. Martens was a former Ferrie roommate. Second, Shaw was asked if he knew Dante Marachini, who had been hired at the Reily Coffee Company the same day as Oswald. Shaw denied knowing him, under oath. Yet Marachini lived next door to Shaw.

65. According to Louisiana law, Shaw would have been liable to five years' imprisonment on each count. Also, would an innocent man have met with Edward Whalen? See Chapter 10.

66. Information on Shaw's early life is drawn from interviews in New Orleans with his cousin Libby Audibert, and in Kentwood with his cousin Clay Starks and his niece Susan Fairburn, January 23 and 25, 1992.

67. Kirkwood, pp. 18-19.

68. Author interview with Arthur Carpenter, January 22, 1992.

69. Hurt, pp. 282-283.

70. *Ibid.*, p. 283.

71. *Ibid.*, p. 288; Garrison, *On the Trail*, p. 234.

72. Oglesby, "The Conspiracy," p. 148. The circumstances surrounding Shaw's death were odd. He was pronounced dead at the Ochsner Foundation Hospital at 1:00 p.m. on August 15, 1974. No autopsy was performed. The death certificate was signed by his personal physician, Hugh Betson, and the body identified by his attorney, Edward Wegmann. On August 16, the body was displayed for 15 minutes at the House of Bultman funeral parlor. (The Bultmans, along with the Sterns, had been major backers of Shaw during the trial.) By 11:30 a.m., less than 24 hours after his death, Shaw was buried in Kentwood, almost 100 miles from New Orleans. The process was so fast that none of his family, except one relative, was at the burial. No family relation saw the body after death was pronounced. There are no directives in Shaw's will calling for such speed. (A new will had been executed on March 7, 1974, naming Wegmann executor.) When coroner Frank Minyard asked Wegmann why everything was so rushed and without an autopsy, the lawyer replied that everything was legal. The coroner concurred, but asked whether so much haste and hush were appropriate over the death of the only man ever indicted for conspiracy to murder President Kennedy. Interviews with Shaw's family; Minyard interview, February 17, 1992. Shaw's will is at the Hall of Records in New Orleans.

73. Summers, p. 161.

74. Helms was convicted of lying to the Church Committee about the CIA's operations in Chile. See Thomas Powers, pp. 298-308.

75. Hurt, p. 247.

76. Summers, p. 163.

77. Marrs, p. 192.

78. Summers, p. 163.

79. *Ibid.*, p. 164.

80. This is the same year that the Agency opened its psychological profile on JFK. See Chapter 4, note 30.

81. Summers, p. 168.

82. *Ibid.*, p. 91.

83. *Ibid.*

84. *Ibid.*

85. *Ibid.*, p. 92.

86. *Ibid.*

87. Melanson, pp. 93-95.

88. Garrison, *On the Trail*, p. 90.

89. Belin, pp. 93-95. See also Ashman, Chapter 1, *passim*; and "The Rockefeller Commission," in Blumenthal and Yazijian, pp. 243-252.

90. Belin, p. 116.

91. Senate Select Committee, Report on Intelligence, Book Five.

92. Sobel, p. 59.

93. *Ibid.*, p. 66.

94. *Ibid.*, p. 59.

95. *Ibid.*

96. *Ibid.*, p. 74.

97. *Ibid.*, p. 80.

98. *Ibid.*, p. 82.

99. Hart said, "I don't think you can see the things I have seen and sit on it.... [K]nowing what I know—I can't walk away from it." Summers, p. 295.

100. *Ibid.*

101. *Ibid.*

102. *Ibid.*, p. 142.

103. *Ibid.*, p. 295.

104. *Ibid.*, p. 296.

105. The HSCA also was authorized to investigate the assassination of Martin Luther King, Jr.

106. Belin, p. 188; Marrs, pp. 33-34; Groden and Livingstone, p. 340.

107. Some analysts have argued that Sprague and Gonzalez were set up to fight as a means to divide and conquer the HSCA and, if possible, to sink it. Afterward, both Sprague and Gonzalez felt this was so. See Policoff, p. 7; Groden and Livingstone, p. 363.

108. Belin, p. 188.

109. HSCH VI, p. 242.

110. HSCH III, pp. 363-65.

111. Groden and Livingstone, p. 475.

112. HSCH VI, pp. 242-257.

113. Summers, p. 77.

114. Groden and Livingstone, p. 241.

115. *Ibid.*

116. *Ibid.*, pp. 242-43.

117. Scheim, p. 27.

118. Groden and Livingstone, p. 245.

119. *Ibid.*

120. Blakey's excuse for not testing other locations was shortage of funds. Yet the committee actually refunded money to the Treasury when it was done. Interview with Committee consultant Robert Groden, November 17, 1991.

121. Groden and Livingstone, p. 245.

122. Groden and Livingstone suggest, p. 245, that the best candidates for a third location are 1) manhole covers in Dealey Plaza; and 2) the Dal-Tex building.

123. Groden and Livingstone, p. 261.

124. *Ibid.*

125. *Ibid.*, p. 262.

126. *Ibid.*

127. It never seemed to occur to Blakey that many young men from a lower

socio-economic background would fit this profile. For example, my boyhood neighborhood had organized crime in it. I hung out at a novelty store that was a front for a bookie joint. One of my uncles was associated with a shady lawyer. Another of my relations ran numbers. But I have an alibi for November 22, 1963, and anyway, I was only eleven at the time.

128. See Blakey and Billings; Scheim; and Davis. The effect in all three is to fit a square peg into a round hole.

129. Summers, p. 335.

130. These, in turn, caused JFK to crack down on the more militant exiles operating independently of White House policy.

131. Summers, pp. 421-26.

132. *Ibid.*, pp. 354-55.

133. *Ibid.*

134. According to Hinckle and Turner, the attacks were launched for the purpose of provoking another Soviet-U.S. showdown and an invasion of Cuba. Hinckle and Turner, pp. 155-56.

135. Summers, p. 353.

136. *Ibid.*, p. 356.

137. *Ibid.*, p. 357.

138. *Ibid.*, pp. 390-91. Phillips, who became the Agency's Chief of the Western Hemisphere Division, had played key psychological warfare and black propaganda roles in the CIA's overthrow of Arbenz in Guatemala in 1954, the Bay of Pigs invasion of 1961, and the overthrow of Salvador Allende in Chile in 1973.

139. According to Summers, Phillips headed the Mexico City CIA unit responsible for the circulation of pictures of the man who was not Oswald. Summers, p. 384.

140. Summers, pp. 388-89.

141. *Ibid.*, p. 392.

142. At the JFK Assassination Symposium in Dallas, November 17-19, 1991, Mark Lane said that shortly before he died Phillips had told a small audience that the CIA was involved in the JFK assassination coverup, and that most of the Oswald-in-Mexico story was a CIA fabrication. If true this would jibe with Victor Marchetti's disclosure in the July 1979 *Gallery* that, at the time of the HSCA hearings, the Agency was seriously contemplating a "limited hang out" stance before the Committee. They would admit certain mistakes, finger a few lower-level people, and cut their losses.

143. Groden and Livingstone, p. 154; Fensterwald, p. 237.

144. Groden and Livingstone, p. 311.

145. *Ibid.*, pp. 258-260.

146. Quoted in *ibid.*, p. 399.

147. *Ibid.*

148. Blakey proudly stated, on the December 23, 1991, CNN program *Crossfire*, that the HSCA held 18 days of public hearings. The Committee under Blakey was in session more than a year.

149. Policoff, p. 6.

150. *Ibid.*

151. Hurt, p. 246.

152. Policoff, p. 6.

153. Blakey tends toward overstatement and disingenuousness. On the *Crossfire* program (see note 148), he referred three separate times to Oliver Stone's *JFK* as "obscene," because it postulates a government conspiracy. He said the single-bullet theory was substantiated by two tests, a tracing of the trajectory back from the car to the Book Depository and the use of neutron activation analysis. Most experts agree that such a tracing is inconclusive at best. And in this case, the Committee's outside expert had to move the back wound *up* for his analysis to work, while the Committee's own medical experts had to move it *down* for their version to work.

The neutron activation analysis (NAA) was conducted by Dr. Vincent Guinn. (Although Guinn denied that he had ever tried to work for the Warren Commission, Jerry Policoff has produced documents that prove he had.) Guinn concluded from NAA tests that trace elements from CE 399 matched fragments taken from both Kennedy and Connally, which would support the single-bullet theory. But there is a problem. Guinn admitted that the fragments he tested were not those tested by the FBI in the original NAA examinations, which suggests that there may have been some switching of fragments (see Chapter 15).

In any event, Sprague's assessment of Blakey is that he did not really want to do any new investigation; he just wanted to review what had already been done. Sprague said, "Blakey was more interested in the points that Blakey might make with people he thought might be helpful for his future career." Policoff, p. 7.

154. See Carl Oglesby's Afterword in Garrison, *On the Trail*, p. 308.

155. Policoff, p. 7. On that *Crossfire* program, Blakey stated about Stone's film, "[if] the shot came from the front, there was a coverup, therefore the military-industrial complex did it, therefore my nation is corrupt, and that's just obscene." Anyone who displayed this kind of ingrained, psychological bias against a military-inteligence coup *and* who came with his own fall guy, the Mob, would be heaven-sent for the Agency. As noted above (at n. 142), the CIA was seriously considering a "limited hang-out" position with regard to the HSCA. With Blakey in charge, this position was apparently abandoned. Why should they buy what they could get from Blakey for nothing?

156. Jerry Policoff interview, April 29, 1992.

157. *Ibid.*

158. Morrow, *The Senator Must Die*, p. 233.

159. *Ibid.*

160. *Ibid.*, p. 236

161. *Ibid.*; interview with researcher Gary Rowell, December 9, 1991.

162. Morrow, *The Senator Must Die*, p. 236.

163. Rowell interview.

164. HSCR, pp. 129-47.

165. HSCH X, pp. 199-205.

166. HSCR, pp. 156-58; HSCH V, pp. 575-86, IX, pp. 137-48, 1122-28.

Chapter 14: The Unmarked Milestone

1. See preface to Texeira; and Nelson, p. 88.

2. Discussions of Church Committee recommendations are in *U.S. News and World Report*, May 10, 1976. And see, for the Rockefeller Commission Report

recommendations, *The Nation*, August 16, 1975.

3. With the notable exception of a groundbreaking 1970 attack on Hoover in *Hoover's FBI*, by former Agent—and Garrison supporter and investigator—William Turner.

4. Curt Gentry, *J. Edgar Hoover.*

5. New York Times, *The Witnesses.*

6. A summary of the *Times*'s early devotion to the Warren Report includes: Tom Wicker's unprofessional failure in November 1963 to follow up diligently on the Parkland doctor's statement that JFK suffered wounds of entry into his throat; Arthur Krock's appraisal of the Report as "the definitive history of the tragedy"; Wicker's unqualified testimonial in the preface for Warren Commission counsel David Belin's book; Harrison Salisbury's endorsement of the *Times*'s abridged version of the Report; the *Times*'s shamelessly doctored and biased selection of testimony in *The Witnesses* (which Jerry Policoff has documented; see *The Realist*, October 1971); its flagrant headline November 24, 1963, when Oswald was killed by Jack Ruby; the systematic violation of the pledge, taken after Oswald's death by then-managing editor Turner Catledge, to refer to Oswald as "the alleged assassin" (November 27, 1963, p. 36); the removal, on December 1, 1970, of searching pro-conspiracy questions in John Leonard's book review of Jim Garrison's *Heritage of Stone* from all but the early, bulldog edition (see Krassner); and managing editor Turner Catledge's disturbing friendship with New Orleans patrician, Alton Ochsner, financier of INCA (see Chapter 13).

7. Kirkwood, p. 418. It is hard to exaggerate how far Sheridan was willing to go in his attacks on Garrison. In August of 1967, Zachary Strate, one of the men Sheridan had helped convict along with Hoffa, testified that Sheridan had offered to help in his attempt to reverse his conviction, if Strate would aid Sheridan in smearing Garrison. Sheridan's attorney, who was in court at the time, did not dispute the fact, only its timing. (Flammonde, pp. 324-325; Joesten, *Garrison*, pp. 138-139.) To this day, Robert Sam Anson asks rhetorically why Sheridan would want to destroy Garrison. If Anson had done his homework on Sheridan's extensive intelligence ties—the NSA was staffed with many Gehlen operatives— he would not sound so lost and spew so much misinformation.

8. See Hertsgaard, *passim.*

9. Wolfe, *The Bonfire of the Vanities.*

10. For an intricate, overstated treatment of these men and the CIA in Watergate, see Hougan, *Secret Agenda.*

11. As discussed in the assassination literature, leading candidates for a breakaway faction (or one under high-level control) are anti-Castro operations attached to JM/WAVE (Theodore Shackley's Miami Station), Operation MONGOOSE (Edward Lansdale's Pentagon-CIA hybrid), and ZR/RIFLE (William Harvey's CIA-based assassination team). Other sources hypothesize a team or teams working under Division Five of the FBI, and/or various mob factions under the control of Santos Trafficante, Carlos Marcello, etc.

12. In the past few years, some writers have observed that JFK's extramarital love life might have provoked a major scandal, particularly if manipulated by enemies like J. Edgar Hoover. Thomas Reeves's recent *A Question of Character* stretches this point to ethically grotesque limits by suggesting that JFK's assassination, however tragic, may have saved the nation an even more wrenching and

demoralizing impeachment or media scandal arising from Kennedy's sexual liaisons.

13. Harper and Krieg, p. 9.

14. Even his most idealistic program, the Peace Corps, had its pragmatic side. He did not want a large number of volunteers sent to any one area in order to prevent the creation of "large American enclaves." In addition, service was restricted to five years so a bureaucratic staff with vested interests would not be built up.

15. Harper and Krieg, p. 12.

16. Nixon's rise to power began with red-baiting smear campaigns against electoral opponents like Jerry Vorhees and Helen Gahagan Douglas and ended in national trauma with his near impeachment over the Watergate scandal. This legacy makes ludicrous the media attempts of the last few years to rehabilitate him as an "elder statesman."

17. Goodwin, p. 105. Kennedy could be wickedly funny about Nixon. In 1959, while in Wisconsin preparing for the next year's primaries, Senator Kennedy said, "Actually, I am not campaigning for votes here in Wisconsin. The Vice President [Nixon] and I are here on a mission for the Secretary of Health, Education and Welfare to test cranberries. Well, we have both eaten them, and I feel fine. But if we both pass away I feel I shall have performed a great public service by taking the Vice President with me." Book Review, *Los Angeles Times*, June 23, 1991, p. 13.

18. Goodwin, p. 83.

19. Harper and Krieg, p. 7.

20. *Ibid.*, p. 31.

21. *Ibid.*, p. 13. See Bernstein for a complete discussion of JFK's domestic achievements. To give an example, in less than three years, Kennedy doubled economic growth and increased GNP by 20 percent.

22. Harper and Krieg, p. 14.

23. Isaacson and Thomas, p. 687. The genesis and aftermath of Acheson's quote is epitomic. After the Tet offensive, during the siege of Khe Sanh, Acheson was asked to attend another briefing at the White House, after which Johnson ranted and raved for 45 minutes. Acheson walked out, and when he was phoned, he made the remark. LBJ got on the phone and Acheson told him the JCS was giving "canned briefings" and he would not listen to them again. He only wanted to hear from people on the scene in Vietnam and would accept only raw data, not finished reports. Johnson complied, and Acheson got the first real picture of the situation in February 1968, one month before Clark Clifford, Secretary of State, went through the same review and told LBJ it was a hopeless situation (Isaacson and Thomas, pp. 683-689). To me, nothing crystalizes the difference between JFK and LBJ in both foreign policy and their relationship to the JCS and the CIA more than this. What it took Johnson three years and untold destruction to discover, JFK instinctively realized by the second half of 1961. See Newman, especially Chapters 3 and 7.

24. See Prouty's "Kennedy and the Vietnam Commitment," in Groden and Livingstone, pp. 467-473. See also Scott's, "The Death of Kennedy and the Vietnam War," in Blumenthal and Yazijian, pp. 152-87.

25. "Oliver Stone Talks Back," *Premiere*, January 1992, p. 70; Hilsman.

26. Blumenthal and Yazijian, *Government by Gunplay*, p. 182.

27. *Ibid.*, p. 171.

28. *Ibid.*, p. 170.

29. Groden and Livingstone, *op. cit.*, p. 466.

30. Stone, p. 72; Newman, p. 449.

31. The Vietnam War was fought without a congressional declaration of war. Congress's Gulf of Tonkin Resolution authorized the President to take measures necessary to defend South Vietnam from "aggression" by North Vietnam. Congress was provoked into enacting the legislation by reports of an alleged attack by North Vietnamese gunboats on an American destroyer. The attack never happened. Robert Scheer interviewed Retired Admiral James B. Stockdale, who was in the Gulf of Tonkin at the time. After 20 years of silence, Stockdale said categorically that the attack *never occurred.* Scheer, pp. 152-162.

32. Wayne Morse of Oregon and Ernest Gruening of Alaska were the only two Senators with the courage to vote against the Gulf of Tonkin Resolution that gave LBJ his blank check.

33. See Newman, *passim.*

34. Groden and Livingstone, p. 466.

35. John Newman writes, "The facts are that Kennedy was withdrawing from Vietnam when he died and that Johnson crossed the line that Kennedy repeatedly refused to cross—the dispatch of American combat troops to Vietnam." See Newman, "The 'Gimmick' in JFK's Withdrawal Plan." *Boston Globe*, January 14, 1992. For an example of the controversy, see *The Nation*, January 6 and 13 and March 9, 1992.

Roger Hilsman, Kennedy's former Assistant Secretary of State for Far Eastern Affairs, insists on Kennedy's genuine commitment to a withdrawal from Vietnam: "[H]e refused every suggestion to send American combat forces.... [H]e laid the groundwork for doing so [withdrawing]. Shortly before his death, he took the first step by ordering the first 1,000 advisors home." Hilsman.

36. Blumenthal and Yazijian, *Government by Gunplay*, p. 166.

37. *Ibid.*, p. 167.

38. *Ibid.*

39. Harper and Krieg, p. 15.

40. *Ibid.*, pp. 39-40.

41. Blumenthal and Yazijian, *Government by Gunplay*, p. 166.

42. Ralph G. Martin, p. 495-499.

43. John Morton Blum, pp. 23-24.

44. William Blum, p. 175.

45. *Ibid.* The memo said: "[H]is talents and dynamism appear the overriding factor in reestablishing his position each time it seems half lost.... Lumumba was a spell binding orator with the ability to stir masses of people to action.... [I]f he started to talk to a batallion of the Congolese Army he probably would have them in the palm of his hand in five minutes."

46. John Morton Blum, p. 23.

47. *Ibid.*

48. William Blum, pp. 175-176. In September, a CIA chemist arrived on the scene carrying a virus to be used in the murder.

49. *Ibid.*

50. *Ibid.*; Stockwell, p. 105.

51. Garrison, *On the Trail*, p. 60; see also Chapter 4, note 30.

52. Lane, *Plausible Denial*, pp. 94-95.

53. Newman, p. 52.

54. *Ibid.*

55. See Hilsman, especially on the instructions JFK gave to Harriman.

56. Fay, p. 189.

57. Newman, p. 55.

58. *Ibid.*, pp. 55-56. For another military man's view of Kennedy, see General Lane's observations in Groden and Livingstone, pp. 427-429, 437-438.

59. North, p. 91, referring to the *Washington Post* of May 14, 1961. JCS Chair Lemnitzer went the following year, and so did Navy Chief of Staff Burke. Hinckle and Turner, p. 112; author interview with John Newman, March 16, 1992.

60. William Blum, p. 196.

61. Morrow, *The Senator Must Die*, pp. 55-56.

62. Newman, p. 98; see also Groden and Livingstone, p. 435.

63. Lane, *Plausible Denial*, pp. 99-100.

64. *Ibid.*, p. 100, n. 2.

65. Newman, p. 138. Roger Hilsman said that Douglas MacArthur had told Kennedy it would be a mistake to get into a land war in Southeast Asia. Whenever someone would suggest sending in combat troops, Kennedy would say, "Well now, you gentlemen, you go back and convince General MacArthur, then I'll be convinced." Hilsman tells another story about Kennedy's reluctance to let the military into Vietnam. JFK had read that a general was going to visit the country and quickly called Hilsman. He was angry at him for letting a high officer visit the place; it would ruin his plan for neutralization. Hilsman replied that he did not know of the visit and had no authority to prevent it. JFK hung up without saying goodbye. *That afternoon*, an NSAM was issued prohibiting any general from visiting Vietnam without Hilsman's permission.

66. William Blum, pp. 164-170; see also Tully, Chapter 4, *passim.*

67. Prados, pp. 171-172.

68. Newman, p. 433. It is interesting to note that in an article in the *New York Times*, October 3, 1963 ("The Intra-Administration War in Vietnam," p. 34), Arthur Krock notes that the CIA had failed to carry out certain administration policies. The article went on to quote unnamed sources as saying that the CIA was a malignancy that the White House could no longer endure, and if the U.S. ever experienced a coup attempt, "it will come from the CIA and not the Pentagon.... The Agency represents a tremendous power and total unaccountability to anyone."

69. *Ibid.*, pp. 434-435.

70. *Ibid.*, p. 447.

71. *Ibid.*, p. 442.

72. Lane, *Plausible Denial*, p. 98.

73. *Ibid.*, p. 101; see also North, p. 52. Hoover was collecting information to use against JFK if he was asked to leave. North, p. 75.

74. "The few officers remaining ... moved up and down the halls like attendants at a sepulcher." David Atlee Phillips, pp. 143-144.

75. The summary of the trip is from WR, pp. 730-736.

76. WR, p. 736.
77. *Ibid.*, p. 735.
78. *Ibid.*, p. 734.
79. Lane, *Plausible Denial*, p. 58.
80. *Ibid.*, p. 66.
81. *Ibid.*, pp. 59-60.
82. Summers, p. 374; on Duran, see p. 377.
83. *Ibid.*, p. 385.
84. *Ibid.*
85. Lane, *Plausible Denial*, p. 61.
86. Rose, "The Trip That Never Was," p. 11.
87. *Ibid.*, p. 12.
88. *Ibid.*, p. 14. Regarding this return trip, the name "Oswld" appears on the manifests of another bus line, Transportes Frontera. This has never been explained. Oswald's name was spelled at least five different ways during the trip, including "H.O. Lee."
89. The Veciana-Bishop incident is treated fully in Summers, pp. 353-362, 508-513.
90. Lane, *Plausible Denial*, p. 271. Hunt denies he was in Mexico City, but Lane quotes two reliable journalists, Joseph Trento and Tad Szulc, who say he was; p. 273.
91. *Ibid.*, p. 78.
92. *Ibid.*, p. 79. Lane reports that when Blakey interviewed Phillips, he told him he had nothing to worry about. HSCA investigator Edwin Lopez has said he believes there was an imposter for Oswald in Mexico City and that Oswald was being set up for the assassination. He adds that Oswald was not trying to get to Cuba and that he was associated in some way with the CIA. See Melanson, p. 104. With the salting away of Lopez's report until 2029, Blakey was right to tell Phillips he had nothing to worry about. Phillips died in 1988.
93. It should be noted that intelligence-Mafia ties go back much further than the Castro plots. The ONI dealt with Lucky Luciano during World War II (see Marrs, pp. 161-163), and the young CIA used the Corsican Mafia to break the Marseilles dock strikes in 1947; see Evica, pp. 240-241.
94. Fay, pp. 189-190. Kennedy's association with this book has three other ironies. The President in the novel—Lyman Jordan—is working to relax the Cold War. He has just signed an arms agreement with the Soviets that the Pentagon frowns upon, which is the reason for the coup. Second, when the book was made into a film, Kennedy was eager to cooperate in its production. Third, its co-author, Fletcher Knebel, became a staunch defender of the Warren Report. In fact, he is named in the Agency directive on counteracting critics of the Report (see Appendix B).
95. *Ibid.*, p. 190.

Chapter 15: Homage to Jim Garrison

1. Details of his life taken from Garrison, *On the Trail*, pp. 254-76.
2. Flammonde, p. 13.
3. Garrison, *Playboy*, p. 68.
4. Flammonde, p. 298.

5. The most sophisticated and superficially cohesive argument against *JFK* and the Garrison case is "The Case Against Jim Garrison," by Nicholas Lemann, in the January 1992 *GQ*. Lemann, who writes often for *The New Republic* and *Atlantic Monthly*, seems to have taken a quick dip into the pool of assassination literature. His article would make the maestro, James Phelan, proud. But to one familiar with the details of the case, it is cheap, tired, shameless, slanted, and illogical.

Lemann states that Garrison's case "had an aspect of persecution of homosexuals about it," but never even tries to back the statement. He could not, because, as noted (see Chapter 12), Garrison has *never* made a negative public statement on the issue and *never* brought it up in the Clay Shaw trial.

Lemann couples this smear with some classic psychobabble. He suggests that Garrison, and Oliver Stone, and even Russell Long, are conspiracy advocates because of personal trauma: Garrison's early separation from his father, the divorce of Stone's parents, and the assassination of Long's father, Huey. Lemann suggests that anyone who believes conspiracies *do* happen is compensating for some psychic tragedy. Presumably, everyone who believes Oswald did it alone is happy and well-adjusted.

These are fitting preludes to Lemann's presentation of the "facts." He says Garrison began his probe in 1966, ignoring the 1963 investigation of Ferrie. He says, wrongly, that Garrison was on the case for a year before the Rosemary James story appeared. He says Garrison's first real insight into the case was the discovery of the meaning of the 544 Camp Street address, ignoring Garrison's earlier questions about the Russian examination. He omits Ferrie's see-through excuses for his Texas trip, his partial confession to Lou Ivon (author interview with Ivon, February 19, 1992), his confession to Raymond Broshears, the Clinton trip, the disclosures of Richard Case Nagell, Permindex and CMC. Lemann calls Shaw's connection to the CIA "possible," even though the CIA admitted it 13 years ago. In sum, he characterizes any evidence of ties between Oswald, Banister, Ferrie, and Shaw as "unsubstantiated." (For a good review of Oswald's relations with these men, see Kurtz, "Lee Harvey Oswald," pp. 7-22.)

Lemann's biases paint him into a dreadful corner: they put him in the clutches of the Warren Report. He concludes that "the Report does manfully shoulder the difficult task of presenting a comprehensive explanation of the assassination." A strange description of a report so many consider cowardly and single-minded.

Lemann reaches the heights of absurdity when he challenges: "When exactly did the CIA decide to assassinate the president? Who gave the order?" Does he really believe there is a memo somewhere in Langley with the date, time, and agenda? That some FOIA request ought to have turned it up?

6. Tommy Lee Jones, the actor who played Clay Shaw in Stone's *JFK*, recently said, "Jim Garrison is considered a 'discredited figure'? By whom? I mean how did *that* get established? Why, all that means is that there were a lot of negative headlines in the newspapers, and that's not reality, now is it?" *Time Out*, p. 18.

7. Garrison, *On the Trail*, p. 26.

8. The best analysis of Oswald's probable role as an intelligence operative is in Melanson, pp. 29-37 and *passim*.

9. Anson, p. 127; Phelan, *Scandals*, p. 146.

10. See Garrison, *On the Trail*, pp. 62-63.

11. Melanson, p. 22.

12. Shaw and Harris, p. 112.

13. Joesten, *Garrison*, pp. 80-81.

14. *Ibid.*, p. 73.

15. Kirkwood, p. 572. Amazingly, speaking extemporaneously, Garrison made much the same argument that Peter Dale Scott did later, from partly declassified Pentagon documents. The DA argued that the withdrawal plan begun with NSAM-263 was reversed by Johnson.

16. Interview with Jerry Policoff, December 26, 1991.

17. Policoff, p. 20.

18. See Groden and Livingstone; also Lifton, *Best Evidence*.

19. Flammonde, p. 298.

20. Kirkwood, p. 71 ff.

21. Garrison, *On the Trail*, p. 251; Lane, *Plausible Denial*, p. 221.

22. Garrison's principal players star in the only two published confessions I know of on the subject. In 1975, former CIA operative Robert Morrow wrote *Betrayal*, a reconstruction of the assassination that helped bring about the establishment of the HSCA. See text of letter on p. 9. His reconstruction, in which, unbeknownst to him, rifles he purchased were to be used at Dealey Plaza, has the same people and motives dug up by Garrison. The key issue is Cuba. The main characters are Clay Shaw, Guy Banister, and David Ferrie. The supporting cast includes Banister's colleague Hugh Ward, Agency-linked Richard Nagell, and Rose Cheramie, who died so mysteriously. A false Oswald also figures in the plot. The real Oswald is a complete patsy.

In 1981, author Henry Hurt received a phone call from a stranger named Robert Easterling confessing his small role in the murder of John Kennedy. Hurt then knew little about the assassination, so he could not judge the man's truthfulness. For the next four years he immersed himself in the literature in the field and produced his own book on the subject, *Reasonable Doubt*. (The phone call and its aftermath are in Hurt, pp. 7-13; the confession and conspiracy details are in Chapter 12.) Hurt treats Garrison somewhat cavalierly, so it comes as a surprise that when he introduces the conspirators who hired Mr. Easterling, they are none other than Clay Shaw, Guy Banister, and David Ferrie. The author seems a mite ungrateful.

Appointment in Dallas, by Hugh McDonald, is a third such book, but there are substantial rumors it was a "black book," *i.e.*, an Agency backed or approved product.

23. In the wake of the opening of *JFK*, there has been a rash of articles, and even fresh witnesses, to proclaim that there was a conspiracy after all, and that the mob did it. One such witness is mob lawyer Frank Ragano, who told reporter Jack Newfield that in 1963, Jimmy Hoffa sent him to deliver the message to Santos Trafficante and Carlos Marcello that Kennedy must be eliminated. See Newfield, pp. 4-5.

One of the things that Mafia advocates never like to admit is that Ferrie *openly* admitted he worked for G. Wray Gill, Carlos Marcello's attorney. He said he was in court on November 22 waiting with Marcello for a decision in a pending case. But Ferrie tensed up when anyone suggested he knew Oswald. Melanson, p. 51.

24. Sparrow, p. 12.

25. Hale Boggs died in a plane crash over Alaska in 1972, at a time he was becoming openly skeptical of the magic bullet theory and increasingly dubious about the Commission's lone-nut solution. (See Chapter 7.) Jim Marrs considers the death suspicious. Marrs, p. 562.

26. For a discussion of the effects of Gehlen's overestimates of both Soviet intent and military strength in Eastern Europe, see Simpson, Chapter 5, *passim*. After Gehlen became part of West German intelligence in 1954, he was the prime mover of the myth that the Soviets would invade West Europe through Germany. *Ibid.*, p. 55. These claims coincided with the interests of Wall Street and Washington lawyers like Dulles and McCloy not just because they increased funding for the Agency and other defense interests, but also because their corporate clients profited in two ways. First it fueled the need for corporate defense contracts, and second the increased paranoia made it possible to smother nascent progressive governments in the Third World, *e.g.*, Guatemala in 1954. United Fruit was a client of both Dulles and McCloy. Brussell, p. 113.

Walter Dornberger of Paper Clip also played a part in this. Simpson notes (p. 64), that he and Gehlen inflated the mythological missile gap of the 1950s, the one JFK used for political purposes in the 1960 campaign. Garrison picked up on this in a May 25, 1989, interview with Dave Mendelsohn. Dornberger's Bell Helicopter was in serious financial straits in the 1960s, before Johnson expanded the Vietnam War and the Army began to purchase thousands of helicopters from Bell. Vincent Salandria told me that he always felt that the secrets of Kennedy's assassination would never come out until the reason he died—the Cold War—was over. When he said that, I thought it was far-fetched; I now think he may have been prescient. Salandria interview, February 23, 1992.

27. Turner, "Garrison Commission," pp. 68, 46. The well-read Garrison was translating a Latin maxim of William Watson (1601), *Fiat iustitia et ruant coeli*.

28. Harper and Krieg, p. 10.

29. Garrison, *Playboy*, p. 178.

30. By design, I mean its intended effect, *i.e.*, a more aggressive foreign policy. By outline, I mean the circumstances surrounding the event, with half the Cabinet in the air over the Pacific, the nuclear code book missing from Air Force One and the SAC planes at Wright Air Force Base, the communications breakdown in Dallas, the telephone tieup in Washington, and the extraordinary military presence at the autopsy (see Appendix A). For a good overview of this phenomenon and how it follows the classic lines of a coup d'état, see Shaw and Harris, pp. 193-206.

The *structure* of the plot was fascist. Fascism has usually been associated with the comingling of power between military-intelligence forces, suitable politicians, and powerful business interests. This book concentrates on the first group. Lyndon Johnson's world view certainly fit into the second role. Two books that describe the business interests most likely involved are Scott, "Dallas Conspiracy," and Marrs, pp. 253-300.

To those who think the concept of a fascist coup is out of place in America, there is a precedent. An attempt was made in the 1930s to seize power from Franklin Roosevelt through just such a conspiracy. There are some jarring parallels between the two cases. In 1933 and 1934, the plotters included big money interests, the military, and a former presidential candidate, in this case John

Davis, the Democrat who ran against Coolidge in 1924. The motivation was the belief that FDR was too liberal, both domestically and in his foreign policy. In fact, the plotters actually sent an emissary to scout the fascist organizations of European regimes like Mussolini's and Hitler's (an eerie echo of Shaw's connections). Third, there was a media smear campaign orchestrated by the plotters' allies against the man who exposed the conspiracy, Marine General Smedley D. Butler. Last, there was a partial coverup of the plot by the official government investigation. The coup failed because Butler, the officer approached by the conspirators, was a former military man who hated fascism as much as Garrison did. He could not be convinced or bribed into leading the plot, and his testimony was sufficient to end it. For a chronicle of this episode, see Archer.

31. Garrison, *Playboy*, p. 178.

32. As Garrison has noted: "Clarence Darrow lost the Scopes trial, but who remembers that now?" Garrison, *On the Trail*, p. xii.

Index